PRAISE FOR *A RETURN TO EROS*

"Marc and Kristina are going where ⟨...⟩ what it means to live a fully erotic lif⟨...⟩
—**John Gray, bestselling author** ⟨...⟩
Are fron

"*A Return to Eros* is the map for the new human. Read it and be forever enlivened and transformed! I believe this is the most compelling invitation ever written to live the Erotic Life. It changed my life."
—**Kristen Ulmer, former professional extreme skier and author of *The Art of Fear***

"Surrender to this book. Erudite, provocative, and filled with lively insights, there is much to be learned from it about the sexual confusion of our times."
—**Adam Bellow, author of *In Praise of Nepotism: A History of Family Enterprise from King David to George W. Bush***

"*A Return to Eros* is a book written with no hang-ups, no compromises, and no holds barred. It rocks!"
—**Jonny Podell, iconic American rock 'n' roll music agent at the Podell Talent Agency**

"I've known Kristina for many decades . . . great to see she is sharing her life work with the world . . . Join the outrageous love train!"
—**Shep Gordon, legendary rock 'n' roll manager and *New York Times* bestselling author of *They Call Me Supermensch***

"*A Return to Eros* evolves our understanding of love, and does it in a way that will transform your own experience of love and Eros. It is a radically inspiring and important book that can help all of us recognize more deeply how love's energy literally drives reality."
—**Sally Kempton, author of *Awakening Shakti***

"*A Return to Eros* should be placed on the shelf next to the great works on emotional and sexual emancipation, including Marcuse's *Eros and Civilization* and O Brown's *Life Against Death*. Gafni and Kincaid remind us that eros and ethics are inseparable, that we must free the erotic from the ghetto of the merely sexual, and in so doing awaken our passion for truth and justice. There may be no more urgent lesson for our culture, which now stands on the brink of another descent into barbarism, that it is through and from love that true power flows."

—Zak Stein, EdD (Harvard), academic director of the Center for Integral Wisdom, faculty at Meridian University, scientific advisor for Neurohacker Collective, and cofounder of Lectica, Inc.

PRAISE FOR MARC GAFNI'S
YOUR UNIQUE SELF

"It is very rare that one comes across a teacher or a book that is 'changing the game.' My friend, Dr. Marc Gafni, is such a teacher. He is a rare combination of brilliance, depth, and heart. Marc's teaching on the Unique Self in an evolutionary context is 'changing the game.'"

—Michael Murphy, founder of Esalen Insitute and author of
Golf in the Kingdom

"*Your Unique Self* could only have been written by someone who passionately lives his own uniqueness. Marc Gafni is a brilliant teacher and heart master with a rare capacity for empathy and a gift for creating community. This book contains the essence of his teaching on what it means to live from an enlightened life from a ground of one's own personal uniqueness. This is a book that deserves to become a classic."

—Sally Kempton, author of *Meditation for the Love of It*

"Dr. Marc Gafni's Unique Self teaching is seminal. What you hold in your hands is a radically exciting and groundbreaking book that will change forever not only how you think about enlightenment, but how you understand, from a post-metaphysical perspective, the very nature of human life itself. The Unique Self work is magnificent, and it belongs among the 'great books.'"

—Ken Wilber, author of *A Brief History of Everything*

"At last—a safe, precise, and potent infusion—Unique Self! Not so much a book, as an antidote, *Unique Self* stands with spiritual teacher, scholar, and master, Marc Gafni's *Soulprints* and *Mystery of Love* as a trilogy of love and healing for humanity. Read and be restored."

—Lori Halperin, leading clinician and theorist in fields of
marital and sexual dysfunction

"With exceptional brilliance and an awakened heart, Dr. Marc Gafni speaks to all of us who are interested in the evolution of consciousness.

His teachings on the Unique Self enlightenment are essential for the next stage in our evolution. They have emerged from his direct experience, and I highly recommend them."

—Michael Bernard Beckwith, author of *Spiritual Liberation:*
Fulfilling Your Soul's Potential

"Marc, a fellow drinker at the holy taverns has written a fine, fine book. Kabbalists say a Day of Tikkun (evolution, soul-repair) is coming. There are great stories here from the Hasidic masters and from Marc's own life, honoring the unique soulmaking that has brought you to this moment. This book will deepen that astonishing mystery and awaken you to the individual beauty of your path."

—Coleman Barks, author of *Rumi: The Big Red Book*

"Marc Gafni's overflowing heart and transmission of the Unique Self teaching profoundly moves me. Dr. Marc holds the lineage energy of the great Hasidic masters of Kabbalah, which he brings with him into the visionary initiative of Center for Integral Wisdom. There is little doubt in my mind that *Your Unique Self: The Future of Enlightenment will become one of the classic texts that* forms the World Spirit vision that our world needs so deeply."

—Lama Surya Das, author of *Awakening the Buddha Within:*
Tibetan Wisdom for the Western World **and founder of the**
Dzogchen Meditation Centers

"At this historic moment, our human mind is passing the border toward a new consciousness. Marc Gafni is far enough ahead of most of us to articulate insights he gained beyond that borderline. Yet, like all great teachers, the author becomes transparent. Here is an invitation and a great opportunity to listen—not to Marc Gafni, but to your Unique Self. Thus this book becomes an indispensable travel guide into the realm of a vast new consciousness."

—Brother David Steindl-Rast, Benedictine monk and author of
The Spirit of Practice

A RETURN

— *to* —

EROS

THE RADICAL EXPERIENCE OF BEING FULLY ALIVE

MARC GAFNI AND KRISTINA KINCAID

BenBella Books, Inc.
Dallas, TX

Owing to limitations of space, permission credits begin on page 489.

BenBella Books, Inc.
10440 N. Central Expressway, Suite 800
Dallas, TX 75231
www.benbellabooks.com
Send feedback to feedback@benbellabooks.com

Printed in the United States of America
10 9 8 7 6 5 4 3 2 1

Library of Congress Cataloging-in-Publication Data
Names: Gafni, Mordekhafi, author. | Kincaid, Kristina, author.
Title: A return to Eros : the radical experience of being fully alive /
Marc Gafni, Kristina Kincaid.
Description: Dallas : BenBella Books, 2017. | Includes bibliographical references and index.
Identifiers: LCCN 2017002508 (print) | LCCN 2017023488 (ebook) | ISBN 9781944648190
    (electronic) | ISBN 9781944648183 (paperback)
Subjects: LCSH: Sex (Psychology) | Sex. | Love. | Erotica. | BISAC:
RELIGION / Spirituality.
Classification: LCC BF692 (ebook) | LCC BF692 .G3194 2017 (print) | DDC 155.3--dc23
LC record available at https://lccn.loc.gov/2017002508

Editing by Jessi Rita Hoffman
Copyediting by Karen Levy
Permissions editing by Sheri Gilbert
Proofreading by Lisa Story and Jenny Bridges

Front cover and text design and composition
    by Aaron Edmiston
Full cover by Ivy Koval
Printed by Lake Book Manufacturing

Distributed by Perseus Distribution
www.perseusdistribution.com

To place orders through Perseus Distribution:
Tel: (800) 343-4499
Fax: (800) 351-5073
Email: orderentry@perseusbooks.com

Special discounts for bulk sales (minimum of 25 copies) are available.
Please contact Aida Herrera at aida@benbellabooks.com.

To Shabbtai and Sara

I come to speak dangerous words.
I ask only that you listen dangerously.
—CHUANG TZU

But to live outside the law, you must be honest.
—BOB DYLAN

CONTENTS

PART THREE: THE FIVE ESSENTIAL FACES OF EROS

PART FOUR: MORE FACES OF EROS

FOREWORD

A Return to Eros is a tour de force of the kind that comes along once in a generation. The way this volume brings Eros to consciousness as the fundamental force direction and "purpose" of reality, on all levels and all quadrants, really is *the* discovery that underlies, directs, and "explains" the sacred purpose of cosmogenesis, the birth narrative of the New Human.

It's the second coming of humanity for the first time in history incarnate as a fully embodied sacred sexual being.

It's the early stages of the next evolutionary unfolding.

A Return to Eros forms the basis of evolutionary spirituality. It captures the glory of its conscious experience from the inside out in the sexuality and Eros of the evolutionary unique self.

It's the experiential basis of the next stage of living and loving.

It's the deepest reason for profound sexual yearning. It's vital and is truly the only path beyond shame. It must not be denied.

It reveals the very nature of "God-in-evolution."

It is the answer to my life question: What is the meaning of our new power that is good?

The answer is the manifestation of what this volume calls Evolutionary Eros in human form to its next level of the supra mental genius as consciously guided self and social evolution.

It's the source energy, which can arouse the Planetary Awakening through Unique Self Symphony.

It is the juicy and delicious fruit of the joining of genius. Sexuality and suprasexuality become one.

God "took the risk" in revealing $E = MC^2$, the genetic code—the language of science—to give humans the powers of our ancient gods to use.

What the authors call "Love or Die" is the new commandment of the ontic human.

It is conscious evolution revealed as erotic evolution made aware of us in our loving.

It is the fundamental sacralization of sex at all levels.

The authors make the radical claim, which I believe is true, that when this force is not recognized, when it is denied, the result is abuse, whether in the form of rape culture or in the false complaints that attempt the rape of a name. It is only, the authors tell us, "when we embrace the full beauty of our embodied Eros, not merely in the sexual but in every dimension of our lives" that we begin to live in integrity.

Marc Gafni, the first author of this book, is an Erotic Radical. He incarnates the evolutionary Eros and articulates its teaching in ways that are several steps ahead of his generation. Like many radicals he has been made to bear the cross of a new vision. He has seen his actions falsified and distorted and experienced the projection and demonization that comes with the territory of incarnating this new vision of Eros. But as I have witnessed myself in a thousand conversations, he has kept his heart open in love, and turned his suffering into a gift and his pain into art. I am proud to stand with Marc as an evolutionary partner in offering this new vision of Eros and identity that is so vitally needed in our evolution.

Marc's co-author on this volume, Kristina Kincaid, herself incarnates evolutionary Eros through her work with the body. Mentored by the leading-edge somatic teachers of our time, she understands the inseparable connection between one's sexuality and one's emotionality, and how that relationship is mirrored through our relationship to life. She brings a deep embodied understanding of the flow of Eros, love, and sexuality through the body. It is this teaching that can radically transform our lives and birth the new human. The new human majestically called forth in this book will walk with unarmored body, will love with unguarded heart, and, through body, heart, and mind, be connected to all of life.

—Barbara Marx Hubbard
Futurist; President of the Foundation
for Conscious Evolution

FOREWORD

A Return to Eros is poetry. And not just poetry in spirituality, where poetry often catalyzes the spirit. Nor in eroticism, to which poetry often opens the door. But poetry in philosophy, poetry in science, and poetry in history—where poetry is often a stranger.

As such, *A Return to Eros* is not a book that will prove the return of Eros footnote by footnote. It is a book that generates the *feel* of Eros sentence by poetic sentence.

A Return to Eros does not fit into any recognizable genre. It is not pure scholarship even as it is scholarly. It is not self-help even as it inspires transformation. It is not religious in nature even as it offers visions that seek to unify the agnostic and the fundamentalist.

In fact, part of the delight of *A Return to Eros* is the element of surprise: Will we be treated to history or the future? To spiritual insight or scientific fact? To philosophy's sustainable gifts or to Gafni and Kincaid's reworking of those gifts toward the deepening of our future erotic wisdom?

When it comes to the future of love, sex, and Eros, what society often sees as black or white, the authors see in shades of gray. They invite us to confront our cognitive dissonance: "Puritanism lives side by side with promiscuity." Or: "We are not sure whether we are living in the golden age of sex or in a rape culture." The authors venture where others fear to tread: for instance, how we deal with rape of the body versus rape of a reputation should there be a false accusation. What is black and white to some is a continuum for the authors: "Regret is not rape, and arousal is not consent . . ."

Yet still greater gifts of *A Return to Eros* are not in its surprises but in its weaving of diverse insights into a vision that is greater than the sum of its parts. The authors' integration of the disciplines presents us with a tapestry that reweaves the source code of culture. We dance to the music of the tango that was sex and Eros and then listen for the tango that sex and Eros can become.

A Return to Eros, then, is paradoxical: It is both the return of Eros and the future of Eros. It is the return of love, sex, and Eros; and the future of love, sex, and Eros. It is about the history of religion's constraints on sex, and about the history of religion's lack of constraints on sex—especially how the esoterics' embrace of sex forges the erotic and holy into one. As we discover religion's esoterics embracing the erotic, we awaken our personal potential to heal our relationship with religion. It soon becomes no surprise when Gafni and Kincaid declare that *A Return to Eros* is all about sex and not at all about sex.

Although *A Return to Eros* is a return to the wisdom of Solomon's temple, the Magdalene Mysteries, and Da Vinci, it is not a book about the past. Rather, it is a vision rooted in wisdoms forgotten from our past that inspire a more erotic future—what Gafni and Kincaid call a "memory of the future."

All of this may make us yearn for simpler answers. But we recall Gafni's warning: When simplicity falls short of reality, it leaves us feeling disappointed and disillusioned. *A Return to Eros* selects for readers who know that bringing the unconscious to the conscious level rewards us with the capacity to control our own lives—even if part of that control is the choice to "let go and let God." And when we bring philosophies like "let go and let God" to the conscious level, we discover when we are using it to avoid responsibility. Eros, like golf, requires our taking control of the way we hit the ball even as we let go of control of the way we hit the ball. To Gafni and Kincaid, holding the paradox of Eros is a taste of paradise.

A Return to Eros considers "Eros to be the center of our reality . . . to live erotically *not merely in the sexual but in every facet of being.*" Their examination of the twelve faces of the Erotic, and of the many wrinkles among those faces, is like being conscious of every drop in the next shower you take. The mere experience of considering every drop of the shower as if they were "all there is" will leave you feeling as enlivened as you will feel after reading *A Return to Eros*.

—Warren Farrell, PhD
Author, *The Myth of Male Power*
www.warrenfarrell.com

PREFACE

THE FUTURE OF LOVE, SEX, AND EROS

TOWARD A POST-TRAGIC SEXUAL POLITICS OF EROS

There are three primary levels of consciousness through whose prism we experience our lives. We will call these three levels the pre-tragic, tragic, and post-tragic.

Pre-tragic is the stage before tragedy. Life is good. Life is delightful. Life makes sense. It is ordered and reasonable. During the pre-tragic state we also experience pain and suffering, but our pain and suffering are not tragic. We are able to explain to ourselves and our intimates what happened. We might use religious, psychological, or scientific explanations. Explanation saves our suffering from being tragic.

The second level of consciousness is the tragic. The goodness of life is broken up by suffering, but we no longer feel able to explain it. The rules break down. Perhaps the suffering is more intense than any we have experienced before. Alternatively, our trust in the religions or philosophies of life that undergirded our explanations have been shaken, often irrevocably. Our lives feel empty and meaningless, "a tale told by an idiot, full of sound and fury, signifying nothing."[1] We are overwhelmed by the tragic nature of life itself. We may continue to function, love, and even be highly effective achievers. But our joy mechanism is broken. We are cut off from the natural joy we once felt from the essential goodness and primal aliveness of life.

Most people live their lives at either level one or level two of consciousness, what we have here termed the pre-tragic and the tragic. Some people move from level one to level two as a result of lost trust in life, usually occasioned by a personal tragedy. Others move from pre-tragic to tragic because they are witness to the virtually unbearable suffering in the world. The laws and principles they had used to make sense of the world no longer seem sensible. Some individuals, after shifting to tragic consciousness, revert back to pre-tragic. This is either because they find some new, comforting explanation for their suffering (based on a superficial reworking of their old beliefs), or because they simply forget their experience of tragedy and fall back into their prior pre-tragic state.

But there is a third level that is available at the leading edge of consciousness. We call this level "post-tragic." Here, the person or culture is able to once again participate in the elemental joy of living. This happens when the individual (or culture) is able to reconnect to the core Eros and aliveness of reality. In "A Dialogue of Self and Soul," Yeats wrote of this third level, post-tragic consciousness, in the understated but raw Eros of his verse. Here is an example:

> When such as I cast out remorse
> So great a sweetness flows into the breast
> We must laugh and we must sing
> We are blest by everything
> Everything we look upon
> Is blest.

What causes the emergence of this third level of consciousness is always the deepening into what we might call emotional maturity or wisdom. Part of it may come from depth work that the person has done with his or her own wounds. Another part comes from the maturity of letting go and letting God. Often the source is the evolution of a more poignant and potent worldview. But it always comes from some process of joyful deepening.

These same three levels of consciousness apply to the sexual. There is pre-tragic sexuality, tragic sexuality, and post-tragic sexuality. Pre-tragic sexuality has three major expressions:

- The first form of pre-tragic sexuality is purely animal sexuality—a physical, instinctual impulse unburdened by human values or narratives. This is the human attempt to partake in the purely animal mode of sexuality, which we will term "the sex-neutral narrative." It does not work because it is basically regressive. While embracing the animal is essential for our sexuality, it is not enough. Most of us experience the sexual as being more than only physical.

- The second form of the pre-tragic sexual is sexuality defined by the laws, strictures, and taboos of religion. Sexuality is pre-tragic in this context because it is clear. Sex in every particular circumstance is either allowed and embraced or forbidden and rejected. Often the religious view is sex negative, but sometimes (for the sake of having children or even companionship), sex is considered positive or even sacred. But it is pre-tragic because it is fully understood. Sex has its place, its boundaries, and its permissions. All is explained. Everything is on firm ground. At this level of sexuality, we deploy law, culture, and taboo to sublimate the sexual and redirect its force to support our committed relationships. We further invest its power as the animating force in our cultural creations. At this level of consciousness, we feel the need to construct vessels of commitment that are sufficient to hold the raw, anarchic power and seductive beauty of the sexual. But this level remains pre-tragic because it is clear to us through laws and customs that are correct and therefore constitute the most right and righteous approach to the sexual.

- The third expression of pre-tragic sexuality is sex that occurred in the West during and in the years immediately following the sexual revolution. Most of the old sexual ways were overturned. For most people, sex no longer needed to be tightly linked to marriage to make it proper and good. The contraceptive pill broke the causal link between sex and children. A new world was born. The sexual revolution gave us the sex-positive narrative. But it was pre-tragic because—like the sex-negative narrative—it boasted an uncomplicated clarity about sex. But all was not sweetness and light. The bland, pre-tragic, sex-positive narrative of the sexual revolution could not hold.

FROM PRE-TRAGIC TO TRAGIC SEX

Many of us today remain largely ensconced in pre-tragic sex. For some of us, that is because we are blithely positive about sex. Our arousal arouses in us virtually no ambivalence or complexity. Others remain pre-tragic because we live firmly within the boundaries of classical religious strictures around sexuality. Even if they are defined largely in their breach, the boundaries are clear. Our actions may be conflicted, but our frameworks remain cogent. We may be both sinners and saints, but we have a clear understanding of what it means to sin and what it means to be saintly.

But for a large swath of people in the Western world, pre-tragic sexuality is over. A second level of consciousness around sex has emerged. We have moved from the pre-tragic sexual to the tragic sexual. The sexual revolution gave way to a world in which sex is no longer innocent. Hidden issues of sexual abuse, sexual violence, and sexual harassment have come to the surface. On the one hand, there is a dramatic evolution of consciousness. A line is drawn in the culture that says, "No more harassment and no more violence." Indeed, before the mid-1970s, even the words "sexual harassment" were not part of our lexicon and certainly not part of our laws. In the West the ascendancy of the feminine in education and in the workforce brought in its wake a vital new vigilance that says no to any form of sexual boundary-crossing that is not welcomed by both parties. This is an important step in healing the deep violation of the feminine that has characterized much of Western history.

And yet there is a loss of clarity around sexuality. With the loss of clarity comes a loss of innocence coupled with a new form of free-floating anxiety and even fear surrounding sex. We might even venture to say that there is a new puritanism in relationship to the sexual. The old sex-negative positions of religion seem to have covertly resurfaced in the campaigns against sexual harassment.

Now to be clear, we all agree that numerous forms of harassment and sexual violence were rampant in the pre-tragic sexual world. Even in the world of sexual revolution, sexual harassment remained a given. Black Power leader Stokely Carmichael famously remarked that the "right position for women in the Black Panthers is prone." Marital rape was legal virtually everywhere. Rape in war was regarded as the spoils of the victors. Sexual enslavement of women of "inferior" culture or religion was common throughout the world. What we would today call sexual harassment or abuse was considered to be relatively normal.

Nonetheless, most men did not harass, were not sexually violent, did not rape, and did not abuse women. The horrific lack of legal strictures allowed the actions of a small minority of men to inflict great pain and to poison the sexual culture of the world. The evolution of love that raised consciousness and made all these forms of sexual violation unacceptable, both legally and socially, is a desperately necessary and long-overdue advance. But a strong fragrance of the old anti-sexual puritanism seems to have crept its way into today's sexual discourse. Legal scholars and social critics alike have pointed out that in the early days of the war on sexual harassment, the core issue was harassment. As years went by, however, the emphasis shifted to the sexual. Major cases of significant harassment with no sexual component were let off the hook, while any case that had even a whiff of the sexual was treated with full severity. Sex, once again, was bad.

The anti-sexual theme is covert, sensed but not articulated in the public mind. This is where the move from pre-tragic to tragic begins to emerge. We no longer have a clear sexual narrative. We are confused by sexuality. We are not sure whether we are living in the golden age of sex or in a rape culture. Rape on campus, date rape, and confusion about what constitutes consent—what is yes and what is no—abound. Regret is not rape, and arousal is not consent, yet all too often they are confused. The hook-up culture of emotionally unattached sex dominates the campus mythos, yet very few college students say they feel sexually fulfilled or liberated. Women feel prude-shamed for not being willing to hook up and then slut-shamed for hooking up.

The anti-sexual attitude is covert. In so many dimensions of our culture, puritanism lives side by side with promiscuity. How else might we explain the national obsession with sexual scandal, such as the affair between Bill Clinton and Monica Lewinsky? The insatiable appetite of Americans for sexual titillation, combined with the fascination with public degradation and shaming around sex, virtually demanded that newspapers—driven by the race for advertising dollars—cover the details of the scandal more than any other event in the world for a period of nearly two years.

Today there are no clear guidelines and even fewer clear values regarding sex. It is true that we're seeing a long-overdue and welcome increase in sexual ethics. We have significantly less tolerance for all varieties of sexual harassment and violence. Yet the new sexual ethics are not rooted in a new sexual ethos. There is no sexual narrative that both dignifies and eroticizes our lives.

Hardly anyone is really happy with sex. If they are, it's only in the first wave of the sexual encounter when the passion is high and the egos are low. After that, most everyone feels like they are not quite getting enough, getting it right, or getting to move on when they are ready. And if they are getting some, they suspect it should be better than it is. Most everyone is quietly convinced that it is so much better for everybody else. Everyone is obsessed with that mythical couple, living somewhere in New Jersey, who are madly in love and having great sex after two decades of marriage. No one, of course, has ever met them, but reported sightings regularly crop up in magazines, talk shows, and self-help books. We live with the rampant dissatisfaction produced by the great tease of sexual satisfaction, which for the first time in history seems to be democratized. Everyone feels entitled, but virtually no one feels fulfilled.

SEXUAL SHADOWS

But if all that were not enough, sex is also a big-time killer. Men are rap-
ing men and killing men over sex. Men are killing women in domestic
violence scenes. In the world arena, men still use sex in war to break
down the social order and humiliate their enemies. While the term "rape
culture" has been powerfully critiqued, more than a million rapes occur
every year, leaving irrevocable damage on the lives of women and men.
There is a powerful and important literature that suffuses culture which
calls men out on this particular form of masculine shadow.

But don't think that women are off the hook. The feminine shadow has
women killing men over sex. According to extensive rigorous data, gathered by leading cultural critics Cathy Young and Warren Farrell, the level
of domestic violence inflicted by women on men is equal to that inflicted
by men on women. The literature of abuse reminds us that women are also
killing men in domestic violence scenes. At its heart, virtually all domestic
violence is connected to wounds around sexuality. Women also engage
in what has been described alternatively as social murder or name rape.
The early feminists were right when they said that the rape of a name is
also rape. For example, to be falsely accused of rape or sexual assault, and
to have those kinds of accusations disseminated over the internet, where
lies live forever, is a devastating experience. In this tragic scenario, name
rape is reenacted every day online. We interviewed women who had been
raped and also had brothers, sons, or partners who were subject to this
kind of severe name rape. According to these women—all with powerful
feminist sensibilities—both are equally egregious.

Often false sexual complaints cluster together when a group of
women (or men in the more classical lynch mob) bypass structures of
investigation and justice in order to socially murder someone. For example, groups of women who feel rejected and hurt—finding out, as feminist
writer Jessica Roemischer writes, "that they are not the only one"—may
get together and use false or distorted accusations of sexual misconduct
to socially kill a man.

In the internet age, disaffected people find each other more easily. Sometimes that is constructive and positive, specifically when the

disaffected have been genuinely victimized. At other times, however, people who gather together via the internet and other social structures manifest more of a moblike energy or group-think mentality. They incite each other's anger. Facts and ulterior motives are never checked or cross-checked and social lynching takes place on the web.

Malice is not limited to males. There is masculine shadow and feminine shadow. Feminist writer Hanna Rosin devotes a chilling chapter in her book *The End of Men* to feminine violence. Feminist writers like Daphne Patai, Katie Roiphe, Laura Kipnis, and Christina Hoff Sommers have long warned of the growing phenomenon of false sexual complaints by women. Of course the sexual shadows at play which generate malice are often hidden. As Milan Kundera reminded us, "malice can never admit to itself so it must plead other motives." As Patai and other writers point out, name rape hides its true intention under the veneer of victim advocacy. The perpetrator is usually disguised either as a victim or as a rescuer who is "protecting other women." There is always some politically correct formula used to cover up wounded ego and genuine hurt, which get lethally mixed with the often strange bedfellows of malice, envy, self-interest, and self-protection. The fig leaf of relatively minor sexual hurt in the normal arc of human relationships often masks the infliction of lethal hurt that is exponentially more destructive by many orders. All of this is part of the confusion of sexuality's tragic phase.

The confusion itself is the source of much of our devastation. It is the loss of clarity that moves us from pre-tragic to tragic sex. The tragic sexual leaves so many mortally wounded in its wake. There is so much pain from something that should be the source of so much pleasure.

All of these phenomena that are rampant in our culture are expressions of the tragic sexual. But that is just the tip of the iceberg. We have not even begun to explore the super complex territory of monogamy, the myth of the white picket fence, polyamory, open marriage, betrayal in its many forms, the great controversy surrounding "recovered" memories, post-facto reinterpretations of old sexual experience, the claims of rape culture, and the list goes on and on. And anyone who, God forbid, does not want the same kind of sex that the majority approves of is in big trouble. Same-sex couples struggle, transgendered couples struggle, and anyone with any kind of alternative sexual drive has a rough start even before the pleasure actually begins and ends. The confusion around all of these issues is simply an expression of level-two tragic sexuality.

There is more than a little that is tragic in the contemporary sexual landscape. We are not sure about anything. Either God is more than slightly sadistic with a significant interest in teasing and even torturing us through the ordeal of sex or in some mysterious way it is the essential key to this whole life journey. We are not sure. Our lack of clarity drains our energy, robs us of passion, saps our vitality, and de-eroticizes our lives.

Given all of the above, along with the fact that our yearning for great sex is such a desperate and central issue in our lives, it stands to reason that the divine designer who set up this ultimate tease must be a flaming asshole. Or worse still, there is no designer, all is random and chance, and there is no "true north" or meaning in our sexuality. It will always be this hopelessly confused. That is the tragic view.

Or, possibility two: the inherent intelligence of the self-organizing universe totally and absolutely rocks. The love intelligence of the cosmos so desires our good that she wanted to place the deepest wisdom necessary to navigate our lives with power and passion right in the center of our experience—in the heart of our sexuality—just to make sure we did not miss it. That's why all wisdom about life was encoded in the sexual. That realization moves us toward the post-tragic view of sexuality.

FROM THE TRAGIC TO
POST-TRAGIC SEXUAL

We are lost in the tragic sexual, searching for a new narrative. We long for a return to sexual innocence. Not a pre-tragic innocence but a post-tragic innocence. We yearn to re-virginate. We are not seeking sexual license as much as we desperately yearn for a return to Eros. We yearn to live the erotic life. We want to live in an erotic society. To return to Eros, we need a new sexual narrative. Core to this new narrative must be a precise and potent understanding of the relationship between the sexual and the erotic. Are they the same or are they different? If they are different, how do they interact with one another? Could it be that our sexuality is collapsing because we have lost contact with Eros? Could it be that when we look to sex to fulfill all of our erotic needs, sex collapses under the weight of a burden that it cannot possibly bear? Is our confused pathos around the sexual actually rooted in the urgent need for a new sexual narrative that clarifies the shocking relationship among the erotic, the sexual, and the sacred?

Until such a narrative emerges, we will weirdly vacillate between being puritans and libertines on alternative days or even during different hours of the same day. We are politically correct during the day while yearning to be sexually incorrect at night. Sexual anthropologist Esther Perel reminds us, somewhat sardonically, that we often demonstrate in daytime against the kinds of sexuality that we yearn for at night. We need a new post-tragic story of sex and Eros.

BEYOND MARCUSE AND BROWN: A RETURN TO EROS

Herbert Marcuse and Norman O. Brown are the two great social philosophers who, in the latter half of the twentieth century, sought to reclaim a vision of Eros that might form the basis of a new human and a new society. But both of them lacked a sufficiently potent worldview from which that new vision of Eros could emerge. Marcuse was lost in the neo-Marxist restructuring of society, which failed to honor the potential, creative Eros of free markets and an emergent conscious capitalism. Brown sought to reclaim a regressive Dionysian innocence by recovering key stands in Freud's more mythical thinking, while recasting and rejecting still other dimensions of Freud.

Today it is clear that whatever their crucial contributions, neither neo-Marxism nor psychoanalysis is the fertile ground from which a new erotic worldview will arise.

In this work it has been our tender and audacious intention to articulate just such a new erotic worldview. We tried to tell a new story about sex whose subplot is the powerful relationship among the sexual, the erotic, and the sacred. We retold the story of love, distinguishing between outrageous and ordinary love. We articulated a new meta meme: The Universe is a Love Story. We are convinced that this worldview is a sufficient basis to catalyze a return to Eros and a sexual narrative that is an affront to shame. Our vision of Eros is rooted in a spiritual, mystical, scientific, evolutionary worldview, which understands that all of reality is allurement, and which experiences the sexual as an expression of the erotic evolutionary impulse that moves all of reality. In this worldview, rooted in the best science and spirituality available on the planet at this moment in time, the sexual is the seat of all wisdom.

In this new narrative, Eros is not merely ordinary love, which human egos deploy as a strategy to achieve security and status. Rather, Eros is the outrageous love, which moves the sun and the stars, which is the very heart of existence itself. When we awaken to the Eros of evolution alive within us, we awaken as outrageous lovers. Our model for outrageous love is none other than the sexual itself. The sexual models the erotic; it does not exhaust the erotic. The erotic and the holy are one. This is the core of the post-tragic narrative of sexuality that will allow us to move beyond the pervasive sexual shame that covertly suffuses our culture and is the root of so much suffering and pain. This new sexual narrative is the necessary basis of a new sexual politics of Eros that has the potency and power to take us all home.

SOURCES FOR THE NEW NARRATIVE

We draw the new narrative from several sources. Systems theory, evolutionary theory, and science are crucial sources. Various schools of psychology, integral theory, attachment theory, and the social sciences all contribute significantly. But the core wellspring from which we drink is a great Hebrew mystery tradition. Mysteries are meant to remain esoteric, secret. Therefore, allow us to share with you why in our generation it is both permitted and even a sacred obligation to share these mysteries.

We live in an age when ancient wisdoms, long relegated to the basements of the spirit, are being reclaimed. The Zohar, the magnum opus of Hebrew mysticism, teaches that our era is the one in which the "gates of wisdom will be opened." For the first time, after several eons of intense spiritual evolution, we have the vessels to hold the light of the ancient secrets. The mystics suggest that we may well be able to hold the light more deeply today than even the ancients for whom the wisdom was initially intended. It is only now, after the vessels of law, science, and ethics have been integrated into our psyches, that we can go back and fully reclaim Eros and enchantment. It is in the service of the great Hebrew Goddess of Eros (Shechinah) that we enter the mysteries.

We, the co-authors of *Return to Eros*, are—or at least aspire to be—erotic mystics. We study, teach, and try to live the sacred erotic texts in our lives. The think tank of which we, Marc and Kristina, are, respectively, president and board director, is committed to envisioning and evolving the future of Eros in every field of human endeavor. The Outrageous Love Project (www.OutrageousLove.com) and the Integral Evolutionary Tantra School (www.IntegralEvolutionaryTantra.com) are two projects that emerged from the Center, which we were delighted to cofound. Both projects are committed to articulating a next-stage vision of Eros and ethics, which humbly and audaciously evolve the source code of culture and consciousness.

The Hebrew mystery texts on Eros, as well as those of other spiritually incorrect traditions, have been our guides and friends for many years. Of course, like all mystics who engage sacred wisdom, we hear the text in accord with the inner melody of our souls. We now share this song with you in the form of this book. You are invited to find the place in your soul where you can receive and integrate this ancient wisdom into your own song.

Let this be not a monologue but a sacred conversation. Share with us your words, your thoughts, the poetry of your soul, and we will be honored to receive at AReturnToEros.com.

With all the outrageous love and blessings in the world and beyond,

Dr. Marc Gafni and Dr. Kristina Kincaid
Carmel, California
New York, New York

PART ONE

THE COSMO-EROTIC UNIVERSE

CHAPTER ONE

A NEW SEXUAL NARRATIVE

If you stop to think even for a short moment, you realize that sex really is the great mystery of our lives. This is truer today than it was in any previous generation. For we have lost the story line of meaning around our sexuality. There are four basic stories about sex that we have inherited in our culture, and none of them addresses our sexual experience. These hand-me-down narratives can loosely be labeled as sex negative, sex positive, sex neutral, and sex sacred.

SEX NEGATIVE

The sex-negative narrative is articulated in our culture to prevent us from having sex. They tell us, of course, that it is for our own protection. According to this narrative, sex is somehow wrong, immoral, or sinful. The spokespeople for sex negative are quite potent. Even when we think we have gotten free of them, they pop up again inside our hearts or heads, wagging their fingers disapprovingly. Even if we have successfully removed them from our minds and psyches, they still show up in the way our bodies respond and behave. And, of course, they remind us

2

constantly of all the trouble sex has gotten the world into—from the Trojan War to the Clinton/Lewinsky drama. Not to mention the trouble it has gotten us into—emotionally, psychologically, personally, professionally, and physically. It's all the fault of sex.

You have to admit that the sexual renunciates and conservatives have a point. If you want to keep life simple, clean, and orderly, foregoing or limiting the sexual experience might be an excellent decision. If you like spiritual exercises—and you are up for it—take a few minutes and write down all the times sex got you into trouble in any or all of the above areas. We predict you will probably generate quite a list.

Lots of religious and conventional moralists fall into the sex-negative category. Religion typically affirms love and passion as virtues but divorces them entirely from sex. Moralist religion works hard to erect boundaries that will protect us from the pitfalls of our sexuality.

But the sex-negative narrative, while it certainly has a point, clearly does not fully capture our experience of the sexual. While we all know that sex requires a dimension of discipline—context and commitment matter for sure—most of us know in our hearts that the moralists are wrong and that sex is ultimately, and overwhelmingly, good. And it's not merely a side benefit of (or a tool for achieving) a loving relationship. As the fourteenth-century Zen master Ikkyu observed:

With a young beauty, sporting in deep love play;
We sit in the pavilion, a pleasure girl and this Zen monk.
Enraptured by hugs and kisses,
I certainly don't feel as if I am burning in hell.

SEX POSITIVE

This brings us to the second story about sex that we hear in our culture: the sex-positive narrative. This story is told by a powerful coalition of forces talking about sex. This group tells us, "Sex is wonderful. If liberated, it's the panacea for all ills; if repressed, it's the source of all dysfunction." Sexual revolutionaries, Freudians in disguise, along with many other intelligent folk and proponents of schools of modern psychology, work hard to strip sex of anything remotely spiritual or even emotional. They want to liberate sex from love, from Eros, and from the myriad existential and emotional complexities. To these individuals, sex is simply positive.

Truth be told, Freud himself was the most influential modern cheerleader at this party. Rooted in a hydraulic model of the psyche, which slightly confuses human beings and steam engines, he taught us that if we could just find a way to release sexual tension in a balanced way, we would be healthy and happy. The problem with this narrative is that, though we may be having much more sex, we are not feeling much more positive.

In fact, after engaging in all of the sex that so many generations thought would signal heaven on earth, we are shocked to find that the same feelings of alienation, depression, and emptiness still plague us. Okay—hydraulic equilibrium achieved—what are we supposed to feel when the sexual revolution failed to bring us any closer to liberation? We remain mired in suffering, just as before.

SEX NEUTRAL

This brings us to the third sexual narrative: sex is neither positive nor negative. The third sexual story is the sex-neutral narrative. This story was articulated by a host of sex researchers, perhaps most prominent the highly controversial, but highly impactful, Alfred Kinsey. Kinsey's father was a fundamentalist Christian who raised his son squarely in the sex-negative camp. Kinsey rebelled, however. Receiving his PhD in biology from Harvard, he argued that sex is simply a neutral biological mechanism. He sought, in both his personal and professional life, to completely disinhibit sex from any sense of being either negative or positive. For Kinsey and the sexual story he put into our culture, sex—all forms of it without exception—is simply biology. "So let's get over all of these inhibitions. Why all the fuss about it anyway?"

The problem with this third narrative is that, like the sex-negative philosophy, it does not fully capture our sexual experience. Sex just does not feel neutral to us. Having sex and having dinner just are not the same. But that's not all. The more neutral we make sex, and the more we make it available, like food, the less satisfied we are. Uninhibited sex is available in infinite variety in almost every imaginable social or commercial context, and yet we do not seem any the better for it. So much sex and so little pleasure. So many orgasms and so little fulfillment.

A few decades ago, a sociologist named David Riesman called sex "the last frontier." If this is true, then we have crossed it and found it wanting. Psychologists report that patients rarely complain about sexual dysfunction or repression anymore (what seemed to be the most common complaint in the days of Freud). Rather, the malaise of our time is the lack of feeling or passion and a disconnect between sex and spirit. Sex is all around, and yet it is hard to tell whether anyone is truly enhanced by it. Indeed, no one even seems to be really enjoying themselves—at least not in any sort of sustained manner.

T. S. Eliot describes this state of affairs in his epic poem "The Waste Land":

> *She turns and looks a moment in the glass,*
> *Hardly aware of her departed lover;*

Eliot speaks of the hidden alienation from the sexual even after the Church's sexual mores have been overturned.

> *Her brain allows one half-formed thought to pass;*
> *"Well, now that's done: and I'm glad it's over."*

The alienation sets in the moment it's over, surfacing our discomfort with our own sexing.

> *When lovely woman stoops to folly and*
> *Paces about her room again, alone,*

We pace—unable to rest in what should be the aftertaste—our confusion around sex darkening what should have been the afterglow.

She smoothes her hair with automatic hand,
And puts a record on the gramophone.

SEX SACRED

The fourth sexual story, often deployed as a counter to the sex-neutral narrative, is sex sacred. Rooted in certain strains of the great religions, this narrative claims that sex is not negative, neutral, or even positive. Rather, it is holy. The evidence of sex's holiness, the sex-sacred story, is taken to be self-evident. Sex creates life, life is holy, therefore sex is holy.

That is a pretty good argument as far as it goes. But again, it does not address our full experience of sexuality. Just ask yourself: is most of the sex that you have for the sake of procreation? For most people, most of the time, most of their sex has nothing to do with making babies. So to root the sex-sacred narrative in sex for babies just does not speak to the truth of our full sexual lives. Besides all of that, are we really sure what we mean when we talk about sex or anything else as sacred or holy? We know it means that sex is not just neutral or even merely positive. But what does "sacred" really mean, anyway?

A NEW SEXUAL NARRATIVE: SEX EROTIC

So although all four of the sexual narratives contain some elemental validity, they are, at best, true but incomplete. They each may be spiritually and politically correct in their respective cultural space, but they do not address our deepest knowing and yearnings about sex.

We need a new sexual narrative. We need a new story. Enter the philosophy of sex erotic. This fifth sexual story, the one that addresses most fully our sexual experience, is that sex is indeed sacred but not only when it creates children. Sex is not sacred only because it creates life. Sex is sacred because it *is* life. Sex is the very pulse of life itself. Sex is the fundamental nature of all existence. Therefore, sex is the ultimate guide to living in alignment with all of reality. Let us call this new sexual narrative "sex erotic."

If sex is life, then naturally sex is the seat of all wisdom about life. Sex is not only our great delight and pleasure—sex is our ultimate teacher about living. For life itself is, at its core, Eros.

SEX MODELS EROS

The paradox of this book is that it is all about sex and not about sex at all. Sex is life. But if we are only alive in our sex, then we are already dead. By contrast, being fully alive in the sexual models for us what it means to be radically alive in every facet of life. The experience of being radically alive is called Eros. To be fully alive in every dimension of your life is what it means to live an erotic life.

That is why we have termed the new sexual narrative "sex erotic." Sex erotic suggests that sex and Eros are not to be collapsed synonyms. Sex and Eros are different but closely related terms. Sex is sex. Eros is the radical aliveness that animates and drives all of reality. The new sexual narrative of sex erotic informs us of two great truths. First, that sex is the expression of the evolutionary Eros that animates and drives all of reality, awake and alive in us. Second, that sex models for us what it means to live in Eros in every facet of our existence.

The purpose of this book is to articulate the new sexual narrative. Sex is neither negative nor neutral nor merely positive. Sex is not even just sacred because it creates life. The new narrative is that sex is life. That's why our aliveness is most directly accessed through sex. To be sexual is to be alive, and to be alive is to be sexual, but our basic yearning is not just to be fully alive during sex but also to be radically alive in all parts of our life. It is this voice of authentic yearning that is our most reliable spiritual guide. To be radically alive in every part of our life is what it means to live in Eros.

What, then, is the relationship of sex to Eros? The answer is as profound as it is simple: sex models Eros. But sex does not exhaust Eros. Sex models what it means to live an erotic life in every arena of your engagement. To be radically alive means much more than simply being sexual. To be erotic only in sex is to live a deadened life of quiet desperation. Sex erotic implies that sex—when it is lived in its fullest form—incarnates Eros even as it models Eros. Sex erotic teaches us how to live in Eros, not only in sex but also in all the nonsexual dimensions of our lives. That is what it means to live an erotic life.

Eros is aliveness. Aliveness occurs as *you*, when the energy of reality awakens in you and through you. Eros is the vitality that pulses through our atomic structure, making our protons and electrons dance in perpetual ecstasy. Eros is the passion that makes our cells and atoms yearn for each other, always allured and constantly sexing. Eros is what makes us want to dance. Eros is—very literally—what transforms a relationship from a strategy for security to an event of cosmic significance. You can be sexually active and in relationship and remain profoundly lonely. It is only when you realize that your own attractions and allurements participate in the attraction and allurement that is the very structure of the cosmos that you begin to live an erotic life.

In the lived sensuality of an erotic life, loneliness makes no sense. Loneliness is the opposite of Eros and aliveness. Eros is wholeness and interconnectivity. It is the essential nature of a cosmos whose core truth might well be: reality is relationship. It is only when you realize that reality is relationship and that your relationship is part of the grand cacophony of relationship at every level of the cosmos that you truly transcend loneliness.

When you really get the scientific truth that your erotic autobiography is an intended outcome of the love intelligence of reality, then you begin to be at home in your life. The scientific reality of your radical uniqueness is shocking when you really get it. You have an irreducibly unique atomic and cellular signature. The extent and precision of your intricate uniqueness is made clearer every day with new studies and evidence. Your level of dazzling uniqueness intuitively implies intention. When you know that you are personally addressed and intended, you fall in love with your life. Your heart beats faster, and your eyes open wider. You realize that the ache of your wetness or the throbbing of your fullness is reality awake as you. The truly alive person does not know the ennui of boredom. Everything is fascinating to the person who is truly alive. It matters not whether it's a piercing pain, a moment of pleasure, a bucket of grief, or a glimpse of beauty.[2]

THE MEANING OF EROS

Eros is the principle of aliveness and magic inherent in all of reality. Something infinitely real animates everything. Reality is realness, which is another way of saying Eros or aliveness. Everything radiates an intense aliveness. The intensification of aliveness is the natural result of living an erotic life. Most people have had the experience of visiting a place and finding it vibrating with aliveness, color, and immediacy. Some years later they may visit the same place again and find it drab and dreary. Most likely it is not the place that has changed, but the person. Beauty is always in the eye of the beholder. When your eyes are alive, then the hills are alive. When your eyes are asleep, then even the most beautiful vista is deadened.

Our lives are a search for passionate aliveness. Our lives are a search for Eros. We remember well Eros lost. Until we are able to recover Eros, we are filled with an inconsolable longing that can be healed by no external balm.

We hunger for the depths of aliveness, for it is only from those depths that we are capable of love. It is only in the quivering of aliveness that we are capable of being all we can be. That is what it means to be holy. The opposite of holy is not unholy. The opposite of holy is superficial. The holy is the real. We long for what is real. That is why we yearn with all of our being to return to Eros.

NOT SYNONYMOUS

When we talk about Eros or the erotic, we suffer from any number of confusions. There's an important relationship between the erotic and the sexual, but as we said above, they're not the same thing. Eros is the essential aliveness of reality—it's the experience of being on the inside, like when you're running and at some point you break through and you're in the zone or the inside of experience.

There is a fullness of presence in Eros and a feeling that your yearning participates in the evolutionary yearning of being. In Eros you have a felt experience that you are not separate; you experience your own interconnectivity with the larger context, with the wholeness of it all. All blessings flow from Eros. The goodness of life, the color in a black-and-white world, and all ethics flow through the channels of Eros. The loss of Eros is the failure of ethics. Creativity, intimacy and relationship, politics, economics—nothing moves without the erotic. When there's a disconnect from Eros, systems begin to break down both in the world of the personal and in the world of the collective.

When you feel fully alive, when you are in Eros, there is no question about the meaning of life. When you are in Eros, there is no question about the essential goodness of life. When you live in Eros, life is self-evidently meaningful and obviously good. Here is an example of how sex models Eros: when you are on the edge of orgasm, you are on the inside of life—yearning, totally present, ultimately connected, lost in the experience, and yet most radically your Unique Self. When you are in Eros, you have no questions about the meaning of life. You are life.

At the edge of sexual explosion, you do not stop in the middle to contemplate philosophical issues or life's meaning, nor do you question the natural goodness of life. You are fully alive and fully in it. In fact, those five qualities—living on the inside, fullness of presence, yearning, wholeness and interconnectivity, and the experience of your unique identity—are the first five of the twelve faces of Eros that we will be exploring in this book. "Sex models Eros" means that sex models the experience of being on the inside, fully present and connected, deeply yearning, and ultimately yourself, in every facet of your life.

ANCIENT ARTICULATIONS

For ancient articulations of this new sexual narrative, we turn to the hidden wisdom of the spiritually incorrect masters. These masters taught the esoteric traditions of all the great systems of spirit. They are the erotic mystics. The esoteric name for this tradition in the earlier sources is "the Secret of the Cherubs." We will meet the cherubs formally in chapter three. For now, a brief introduction will suffice.

The cherubs are two figures that live atop the Ark of the Covenant in Solomon's temple in Jerusalem. According to the sacred text, the voice of God "speaks from between the two cherubs." What is not known other than to initiates in the esoteric tradition is that these two cherubs are locked in ecstatic sexual embrace. The voice of God speaks from between the sexually entwined cherubs.

The spiritually incorrect Tantric masters were not limited to the Hebrew mystics. They appeared in different guises in all the great traditions. Their true teachings were always esoteric, hidden from public access. Only the initiates truly understood their radical intention. These masters are called the Kabbalists in Judaism, and the Tantric masters in Hinduism and Buddhism. Rumi and Hafiz in Sufism were initiates, as were the Cathars in mystical Christianity. One master of the Zen tradition was named Ikkyu. Mary Magdalene was a master in the hidden Christian tradition. We add to these ancient traditions a vital modern wisdom tradition that we will refer to as Evolutionary Spirituality. This contemporary wisdom lineage is rooted in evolutionary science, systems science, modern physics, biology, chaos theory, and complexity theory. (More about Evolutionary Spirituality in later chapters.)

Veiled in all of these great traditions is a hidden, subversive, mystical teaching. It is either ignored or reinterpreted to avoid its full implications. The great teachers were literally killed, socially murdered, or otherwise sidelined from positions of influence. They were destroyed because the fear of Eros overwhelmed both the goodness of Eros and the wisdom of Eros.

The ancient religions, in their public teachings, sought to impose a measure of order and stability on the ignorant masses. To do so, sex had to be controlled before anything else. This is the legitimate reason for the sex-negative teaching of the great religions. Today, what we need most desperately, however, is not to control sex. Rather, we need to reinvest our sex with a meaning and purpose that is equal to the central role that sex plays in our lives. We have killed all the gods except for Aphrodite, the goddess of sex. It is in the sexual that we still hear the murmuring of the sacred. But we cannot quite make out the words. We need to articulate a new sexual story. We need a story that invests not only our sex but all of our life with fresh aliveness and a new plot line of meaning.

The source of this narrative is in the spiritually incorrect teachings, which understood implicitly that embedded in the sexual, in the full panoply of its gorgeous and graphic detail, is all that is holy, all that is wise, and all that is good. The masters of spiritually incorrect Tantra viewed the sexual act itself as the great wisdom mystery reflecting all the deepest truths of the spirit. In a world torn apart by fanatic fundamentalisms and insipid liberalisms, we need a new teaching that all of us can recognize and take home.

Contrary to conventional religion and much of psychology, the post-conventional, spiritually incorrect Tantric masters insisted that sex is integrally related to love and Eros. There is no disconnect. And not because it is nice, secure, and comfortable if you are able to love the person you are sleeping with. But far more powerfully—and this is the heart of the secret—because the sexual is the ultimate model for Eros and love. The erotic and the holy are one. In every ethical sexual encounter, one can create an energetic container for the sacred, for opening up fully and absolutely into the radical aliveness and love that are already there. The sexual in all of her intricate detail is a most potent teacher, ripping us open, if we will but let her, to the radical fullness of spirit that seeks our pleasure and goodness.

One thirteenth-century Kabbalist put it this way: "Whoever has not desired a woman is like an ass and even less than an ass, for it is from the sexual one understands divine service."[3]

Or in the language of Zen master Ikkyu:

Rinzai's disciples never got the Zen message,
But I, the Blind Donkey, know the truth:
Love play can make you immortal.
The autumn breeze of a single night of love is better than a
    hundred thousand years of
sterile sitting meditation . . .

And just in case he was being too subtle, and to avoid being piously misinterpreted, Ikkyu continues:

Stilted koans and convoluted answers are all monks have,
Pandering endlessly to officials and rich patrons.
Good friends of the Dharma, so proud, let me tell you,
A brothel girl in gold brocade is worth more than any of you,

Emerging from the world's grime, a puritan saint is still nowhere
    near a Buddha.
Enter a brothel and Great Wisdom will explode upon you.
Manjushri should have let Ananda enjoy himself in the whorehouse –
Now he will never know the joys of elegant love play.

Sex stands as the ultimate symbol, both signifying and actually modeling the sacred wisdom, which needs to animate and guide all areas of life. The goal of life is to live erotically in all facets of being, and sex is the model par excellence for sacred erotic living in all of the nonsexual arenas that make up most of our lives. The sexual is in the hidden teaching of the spiritually incorrect Tantric masters. It is the ultimate spiritual master. Thus, deep understanding of the sexual is the ultimate guide to accessing the spirit in every dimension of our reality.

We are not talking about sexual technique. Even when important, sexual technique is technical at best. Sexual technique can never make you a great lover. You can only be a great lover if you are fully alive. To be a great lover in all facets of your being, you must listen deeply to the simple yet elegant spirit whisperings of the sexual. Nietzsche, the great German philosopher, got something right when he said, "The degree and kind of man's sexuality reaches up into the topmost summit of his spirit."

SEX IS THE ANSWER

Is there anything except sex that so grabs our rapt attention; incessantly pursues us; and occupies our daydreams, fantasies, and yearnings? The mystics are just stating the obvious when they say that, with sex, God is trying to GET OUR ATTENTION. "Hello . . . over here! Pay attention!" Now we are not talking about the God who sends good people to burn in hell because they slipped up on one of his impossible demands. Nor even the Grandfather in heaven who hands out chocolate to do-gooders. Forget that God. The God you don't believe in doesn't exist. Rather, the God that exists for us is the personal, erotic life force that courses through reality and knows our name. The God we believe in is the vitality of an intelligent Eros that initiates, animates, and drives all of reality and addresses us personally. The God we believe in is the force for healing and transformation in the world. The God who knows our name is the God who so clearly calls out to us that sex is the answer.

When religion splits us off from our sexuality, we correctly intuit that something is deeply askew. But sex is not a panacea. Sex is not a drug that will soothe away the lurking feeling of ennui and that this cannot be all there is. Good orgasms will not a good life make. Sex is also not merely neutral or simply sacred because it is the method of procreation. Rather, sex is the answer as a model and not as the sum total of all Eros, holiness, and wisdom. Sex, if we will but listen, is a great master of the spirit—better than any guru, psychologist, rabbi, or priest. Sex can teach us how to reclaim the erotic in every nonsexual aspect and element of our lives. For Eros is not sex. The sexual models the erotic; it does not exhaust the erotic.

EROTIC AND NONEROTIC SEX

When we say that sex models Eros, we are not talking about the merely sexual. We are talking about erotic sex. The merely sexual involves a few pathetic grunts, maybe an occasional kiss and nice word, the titillation of the narrow section of the genitals for a few minutes at the most, and a brief fleeting pleasure at climax. If you are lost in mere sex, then you will never penetrate and never be penetrated.

We all know that titillation of the sexual instruments feels good. That is not, however, the sum total of Eros. Superficial feeling good is for people who are afraid of the full divine power of the erotic sexual. When the sexual awakens as the erotic sexual, it takes on an entirely different quality of power, potency, and pleasure. Sex is not a path unless it cracks you open to the divine.

People cling to the outside of the sexual, to breasts and pallid orgasms, because they are afraid to open up to the full power of Eros. It is the fear of Eros that keeps most people fixated on pathetic titillation. Sex invites us to be open as love. Not as ordinary love but as outrageous love. Outrageous love is Eros. The Hebrew mystics teach together with Ikkyu that the universe in every second is always making love. The Kabbalists call it *zivug*. In this world, the incarnation of that divine movement, the perpetual divine lovemaking, is not ordinary sex but erotic sex. Enter into the inside of sex, and you will find God, the sacred lover and gorgeous, divine paramour of the cosmos. The inside of sex is outrageous love. The inside of sex is Eros.

ORDINARY LOVE AND OUTRAGEOUS LOVE

Understanding the distinction between ordinary and outrageous love is the doorway to all that is magical and mysterious both in the cosmos and in life. We need to realize that Sex with a capital *S* is a love story. Not an ordinary love story, but an outrageous love story, an erotic love story. Because outrageous love is Eros. It is the radical aliveness and purpose that animates and drives all reality on every level of creation, all the way up and all the way down. Ordinary love is an experience of the human personality, which feels separate from all that is, grasping for some measure of security and comfort. Ordinary love is a strategy of the ego desperately fleeing the feeling of lonely desperation.

The Bengali mystic Tagore alluded to the distinction between ordinary and outrageous love when he said, "Love is not mere human sentiment but the heart of existence itself." The love that he called "mere human sentiment" is what we are referring to as ordinary love. The love that he calls "the heart of existence" is what we are calling outrageous love, or Eros.

The mystics of the Kabbalah called ordinary love "the love after creation." They called outrageous love "the love before creation." Love after creation is in reaction. It is all too often culturally conditioned and imposed. Love before creation is what the great writer Dante called *l'amor che move il sole e l'altre stele,* "the love that moves the sun and the other stars." It is the love that moved the Infinite to manifest reality in the explosion of the big bang. It is the love that is the evolutionary impulse driving all reality to higher and higher levels of consciousness and love.

Ordinary love is valid and good, but it is a strategy of the ego. It is a legitimate and even necessary human experience. It may win you comfort and some measure of illusory security, but ordinary love cannot take you home. Home is the experience that there is no place to go because you have already arrived. Home is when you stop seeking the meaning of life because it becomes outrageously self-evident. Home is when you fall in love with your life anew every day. Home is the knowing that every place you go you are being carried. Only outrageous love takes you home. Outrageous love is the dance of allurement and attraction at the very subatomic level of existence. Outrageous love is the ceaseless, ecstatic, creative pulsation that drives the entire process of emergence. Outrageous love is the field of allurement, at every level of reality—from atom, to plant, to animal, to human—that holds all creation together.

But outrageous love can become part of your human experience. Living becomes extraordinary when we access outrageous love in the course of what we like to call ordinary life. When you love your beloved not merely as an unconscious strategy of ego but as an expression of the Eros of existence, outrageous love is awakened in you, and your entire experience of life changes. When you hold your beloved's hand with ordinary love, your hand gets clammy rather quickly. You can't quite find the right position, and soon you want to unclasp. When you hold your beloved's hand with outrageous love, you feel like all is perfect and you want the moment to last forever.

Another scenario. Your baby is crying. Pick up the baby with the hands of ordinary love, and the baby continues to cry and fidget, often more intensely than before. But pick up the baby with outrageous love, and the baby literally melts into you. The crying naturally recedes, and the baby falls into a profound and deep state of rest. The infant has been lifted up into the lap of Eros, and she knows it. You feel the bliss of her resting in the depth of your being, which is the Eros of existence—outrageous love itself. This shift inside you, from emptiness to Eros, from ordinary love to outrageous love, is the change that changes everything.

When the very Eros of existence is awakened in you, you are awakening as outrageous love. You become an outrageous lover. You begin to live an erotic life. Sex transforms from the pitiful grasping for fleeting fulfillment that is not working for virtually anyone, to something else entirely. Sex is revealed as the potent prose and poetry of reality itself, incarnate as your body and your desire. Sex is revealed as the love story of all of reality, happening in and as you. Sex is revealed as the source of all wisdom, pointing us toward the erotic and the holy in every dimension of life. It is a virtuous circle. Sex models Eros. You begin to live the erotic life in every dimension of your nonsexual life. As you re-eroticize your life, you are personally transformed. At the same time, regular sex transforms into erotic sex. Ordinary sex becomes outrageous sex.

SEX: A LOVE STORY

We need to realize that sex is a love story—not an ordinary love story, but an outrageous love story. An erotic love story. Outrageous love is Eros. Ordinary love is legitimate, but it is limited in the gift it can give you. In this world, that incarnation of the divine movement called outrageous love is the perpetual divine lovemaking. Participate in that perpetual movement of reality's lovemaking through your body and the result is not ordinary sex, but outrageous erotic sex. Enter into the inside of sex and you will find God, the sacred lover and gorgeous divine slut of the Cosmos. The inside of sex is outrageous love. The inside of sex is outrageous Eros. The qualities of Eros are the qualities of the sacred; the erotic and the holy are one. The goal is to re-eroticize all of your life, and your teacher and your guide is the sexual, the seat of all wisdom.

In the upcoming chapters through the end of part two, we will explore in depth the Secret of the Cherubs. At the heart of the secret is the new sexual narrative: sex erotic. These chapters form the essence of the Secret of the Cherubs. Parts three, four, and five will explore the twelve faces of Eros—erotic qualities that are, at the same time, characteristics of Eros and paths to Eros.

Each face of Eros is an expression of a different texture of radical aliveness. When all of these awaken in you, you are living an erotic life. Each face is a portal through which to return to Eros. The twelve faces are:

- The First Face: Interiority: Living on the Inside
- The Second Face: Fullness of Presence
- The Third Face: Yearning and Desire
- The Fourth Face: Wholeness and Interconnectivity
- The Fifth Face: Uniqueness and Identity
- The Sixth Face: Imagination
- The Seventh Face: Perception
- The Eighth Face: Giving and Receiving
- The Ninth Face: Surrender
- The Tenth Face: Play
- The Eleventh Face: Creativity
- The Twelfth Face: Pleasure and Delight

The experience of being radically alive comes from all of these faces of Eros taken together. To live the erotic life is to have the most potent and powerful access to each of these faces. In each of them, sex is our teacher. It is our portal to accessing the radically alive experience of each face. But our experience of the faces does not end in their sexual expression. Quite the opposite. It is all about sex and not about sex at all. Sex models each of the faces of Eros, and in so doing, gives us a vision of what it might mean to live them fully in every dimension of our lives.

It would be a great tragedy of the spirit if the only place where we experienced the faces of Eros were in the sexual. That would be to relegate Eros to the narrow confines of the bedroom, when it needs to soar through our kitchens, our offices, our carpools, our classrooms! In erotic living, we seek the realization of these qualities in every dimension of our existence. From work, to play, to politics, to intellectual pursuits—in all of these we seek erotic experience.

Erotic engagement could become our daily fare if we just freed our Eros from its old casing. These hand-me-down ideas of an Eros that is only about sex have become threadbare. We must reweave the fabric. The full pleasure of living, the joy of fullness and creativity, can come only when we re-eroticize our lives. Until then, human beings will turn to the shadows of Eros—rage, abuse, and violence—to remind themselves, through the intensity of those experiences, that they exist.

FACES AND PATHS

One of the fundamental principles of Eros is the path is the destination. In a true path, there is no split between the path and the goal. We are creative not only for the sake of the product that emerges but also for the sake of the creative experience itself. We do awareness practice not merely to get to awareness but also because the practice is awareness. We have sex, among other reasons, to feel intimate, but the experience of sex is intimacy itself. In the same way, the authentic and potent experience of each face of Eros is also the path to Eros.

The path and the destination are the same. Each face of Eros is a distinct path of Hebrew Tantra. In each, the sexual opens the door, giving us a taste of that particular face of Eros, so that Sex models for us each face of Eros so we can live that face in every dimension of our lives. The return to Eros cannot bypass sex because erotic sex models for us how to live erotically, how to be radically alive in all of the nonsexual dimensions of our lives.

CHAPTER TWO

EVOKING EROS

Our lives are spent teetering on the edge of the void. You know, the void—the big hole you feel inside. Usually it is a dull and throbbing pain, the background noise of most lives. We rush around, doing everything we can to fill the hole. We have a handy word for this rushing about: avoidance. A dance around the void. We develop the most elaborate maneuvers we can imagine, never realizing that it is all a-void-dance. That if we could but taste fullness for a moment, then the vacant dances of consumerism, addiction, empty sex, and violence would be transformed into the erotic dance of Being.

The emptiness is so palpable and overwhelming that we would fill it at virtually any price. We seek immediate gratification, a quick fix—a book, a drug, a relationship, a job—anything to fill the gaping chasm, the hole in our wholeness. We run desperately looking for the next watering hole that might fill up the emptiness we feel so deeply and try so hard to hide.

On the outside our mad dashing about may look like a dance, but we are really gasping for air. Picture a bee in a bottle. Seen from the outside, the bee darts from side to side in an ecstatic dance. On the inside, however, there is neither dance nor ecstasy. The bee is slowly dying, suffocating. It was not meant to be this way. Life should not be a pathos-filled scramble for some snatches of authenticity in between empty charades.

THE EROTIC MYSTICS

The ancient wisdom of the erotic Hebrew mystics makes one essential promise: There is a better way to live. In the midst of uncertainty and anxiety, joy and meaning remain genuine options. We can choose life and love, or death and fear. To experience the fullness of every moment, to move from isolation to deep connection, is our birthright if we but claim it.

The great invitation of the spirit is to heal our pain, opening us up to the possibility of joy, ecstasy, and love. There is another way to dance: the dance of Eros, the dance in which we all have a place. This book is about sharing the dance of Eros with you.

As you probably know, most people assume that Eros is merely a synonym for sex. It is not. The fact that we so often confuse Eros with sex merely reminds us of how distant we are from true erotic engagement. To dance with Eros is to live and love erotically in all the arenas of our lives, beyond the merely sexual. That is what it means to be holy. Just as holiness should not be limited to our houses of worship, Eros should not be limited to our bedrooms.

Eros is to be fully alive. Eros is to be fully present to what is. It is to open your eyes and see for the first time the full beauty and gorgeous-ness of a friend. To smell the richness of an aroma, to feel the fullness of throbbing desire, and to taste the erotic experience that connects you with every being. It is to feel the palpable love that dissolves the walls of ego, anger, and anxiety.

Eros is the feeling you have when you stop trying to get someplace because you realize with great joy that you are already there. To be erot-ically engaged is to feel the radical interconnectivity of being as a living reality in your life. For the spiritually incorrect mystics, neither dogma nor doctrine will take us home. We need Eros. Eros is the key that pro-vides deep meaning to everything—satisfying work, joyful relationships, effective parenting. Starvation, fundamentalism, greed, war, and the rape of the Earth are all the result of lack of Eros.

It is the mystery of Eros that was at the core of the teachings of the temple in ancient Jerusalem. The dance with Eros was called the dance with the Goddess. In the hidden tradition of the erotic mystics, it is the Shechinah, the Goddess whose presence suffuses reality. The mystics render the sacred text as follows: "Make for me a temple" and the Shechinah, the Goddess—literally, the erotic presence—"will dwell in your midst." She is Eros incarnate.

We will call these teachings the path of Hebrew Tantra. One of the meanings of the Sanskrit word *tantra* is "to expand." Hebrew Tantra is about expanding Eros beyond the sexual to include all the nonsexual areas of our lives. To dance with the Goddess is to live the erotic life not only in sex but also in every facet of our existence. Hebrew Tantra is a means of accessing the aliveness of erotic energy to become one with the divinity that courses through us at every moment.

These teachings on sex, love, and Eros were secret. Sourced in the temple mysteries, they were transmitted in secret by the erotic mystics in all the great traditions, often at great risk to both the teacher and the student. Modern popular books, like the fiction best seller *The Da Vinci Code*, are potent because they are perfumed with the fragrance of this ancient mystery tradition. *The Da Vinci Code* is a popularization of the Mary Magdalene tradition, which asserts that Mary and Jesus were sexual. It understands sex in a very different way than sex was viewed by the classical Christian tradition. The erotic love between Jesus and Mary is a model for living the scared life. The Magdalene tradition is rooted in the mysteries of the Jerusalem Temple, which understood that the erotic and the holy are one.

The ancient teachings about Eros have never been taught publicly, and for good reason. They were thought to be too explosive to be taught to the general public. Read superficially, they could be misunderstood as merely sexual license or an abandonment of interpersonal ethics. As we shall see, however, they are neither. Rather, the temple mysteries are a profound and powerful path of love and Eros. For the temple mystics, the goal of life was erotic living. The essence of their teachings was to transform sexuality into a loving guide to fullness, Eros, and joy.

THE QUESTION OF MEANING

When we live from the lap of Eros we stop searching for the answer to the question of the meaning of life. The meaning of life becomes self-evident. The split between the ordinary and the extraordinary disappears. It is not that we come up with a great answer. The question simply falls away. Imagine that you are having the best sex of your life with a person you love deeply. Do you stop before the explosion to ponder the meaning of life? We think not. Not because you have come up with the answer but because the question falls away in the fullness of the moment.

When all of your activity has the same level of self-evident meaning, then you are living the erotic life. T. S. Eliot once referred to this as "living an autotelic life." *Auto* derives from the Greek word for "self," and *telic* comes from the Greek word *telos*, which means "goal" or "end." An autotelic person means one who is so fully immersed in the current of life that every activity is not merely a means to an end but an end in itself. For such a person, every activity is an expression of the fullness of life rather than a grasping for happiness or achievement. According to the *Oxford English Dictionary*, an activity that is autotelic "is one which has a purpose in and not apart from itself." The autotelic life is the erotic life.

THE RETURN TO EROS

In the language of the erotic mystics of the secret temple lineage, the return to Eros transforms reality and liberates the Goddess. Eros is outrageous love, the love that is the essence of all reality. The return to Eros happens when outrageous love becomes alive in our lives.

Eros is what we are talking about when we say God is love. God is not ordinary love, a strategy of the ego. God is outrageous love. God is Eros. Or said differently, in the language of the leading edge of evolutionary theory, reality is Eros. Reality is animated and motivated by Eros, and it self-organizes toward higher and higher levels of complexity and consciousness.[4]

Finally we will evolve the very source code of consciousness and transform our core experience of life by closing the tragic gap (which has persisted both in our personal lives and throughout human history) among the erotic, the sexual, and the holy. We will see that you can only be fully alive, powerfully ethical, and in love if you are living a full erotic life. The erotic life is purposeful even as it is powerful and poignant. But Eros is also potent in that it is always potentiating new possibility. As the great philosopher of science Alfred North Whitehead reminds us, the constant emergence of novelty is the very nature of Eros. In the fullness of erotic living you are literally a virgin, always touching for the very first time.

THE FAILURE OF EROS

We will demonstrate the surprising counterintuitive principle that the failure of Eros leads directly to the collapse of ethics. Virtually all forms of acting out, addiction, depression, violence, and abuse are rooted in the loss of aliveness—what the mystics allusively call the fall of Eros. Every form of success, fulfillment, and joy is the natural result of living the erotic life. It is only in the erotic life that we experience a life well lived. In the erotic life, we not only love on occasion; we are actually lived as love. When we live in the lap of Eros, we are able to keep our hearts open in all situations. Eros does not bypass the hurt; rather, it fills it with aliveness and love. Eros is not tepid and polite; Eros is dynamic and outrageous. The credo of Eros is simple: we live in a world of outrageous pain. The only response to outrageous pain is outrageous love. Outrageous love is Eros.

Even if we could somehow put aside the starvation and the wars, an even superficial view of our own society reveals that something is seriously askew. This is not a detail problem but an essential flaw in the plumb line of our culture. Every forty seconds someone kills themselves. Every year upward of one million people will experience a failure of love so intense and painful that they will voluntarily end their lives. In the last forty-five years, suicide rates have increased by 60 percent worldwide.

The figures are highest in Western democracies like Belgium, Denmark, Sweden, New Zealand, Finland, and, of course, the United States.

Suicide used to be largely limited to the elderly—people who had, at the end of their lives, looked back and been unable to make sense of their story. Not particularly comforting news, because all of us want to, and most of us will, reach old age. But the jolting news is that the average age of suicide is going down. Suicide is now one of the three leading causes of death among those aged fifteen to forty-four. Now of course it would be nice to dismiss this unpleasant information with the thought that only crazy or severely depressed people commit suicide. Note, however, that for every actual suicide there are ten suicide attempts. Suicide attempts have increased in the last forty-five years twenty times more than "successful" suicides.

Add to this the easily inferred truth that for every person who attempts suicide there are a lot more people in just as much pain. They are just as lonely, just as alienated, and just as depressed, but they simply are unable to do anything about it. So they live in limbo, suspended between hells, all the while maintaining the facade of normal and even successful lives.

And yet our guilty feet have got no rhythm. Beneath our desperately dancing steps lurks a yawning abyss of emptiness that kills our joy and poisons our satisfactions. We need another way to dance.

We will introduce you to a dancing master in chapter four who will show us this new way. He reminds us that Eros is a genuine possibility in our lives. Stay in the emptiness, he tells us, and it will become full. Where before you danced to the music of competition and grenvy (greed and envy), you are now aroused by the alluring melodies of Eros in every sphere of your life. You no longer feel like you must obey God; rather, you participate in the divine.[5]

Eros is revealed in the sound of a woman singing, the caress of a small deed of loving, or a tear quivering with tenderness. Eros is found in the silence of presence between close friends working side by side, or in the ecstasy of lovers screaming the name of God. Eros is when you explode in pleasure that affirms the very goodness of existence. Eros is when you delight in giving or receiving a gift that makes life worth living. Eros makes itself known in all genuinely felt pain and joy, anger and ecstasy, in which we enter the feeling so deeply that we come out the other side more whole and more alive. All of these fill our emptiness and enliven our days. We are no longer alienated from our own lives, living externally, wondering, "Is this all there is?" To dance with Eros is to step inside to the full glory and wonder of your life. To live and love with passion, purpose, and poignancy—to be radically alive in all the facets of our being—is what it means to live an erotic life.

EXPANDING LOVE LISTS

One cannot be told that life is worthwhile. One must experience the erotic love of living firsthand. Yet so few people have an unmediated sense of the radical aliveness and infinite dignity of their lives. It is this very erotic sense that is so essential to making our lives a triumph. This is the experience that we call the erotic life. So many of us today are secondhand consumers of secondhand joy, never touching Eros directly. And when our Eros fails, there truly is nothing left to live for.

When we exile the essential Eros of love into the experience of romantic love with only one person—beautiful as that may be—the erotic is in exile. For there is no one person to whom we can give over the power to make our life meaningful or meaningless. When we exile Eros into the sexual, when the sexual becomes the only place that we taste the erotic, the erotic is in exile. And then sex collapses under the weight of a burden it cannot bear.

In every chapter of this book we will further unfold the stunning relationship between the erotic and the sexual. This relationship articulates a new narrative of sexuality that radically transforms both your understanding and your experience of the sexual and of sex in your life. Sex will become not the sum total of your erotic experience but the portal into ever deepening Eros in every dimension of your life.

Eros is experiencing that your existence drips with aliveness and overflows with meaning, no matter what your particular circumstance may be at a given moment. The universe feels, and the universe feels Eros.

Eros is not hard to find and impossible to avoid. For Eros is the very nature of reality itself. We are drenched in Eros. We just need to open the door and realize we are already on the inside.

When you live in Eros, you fall in love with life itself, and with your own life, again and again. From that place of being in love with life you fall in love with many people, not necessarily romantically or even sexually. But you realize that your love lists are too short. Love cannot be limited to the people who give you economic security or to whom you are connected biologically. Love rooted in Eros is not ordinary love. Ordinary love is a strategy of the ego seeking security and comfort. All too quickly, ordinary love becomes comfortably numb. Love rooted in Eros is not ordinary but extraordinary. It is radically alive. Eros is not mere fancy or passing sentiment but rather the essence of existence itself.

LOVE OR DIE

We are confronted, personally and globally, with a stark choice: love or die! It is that simple. Again, by love we do not mean ordinary love but outrageous love, that which we have called Eros. Eros is no longer a luxury—it is an absolute necessity for the survival of the individual and the planet. In the last half century, modern psychology has documented an age-old truth: a fully nourished baby who is not held in loving arms will die. The loving arms that ensure a baby's wholeness and health are not the arms of ordinary love. It is not the love of an ego seeking security. Rather, the love of a mother or father is the Eros of existence holding the baby and keeping her safe. This is outrageous love, the fabric of existence itself. This is the love about which Solomon, builder of the Hebrew Temple, wrote, "Its insides are lined with love." Just like a baby will die if not held in love, so too our world—even with all the resources, intelligence, and technology at our disposal—will die if not held in outrageous love. A de-eroticized world cannot survive. We must embrace a personal path with heart and a global politics of Eros.

Life is a choice. What is the rhythm of our dance? Are we dancing masters or bottled bees that appear to be dancing but are gasping for air?

Who are our dancing partners—desperation and emptiness or Eros and the Goddess? Are we outrageous lovers in all facets of our lives or are we apathetic, deadened, and indifferent? Bees in bottles always sting. But everyone knows that to sting is to die. The only way to not sting is to learn to be a dancing master.

The great mystery tradition of Hebrew wisdom is about a radical and profound path toward becoming just such a dancing master. The ancient Temple in Jerusalem was the center of a society, where the Hebrew mysteries were practiced and taught. At the core of the temple mysteries lay an ancient set of radical understandings about sex, love, and Eros. The Hebrew mysteries gently but powerfully charted a path that, if we but have the courage to walk it, will teach us how to live erotically in every facet of existence.

The invitation and the challenge of the spirit in our generation are to create a politics of Eros and love. That can only begin to happen when each person in the polis takes responsibility for the erotic quality of his or her life. We need to, and we can, realign our souls with the vital currents of loving energy that course though our universe. We need to return to Eros. We can decide to enter the flow, and from that place on the inside, transform first our lives and, ultimately, our planet.

At the epicenter of holiness in the ancient Hebrew Temple in Jerusalem was the Ark of the Covenant. You may remember it from the cinema—it is the very same Ark that Indiana Jones sought to retrieve in the classic movie *Raiders of the Lost Ark*. As we said earlier, atop this Ark was carved a pair of figures called cherubs. Surprisingly, the cherubs were locked in sexual embrace. These entwined cherubs were not only atop the Ark but were also the major decorative motif all over the temple walls, doors, and sacred vessels. Even if you absolutely affirm the sexual as a wonderful part of your life, sexually entwined cherubs at the axis mundi of holiness in the Jerusalem Temple? What might this possibly mean? We will explore this mystery in the next chapter.

CHAPTER THREE

SEX IN THE TEMPLE

Imagine the scene: You walk into your local place of worship—church, synagogue, mosque, meditation center, or whatever. The pastor or rabbi has apparently decided to redecorate while you were away on vacation. You find that he has installed atop the Ark or altar a statue of sexually intertwined golden figures. In addition, he positions among the pews another freestanding set of sexually embracing figures. And just in case you missed the point, vivid pictures of these effigies adorn most of the sanctuary walls.

We daresay that as sexually open as we are, and much as we affirm sexuality as a wonder and a central good in our lives, the pastor's contract would not be renewed. However, in the pastor's defense, let me share with you a secret. These precise images were the central display in the archetype of the holiest of places: the ancient Temple of Jerusalem.

The figures were called cherubs. The primary set was positioned in the center of the temple, atop the Ark of the Covenant. According to Hebrew myth, this spot is the Earth's epicenter, the axis mundi, the place where heaven and earth kiss. A second set of golden cherubs was freestanding, and the rest were in pictographic form on the walls and even on some of the temple vessels. The provocatively entwined cherubs were, for the mystics, the very key to the mystery of love, a mystery that lay at the heart of the Jerusalem Temple, a mystery that lies at the heart of all of our lives. Unraveling this mystery is the purpose of our journey together. Let the mysteries begin!

THE SEAT OF THE SECRET

Remember the movie *Raiders of the Lost Ark*, featuring Indiana Jones adventuring through the dusty Middle East in search of the Ark of the Covenant? Lives are lost, blood is let. One was tempted to ask why he shouldn't just let the Ark stay lost!

The answer is that the Ark, perhaps more than any other earthly object, is of overwhelming mystical significance. The Ark was an elegant container that held the original tablets on which were inscribed the Ten Commandments. Described in the sources as something akin to a spiritually creative, life-giving nuclear reactor, it was lost when the Temple of Jerusalem was destroyed some 2,500 years ago. It has been sought after, physically and metaphysically, ever since. The search for the Ark is the original grail quest of biblical myth.

Jerusalem holds the secret. It is the cradle of three faiths, each today in its own way in desperate need of renewal and re-souling. At the center of Jerusalem stood the temple built by Solomon and destroyed by the Greeks, then rebuilt by Ezra and destroyed by the Romans. It is a temple that awaits rebuilding in our own inner lives, for the temple in the Hebrew mystery tradition of the Kabbalah is not so much a place on Earth as a powerful idea of the spirit. The essence of Hebrew mysticism lies hidden in the grain of the temple's wood and the folds of her curtains.

The loss of the temple is considered by the biblical mystery tradition to be the greatest spiritual disaster in history. The rebuilding of the temple through the reclaiming of its energy in our lives is the overarching goal of the entire biblical project. This is the desire that is expressed time and again in a thousand different ways in Hebrew ritual and liturgy. It is the idea that shaped all of the spiritual offspring of Hebrew religion—that is to say, much of civilization as we know it.

The temple myth is so powerful, so fertile and teeming with life, that it has given birth to most of the great systems of the spirit created by humanity. Hebrew mysticism, beginning with Abraham, gave birth to Judaism, Christianity, and Islam. All three religions in their inner forms are rooted in the Temple of Jerusalem, hence the mythic power of the Christian Templars, the Islamic Dome of the Rock, and the Hebrew Temple Mount.

Further, Kabbalistic tradition tells of the sons of Abraham, who in the book of Genesis are sent eastward to the land of the Buddha. The Kabbalists teach that Abraham's heirs are the progenitors of Buddhism. There is even an old oral Kabbalistic tradition that claims that the builder of the temple (King Solomon) and the Buddha are, if not the same person, at least masters in the same sacred tradition. While historically inaccurate, the story points to the deep spiritual affinity between Solomon's teachings and those of the Buddha hundreds of years later.

So the Hebrew Temple with her eternal flame is the source of the fire that sparked, and continues to light, so many of the pure wicks of the spirit that illuminate our world. Those who have lost touch with the mystery kill one another today in order to control the temple's geographical site, a sad betrayal of the spirit for which the temple was incarnated. For the great mystics, the devotion to the temple is not about a commitment to a particular building on a particular hill in Jerusalem. It is about what we might call "temple consciousness." This consciousness represents a potent wisdom that defies convention. Temple consciousness is subversive in that it defies the petty power plays of the ego and the contorted contractions of our superficial identities.

But what is the great wisdom hidden in the temple myth? What perennial message of the spirit does it yearn to share with us? The simple answer is Eros. The temple plans were drawn up by David and manifested by his son Yedidya, better known as Solomon. Both names, David and Yedidya, mean "loved by the spirit." These kings are the great lovers of biblical myth. They loved greatly and were greatly loved—Solomon by God, the Queen of Sheba, and a thousand wives; David by God, the people, Jonathan, and biblical myth readers throughout history. The temple mystery was thus born and sired by men whose name was love. Not ordinary love but outrageous love.

What is the secret of this ancient love hidden in the temple's origins? What is the mystery of the lost Ark, crowned by her sexually intertwined cherubic lovers? Why is the mythic Ark's metaphorical recovery so absolutely crucial for our lives? Could this ancient and esoteric wisdom have something radically new and important to say about the love lost in our lives and the road to its recovery? Can the cherubs lead us home?

THE SECRET OF THE CHERUBS

To understand the mystery of the temple and what it has to teach us, we need to approach it more carefully. Indeed, gradually approaching the center is always the essential formula in the quest of the spirit. The temple itself was built somewhat like an exquisite mandala. A mandala invites the gazer to pass through layer after layer of imagery before beholding its wondrous core. Similarly, we find that the temple was a layered structure. The high priest would ascend the great staircase to the outer Courtyard of Song, pass through the courtyard into the chamber called the Holy, and from there into the innermost sanctum, the Holy of Holies. In this sanctum sanctorum of the temple, behind fine brocaded curtains, stood the golden Ark of the Covenant. The Ark contained within it the two tablets of stone upon which were carved the Ten Commandments. They were magical lapidary tablets, sculpted by the God-gripped hand of Moses himself.

Most significant, though, is that which rests atop the Ark. Sitting perched aloft the Ark are our two winged figures, the celebrated cherubs. Indeed, their cherubic faces have graced everything from the greatest works of art to countless covers of Hallmark cards. Yet here, according to the esoteric tradition, these images were not of the Hallmark variety. These two cherubs were male and female, face to face, *meurim zeh b'zeh*—intertwined in sexual embrace. In the language of the biblical source text, the cherubs were "as one embraced with his lover." These carved creatures were the focal point, the epicenter, of the mandala-like temple space. They sat, like the guarded pupil of the eye, at the source of the sacred.

That such provocatively sexual figures would have such prominence in the Holy of Holies is a mystery indeed. It is called by the Kabbalistic initiates the *sod hakeruvim*, the Secret of the Cherubs. And though full initiation into this secret cannot be wholly transmitted in the pages of a book, together we can at least hint at its wonder and strive to scrutinize the inscrutable.

THE LION OF FIRE

The best way to behold such mysteries is through the gleaming prism of story. Thus we begin with a spellbinding ancient text that sits at the core of the mystery tradition. This esoteric tale describes an extraordinary scene that takes place in Jerusalem in roughly 500 BCE, almost two centuries before Plato and Aristotle.

The masters of the day were distressed. Adultery was spreading rampant as plague among the people. The authorities were at a loss as to how to curb this powerful urge. Finally, driven to desperation, they began to pray. For three days, they fasted, weeping and pleading with God, "Let us slay the sexual drive before it slays us."

Finally, God acquiesced. The masters then witnessed a lion of fire leap out from within the temple's Holy of Holies. A prophet among them identified the lion as the personification of the primal sexual drive.

They sought to slay the lion of fire. But the result was that for three days thereafter the entire society ground to a standstill. Hens did not lay eggs, artists ceased creating, businesses faltered, and all spiritual activity came to a halt.

Realizing that the sexual drive was about more than just sex, that it somehow echoed the divine, the masters relented. They prayed that only its destructive shadow be removed. Their request was denied on high with the insightful psychological response, "You cannot have only half a drive." The greater the sacred power of a quality, the greater its shadow; the two are inseparable. So they prayed that the lion at least be weakened, and their prayer was granted. The lion, less potent but no less present, reentered the Holy of Holies. The text is alive with myth, magic, and mystery. The most startling revelation is the radical claim as to the originating place of the sexual drive. Why does this drive, personified as a lion of fire, emerge from the temple's Holy of Holies? Apparently, this is its eternal abode. Remarkably, the text is telling us that the seat and source of the sexual drive is none other than the Holy of Holies.

In fact, the Holy of Holies is often depicted in the mystical sources as the marriage bed. The tablets and the Ark are depicted respectively as the phallus (the penis) and the yoni (the vagina) or the clitoris. This sexual model of Eros and the virtual identity between the erotic and the holy are perhaps the most vital and provocative insights of the Kabbalists. They taught it implicitly in a thousand different ways in their writings. They rarely said it overtly for fear the message would be misunderstood, leading to a kind of sexual anarchy, which would bring in its wake the collapse of family. So the dominant impression we are left with is that while sex is good, as it is created by God, it is exceedingly dangerous and is to be handled with great caution. One gets the impression that the attendant dangers may even override the essential good. Thus, nothing as audacious as the Secret of the Cherubs was written about openly. And, yet, once you see it, you realize it is there, subtly calling out, whispering from the folds of literally hundreds of texts.

Sex in the temple!? Sexually entwined cherubs atop the Ark, and a fiery feline sexual drive living in the Holy of Holies? What are these mythic images trying to express? At first blush, they seem to describe sex as a central preoccupation of the Holy of Holies, portraying the temple as some kind of ancient Hebrew Playboy mansion. While Hebrew mysticism may wholeheartedly embrace a positive and healthy sexual ethic, one would not have thought that sex is the essence of the sacred! What is being pointed toward here is not merely a sex-positive moment. Rather, hidden in the folds of the ancient manuscripts is a new narrative of the sexual that is well beyond a prosaic affirmation that sex is good or even that sex is holy because it creates babies. The answer lies in the story itself.

When the lion is subdued, the world does not wake up with just its sexual drive lobotomized. Rather, the world wakes up to an overwhelmingly dull and driveless existence. The passionate engagement in all activity has suddenly withered and vanished. Whether it is in sex, art, work, or creativity, the thrill of existence is gone. Clearly, that fiery feline inhabitant of the Holy of Holies represents not merely sexuality. She is the incarnation of a more potent energy force. She is the embodiment of the Shechinah. She is the incarnation of Eros.

THE SHECHINAH

The Shechinah is the Hebrew name for the feminine Divine. Her name means "indwelling presence" and "the one who dwells in you." She is presence, poetry, passion. She is the sustaining God force that runs through and provides a womb for the world. She is the underlying erotic, sensual, and loving force that knows our name and nurtures all being.

Shechinah captures an experience, a way of being in the world, for which we do not yet have an English word. For this is a way of being that we in the West are hard-pressed to articulate. It is the experience of waking up in the morning full of utter joy for the arrival of the day. It is weeping over the splendor of the sunset or the scent of the ocean or the fragility of a newborn. It is a way of living in love. It is a way of being lived by love. It is a way of living the erotic life.

Indeed, it is one of the great failures of love that we do not possess such a word for this fully charged way of living. The main reason we lack a word for the type of love we will be exploring in this book is that such an expanded notion of love is still so foreign to the fabric of our lives. Our vocabulary reflects our reality. Just as the Eskimo has an ample supply of words to describe different types of snow, a society infused with love would likewise have a menagerie of terms for different types of love. We should wonder over the paucity in the English language of our "terms of endearment."

Our best choice in the English language is to turn toward the term Plato introduced in *The Symposium*: Eros. For Plato, Eros is love plus. It is precisely the kind of fully charged life experience that is evoked by the Hebrew term *Shechinah*.

But over time the word *Eros* has been so narrowed and limited that it has lost most of its original intention. Usually when we hear the word *erotic*, it evokes only the sexual. The erotic life has been reduced to but one of its dimensions. And although the sexual is a part of Eros, it is only a limited part. The type of full Eros we have been describing in this book is way beyond the mere sexual. We must work to reclaim this original meaning of Eros, a meaning infused by its Hebrew counterpart, Shechinah. Temple consciousness incarnates in the lion of fire, the sexual drive, which lives in the Holy of Holies. The Holy of Holies, remember, is the place where the sexually entwined cherubs make love, above the Ark of the Covenant. And the sacred text reminds us that the voice of God speaks from within raw Eros—the radical aliveness of their sexual play.

CHAPTER FOUR

THE DANCING MASTER, AN EROTIC STORY

A Tibetan story wonderfully evokes the erotic experience we are exploring together.

Reports had reached the young Dalai Lama that a certain master of Kung Fu was roaming the countryside of Tibet, converting young men to the study of violence. Rumors even began circulating that this Kung Fu master was an incarnation of Shiva Nataraja, the Hindu god in his aspect of the Lord of the Dance of Destruction. The Dalai Lama decided to invite the master for a visit.

Pleased with the invitation, the Kung Fu master strode into the Dalai Lama's ceremonial hall some weeks later. The master was beautiful indeed, with thick blue-black hair falling down over the shoulders of his black leather suit. "Your Holiness," he began, "be not concerned. I would not think of doing you harm."

"Well, when you do want to harm," asked the Dalai Lama, "what kind of harm can you do?"

"Your Holiness, the best way to show you would be for you to stand here in front of me while I do a little dance. Though I can kill a dozen men instantly with this dance, have no fear."

The Dalai Lama stood up and immediately felt as if a wind had blown flower petals across his body. He looked down but saw nothing. "You may proceed," he told the master of Kung Fu.

"Proceed?" said the other, grinning jovially. "I've already finished. What you felt were my hands flicking across your body. If I had done it in slow motion, extremely slow motion, you would have seen how each touch of my hand would have destroyed the organs of your body one by one."

"Impressive. But I know a master greater than you," said the Dalai Lama.

"Without wishing to offend Your Holiness, I doubt that very much," said the Kung Fu master. "Let him challenge me, and if he bests me, I shall leave Tibet forever."

"If he bests you, you shall have no need to leave Tibet." The Dalai Lama clapped his hands. "Regent," he said, "summon the dancing master."

The dancing master entered. He was a wiry little fellow, half the size of the master of Kung Fu and well past his prime. His legs were knotted with varicose veins, and he was swollen at the elbows from arthritis. Nevertheless, his eyes were glittering merrily, and he seemed eager for the challenge.

The master of Kung Fu did not mock his opponent. "My own guru," he said, "was even smaller and older than you, yet I was unable to best him until last year when I finally caught him on the ear and destroyed him, as I shall destroy you when you finally tire."

The two opponents faced off. The Kung Fu master assumed a jaunty, indifferent stance, intending to tempt the other to attack.

The old dancing master began to swirl very slowly, his robes wafting around his body. His arms stretched out, and his hands fluttered like butterflies toward the eyes of his opponent. His fingers settled gently for a moment upon the bushy eyebrows.

The master of Kung Fu drew back in astonishment. He looked around the great hall. Everything was suddenly vibrant with rich hues of singing color. The faces of the monks were radiantly beautiful. It was as if his eyes had been washed clean for the first time.

The fingers of the dancing master stroked the nose of the master of Kung Fu, and suddenly he could smell the pungent barley from a granary in the city far below. He was intoxicated by the aroma of the butter melting in the Dalai Lama's fragrant tea.

A flick of the dancing master's foot at the Kung Fu master's genitals, and he was throbbing with desire. The sound of a woman singing through an open window filled him with exquisite yearning to draw her into his arms and caress her. He found himself removing his leather clothes until he stood naked before the dancing master, who was now assaulting him with joy at every touch.

His body began to hum like a finely tuned instrument. He opened his mouth and sang like a bird at sunrise. It seemed to him that he was possessed of many arms, legs, and hands, and all wanted to nurture the blossoming of life.

The Kung Fu master began the most beautiful dance that had ever been seen in the great ceremonial hall of the Grand Potala. It lasted for three days and nights, during which time everyone in Tibet feasted and visitors crowded the doorways and galleries to watch. Only when he finally collapsed at the throne of the Dalai Lama did he realize that another body was lying beside him. The old dancing master had died of exertion while performing his final and most marvelous dance. But he had died happily, having found the disciple he had always yearned for. The new dancing master of Tibet took the frail corpse in his arms and, weeping with love, drew the last of its energy into his body. Never had he felt so strong.

What a holy tale of Eros. The darts and lunges of emptiness and violence become the erotic soarings of fullness and love. The great mystery tradition of Hebrew wisdom is about a radical and profound path toward becoming just such a dancing master. It is about the dance with Eros, with Shechinah, the dance with the Goddess Divine.

Eros has many expressions. Each expression is hinted at in the temple mysteries.

Now that we have sensed at least a fragrance of Eros, how do we find our way back to it? Through what doors might we return? This is the great mythical question of all the mystical traditions. We are exiled from Eden. Eden is Eros. How do we find our way back to the Garden?

The answer is startling and beautiful. The way back to Eros is through sex. Sex is the portal for the return to Eros.

CHAPTER FIVE

THE SECRET OF
THE CHERUBS

REALITY IS EROS

N
ow that we understand that Eros lies at the heart of the temple mysteries, we can turn to the core question: If, as we have seen, the essence of the temple (and of every journey of spirit) is Eros, not sex, then why is sex such a prominent feature of the temple? This chapter will begin to unfold that information, which lies at the heart of the mystical Secret of the Cherubs.

The Secret of the Cherubs tells the story of the relationship between the erotic, love and the sexual. Sex models Eros. Erotic sex models what it means to be radically alive in every single facet of our lives. This is the new sexual narrative that is an affront to shame. The Secret of the Cherubs shows us the way to erotically reweave the very fabric of our lives in more vivid patterns, sensual textures, and brilliant hues. This is the path of what we have called Hebrew Tantra. Hebrew Tantra is both the invitation and the divine demand that we re-eroticize our lives.

The Secret of the Cherubs tells a new sexual story, one we have alluded to that now needs to be spelled out in its full erotic delight.

All great mysteries arise in response to powerful yet simple questions. If we were in a classroom, with the blackboards whitened with sketches of cherubs and notes on Eros, Shechinah, and sex, I would at this point step back and ask for questions, for all good spiritual maps should give rise to questions. Slowly a hand would be raised in the classroom . . . a second hand . . . a host of hands. The questions would begin: "If all that you have said so far is true, if Eros is not sex, then why in the temple of Eros is the centerpiece two sexually intertwined cherubs? Why sex? Why wouldn't the temple use some other image of Eros? Wouldn't a statue of a runner who has become the wind or a painter engrossed in his colors be a more fitting figure to perch atop the Ark? If Eros and love are, as you say, more than sex, then why does the temple insist on using a blatantly sexual image?" I would add a question of my own: "What is the magnetism of the cherubs and the Ark that has so fascinated the world for millennia?"

The Greek historian Thucydides reminds us that when words lose their meaning, culture collapses. A movie called *Raiders of the Lost Ark* goes blockbuster toward the end of the twentieth century. But why is the lost Ark so precious to us? Why are people so passionately committed—willing to risk it all—to recover the Ark? Why does the Ark have sexually entwined cherubs adorning its cover? These same cherubs appear in a sacred text in the book of Genesis guarding the entrance to the Garden of Eden. What precious secret do these cherubs hold in their embrace?

QUEST FOR THE GRAIL

Think of King Arthur and his valiant knights, who are all committed to the great quest for the Holy Grail. The grail is a goblet, in the mystery tradition, in the shape of the feminine yoni. In some Middle Eastern languages the very word for "grail," *kos*, connotes the wetness of the feminine yoni. The phrase "My cup runneth over" alludes to this hidden meaning in the mysteries of the grail. Arthur's knights of the round table are in devotion to the saving of the damsel in distress. For the grail tradition, this refers to the "redemption of the Shechinah"—the Goddess—which is the liberation of Eros. The table is round, a circle, alluding to the curves of the feminine. The popular *The Da Vinci Code* novel evokes the Mary Magdalene tradition, which sees Jesus and Mary in sexual embrace. Both the knights of Camelot and the Magdalene mysteries are sourced in the Secret of the Cherubs. Indeed, Jesus and Mary are no less than the cherubs above the Ark. The voice of God cannot be heard other than through their embrace. A church that denies Magdalene cannot hear the voice of God. Then, of course, there is the source of it all, Solomon, the great builder of the Jerusalem Temple, who marries a thousand wives. In the cherub tradition, the thousand wives symbolize the great erotic project of Solomon. The intention of his project was no less than the restoration of Eros to its proper position as the North Star of our lives.

Solomon, Wisdom of Solomon, Ark, lost Ark, grail quest, Temple in Jerusalem, Mary Magdalene, cherubs, damsel in distress, Da Vinci code—all of these are words that have lost their meaning in our culture. All of them are allusions to Eros. All of them have their source, in one form or another, in the Secret of the Cherubs, which lies at the epicenter of Solomon's temple. In recovering the meaning of the lost words, we both return to Eros and evoke the possibility of a new human and a new culture.

Contrary to the tenets of classical religion and much of psychology, Hebrew Tantra insists that sex is integrally related to love and Eros. Let's look again, one step deeper, at these three words and their relationship to one another. When we use the word *love* in this book, we mean what we referred to earlier as outrageous love. Outrageous love is the ceaseless inherent creativity of the cosmos that animates and seduces all of reality to ever higher and deeper emergence. Hebrew mystics teach that the universe in every second is always making love. The Kabbalists' word for it, *zivug*, connotes the outrageous erotic coupling that characterizes the cosmos at every level of reality. Outrageous love is Eros. Eros is love writ large, which is the essence of existence itself.

A NEW DIMENSION OF EROS

Eros, as we have seen, is the experience of radical aliveness.

Now let's point to a new dimension to Eros. Inextricable from the erotic experience of radical aliveness is the powerful drive for union, the drive to make contact. One succinct definition of Eros therefore might be: *Eros is radical aliveness passionately seeking contact.* The drive for contact is, however, not merely an additional dimension of Eros. Radical aliveness is how the drive to contact feels.

Now let's add yet another dimension of Eros: Contact always births something new. New intimacy, new creativity, new emergence. We can now reformulate our definition of Eros. *Eros is radical aliveness, passionately seeking contact, which always births something new.* The erotic equation might be formulated as Eros = Radical Aliveness + Contact + Creativity.

Now we turn to sex. The sexual expresses the fundamental eroticism of all of reality, from the subatomic to the celestial to the human. But sex does not exhaust the eroticism of nature. The sexual is an expression of Eros; it is not the whole of Eros. Eros is the inner texture of reality that lives awake, alive, and aware in every moment. To wake up to Eros is to wake up to the shocking yet stunning realization that the universe is passionately making love all the way up and all the way down creation. Sex in the human realm is an expression of that same core yearning for contact—Eros—that drives all of reality. *Sex is cosmic Eros performed in the flesh.*

Cosmology tells us that we are made from stardust in constant equilibrium—attracted and held together by gravitational pull, kept apart by centrifugal force. We are partnered and yet separate—all part of the great cosmic Eros of reality.

FOUR DIMENSIONS OF THE SECRET OF THE CHERUBS

Let's now state clearly the four major dimensions to the Secret of the Cherubs. The first dimension is that God is Eros. For the mystics, God is identical to reality, or life. To say that God is Eros is to say reality is Eros or life is Eros. The second dimension is that the sexual is an expression of the Erotic movement that characterizes every level of the cosmos. The third dimension is that the sexual in its ideal form models what it means to live radically alive and on purpose, in every other nonsexual dimension of life. Sex models Eros. It is in this precise sense that the sexual is the seat of all wisdom. The fourth dimension, central to the cherub mystics, is that conscious human sex actually transforms reality itself. Human sex does not only participate in the Eros of the cosmos; it is much larger than that. When human beings perform the cosmic Eros in their own flesh with the intention of *tikkun*—the healing and transformation of all that is—then, in the language of the mystics, a "great evolutionary fixing" takes place in all worlds above and below. For the cherub mystics, the miracle of life is not realized in some future world. The wonder of life is that we've met and been together in sexual union, making love here, "in this half-made world, where love is yet to take its hold."[6] When we are together with the intention of restoring wholeness in a world of broken hearts, then we are living the erotic life.

Eros is the very aliveness of the cosmos expressed in all of its potency. When that potency awakens in you, your life becomes naturally good, true, and beautiful, and you become appropriately powerful beyond imagination. This is not a surface power that you wield against others, but a depth of power that allures others into the noble grace of your own full potency. When you awaken to the fullness of your own sexual power, you have the ability through your own erotic life to participate in the healing and transformation of all that is.

For the cherub mystics "the sexual union of man and woman" both models and participates in the more primal union of Shechinah (the divine feminine) and Tiferet (the divine masculine). By masculine and feminine, we do not mean man or woman but rather two essential forces of the universe. These universal cosmic forces are often referred to by the cherub mystics as lines and circles. They are different faces of the greater union, the force of divinity that courses through the cosmos and our own bodies. Their integration is the highest erotic expression of a healed world.

Now comes the truly radical insight! The human being is responsible for effecting the uniting of the masculine and the feminine in the God force. Entrusted to us is the sacred task of erotically merging the Shechinah and Tiferet, the Goddess and the God. We are the erotic mystics invested with the power to influence the force in powerful and profound ways.

This is possible because we reside in the undivided heart of God. It is not that we have power over God; rather, we have power as *part of* God. In our sexing we unite and balance the Shechinah and Tiferet poles within us. We heal the split in divinity. This is a sacred Tantric practice to unify, balance, and integrate the Shechinah and Tiferet, the circle and line poles within ourselves and in all of reality. We are bridge and balancer. It is we who bring home the exiled Shechinah. This erotic activism is modeled by the sexual but not exhausted by the sexual. That is what we mean when we say that sex models Eros. When we live the erotic life, in every dimension of our existence, then a *tikkun*, a "great evolutionary fixing," takes place in all worlds. The twelve faces of Eros, each modeled by the sexual—which we will unfold in the second half of this book—are the path to living the erotic life.

This fourth core dimension of the Secret of the Cherubs makes natural sense in light of contemporary science. Modern chaos theory grounds this activist principle in the material world in a phenomenon called "the butterfly effect." For example, the gentle breeze from a butterfly's wing on one side of the world can, two months later, be the "cause" of a windstorm on the other side of the world. If that is true about the effect of a butterfly, then imagine the impact of human beings consciously coupling—performing cosmic Eros in the flesh—with the intent of healing and transformation. For the cherub mystics, this kind of erotic activism is a core principle of human ethics.

Let's look more deeply at each of these dimensions. Eros is the fundamental movement in the universe toward contact. Sex is an expression of the core Eros of the cosmos. Sex is the drive for contact, the drive to bond, to connect, to be intimate. Sex is an expression of the drive to greater union, which is the creative essence of reality itself. In union, we all come home. But for the erotic mystics in the cherub tradition, home is not the boredom of perpetual rest but ground for ever greater and deeper union. Sex models the ecstatic urgency, which is the feeling of the drive to union.

In union, two separate parts do not fuse but rather make contact through intimate bonding to create newness. This newness is the greater union, the higher love, which is the yearning of reality's Eros. From quarks, to atoms, to molecules, to cells, to early organisms, to plants, to animals, to mammals, to ideas themselves, this core drive for contact is the Eros of all of reality.

Said differently, the great realization of the spiritually incorrect Tantric masters is that reality is allurement. Allurement is the quality of attraction, which is the very fabric of existence. From electromagnetic attraction to gravity to rungs of evolutionary emergence to the intellectual sex between ideas that generates newness—all of reality is moved by the intense allurement for contact, which generates new creations.

Way before sex appears on the scene, allurement is at work throughout the cosmos, attracting all expressions of creation to each other. From the first nanoseconds of the big bang to the first quarks that generated your body, to your own life, unique allurement is what drives all of life. Who are you if not your unique set of allurements? Your physical structure is the composite of the allurements that caused its atoms to form into molecules, its molecules into cells, and its cells into organs. Everything in creation is attracted to everything else, and this urge to know each other, to communicate, to join and make something greater, is the allurement that lies at the very heart of life.

Sex is an expression of this erotic drive. In human sex, Eros becomes conscious of itself. In conscious human sex, all levels of one's being are brought into higher union. This is the new sexual narrative that we have called sex erotic. Cosmic Eros is enacted in the flesh. Sex erotic transcends and includes the physical. The human being becomes the creative drive of the cosmos, all levels of body, mind, emotion, and spirit moving toward union. This is the core of the Secret of the Cherubs. We will go deeper into this truth about the nature of reality in our conversation about allurement, which is the third face of Eros.

HIEROS GAMOS

The esoteric term for the great love affair of the cosmos is Hieros Gamos. The Secret of the Cherubs is the primary source of this great mystical secret. *Hieros Gamos* is Latin for "the divine marriage." The divine marriage is the hidden mystical doctrine of the spiritually incorrect Tantric masters in virtually all of the great traditions. What does the divine marriage mean? It is not about God going shopping. Hieros Gamos is the hidden way of saying nothing less than "God is Eros." Or we might say even more directly, reality is Eros.

At every level of existence, two expressions of reality seek contact with each other to birth not only new but also higher and deeper orders of existence. These two forces used to be called masculine and feminine, but they are not gender specific. We can no longer exclusively identify them with men or women. They are two energetic qualities of the cosmos that live in all of reality, including in every human being. Borrowing a term from the erotic mystic Isaac Luria, we call these cosmic forces lines and circles. In Luria's evocative image, *every moment of reality, on all levels and in all worlds, is born from the [unique] interpenetration of lines and circles that takes place in that moment.*[7] In other words, all of reality is erotic union.

Lines and circles were qualities of reality way before any gendered masculine and feminine existed. Line qualities include the forces of autonomy, independence, thrusting, and direction. In physics, these forces express as the particle (in contrast to the wave), centrifugal force, and the force of repulsion that opposes attraction. Circle qualities include the forces of allurement, attraction, reception, and cycle. In physics, these forces might be expressed as the wave (in contrast to the particle), centripetal force, and the quality of attraction that opposes repulsion. Physicist Niels Bohr insisted that a wave and a particle cannot exist separately from each other but are in a complementary both/and relationship, a sacred marriage of energy and matter.

The primary forces of lines and circles were already well known to the ancients. They are identified in the great traditions as God and Goddess or King and Queen. In Hinduism, they are called Shiva and Shakti, in Taoism yin and yang. In Kabbalah, they are known by many terms, including Shechinah and Tiferet as well as the upper waters and the lower waters. In ancient Egypt, there were earth and sky. In the grail tradition, the knight with his linelike lance seeks the Holy Grail, the circlelike chalice. While these traditions often had markedly different visions of what constituted masculine and feminine, in all of them the goal is Hieros Gamos, some form of divine marriage in which the polarities are integrated into a larger whole. In science it was Niels Bohr who insisted that a wave and particle cannot exist separately from each other but in complementary both/and relationship, a sacred marriage of energy and matter.

SEX EROTIC

All of this forms the matrix of the new sexual narrative: sex erotic. Evolutionary theory, systems science, the new physics, the Kabbalistic Secret of the Cherubs, and the ancient knowing of Hieros Gamos all come together to weave this new sexual story. Reality is erotic. Human sexual Eros participates directly in the erotic nature of the cosmos. Or, said differently, human sexual eros models the great Eros of the cosmos at every level of reality. Reality is Eros, God is allurement, reality is allurement, the sexual models the erotic, God is Eros—all of these are potent expressions of the new sexual narrative for our time.

None of the classical sexual narratives—sex positive, sex negative, sex neutral, or sex sacred—have the capacity to address the fullness of our sexual experience. All are true, but only partially. Moreover, none of these four narratives is an affront to shame. It is only this fifth sexual narrative, sex erotic, the sexual story for our time, that has the potency to deconstruct shame. When you understand that at its source, sexual desire arises in you as the allurement of life itself yearning for contact, shame is eviscerated. The universe is erotic, motivated and animated by allurement and attraction. The sexual drive is but an expression of the core evolutionary Eros that moves all reality. It is only this spiritually incorrect but scientifically accurate understanding of reality that can birth a sexual narrative that honors the radical dignity of our desire.

FROM ETHICS TO ETHOS

If you are with us up to this point, it will be self-evident to you that "reality is Eros" has absolutely nothing to do with inappropriate sexuality. Reality is Eros takes radical sexual ethics as a given. It addresses the next step beyond sexual ethics, upon which all sexual ethics depend. It is the articulation of a sexual ethos—that is to say, a sexual story that is true both to spirit and science and to our own deepest experience and yearning.

Reality as Eros is an ethos that speaks equally to liberal Protestants, progressive devout Catholics, Orthodox and liberal Jews, Southern Baptists, Colorado New Agers, singles, hipsters, Millennials, yuppies, and entrepreneurs of every color, nationality, creed, and orientation. Reality is Eros has nothing to do with whether you are monogamous, celibate, or polyamorous. It has nothing to do with your particular sexual style or code of behavior. The knowing that reality is Eros is, however, is core to your most fundamental vision of reality, and therefore your core experience of both your sexual and your erotic self. A complementary way of saying this is that God is Eros or God is love. Reality is love. Not ordinary love but outrageous love, the love that is Eros.

The reason that we add the words *outrageous love*—as we noted above—is because it has a power that the word *love* does not have by itself. Outrageous love is caring, compassionate, and kind. But outrageous love also has a fierce quality. This is the quality that the word *outrageous* connotes. In English, we do not have a word that captures the quality of reality that seamlessly arouses, attracts, allures, enchants, shatters, demands, and delights. We are so overwhelmed by the power of this quality that we assign to it a word—outrageous—that is on the one hand confronting and demanding and on the other raw delight, desire, and amazement. Outrageous love is Eros.

Eros is not just sex. Sex is too small a word to contain the wholeness of Eros. Sex merely points toward Eros. Eros is so much greater. The erotic is the pulse of God beating at every level of reality. So, by Eros we do not mean human sex, but rather the cosmic Eros of which sex is but one potent expression.

If we trace sex to its source we realize that the body electric is plugged straight into God. Once you discover that current, you will never be the same.

LOVING THE MOMENT OPEN

One of the principles that emerges from chaos theory contributes to a deeper understanding of the Secret of the Cherubs, and it is this: Every moment is either open or closed. Alfred North Whitehead, the great philosopher, reminds us that the "creative advance of novelty" is a defining feature of the cosmos. This means that reality opens to novelty in every moment. Or, as physicist Stuart Kauffman points out, we live in a ceaselessly creative universe. At the human level, the evolutionary impulse that drives the universe toward new depth moves us from unconscious growth to what evolutionary biologist Julian Huxley calls "conscious evolution." In Hebrew, the word *development* or *evolution* is the same word as *opening*. To evolve means to open. To awaken to conscious evolution is to come to realize that there is only one great human choice in every moment: to open or to close. The Secret of the Cherubs integrated with the leading edge of science informs us that the moment and the human being are not separate from each other. In every moment we have the choice to be open or closed. In other words, we have the choice to actually love open the moment—EVERY MOMENT—and the moment opens, or we can choose to remain closed, and the moment remains closed.

When we stay open in love we are pulsing alive in the flow of life. We then have the capacity to love the moment open. When the moment is opened, new life is created. If the moment remains closed, the potential new life is stillborn. It is therefore a simple evolutionary truth that to open or to close is no less than to love or to die. Those are the two evolutionary choices available in every moment.

CREATION EVERY SECOND

The reason that in every moment you must decide whether to be open or closed is because every moment is new. In every new moment you either love the moment open or you let the moment love you open. To love the moment open is to penetrate the moment. To be loved open by the moment is to let the moment penetrate you. That is what it means to be open and alive. The alternative is to be closed and dead.

The pivotal insight that every moment is a new quality of intimacy is core to the realization that reality is Eros. The erotic explosion in which the unmanifest becomes manifest is not a one-time event. Said differently, the big bang or creation did not happen once upon a time. It is—both mystically and scientifically—happening right now.

Eros is the initiating energy of the cosmos, the evolutionary impulse that creates all worlds; countless planets; myriad suns, moons, and stars; and every single particle of cosmic dust. Originally, creation, or the big bang, was thought to have been a one-time, initiatory event, an erotic divine implosion in which the primal line bisected the primal circle and the cosmos poured forth. Mystics and leading-edge quantum field theorists tell us differently. The erotic Hebrew mystic Levi Isaac opens his commentary with a radical assertion: creation is happening every second. The great flaring forth of reality is enacted anew every moment. As some quantum field theorists put it, reality flashes in and out of existence every moment. The very force of Eros, which is divinity, is constantly pouring through existence. God is Eros!

My (Kristina) eighth-grade science teacher, who was an avowed atheist, used to say, "You can't get something from nothing." He was only partially right, however. Within the atomic world, governed by the classic laws of physics, indeed, everything comes from something. But both the universe itself and the subatomic world—which contains the core building blocks of all of reality—literally come from nowhere. Reality is *creatio ex nihilo*—something from nothing.

In the language of the cherub mystics, we might say that reality was ecstatically exploded into existence by source. Creation is not from nothing but from no-thing. They call this *yesh me-ayin. Yesh*, "something," comes from *ayin*, which is best translated as "no-thing" or "the realm of pure possibility." But this erotic explosion that births reality is not a discrete event. The pulsing throb of outrageous love is the constant nature of reality, right now and now and now. Reality births new intimacy and new possibility in every moment.

All of reality as we know it is created out of subatomic particles. Quantum physics tells us that these particles flash in and out of the quantum field in every second. They are constantly popping in and out of existence. The particles pop out of our time, space, matter, energy, and the reality that we know into what is technically called a virtual state. This is a state of pure potentiality. It is in this sense that God is referred to by mystics as the possibility of possibility. Pure potentiality fiercely loves reality into existence in every moment. The two sexually intertwisted cherubs above the Ark in the Holy of Holies represent the constant movement of pure potentiality loving reality into existence anew in every second. This rhythm of reality is the core nature of all existence.

The brain operates in much the same way. Millions of separate signals throughout the brain are constantly flashing on and off. The place in the brain in which reality "disappears" before it turns back is in the synapses between neurons, the empty space that scientific language refers to as the gap between all neuronal connections. In the language of the cherub mystics, we might say that the gap is "the space between the cherubs." Mind the gap, for it is where creation mysteriously takes place.

According to neuroscience, there are some quadrillion synaptic connections that flash in and out of reality in the adult brain. It is in this gap that creation mysteriously takes place. Reality thus flashes in and out of existence through the perpetual Eros that emerges in the spaces in between. In the sacred texts of the Secret of the Cherubs, "the voice of God speaks from the space between the cherubs." The voice of God is no less than the constant ecstatic creativity birthed from pure potentiality, activated from synapses "in between."

What is so vital to realize is that this is not a one-time event but is the constant nature of existence.

In Hebrew, the implication of this perpetual Eros—the constant hidden intercourse of the cosmos—is captured in the word *zeman*. *Zeman* has three related meanings: "time," "invitation," and "radical readiness." The implication is that every moment in time is a new invitation. There is unrelenting optimism in this insight. The very depths of reality can be recreated in every moment. Yesterday can never define today. New possibility is constantly available. The pure potentiality of this moment births that which did not exist a moment ago. All trauma can therefore be healed. All pain can be transformed in the new moment.

What is required for that transformation is the third meaning of *zeman*: radical readiness. The image of a runner primed to sprint at the beginning of a race is helpful here. "Ready, set, go." It is that sense of being fully entered by the moment and fully penetrating the moment with your readiness that embodies the understanding that reality is *zivug*, reality is Eros. This is what St. Thomas knew when he said, "The dynamic pulse and throb of creation is the love of all things for the infinite." We might slightly reframe the end of the sentence to say, "the love of all things *within* the infinite." There is nothing apart from the infinite field of pure potentiality yearning to emerge. All of reality is penetrating and being penetrated all the way up and all the way down. All of reality is constantly making love with itself. *This love awakens from hardwired instinct to human choice when we move from unconscious to conscious evolution.*

Every moment waits for you to love it open. To love the moment open you must be fearlessly present, facing everything, avoiding nothing. In denial, the moment closes. In radical recognition coupled with audacious yet humble embrace, the moment opens. For the cherub mystics this is what it means to continuously make love with the divine one. This is what it means to live an erotic life, to be an outrageous lover. For the cherub mystics, the human being who awakens into full consciousness incarnates the throb and pulse of evolution.

Remember the story of the dancing master in chapter four? Had the Kung Fu master merely killed the dancing master with his superior skill, the moment would have remained closed. Even if the old dancing master had succeeded in besting the Kung Fu master, the moment would not have fully opened. No new quality of consciousness would have been achieved. It was only when a new dance emerged, in which the dancing master and the Kung Fu warrior were both transformed, that a new quality of consciousness was birthed into reality. Both the dancing master and the Kung Fu fighter claimed the full aliveness of his being as each met his unique destiny.

We are all dancing masters. When we succumb to smallness, contraction, corruption, or unlove, the moment closes. When we expand into the full aliveness of our Unique Selves, we have the power to love the moment open and to receive the potent promise of that specific instant in time. When we talk about loving the moment open or letting the moment love us open, we are not talking about a sweet or even a gentle movement. We are talking about an intensity of presence, receptivity, and thrust that opens the moment to meet the implicit creative demand of its and our raw potency.

A SEXUAL UNIVERSE

We live in a sexual universe. From subatomic particles to the plant world, where the birds and bees are symbolic of the great pollination dance, to animals, plants, and humans, to the celestial attraction between planets, the fundamental structure of reality is allurement and attraction that creates profound contact at every level of the evolutionary chain. This is what we mean by Eros. We live in a universe driven by allurement. In that sense, we could say that reality is Eros all the way up to the highest spirit forms and all the way down to the smallest subatomic particles and the most essential forces of the universe.

A COSMOS DRIVEN BY EROS

We live in a cosmos driven by Eros. The universe is a perfect, interconnected whole that at the same time seeks greater wholeness. The universe is radically alive, infused with presence and infinite vitality, even as it is infinitely intimate and whole. Everything rests in the being-ness of spacious perfection.

And yet the universe is driven by evolutionary Eros. The cosmos is not only being but also becoming. Whereas being is characterized by harmony and equilibrium, becoming is characterized by a kind of ecstatic urgency and disequilibrium. Evolutionary Eros is constant becoming. It is the inherent, ceaseless desire for more and more contact and creativity. Consciousness yearns for contact. More contact always births new creativity. New creativity creates new babies of all kinds, or what science calls new evolutionary emergents. This is not an accident but the essential, sacred nature of an erotic universe. This is the lure of becoming that animates and drives all existence.

Walt Whitman caught a glimpse of this reality in his poem "Song of Myself":

> *Urge and urge and urge,*
> *Always the procreant urge of the world.*
> *Out of the dimness opposite equals advance, always substance and*
>   *increase, always sex,*
> *Always a knit of identity, always distinction, always a breed of*
>   *life.*

WHY SEX IS THE ULTIMATE MODEL

The sexual models the erotic for two simple reasons. First, because reality is Eros. Second, because sex or allurement is the structural nature of reality, Eros all the way up and all the way down, it is utterly natural that the sexual models the erotic. It is almost self-evident that Eros should be the seat of all wisdom about reality. How could it be otherwise? *Sex models the Eros of all reality, which inherently seeks more and more contact, mutuality, recognition, union, and embrace.*

To paraphrase the evolutionary mystic Teilhard de Chardin, the fragments of the world, driven by the forces of Eros, seek each other so that the world may come into being. Desire is, at its most fundamental level, the desire for contact. Contact always births newness. The new thing might be a baby. Or it might mean a new level of intimacy. New might mean new creativity or possibility. In what evolutionary theorist Matt Ridley calls Idea Sex, "new" means new insight and new discovery that comes from intimate contact between ideas and people who are attracted to each other. Sex is an expression of the evolutionary Eros. The desire for contact is an expression of the core nature of the evolutionary Eros that drives all reality. This Eros animates every dimension of life. Sex models Eros means that sex is the arena where the ecstatic urgency of our drive to make contact is most apparent, most obviously pleasurable, and most self-evidently creative.

CHAPTER SIX

EROS

FROM FEAR TO LIBERATION

Eros—as we will see more clearly in the unfolding of the Secret of the Cherubs—is the core nature of reality, all the way up and all the way down the evolutionary ladder. When Eros awakens in us, it expresses itself as the radical drive for contact and connection. It is not a uniquely human impulse but rather the impulse of all of reality becoming conscious of itself in us. When we feel our Eros we feel radically alive and at home in the cosmos. We are filled with an unmistakable telos. We begin to live purpose-driven lives, which drip with the nectar of Eros itself. *Our lives become telerotic.*

EROS IS OUR BIRTHRIGHT

Our bodies and hearts know that Eros is our birthright. It is not merely an intensifier of the ordinary. Rather, it points to the extraordinary energy at our core, which is the true marker of our deepest desire. The failure of Eros is the loss of aliveness that psychoanalyst Wilhelm Reich correctly diagnosed as the "emotional plague of man." It is not the loss of a particular privilege or experience. It is a deadening of all experience. The disconnection from Eros is cause for the loss of our unmediated knowing that life is good. When we become alienated from Eros, we forget our true identity and lose our dignity. We forget that we are good children of the universe that seeks our transformation. It is in the dignity of Eros that we recognize the glory of our true situation. It is in the dignity of Eros that we are personally addressed by reality. It is in the dignity of Eros that we know that we are needed, desired, and chosen by all that is.

BYPASSING EROS CREATES ABUSE

The loss of the larger sense of Eros reduces Eros to mere sex. This, by its very nature, creates the rupture of contact and severing of connection that fosters the abuse of sex in all of its forms. Sex is abused when it is cut off from the larger context of Eros in which it lives. When sex is disconnected from the larger Eros, it cannot help but collapse on itself because we are asking far too much from it. Sex then implodes in every form of addiction and abuse. It is only when sex becomes a portal to the unique potency that flows through us from source—what we have called sex erotic—that the dignity and delight of Eros are restored.

When sex is cut off from our total being, from our deeper wholeness, and we ask it for favors it cannot grant, then Eros is degraded. It devolves from a blessing that bestows joy to an abusive curse that inflicts suffering. Abuse may appear as sexual harassment, rape, name rape, or false sexual complaints. Abuse results from the denial of our core equation, Reality = Eros. To deny Eros is to deny reality. Eros then reappears in degraded forms of sexual acting out or in the weaponizing of sex through false sexual stories. We must always remember that arousal is not consent and regret is not rape.

We must always stay connected to the goodness of Eros. Our disconnection from the aliveness of reality's inherent Eros results from our exiling of the larger Eros that animates all of reality into the constraints of merely sexual Eros. Sexual Eros comes alive when it begins to enact cosmic Eros. This is the narrative of sex erotic.

SHAME AND GUILT

Let's now revisit the principle that we introduced above. Shame is the root of all evil. Shame is different from guilt. Guilt is a healthy human emotion that arises when we have done something bad. Shame, by contrast, is the experience not that we have done something bad but that we *are* bad. Shame is the feeling that we are somehow broken and cannot be fixed. More often than not, shame is rooted in something sexual. Self-images of control, artificial dignity, status, appropriateness, and more all need to be surrendered at the altar of the sexual.

Because the sexual challenges our conventional sense of identity, to heal shame we must articulate the new sexual narrative of sex erotic. In sex erotic, the sexual models the erotic. It is paradoxically the greater Eros that illuminates and eroticizes the small eros. *Shame is when sex stops short of infinity.* We heal shame when we realize that the sexual does not regress our identity but rather it expands and evolves our identity. The sexual, as we will show when we discuss the twelve faces of Eros, offers us a glimpse into who we might be if we realized who we already are.

THE UNIVERSE FEELS

The universe feels, and the universe feels the pulse and throb of Eros. It feels the intensity of desire and passion that is expressed in the word *erotic*. The greatest human desire is to participate in the Eros of reality. But we are afraid of the feeling of the erotic. It makes us feel out of control or vulnerable in a way we would rather deny or repress. It is only by entering the pounding surge of Eros and tracing it back to its original divine source that we begin to live the erotic life. But if we bypass the pounding surge it will demand its pound of flesh. The feeling of erotic desire is the incessant longing of the universe to meet other forms of itself in order to birth new creations from the joy of that contact.

RECOVERING OUR MEMORY OF *ZIVUG*

The great *zivug* of the cosmos has been forgotten. We forget that we live in a reality whose core principle is allurement. For the Greeks, the loss of knowledge is the source of all evil. For the erotic mystic, the loss of memory is the source of all evil. Our failed memory of *zivug* is the source of great pain and confusion. On the one hand we forget that, according to the leading edge of quantum theory, reality is coming in and out of existence in every second. Mystics call the interior of this same phenomenon "constant creation." Constant creation is the outrageous love, what the mystics call *zivug matmedet*—perpetual Eros—which fiercely and tenderly loves reality into being in every second.

However, it is not only that we have forgotten. In addition, our denial of the erotic is so desperate and intense that we have forgotten that we have forgotten. And yet, in the midst of our amnesia, we yearn to participate in the Eros of the cosmos. Anything less will not satisfy us. We yearn for what we have forgotten, and so we cannot explain our yearning to ourselves. We no longer understand our innermost drives. We have lost touch with the radical yearning for intense contact that is the axiomatic desire of reality alive in us.

FEAR OF EROS

Why are we so afraid of Eros? The erotic, at its core, is the primal drive to make contact. It is the urge to merge—at least temporarily—with another being. It is an urge that is so intense that we are willing to give up much of our vaunted sense of dignity and self to accomplish it. But we are afraid of this urge because it undermines our sense of identity. The illusion of being a self-sufficient, separate being, independent and autonomous, is significantly challenged or shattered by Eros. We assume that this undermining of identity is regressive. Therefore, we fight it—personally, religiously, and culturally—with everything we have, because identity is the lifeboat we desperately need to feel safe in the world.

But what if the undermining of identity catalyzed by the erotic was not regressive but expansive and evolutionary? What if we really understood that Eros is the stirring within the infinite awakening as our arousal? What if erotic desire in all of its expressions simply reminded us that we are interconnected—that we need each other? What if the beds of our delight invited us to the practice of our devotions?

That is what we mean when we say that sex models Eros. This is the hidden Tantric teaching of non-rejection that appears in every great tradition. In Hebrew Tantra—the Secret of the Cherubs—we enter desire and trace it to its root, the ceaseless creativity of the cosmos that is perpetually birthed through ever more intimate contact. Desire is the doorway into the elemental Eros and allurement that drives all of reality. Desire models the great yearning for connection and contact.

Because we can't see that Eros is a doorway, we make it into a closed room with no way in or out. We then proceed to identify the erotic with its most degraded forms, hence our intense and even desperate fear of the erotic.

The Secret of the Cherubs is simple: we degrade Eros because it makes us feel out of control, but hidden in the erotic is the very source code of the cosmos itself. Reality itself is Eros. Awakening to our sexual longing models our desire to live a fully erotic life in every dimension of existence. The Secret of the Cherubs is that the great Eros of the cosmos is hidden in the small eros of sex.

SHRINKING FROM ALIVENESS: THE FEAR OF PLEASURE

The Carousel Nightmare

Our close associate, Holly, whom we have worked with for many years, brought a recurrent childhood dream into our Holy of Holies space.

(The Holy of Holies, you may remember, is the term for the inner sanctum of the Jerusalem Temple. In working with students at our Tantric institute, we refer to our study space, also, as "the Holy of Holies." It is a re-creation of the "space between the cherubs." It is neither a therapeutic nor a coaching space, and certainly not any form of guru relationship. It is an ecstatic yet rigorous context where we meet, as fully autonomous spiritual friends. Our intent is always to support the full emergence of the Unique Self of the person doing the work.) Here is Holly's dream:

As a child, I had a recurring nightmare of a carousel spinning very near me, with its lights, colors, bells, and shouts of adults on painted horses reaching for the brass ring. Sometimes the riders succeeded and sometimes they reached for the ring in vain, carried around the circle until another turn for glory or another shot at victory was lost.

I didn't know much about carnival rides yet—I was three and had only ridden a couple of times on an actual carousel, with the brass ring mechanism offering its prizes high above my reach. I loved riding painted horses, but I had that dream countless times, waking up screaming and drawing someone, parent or babysitter, to my room. I had no words to explain, just fear enveloping me as I saw myself swept under the wheel of the carousel or dragged aboard it, circling endlessly with no control over its direction or my own.

In my earliest memories, this dream was somehow familiar to me—I knew I had had it before—but what I remember on one particular occasion is my father coming to my rescue, standing beside me near the window, holding a stuffed toy bunny that was my frequent companion in waking life.

I imagine the words my dad must have used, "Wake up, Holly, it's just a dream. I'm here. Mom's downstairs. You're safe." I remember him asking with a gentle and quizzical smile, "What is this dream that scares you about?"

I remember feeling it was impossible and maybe useless to explain. I had probably tried to describe it before, and I could

see that it was upsetting to him to see me so distraught. So
instead, I invented a more solvable problem. "I dreamed that I
lost my bunny," I said tearfully. "I couldn't find him anywhere.
He was gone." My father held the missing bunny out to me. "But
look, he's right here!" he reassured me. I took the bunny under
my arm, thanking Dad for returning him to me. He had solved
the problem, and I went back to sleep. But of course, it was a
false problem—and the carousel spun on in my dreams.

I don't entirely know what the carousel dream was about,
but I had it frequently. And I seemed already to know there
were some things it was better not to talk about.

In our conversations, Holly added the following reflections about her
dream:

I was learning not to feel, or more accurately, not to know or
to admit to what I felt. I still did feel it, of course, or I wouldn't
have had a recurring nightmare about it, but I hid it even from
myself—a terror and attraction that I could not explain.

As our conversation deepened, Holly began to grasp the dream's
meaning:

As I look back on my carousel dream, I think what frightened me was what frightens us all at times: the threat of being
crushed by the enormous and potent energy of the world. Of
course, I had no words for this. Just to feel it takes courage. We
are all ambivalent about it—something attractive and alluring,
something scary and dangerous.

As we worked with the dream together over the years, its meaning
came into clearer focus. The carousel represents Eros. The carousel moves
in a circle. The circle is a classic expression of the primal Eros of nature
in its cycles. It is potent, enlivening, and sometimes deadly. The brass
ring—another circle symbol—is the prize of erotic fulfillment. It always

seems just beyond our grasp. The horse—a potent symbol in classical myth—represents the raw experience of radical aliveness. The dream is about the fear of Eros. The carousel, with its colors, lights, and sounds, is deeply alluring, but it is also seriously frightening.

Holly's fear that "envelops" her is that she will be "swept under the wheel of the carousel or dragged aboard it." That is the fear of being overwhelmed and destroyed by Eros. This is the primary fear of Eros. Then there is a secondary fear of Eros, that of "circling endlessly with no control over its direction or my own." Holly understands that Eros is both "attractive and alluring" even as it occurs to her as "scary and dangerous."

Naturally, Holly could not share the dream with her father. The father principle is order and safety. Holly intuitively knew, even though she could not express it in words, that she could not share either her attraction or her fear of Eros with the person who represented safety and order in her life. So she lied. She told her dad she lost her bunny. This was a problem he could solve. He retained the illusion that he was in control and could make his daughter happy. Holly, however, in hiding the dream, split herself off from Eros—both her own and that of the world, for the two are indivisible.

Holly's father represents the values of conventional culture, which seek to protect the child against Eros. The fear of Eros held by the father is transmitted to the child. Because all children seek the blessings of the father, the child naturally adopts into her psyche the father's fear of Eros.

In the earlier stages of life, Eros is very bound up with pleasure, and specifically with the most basic pleasures of food and sexuality. A key subset of the fear of Eros is naturally the fear of pleasure. Wilhelm Reich was not wrong when he wrote that "the pleasure of orgasm and the pleasure of living are identical" and that "extreme anxiety" about sexual pleasure "forms the basis of a general fear of life."[8] Fundamental pleasure is a core quality of Eros.

Pleasure is one of the twelve faces of Eros that we will explore later in this book. At this point, let us simply consider pleasure from the perspective of our fear of it. A very young child intuitively knows that cosmic

Eros is expressed in pleasure. Pleasure is the child's natural early connection to the larger field of Eros and existence. But, as we saw with Holly, our parents often rupture that intuitive currency of connection.

PARENTS AND THE SEPARATE SELF

Our parents call our separate self into existence. The default identity of most people, the separate self is our sense of being a skin-encapsulated ego. We experience ourselves as ultimately separate from each other, from nature, and from spirit. Our identity as a separate self is not actually a true identity. As we will see in later chapters, it is not our ultimate identity. It has been called by some of the wisest among us "an optical delusion of consciousness,"[9] but it remains the persona of most people most of the time. This identity is only transcended if a person evolves her consciousness and undergoes a genuine developmental identity transformation.

We will talk about this in depth in our chapter on uniqueness (the fifth face of Eros) and in our final chapter on union. But for now it is important to note that both our fear of Eros and our first experience of separate self are inextricably linked and virtually always come from our parents.

Our parents, hopefully, love us. But they also see us as fragile separate selves in need of protection. On the one hand, this is good, for they are inspired to protect us and to teach us how to protect ourselves. This is one basic aim of education. We learn how to navigate society so we will be able to "take care of ourselves." Because our parents experience us as vulnerable separate selves, they move to limit our unmediated contact with the forces of nature, both human and elemental. We are taught from birth the rules of navigation that will buy us safe passage through the turbulent and dangerous Eros of existence.

Part of the protection they afford us, against our will, is the protection from pleasure. Pleasure is seen by society (and by our parents as representatives of society) to be part of the inexorable force of reality that might seduce us away from our responsibilities or otherwise sweep us away. So when Holly is allured to the carousel, she knows—even though she has no words for her knowing—that she cannot share that truth with her father. Her fear of pleasure gets tangled with her desire to receive her father's blessing. The result is that the fear of pleasure—a corollary to the fear of Eros—goes underground. She cannot express it, even to herself. But it remains an omnipresent if unconscious force in her life that appears recurrently as the carousel dream.

Pleasure represents—not just symbolically but also experientially—the world beyond the separate self. We see that in our own daily experience. Pleasure attenuates the experience of separate self. When we feel pleasure, the boundaries of separation soften. The simple experience of eating relaxes the anxiety of separation. That's why our love of food goes far beyond the need to sate our actual hunger. Like food, sex also eases the pain caused by the sharp boundaries of alienation and loneliness.

ADDICTION AND "NEGATIVE PLEASURES"

In its unhealthy expression, this quality of pleasure, which relaxes separation anxiety, is the source of addiction. For example, when we are feeling depressed or lonely, we may feel drawn to eat or to masturbate. In the pleasure that is aroused, we are able—even if only for the duration of the physical sensations—to feel less scared and alienated.

When physical pleasure is misappropriated as our sole source of Eros, it becomes addictive and therefore ultimately destructive. Because our original relationship to pleasure is distorted so early in our lives, it loses its ability to hold us in its lap. The primal pleasures of eating and sex are sharply regimented by our parents, who impose myriad cultural rules and restrictions. As a result, we do not feel the spacious holding and radical affirmation of our belonging that reality intended to communicate through pleasure. We do not feel pleasure caressing our hearts and whispering in our ear, "You are honored and desired by all that is. You are a good child of the universe. You deserve to live an erotic life filled with every sacred pleasure."

Too many of our parents communicate in countless ways that pleasure by itself is not good. One of their most subtle messages is that pleasure is not a good in itself but is rather a reward for doing something good. Cleaning up your room is the good act; your reward is ice cream. Parents writ large as culture have long ago lost touch with the elemental insight on Eros and pleasure that lies at the heart of the cherub tradition: "God saw that it was good."

When the parent moves to control the child's life impulses, then the child starts to turn away from life. This is the beginning of the exile of Eros. The child begins with open hands, shouting a resounding "yes!" to life. But when that "yes" is sharply rebuked, then the child closes not only his hands, but also himself. The natural energy of Eros distorts, and life turns in on itself.

Since reality is Eros—one core expression of which is pleasure—a vacuum of Eros or pleasure is intolerable. So the child begins to fill himself with what might be called "negative pleasures." Both the term and the idea are rooted in key passages in Freud's writing. When you lose contact with the larger erotic life force, you turn away from life. You take the energy of pleasure back into yourself, where it twists and distorts. It appears as withholding, anger, resentment, and inappropriate aggression. The natural erotic current of "yes" energy is turned into "no." The child defines herself by protecting her separate self from all that is outside of her boundary. At the same time, her natural allurement to Eros and pleasure is disowned and goes underground.

Materialist psychology tries to subdue Eros and pleasure by identifying it with personality dysfunction or neurosis. But pleasure is not an aberration from reality. At its core, the pleasure principle is the reality principle. The rupture of our experience from Eros and pleasure is therefore a primal alienation from reality itself.

Denial, as psychology has well documented, always demands its proverbial pound of flesh. Denial of our essential erotic nature will always create distortion of the most tragic kind. As social philosopher Norman O. Brown writes in explanation of Freud, when taken too far, the alienation from Eros is the path of sickness and self-destruction. The repression of libido turns the lack of Eros into pain.

Wilhelm Reich calls this alienation from Eros the emotional plague of man. When man's erotic force is blocked, it turns in on itself, seeking expression. The result, he says, is that "man can murder, rape, and pillage."[10] Reich was perhaps Freud's most brilliant student. Reich broke with Freud over the latter's inability to understand the cosmic nature of Eros.

The hidden fear of the full power of Eros remains with us throughout our lives, expressing itself in many ways. One way the fear manifests is in our relationship with pleasure. Whenever we go to engage pleasure, the original "no" of culture or parents shows up. That first "no" was sharp and painful. We experienced it not as a "no" to something external to us but as a "no" to our essential selves. Our core desire, our most primal "yes," was rejected. The pain of that originally rejected Eros is reawakened every time we move toward Eros or pleasure. The original fear of Eros, learned in our earliest years, is layered with the pain of rejection that our original erotic "yes" occasioned. The fear of Eros is thus a kind of double loop that shapes our entire lives.

Fear of Eros fosters the alienation that lies at the heart of our culture. Freud is a primary example of this disconnection from Eros that has contributed so much to our modern disease. Freud identified the pleasure principle as being characteristic of the earliest stages of life before a child matures. At maturity, he argued, the reality principle supplants the pleasure principle: the ego then guides the id as the child's new North Star. Should the pleasure principle reappear inappropriately in the child's life, that is considered "regressive." But this Freudian philosophy sets up pleasure and Eros in opposition to reality. In fact the opposite is true: Eros is the very nature of reality all the way up and all the way down the chain of being. To set up a semantic field in which pleasure and reality are antonyms is a potent expression of our fear of Eros. To return to Eros, we must therefore establish the core principle of reality as Eros. That is the intent of these chapters.

THE HIDDEN LIGHT

There is a beautiful teaching in the cherub tradition about the hidden light. It is written that when God created the world, he hid the most intense light until the time of the world to come, when it would be available for the righteous. Simply read, this is a mythic story about the anthropomorphic God saving the really good stuff for the really good people at the end of time. The cherub mystics, however, read it differently. The world to come is the space of liberated consciousness that is already present right now. The righteous are those who are able to access that liberated consciousness, the full intensity and beauty of the hidden light.

"But where," ask the cherub mystics, "is the light hidden?" They answer elliptically, "The light is hidden in the darkness." By "darkness" the mystics mean the same thing that Eastern sages refer to as ignorance—the blindness of unconscious drives. Blind need or desire is the nature of the sexual in the experience of the vast majority of people. It is when the sexual wakes up to its true erotic nature that the hidden light is revealed. Said directly: For most of us, the great realization of Eros is hidden in the small eros of the sexual. Eros is the ultimate nature of reality. Reality desires ever greater contact and ever greater intimacy. This is true on every level of reality, from the subatomic all the way through the human. This is the "hidden light" secreted in the darkness for the "righteous ones" in the "world to come."

The great gnosis of reality as allurement—reality as Eros—is hidden in the sexual. The hidden light is too intense for ordinary reality. Ordinary reality is—as it should be—based on boundaries and separation. But on a deeper level, we are all so profoundly interconnected and interdependent that the notion of separation becomes ludicrous. Imagine if you met a person and you could clearly see all the myriad lines of connection between you. Imagine if you could see through the veil of separation and witness the thousands of seemingly random events in previous generations that were intended by the self-organizing universe to bring you together with this person, in this precise moment, for this precise meeting. Imagine that you also were able to hold in your mind's eye the dazzling meshwork of allurements holding your world together. You would see level upon level of stunning beauty and symmetry, beginning with the atomic level and then moving to the chemical, cellular, biological, and cultural structures of allurement at each level of reality.

Holding this paradox between our radical uniqueness as distinct beings and the realization that we are not in any way separate from the seamless coat of the universe is what it means to be awake. This is the hidden gnosis that animates the erotic life.

This knowing is hidden in the erotic. The erotic in its degraded forms is precisely the darkness that the mystics referred to. When Eros is in its degraded form, we are repulsed and filled with shame. The edifice of our nobility and goodness seems shattered by the irrational urges that threaten to overwhelm many of the values and principles that we hold so dear. As cultural critic and sexual therapist Esther Perel once remarked, "We long to do at night what we protest against during the day."

Desire is politically and socially incorrect. The solution, however, is not to act on every desire. Sex requires a radically awake sexual ethics that protects every man and woman from every form of unwelcome sexual advance. Rather, what we need to do is to trace Eros back to its source. Degraded Eros must not be bypassed but excavated. We need to find the root of our desire, which is desire itself. When we trace our desire back to its source we realize that it is not personal to us. Rather, allurement is the nature of reality itself. Reality then awakens in us personally.

But allurement is not only the nature of reality—it is also the glory of reality. All parts seek to make contact. All parts yearn for ever greater mutuality, recognition, union, and embrace. It is only in the evolved human being, however—the superior man and woman—that desire awakens to its true nature. In humans, Eros awakens to itself. We move from unconscious desire to conscious desire. We move from chance to choice. More than that, we realize that sexual desire models all desire. Our deepest desire is for radical aliveness, contact, and creativity. We yearn to awaken as outrageous lovers. Said simply, we long for Eden. We long for the return to Eros. This is the hidden light to which the cherub mystics refer, the light hidden in the darkness of Eros in its most limited and even degraded of forms.

ORGASM: THE EXTREME LIGHT

One of the core expressions of the erotic is orgasm. It has been playfully suggested that orgasm derives from the Hebrew word *mugzam*, "extreme light." This is the hidden light to which the Zohar refers. Orgasm triggers an intensity in consciousness that is not sustainable within what we normally experience as ordinary life. Orgasm is marked by a sense of radical vulnerability and openness, an extreme sense of connection, the obliteration of ego, and the radical intensification of pleasure. All of these are at odds with our story of how ordinary reality should feel.

The word *orgasm* itself has been exiled to the sexual. Orgasm, however, refers to a moment of radical clarity and aliveness in which all the masks drop. In these moments the natural devotion and delight that exist between us all is nakedly revealed.

The great philosopher of dialogue Martin Buber wrote a book of Hasidic stories that he titled *The Hidden Light*. They are stories of rare and intense contact—of outrageous love—between human beings, and between humans and God. They are "orgasm stories," tales of extreme light that attracts and allures us beyond ordinary consciousness. These are stories of Eros even through there is no sex in them. They are stories of Eros because they describe moments when all walls fall down, allowing for radical contact while at the same time retaining the irreducible dignity and uniqueness of every individual in the tale. In these holy stories—stories of holy Eros—the invisible lines of allurement that animate all of reality in every second become visible to the naked eye. The curtains of the Holy of Holies are drawn back, the intertwined cherubs are revealed for all the pilgrims to see. Whereas Buddhist meditation might be said to focus on awareness, many of the meditative practices of the cherub mystics might be said to focus on allurement.

To wake up is to begin to integrate the extraordinary truth of orgasm consciousness into our seemingly ordinary lives. This is the hidden light secreted in the hidden teaching of the Secret of the Cherubs.

The teaching is secret because it threatens the fabric of ordinary existence. It challenges the very core of our limited experience, with its contraction and separation. The Secret of the Cherubs locates the gravitas of our human experience in the dignity of Eros. This is the erotic realization of awakening: that we are all interconnected, that we all yearn for contact, and that we all need each other.

When we cannot access the dignity of Eros, then we experience the erotic as undermining our dignity. That is the source of our radical fear of Eros. We reject the Secret of the Cherubs because, like the intensity of orgasm, the erotic intensity of our true interconnectivity simply overwhelms us. Our dignity lies not in the posturing of a separate self but in knowing that we are an inextricable part of all that is—and all that is desperately needs our service. All that is needs our outrageous love, our erotic potency.

CHAPTER SEVEN

THE COSMO-EROTIC
REALITY UNVEILED

To live an erotic life is to know that you are part of a cosmo-erotic universe. We live in a cosmos driven by Eros. Eros is not an aberration but the natural pulse of reality. Our purpose in this chapter is to enter into some depth in describing the cosmo-erotic nature of our universe. This is what theologian and mystic Meister Eckhardt understood when he allegedly wrote, "We must learn to penetrate things and find God there."[11]

To get a sense of the Eros of the cosmos, we need to go back to how it all began. Let's first recap what we have learned so far. The innate design of the cosmos is one of attraction and allurement. The interior face of the cosmos is Eros—the motivational force of evolution itself, participating in the yearning force of being. Written in lowercase, eros is sex; written as a proper noun, Eros is the cosmic pulse of reality. The sexual models the erotic. Reality is Eros and God is Eros are precisely the same thing. For what is reality if not God, and what is God if not reality?

THE PLOTLINE OF REALITY

What evolution teaches us is that reality is not a fact, but a story. A story has a beginning. It has a plotline. The action has direction and is driven by underlying forces. Scientists say that it appears there really was a beginning known as the big bang. The cosmos was birthed through a great flaring forth of light and matter, animated and driven by a force of wild attraction, emerging from a single point that expanded and is still expanding. This is the radical beginning of the most outrageous love story ever told.

The universe is not a fact, but a story. A story means that reality is not static. It is going somewhere. Reality has direction and purpose. But it is not an ordinary story; it is a love story. And it is not an ordinary love story; it is an outrageous love story. Outrageous love, as we have seen, is but another descriptor of Eros. Based on our deepest scientific and mystical understanding of reality, it is entirely accurate to say that the purpose of existence is fulfilled through ever-deeper manifestations of outrageous love. Outrageous love, or Eros, is the force that drives what scientists have taken to calling the self-organizing universe.

Cosmologists at the Santa Fe Institute like to call this self-organizing property, which moves reality to ever-higher levels of order and love, the fifth force of the universe. Besides the electromagnetic, the nuclear, the strong, and the weak, there is a fifth force that drives the whole story. This fifth force is an inherent, ceaseless, creative force of attraction, Eros by any other name. The gravitational and nuclear events that shape and mold the universe come from the power of allurement. Everywhere we look, we see examples of this urge to merge and emerge, from the vast galaxies to the smallest particles, across the animal kingdom and into humankind. Eros is the most powerful force in the cosmos, binding us and everything else together. It is both the currency of connection between human beings and the essential force that drives the evolutionary process as a whole.

THE EROTIC MOTIVE OF THE COSMOS

Science looks through the eye of the mind and the eye of the senses. Spirit looks through the eye of the heart. At this moment in history, which we are seeing with growing clarity, all three eyes are describing the same reality. Our contemporary understanding of Eros at the subatomic and cellular levels augments the realization of the great traditions, which saw erotic love as the primary motivating force of the cosmos. This is the primary position of the Kabbalists, such as Isaac Luria and Moshe Chaim Luzzatto, rooted in the earlier Zoharic texts, as well as of many Christian thinkers like St. Thomas Aquinas and Mechtilde of Magdeburg. St. Thomas spoke of the "dynamic pulse and throb of creation" as the love in all things. Mechtilde understood herself to be participating in this very throb and pulse when she wrote:

> Lord, love me hard,
> love me long and often.
> I call you, burning with desire.
> Your burning love enflames me constantly
> I am but a naked soul, and you, inside it,
> are a richly adorned guest.[12]

Similarly, a Tantric text called the Mahartha-Manjari describes how Shakti, the creative power of the divine, leaping forth in her own bliss, manifests this universe as an expression or even an outpouring of love.

My (Marc) lineage master, Mordechai Leiner of Izbica, refers to Eros as *teshuka*, or desire as the essential structure of reality. This refers not to superficial desire but to the desire that lies at the heart of reality. Evolution is reality's desire. It was to this that Buddha may have been referring when he said, "Have few desires but have great ones." He was distinguishing between authentic desire, which is source itself, and superficial desire, which seeks to cover up the experience of alienation from source. This ability to discern between authentic and pseudo desire is what Leiner called *birur*, and was for him the mark of the enlightened one.

Leiner emerges out of an older erotic lineage of cherub mystics known as *Hasidei Ashkenaz*, who describe God in sensual terms as the "delight of all delights." In one highly sexualized passage, they describe erotic longing, the core motive of the cosmos, as it shows up in the human being.

> And the joy is strong and overwhelms his heart so much that,
> even a young man who has not gone to a woman for many days,
> and has great desire, when his seed shoots like an arrow and he
> has pleasure, this is as naught compared with the strengthening
> of the power of the joy of the love of God.[13]

Remember in reading this passage that these mystics had already attained the realization that God and reality are one. So the phrase "love of God" should be read as "love of reality."

All of these interior qualities of the cosmos have now been shown to have exterior form as well. We have seen that we are all made of stardust delicately balanced in a constantly recalibrated equilibrium—attracted and held together by a gravitational pull, while kept apart by centrifugal force. We live in a continual, divine erotic tension of radical urgency and ecstasy. We are partnered, yet separate—we are all dancing madly in the great erotic force that is Eros.

The big bang is happening in every moment of reality. The core essence and very nature of reality is erotic. All of reality is moved by the insatiable urge to merge. Eros is the unbearable yearning to make contact, which is the inner and outer form of reality, all the way up and all the way down, from subatomic particles to atoms to molecules to complex molecules and more and more complex molecules—all of it yearning for ecstatic union.

ALWAYS TWO COMING TOGETHER

In the initiating orgiastic movement of the big bang, separate subatomic units, which physicists call quarks, are elemental forms of existence. Quarks, however, cannot live by themselves. Paraphrasing the Bible we

might say, "It is not good for a quark to be alone." Quarks live only in intimate relationship with other quarks. The inexorable force of Eros moves
these elementary particles to transcend what might have otherwise been
their merely separate existence and form a higher union with other quarks.

These higher and deeper units are called hadrons. The most stable
of these hadrons are protons and neutrons, the components of atomic
nuclei. Atoms are born because subatomic particles are attracted to and
allured by each other. And so it is all the way up the evolutionary chain.
This implicit allurement is the face of mystery itself, because it did not
have to be this way. The mutually attracted and allured atoms recognize
each other and embrace. Separate subatomic units are moved to form a
single unit. A boundary drops around them. Whole atoms are formed.
What moves them? The Eros of evolution, which is the Eros of love.

To live an erotic life is to know that sexual play between beloveds is
part of the great love play of the universe. Updating the biblical verse we
might say, "It is not good for either humans or quarks to be alone." Lovers
are electrons and neutrons who have consciously awakened to their own
nature. The Persian poets of Eros from the Sufi lineage wrote much of
their verse in ecstatic affirmation of this great identity between the personal and cosmic journeys of love. Hafiz, probably the most well-known
of these poets, writes in "What Happens":

What happens when your soul
Begins to awaken
Your eyes
And your heart
And the cells of your body
To the great Journey of Love?

First there is wonderful laughter
And probably precious tears

And a hundred sweet promises
And those heroic vows
No one can ever keep.

But still God is delighted and amused
You once tried to be a saint.

What happens when your soul
Begins to awake in this world

To our deep need to love
And serve the Friend?

O the Beloved
Will send you
One of His wonderful, wild companions

ALLUREMENT AND AUTONOMY

What is essential to understand about Eros is that it is not only a force of allurement. Eros is no less than the assertion of independence and autonomy. Desire is both an expression of allurement and a unique presence. When you are filled with desire, you feel wildly attracted to make contact, but not to disappear. Desire is presence. In desire you potently incarnate the unique quality and force of your radical being-ness. Eros therefore is both the urge to merge as well as the urge to emerge.

Early electromagnetic allurement is a physical illustration of these two qualities of Eros. What science terms "the forces of attraction and repulsion"* express precisely the dance between merger and emergence. Eros is not fusion but merger, which catalyzes new emergence. For example, when human beings come together in Eros and love, we both merge and emerge, disappear and appear at the same time. A larger whole is formed without losing the integrity of the separate parts.

The force of Eros is the force of desire itself, built into the very fabric of reality. Desire, or what cosmologists call "allurement," is the essence of

---

* Repulsion means the establishments of a boundary, the refusal to fuse, the assertion of independent integrity and autonomy.

reality itself. Quantum physics shows us that every particle that comes into existence is paired with another particle. Each has both a point and a wave, called a wavicle. The creation of all life—sexual reproduction, in almost all instances—involves two coming together. Our DNA splits into two, generating the missing half. Our cells divide into two during the mystery of mitosis and meiosis. Similarly, most primal creation myths portray human beings as coupled, not as separate individuals. Our brains have two parts: right and left hemispheres. Our spoken language is binary, as are our computers. Our blood circulates in an oscillated dance between the right and left sides of our bodies. Stars, we now know, have companion stars, and they are wildly attracted to each other by this potent force. It is Eros that both allures the stars to each other as well as keeps them from collapsing and disappearing into one another.

When we say God is Eros, we are describing an evolving reality that births new love, new tears, new creativity, and new ideas in every moment. Reality as Eros is the only force that can give birth to the next great stage of our evolutionary awakening. Let's take another look at the origins of Eros in order to understand this point. At the inception of the big bang, the elementary particles called quarks and leptons merged, and within microseconds birthed protons and electrons, which then birthed the first atoms. Reality is Eros all the way up and all the way down the chain of being. Atoms, through their oppositely charged particles, were allured to each other. In their meeting, they created an electromagnetic field, producing an interaction that formed new helium and hydrogen atoms. These elementary particles bonded together, and then formed increasingly complex elementary particles. They were required to relinquish part of their identity in order to merge. Such is the nature of all erotic relationship. The first seconds of creation necessitated a sacrifice and a bonding in order to allow the great genesis of existence to begin.

These intimate relationships led to a complex relational process that continued to deepen, ultimately allowing photosynthesis to appear. Some three hundred million years later, sexual reproduction through vertebrate genitalia emerged, creating an even deeper intimacy. We live in an intimate universe—a universe that is not just radically committed to life, but to ever deeper levels of intimate connection in life! This awareness explodes our identity as limited separate selves. We are allured to see ourselves in a larger context, where our interconnectedness and intimacy become undeniably self-evident.

DESIRE: THE HEART OF ALL MATTER

Allurement is the "strange attractor" at the heart of all matter, the very real and pervasive attractive energy that animates all forms of life. Allurement is at the root of what shapes us and is responsible for bringing together galaxies and planets, as well as lovers. From the union of two individuated beings comes the possibility of new creativity—unimaginable emergent capacities that did not previously exist.

Scientist Brian Swimme reminds us that allurement expresses the deep need of life for life. It is extraordinary to realize that the ecstatic force of allurement, sparked fourteen billion years ago and which gave rise to all life, lives in us. Ecstatic urgency, the urge to merge, the very nature of this attraction is seen all the way up and all the way down the evolutionary ladder, and yet its origin remains a total mystery.

Let's take a deeper look at this magnetic attractor called desire and its luring and seductive appeal to thrust all life forward to greater and greater levels of wonder and complexity.

As we continue to observe evolution within visible matter, we can more readily begin to feel the tangible passion of this primal thrusting forth of desire. We begin to see it enfleshed, not just in the stark imagined world of chemical interactions but also in the passion and desire throbbing in and through all of evolution, in plants, insects, vertebrates, fish, reptiles, and mammals—all the way up the great chain of being and becoming. We can hear it and see it, calling us to its persuasive impetus and its seductive siren song. It is to this that the great philosopher of science Alfred North Whitehead referred when he said that evolution is moved by the "persuasion of love."

If we can let ourselves awaken to the intimate nature of what science sees as objective reality, we feel it deeply in our being, in our hearts, and in every cell of our bodies. If we allow it all the way in, we might feel it as a burning impulse or an unbearable longing to reach out to and make contact or even temporarily merge with another. When felt through the flesh, there is a stunning, visceral realization that the very same desire and yearning that lies at the core of the evolution of life itself is quivering alive in us! As we rise up the evolutionary ladder, we begin to see the carnal causal design of the entire cosmos, amazingly expressed as we observe the dramatic mating rituals among living things.

FLOWER LOVE LESSONS

Zen master Basho pointed to the cosmo-erotic universe in his own implicit yet enigmatic way. He writes:

> *Having sucked deep*
> *In a sweet peony*
> *A bee creeps*
> *Out of its hairy recesses.*[14]

Zen master Ikkyu is more explicit, pointing out that human allurement and the allurement of plants are part of the same cosmo-erotic field:

> *Plum blossom close to the ground her dark place opens*
> *wet with the dew of her passion wet with the lust of my tongue*

Flowering plants have created deeply intimate relationships with their pollinators that have evolved over millions of years, producing a fascinating diversity of strategies to lure them in. Using sweet scents, bright colors, and perfectly designed forms, the blooms entice their pollinators with the promise of a scrumptious feast. Flowers provide visual clues and formations, through their shapes and sizes, that allow pollinators to make contact. Some flowers also feature nectar guides, which contain patterns visible from the air, showing pollinators the way to the sweet spot. Plants pollinated by beetles, for instance, have large open blooms, making for a wider landing area to accommodate larger guests. Irises are prolific producers of flowering petals that take an enormous amount of energy in order to stay in competition with nearby flowering plants, in hopes of alluring the services of bumblebees. Flower receptacles and displays uniquely vary from gullets and spurs to flaps and tubes. With a narrow tubule and a long tongue, the right pollinator, and the right plant part, contact is made. The propagation of new life continues.

We have all been delightfully intoxicated by the scent of a flower. Flowers use potent aromas to attract their pollinators as well. Those with alluring fragrance are often those that are quite plain in their appearance. Some flowers exude scents that can be detected at a distance of over a mile away.

Food produced by flowers is also a major attractor for pollinators. Nectar is primarily a sugar water that contains amino acids and minerals. Plants dependent on pollinators with high-energy diets, such as hummingbirds, produce massive quantities of nectar. Pollen, high in protein, is produced by flowers in large amounts to ensure an appropriate feast. Along with the need for sustenance, pollinators also need to reproduce in order to propagate the next generation of their species. The warty hammer orchid of Australia, for example, takes advantage of this evolutionary impulse to reproduce by mimicking a chemical scent identical to the pheromone of the female thynnine wasp. In addition, the orchid's labellum, or lower lip, is shaped like the body of the female wasp. The male wasp tries to grab the faux female and fly off with her to mate but, instead, he crashes into the flower, releasing its pollen. The male thynnine wasp is a rather randy guy, and his constant desire to make contact through mating over and over is advantageous to the warty hammer orchid by causing its ongoing pollination and propagation.[15]

ANIMAL LOVE LESSONS

Desire and its passionate declaration can be found throughout the natural world in examples of animal courting behavior within many species. Expressions of such passion fascinate in the incredible intricacy of their spectacle. From bizarre mating rituals and courtship displays that offer up explosions of color to melodic song and ecstatic dancing, they all express a lavish display with the sole motivation to evoke desire, pleasure, and the deep impulse to merge with the other.

Most of us don't think of spiders as sexy, yet have you seen a peacock spider perform his mating ritual? No larger than a quarter-inch long, male peacock spiders are remarkable for their beautiful bright colors and butt-shaking dance. As a female approaches, the male begins to shake his body, sending waves of vibrations into the ground that a female detects through her legs. As he moves and splays the incredible iridescent fan on his rear end back and forth, he begins to perform a sensual, tribal-like dance that involves leg waving and drumming on the ground. Spiders, not having ears, hear the drumming on the ground through organs on their legs. The vibration of the drumbeats travels up the legs of the female, which seems to be a great turn-on for her. If the male's routine is met with approval, then—well, you know the rest.[16]

The word *romance* evokes images of a love letter, a box of delicious chocolates, a bouquet of flowers, or maybe a table for two at an intimate restaurant. And although we never really think much about other species on this planet having romantic lives, the worlds of mammals, birds, and creatures of the ocean reveal astounding beauty and untamed passions in their mating rituals from which we humans might take some erotic cues.

Brolgas, elegant birds from the crane family, mate with their partners every year in nesting areas that remain the same throughout their lives. For them, keeping the passion alive is of utmost importance. For the duration of their bond, they continue their dance of tossing clumps of grass in the air and flapping and extending their wings while bobbing and bowing their heads. We humans might do well to notice, for example, how the brolgas take responsibility for their sustained arousal. In doing so, they ensure that no matter how long they have been together, passionate expression, which is vital to keeping the relationship alive, continues to flourish.[17]

TRIBAL LOVE LESSONS

Each year, the Wodaabe tribe in Niger holds a beauty contest with an interesting twist. The men of the tribe dress up for the women, who pick the winners. At the annual festival, hundreds of people gather to watch the young men, who have spent hours painting their faces using colorful red, white, and yellow clay paint along with black eyeliner made from charred egret bone. They ornament their bodies with long strings of cowrie beads and place ostrich plumes on their heads to emphasize their height. The men then begin to dance vigorously for seven nights, showing off physical qualities of strength, stamina, and endurance. At the end of the week, an intricate ceremony is held for the women to choose their favorite man. The men line up, grinning widely so as to show their bright white teeth while displaying their handsome beauty and charisma. Each woman invites the man she finds most attractive to be her lover. Wodaabe women are known to be attracted to the tallest men with the whitest teeth, the largest eyes, the most angular nose, and the most stunning bodily decorations. There is no surprise, then, that Wodaabe men have evolved to become taller with whiter teeth, larger eyes, and more Romanesque noses.[18]

In human beings, this evolutionary desire for contact bursts forth in its fullest conscious form not just in sex. It is also expressed in the form of poetry, of caring for the weak and helpless, and in a thousand other ways. Human beings manifest love more fully and outrageously than any earlier species in the evolutionary chain. But the authentic love expressed so dramatically and poignantly between human beings is the same impulse of outrageous love that moves quarks to make contact with other quarks to form an atom. It is one love. Evolutionary love—outrageous love—all the way up and all the way down the evolutionary chain.

AN AFFRONT TO SHAME

One of the recurrent motifs of the new sexual narrative is the realization that shame is the root of all evil. By shame, we mean the feeling that something intrinsic to our being is essentially wrong and can never be fixed. Sex is a primary source of shame. Cultural critic Warren Farrell makes this point powerfully.[19] Imagine a parent passing by his two teenagers, who are watching a brutally violent action movie. Chances are that the parent walks by, perhaps makes a remark about violence (or not), and then goes on about his business. Or perhaps the parent sits and watches with the teenagers for a while. Imagine the same parent passing the same two kids, and they are watching an erotic movie in which there is graphic sexual intercourse. Almost certainly the parent will stop, somewhat aghast, and will turn off the television or at least change the channel. There is virtually no possibility that the parent will sit and watch erotica with her teenage son or daughter.

Whatever the wisdom of the parent's action, the message is clear. Brutal violence and murder are acceptable, and sex is shameful. Why, even after the old religions have lost their hold on us, does sex remain so insidiously shameful? The reason is our confused relationship to three primary human experiences: control, desire, and pleasure.

Control: We are taught to be "in control." The dangerous people are those who are "out of control." We critique a person's level of development by saying, "He has no self-control." We emotionally shake our angry partner or child with words like "control yourself." And yet the sexual experience requires that we—at least on some level—relinquish control. We are shamed by our loss of control.

Desire: We are taught that our desires, particularly our desire for pleasure, are both ignoble and dangerous. They are ignoble, we think (whether consciously or unconsciously), because they are selfish. In most of the public teaching of most of the great religions, desire is the ultimate enemy. And yet the fulfillment of the sexual is directly dependent upon desire. The more intense the desire, the more pleasurable the sex. We are shamed by our desire.

Sex is thought shameful because we cannot control it fully. This is also tied into control, because we do not fully control whom we desire, the intensity of our desire, or even when we act on our desire. People who think they can completely vanquish sexual desire are foolish indeed.

Pleasure: There is an implicit sense that pleasure is narcissistic and selfish, in contrast to virtue, which is holy and devout. And yet sex is uniquely pleasurable. It is virtually impossible to split the experience of sex from the experience of pleasure. Moreover, we cannot even control what form of sex causes us pleasure. We are shamed by our idiosyncratic desire for pleasure, which we cannot control.

Clearly, the requirement for elemental self-control in sexuality, the regulation of desire, and the commitment not to spend life pursuing merely superficial pleasures are all noble impulses. But the result is a profoundly ingrained sense of shame in regard to sexuality. That shame is massively destructive on both a personal and a cultural level. It is shame that causes us to split off from our sexuality, which nearly always brings disaster. It is shame that causes us to hate ourselves for sexual desires we cannot control. Sexuality challenges our cultural, spiritual, and psychological self-image. Are we really the person that we claim to be? Just think for a second, beginning with your early teenage years, about the hidden shame around your sexuality. Take a moment and list five direct results in your personal life from the deeply ingrained sense of sexual shame.

On a cultural level, shame is no less insidious. The violence of Islamic fundamentalism, for example, and the cruelty of Nazism have both been correctly traced to different forms of sexual shame. The attempt to split sexuality off from life must always fail, for sexuality is life. The failed attempt at repression turns life against itself in revulsion and disgust. That is the root cause of the cruelty and violence. In democracies, sexual shame is regularly deployed as a political weapon. The director of the FBI, J. Edgar Hoover, tried destroying Martin Luther King Jr., the head of the civil rights movement, by shaming him for his extramarital affairs. Al Gore lost the presidency, according to many, because Bill Clinton was unable to campaign for him as he had been widely shamed for his affair with White House intern Monica Lewinsky. The result was the presidency of George W. Bush, which led the United States to invade Iraq. The destruction wrought by that invasion in post–Saddam Hussein Iraq is incalculable. If not for the massive public shaming of Clinton over a consensual affair with an adult woman, all of that pain and suffering may not have happened.*

---

*   It is not that Clinton was right—clearly, he did not have an agreement from Hillary to engage with Monica. However, the level of shaming—as it always is in sexual issues—was insanely disproportionate to the level of infraction both for Bill and for Monica. The source of the obsession is our confusion around sexuality, rooted in large part in our own hidden sexual shame.

Desire, pleasure, and the loss of control are all shamed. Shame is the root of all evil. Neither the sex-positive, sex-sacred, nor sex-neutral narratives truly move us to sex beyond shame. It is only when we articulate the new sexual narrative of sex erotic, rooted originally in the Secret of the Cherubs and deepened by modern science, that we understand allurement and desire to be the essence of the cosmos. Then we can begin to live our sexual desire as an affront to shame. It is the new sexual narrative of sex erotic that reclaims pleasure as the motivating force of evolution and the inner feeling of divinity. In the cherubic mysteries, our desire is our devotion. Devotion merges with delight even as pleasure screams the name of God. We give up control as an act not of reckless abandon but of wild and holy surrender.

DESIRE IS THE PORTAL

Sexual desire is the portal to the sacred in us. The universe feels, and the universe feels desire. Desire is evolution. Desire is allurement, Eros, and Eros knits together all of reality even as it drives it to ever higher and greater levels of uniqueness, consciousness, creativity, and love. Desire is, at its core, the desire for contact.

The sexual impulse is the gorgeous manifestation of that very desire for contact. Desire is no less than the evolutionary impulse in us, awake and alive. The great traditions, East and West, which taught that subduing desire is the great work of man, were not wrong. They were a necessary step on the evolutionary journey. We needed structures to contain desire so it would not overwhelm us. That was but the first step, however. It is not the overcoming of desire but the clarification of desire that is the core spiritual work of the human being.

Desire is personal at its very core. To step up and play a larger game in life is to identify and incarnate the unique desire of your personhood. That is the desire that reality seeks to live through you. That is what we refer to when we speak of outrageous love. To awaken as an outrageous lover means to commit your unique outrageous acts of love to incarnate the personal face of evolutionary desire that desperately needs to be lived by you.

Finding the right gorgeous expression of your sexual desire is essential to living your desire in every other frame of life. Sexual desire models desire in every dimension of life. The sexual models the erotic. The sexual is an expression of the evolutionary Eros that initiated, animates, and motivates all of reality. The two cherubs above the Ark in the Holy of Holies, lost in the rapture of their sexual desire, incarnate the nature of reality on all of its levels.

CHAPTER EIGHT

DECODING THE
SOLOMON MATRIX

We, the authors, have spent years of our lives praying to enter the inside of the inside, to know the mysteries of Eros and sex. Early in my (Marc) journey into Eros, I entered deeply into the sacred Aramaic texts of the Hebrew wisdom tradition. I have spent most of my life immersed in, enlivened by, and in devotion to these manuscripts. In my early twenties, I had the first glimmerings of a slowly dawning realization. Deep in the Hebrew mysteries was a radical vision of the erotic, the sexual, and the sacred, which fascinated me. As this vision gradually clarified through several decades of study, I realized this wisdom was essential to the next stage of human evolution. I began to understand that the future of our planet rested upon a return to Eros. Eros was the key. If we could but understand that mystery, ethics would become clear, and the sacred would sort itself out.

I knew intuitively that the sexual was the key. After all, how could it be otherwise? Either God is more than slightly sadistic with a significant interest in teasing and even torturing us through the ordeal of sex, or in some mysterious way it is the key to this whole life journey. Solomon's temple was the center for the mysteries. The sexually intertwisted cherubs were the clue, but what did it all mean?

In 2000, I went to Oxford University to write my doctoral thesis, which was long overdue. I wrote about my teacher, the great mid-nineteenth-century mystic Mordechai Leiner of Izbica. Leiner was a Hasidic master. Hasidism was the ecstatic movement of God-intoxicated, mystical activism that swept through Europe in the late eighteenth century. At some point it dawned upon me that Leiner was keeping secrets. And why wouldn't he be? He was, after all, writing in the traditional pious setting of classical Jewish orthodoxy, where one cannot be too careful. Institutional politics, egos, hidden fear, and even demonization of the sexual were all at play then as they are today.

I desperately wanted to enter the inside of the texts and know their secret. I somehow knew that my life, and the life of all that is, depended on it. "Love or die" was the phrase that ran constantly through my mind. I knew that I could not conquer the texts. Instead, I surrendered to them and pleaded with them to take me home. But surrender is not sufficient. To learn secrets, seduction is also necessary. It is only that sense of radical commitment and utter devotion that allows one, with grace, to seduce a sacred text into disrobing and revealing her secrets. Leiner himself called such a text "the Goddess without her garments."

Slowly, after years of reading and then many intense months of poring over the same material for almost fifteen hours a day in the Oxford library, with thousands of pieces of paper filled with scrawls and textual clues strewn all over my apartment, the outlines of a secret code began to almost miraculously appear. I was stunned to tears. I sat for weeks and months on end with fifty yellow notepads, following the faint paths of what I called "word clusters." For example, every time Leiner would talk about wine, I would jot it down on a yellow pad. I would collect and note all his seemingly random references to wine. Then I would look for patterns in the references. I began to see that these seemingly out-of-place, random mentions were anything but random.

Then I would look up all of the earlier Aramaic sources he alluded to with the wine references. I wanted to see whether his symbolic understanding of wine was original or whether he was part of a lineage. If he was part of a lineage of sources with a hidden understanding of the symbolism of wine, then was he simply transmitting the lineage, or was he adding some novel dimension to it? I would then pray to intuit the next right word cluster to gather. I would then collect all of those words and search for the intentional pattern in the way Leiner was using the target word. Then I would look up the earlier sources he referenced with that word, searching again for pattern, lineage, and originality. I repeated the same process with many dozens of words. A few led nowhere, but most did not. Slowly and surely, a clear and astonishing picture began to emerge. The code began to crack open, and the erotic text began to show itself, revealing her secrets.

Leiner had hidden in the folds of his text a great secret. Said simply, Leiner was the lineage heir and inheritor of the ancient Wisdom of Solomon. According to Leiner's hidden code, the covert teachings of the Wisdom of Solomon had been transmitted personally from master to student, down through the generations, until they reached him. But it was more than that. The very core of my being shuddered with some mixture of fear and joy when I realized that Leiner wanted to transmit these same teachings to me.

I was shocked, amazed, and delighted by what emerged as the text began to reveal her secrets. I realized that according to him, the hidden Wisdom of Solomon was all about Eros. This was not a word that Leiner ever used. He knew neither Greek nor English, but *Eros* is the closest English approximate that I have been able to find. He deployed a cluster of code words like "Shechinah" (the sensual feminine goddess divine), "fragrance," "King Solomon," "wine," "Judah," "temple," "ravished by God," "deep feminine," and "God's unmediated will, known directly and not through the law." The meaning of the code words was well hidden. It was only by collecting every single reference to the word and then checking them against earlier Aramaic sources that I came to realize these were code words. I understood they were being intentionally deployed by Leiner in highly consistent and deeply erotic patterns. Leiner, in one veiled reference, makes it abundantly clear that he is transmitting the Wisdom of Solomon to the reader who can pierce the veil. The process of cracking the Leiner code of the Solomon matrix was erotic, exhausting, and ecstatic at the same time.

At some point I understood that my mind would not take me there. The text had revealed something of her nakedness to me in an act of grace. But she would reveal no more until I surrendered even more deeply. She demanded my utter devotion to her truth. My relationship to the text was purely erotic.[20] If I would falter, she would close. When my heart opened, she would spread herself to reveal her gifts and drip her nectar into my soul. There was a moment in which She, the text, consented to disrobe, to appear as the "Goddess without her garments." The puzzle started to piece itself together. During the entire process, She was always in charge. That was self-evidently apparent. Even when I appeared to be seducing her, she was in charge.

It became clear that the Wisdom of Solomon was connected to the temple. Remember this is the same Solomon who built the Temple in Jerusalem. This is the temple that had the famed Ark, as in the cinematic phenomenon *Raiders of the Lost Ark*, at its epicenter. I remembered again the terse epigram of the Greek historian Thucydides: "When words lose their meaning, culture collapses."

The movie's cultural reference to the lost Ark was not lost on me. It was then that I began to wonder: Why shouldn't we just let the Ark stay lost? What do we seek in the recovery of the Ark? Remember that the Ark is the center of the Holy of Holies in the inner precincts of the temple. Atop the Ark were two cherubs, sexually intertwined one with the other. The sacred texts read, "I will speak to you from between the two cherubs."[21] The voice of wisdom emerges from between the sexually intertwisted cherubs. This is the core transmission of the Holy of Holies and the essence of temple consciousness. What did the hidden tradition of Solomon mean by all this?

It is worth remembering that Solomon did not fare well in the Bible. The rabbinic voices that canonized the Bible marginalized Solomon. They said he was led astray by his thousand wives and lost his way. There is not one classical source in the entire rabbinic cannon that excuses Solomon entirely of sin in relation to the feminine—except for my teacher and his direct teachers, who were the direct holders of the actual lineage of Solomon. Mordechai Leiner was able to transmit to me in the Oxford library the deeper truth hidden in the Solomon matrix, the truth that forms the core of his teaching. Solomon was not led astray by the feminine. He was guided by Eros.

He was right, but he was also before his time. Solomon saw clearly that the entire world was dripping with divine Eros. Therefore, there is no need to search for meaning because everything is always, already, filled with meaning. There is no place to go other than where you are. You cannot be late, because it's happening now. The experience of being radically alive—on the inside of all the faces of Eros—is fully available to you in this moment. You must simply step through the portal to the inside. All the faces of Eros are revealing themselves to you right now. You can enter the inside of the inside, live in the fullness of presence, participate in the yearning force of being, feel that you are indivisibly enmeshed in the larger fabric of reality, and know that you are an irreducibly unique expression of that seamless fabric, right now.

When you unfurnish your eyes and cleanse the doors of perception, you will realize that you are a uniquely needed, chosen, honored, and loved expression of reality. You are a good child of the universe. You will know the will of God, without need for recourse to any external authority or text. You will feel completely humble and wildly powerful. You will realize there is a gift that you can give to life, which can be given by you and you alone. Giving that gift, nurtured by all the faces of Eros, will sustain your experience of radical aliveness. That is what it means to live the erotic life.

These were core teachings in the hidden Goddess sources that lay at the center of the hidden temple wisdom. This is the secret of the sexually intertwined cherubs atop Solomon's Ark. This is secret of the Mary Magdalene line in Christianity and the inner truth of the grail quest. The grail is the chalice, the feminine form, the goddess, Eros herself. Eros is the plentitude of meaning when all questions are not answered but simply fall away. The goodness of life, of every breath, becomes self-evident. The erotic delight in aliveness suffuses our hearts, minds, and senses. This is what the true evolution of consciousness will yield: a world in which each person's unique creativity will be desired, honored, and needed in the great Unique Self–symphony.

DECODING THE SOLOMON MATRIX

But that is not all. Solomon understood that consciousness would not be fully awakened or evolved unless we came back to our senses. Solomon's sexually intertwisted cherubs speak the great truth of his wisdom. The sexual models the erotic. The sexual is the ultimate teacher. The sexual is the great instruction taking us home to the utter goodness of reality. It is the goodness of Eros that whispers to us of the goodness of all of existence. For reality is Eros.

More than that, the cherubs point to a subversive vision of society rooted in the wisdom of ever-awakening aliveness, pleasure, and transformation. We will talk more of the subversive nature of Eros in later chapters. For now, let us recognize that Eros undermines convention and invites us to live on an entirely different level of delight and devotion with each other.

The erotic and the holy are one. It is for this reason that the word for "temple" in Hebrew is simply *mikdash*, which means "holy." It is for this reason that the epicenter of the temple was the Ark with its sexually intertwisted cherubs. It is for this reason that the word of God, the way of wisdom, poured out from between these cherubs.

The gift I received from the Goddess in her transmission of the Secret of the Cherubs was not made possible by any capacity of mine. It occurred purely as a gift of grace from Her, and it came with many demands. It is a gift that has required intense sacrifice and commitment from me. It is a gift that until today I am hesitant to fully receive because of the immensity of its power and the ever-present potential for misunderstanding. But it is a gift that I know the world desperately needs, so I am committed to giving it in the best way I can for as long as it right to do so.

This great teaching, that the sexual models the erotic, is the core of the Secret of the Cherubs. The teaching was transmitted in an unbroken chain from generation to generation. It was transmitted from Solomon to Luria to Nathan to Leiner to me. I transmitted it to my co-author, Kristina. She and I have founded the Integral Evolutionary Tantra School to create a band of outrageous lovers who will know and teach this truth. It is not merely a cognitive truth or even a truth of only the heart. It is a truth of the body. The Secret of the Cherubs is a truth where the holy trinity of body, heart, and mind merge into the sustained pleasure and passion of radical aliveness directed toward great purpose.

CHAPTER NINE

THE SEXY SONG
OF SOLOMON

In the great chain of transmission beginning with Solomon, there was a teacher who lived historically around the time of Jesus, who walked in Israel not long before the fall of the Jerusalem Temple. He was one of the great lineage masters who both received Solomon's transmission of the Secret of the Cherubs and added to it in a significant way. His name was Akiva.

AKIVA: MYSTIC AND LOVER

In the Kabbalistic tradition, Akiva was an archetypal lover. He witnessed the destruction of the temple and understood deeply that the temple is the axis of Eros and that Eros is the essential force of attraction, the clasp upon the jeweled necklace that holds the whole world together.

Akiva, however, initially learned of Eros not from books or old wise masters. His life's journey began as a poor shepherd. He was an outsider, not part of the rabbinic or priestly power classes in the Jerusalem of the time. He was a shepherd in the fields, playing the flute for his God and his sheep. He was beheld late one afternoon by Rachel, the beautiful daughter of Kalba Savua, patriarch of Jerusalem's wealthiest aristocratic family. She saw him and she knew. Great love and passion were kindled. They married against the fierce objections of her family. She was disowned for marrying a "simpleton," but erotic love and Eros became Rachel and Akiva's spiritual master.

Akiva was so madly in love with Rachel that he yearned to trace that love back to its source. Aflame with love, he made his way to the academy and emerged twelve years later as the greatest spiritual master the Hebrew tradition had ever known. He was master of the law, not because he was the most cognitively gifted among scholars but because he was in love with the Eros of every letter that formed every word that formed every sentence that comprised the Hebrew law. He felt ideas before he spoke them. He was ravished by the Divine and impregnated with wisdom.

To all his disciples, he made clear: his true teacher was Rachel. Not just because, as is usually understood, she urged him to study for many years away from home in the academy, but also because the erotic love they shared was the greatest teacher of the spirit Akiva had ever known. Indeed, the Kabbalists understand "Rachel" to refer both to the real woman who loved Akiva and as a metaphor for the Goddess—for Shechinah, for Eros. The temple, which stood for most of Akiva's life, was the center of Eros. Akiva saw the sexually intertwisted cherubs above the Ark and received their erotic transmission. So when the temple fell, he needed to make people understand that for all its magnificence and even holiness, in the end it was but a symbol of something more. It was the symbol of Eros.

Most people fall when their temple is destroyed and they are exiled from their land. Akiva taught that temple consciousness was more potent than the physical temple, sacred as it might have been. Temple consciousness was all about living the erotic life. Akiva instituted, within Hebrew mysticism, a profound yearning for the rebuilt temple of Jerusalem. But he was not talking about a building on a hill. He was talking about a return to Eros. Eros was the New Jerusalem. But unlike the ancient days, when the erotic life was the province of only the elite, Akiva yearned for a democratization of Eros, in which there is no longer a need for priests because "everyone will erotically know me from young to old."*

THE SONG OF SOLOMON

Akiva taught: "If the Torah would not have been given, then we would have learned all wisdom from the Song of Solomon." The Torah in the Hebrew tradition is the divine source of all wisdom in every dimension of life and in all sectors of society. The Song of Solomon is the biblical poem of outrageous love and Eros, which speaks of spirituality in explicit sexual terms.

The essence of the Solomon tradition is that all wisdom is written not in the law books but in the law of our bodies, the law of the sexual. Even if the Torah, the classic law book, did not exist, we could learn all Torah, all wisdom, from the Song of Solomon, the song of the sexual. Here we have again the Secret of the Cherubs: the sexual models the erotic. But the sexual does not exhaust the erotic. The sexual teaches us how to live in Eros in all the nonsexual dimensions of our lives.

HOLY OF HOLIES

Akiva had a second teaching, which dances us one step further on the path of Eros and love. Akiva participated in a great debate with the other sages over whether to include the Song of Solomon (also called the Song of Songs) in the biblical cannon of sacred books. The song was written as a dialogue between two lovers. "Let him kiss me with the kisses of his mouth.

---

* This is how the erotic cherub mystics read the sacred text in Jeremiah 31:34: "No longer will they teach their neighbor or say to one another—know the Lord—because they will all know me, from young to old." *Me* refers to essence or spirit. The word *know* in sacred text refers to carnal knowledge (see Genesis 4:1: Adam knew his wife Eve," where the word *know* refers to sexual coupling). Jeremiah is a receiver of the Solomon lineage that yearns for the democratization of Eros, "everyone will erotically know me" without need for the mediation of external authority. Akiva is in the direct lineage of Solomon to Jeremiah.

His fruit is sweet to my mouth . . . His thrust is upon me in love." The man responds, "Your lips are like the thread of scarlet . . . Your breasts are like two roses . . . Your closed garden, your secret fountain . . . is my delight."

As you can imagine, the sages of the day protested. The song appears to be a sexual love song, perhaps to be sung in ancient taverns and beer halls; what place could it have in the sacred writ, they said? To this argument of the sages, Akiva had a twofold response. First, he pointed out that the Song of Songs is a *mashal*, an allegory. Second, he argued that while all the books are holy, the Song of Songs is the Holy of Holies.

The traditional sources agree that Akiva was saying two distinct things: do not be afraid of the content of this book; it is not about sexuality; the sexual is but an allegory for the spiritual love between the human being and God. Second, he was saying that this lofty spiritual love is central to religious endeavor. This book therefore was not only holy but the Holy of Holies. This was the classical reading given to Akiva and the Song of Solomon by virtually two thousand years of tradition.[22]

That reading, however, was but a cloak, allowing Akiva to hide his truly radical esoteric doctrine. That doctrine was none other than the Secret of the Cherubs, the spring of enlightenment from which we have been sipping. When Akiva said the Song of Songs is a *mashal*, he meant not an allegory but a model. That is to say, the sexual story of the lovers in the Song of Songs is a model for the erotic. The erotic, as we have seen, is identical with the sacred itself. This was Akiva's intent when he cried out with such passion and pathos that "the Song of Solomon is the Holy of Holies!"

This was not a casual metaphor affirming the importance of the book. Rather, it contained Akiva's deepest mystical intention. The Holy of Holies in the temple, destroyed just a few years earlier, was for Akiva and the people the personification of Eros. The cherubs reminded the people that the sexual was the window to the sacred. The secret of the sexually intertwined cherubs atop the Ark was, you remember, not that sex is all of the erotic but that sex models the erotic, which yearns to be lived in all dimensions of life.

The power of this idea did not fall with the destruction of the temple. The fall of the temple, insisted Akiva, must not be the fall of Eros. For every moment when life was engaged erotically, the temple was rebuilt. Moreover, Akiva was reminding a people who had just been disempowered politically that in the end political power structures are but an illusion. Humans are powerful because by living erotically a person participates in and creates the divine union, because consciousness and action are the touchstone of divinity. That is what Akiva meant when he said the Song of Solomon is the Holy of Holies. The Song of Solomon holds the temple consciousness, hidden in the Secret of the Cherubs.

The entire thrust of the Western tradition was to rebuild the temple and return to the Garden of the Eden. Both refer to the same movement in the evolution of consciousness. That is the implicit cultural image of the lost Ark. This was the spark that ignited the popular best seller *The Da Vinci Code* that allured so many when it was published at the beginning of the twenty-first century. This is the true meaning of the grail quest, the orienting myth of Western culture. This is the yearned-for desire at the heart of Jewish culture, to rebuild the temple in the New Jerusalem. The grail, the Ark, the cherubs, all point in one direction: to Eros. And particularly to the precise relationship among the erotic and the sexual and the holy. The sexual models the erotic. The erotic and the holy are one.

EROTIC TASTES AND TEXTS FROM THE SONG OF SOLOMON

Let us sample segments from the Song of Solomon to taste something of the power and poignancy of the Secret of the Cherubs. As we read, remember with delight that the Song of Solomon is part of the biblical canon. Remember again that it is about this book that Akiva says: "All [biblical] books are holy, and the Song of Solomon is the Holy of Holies. The Song of Solomon is the new Holy of Holies. It is the New Jerusalem. The sexual is the great teacher of Eros."

The song is written in the heteronormative world of biblical sexuality. It needs to be recontextualized to honor the full range of sacred sexual possibility. So please read your sacred sexual preference into the text.

The song opens with kissing. This is not a peck-on-the-cheek kind of kiss but rather a passionate kiss of radical arousal. "Let him kiss me with the kisses of his mouth: for thy love is better than wine" (Song of Solomon 1:2). In their kissing she discovers that "his mouth is most sweet" (Song of Solomon 5:16). He finds that "the roof of her mouth is like the best wine" (Song of Solomon 7:9).

The English translators were accurate here. The verse does not describe kissing that is limited to lips. *Yeshakeni* reads the Hebrew text, literally translated as "kiss me," implying, "kiss me all over, all of me." In the original Hebrew, the reader feels the full passion of these highly sexualized kisses. One translation captures this sense of the original Hebrew with the words: "Your lips cover me with kisses" (Song of Solomon 1:2).

The Song of Solomon, aroused by the delight of the passionate kiss, continues: "I have compared thee, O my love, to a mare harnessed to one of the chariots of Pharaoh" (Song of Solomon 1:9).

Mares excite stallions. He is the stallion; she is the mare. This is a powerful ancient sexual symbol. He is fully aroused by her to the rawness of his sexuality. The mare and stallion suggest images of fully aroused wild Eros.

She is no less aroused. In the full heat of sexual allure, she says, "While the King was on my couch, my perfume gave forth its fragrance" (Song of Solomon 1:12). The fragrance of her wetness allures the air.

She invites him to drink her wetness with the words: "I would cause thee to drink of spiced wine of the juice of my pomegranate" (Song of Solomon 8: 2). The pomegranate is a classical ancient symbol of the feminine yoni, or vagina.

TEACHING THROUGH AROUSAL

The Song of Solomon, to the reader who knows how to decipher its symbols, is a book of highly intense erotica. It would be very hard for the spiritual seeker reading this sacred text not to be aroused. The allure of the graphic sexual imagery works its magic on the mind, the heart, and the body. The descriptions intentionally invite awakening of the sexual imagination. The text seeks to teach through arousal.

The Hebrew mystics talk about the gift of enlightenment as *it'aruta de'le'eyla*, meaning "arousal from above." This is the gift of divine arousal that lives available to all, written into the script of our bodies. In the realization of the wisdom of arousal, we awaken to the utter goodness of our lives. When the goodness of arousal merges with our core experience of being irreducibly unique, we begin to feel at home in the world.

As we will see, uniqueness is the fifth quality of Eros. In the sexual we feel personally addressed, even as we feel the common quality of allurement that threads through all of reality. The realization of the goodness of Eros, coupled with awakening to our Unique Self, is the elixir of greatness for every life. The goodness of Eros integrated with Unique Self–realization is the portal to our authentic knowing. Through this portal we know that we are held, loved, chosen, and desired by all of reality in every moment. The Song of Solomon addresses the seeker, each of us, personally, and calls us to the full Eros of our lives. It is in the personal address of the sexual to every human being that the democratization of greatness is born. For it is the dripping nectar of sexual pleasure gifted uniquely to each of us that affirms that our lives are dignified, worthy, and desired by all that is.

POWERFUL SEXUAL IMAGES

Let's further explore the sexual images inviting us to Eros that form the matrix of the Song of Solomon.

"His left hand should be under my head, and his right hand should embrace me" (Song of Solomon 8:3). They are lying down. In this position she tells him to "drink of the juice of my pomegranate."

"How beautiful and pleasant you are, O loved one, with all your delights! Your stature is like a palm tree, and your breasts are like its clusters. I say I will climb the palm tree and lay hold of its fruit. O may your breasts be like clusters of the vine, and the scent of your breath like apples, and your mouth like the best wine. I am my beloved's, and his desire is for me" (Song of Solomon 7: 6–10).

The man is an apple tree with dangling fruits of delight, and the woman is a palm tree to be climbed in love. The invitations imaged in the explicit sensuality of all the most recognized symbols of blessing in an agricultural world are designed to arouse. Climbing the palm tree, opening the garden, eating the lush fruits, drinking the wine and milk—all are images of a life whose value needs no explanation or justification to a society rooted in the rhythms of nature. Giving one's beloved the gift of one's arousal is a great source of aliveness. Radical intimacy is to let your beloved witness your arousal.

"I was a wall, and my breasts were like towers; then I was in his eyes as one who finds peace" (Song of Solomon 8:10). The name of God in one biblical verse is Shaddai, literally translated as "breast." The beauty of the feminine invites man to a state of contentment where he may find peace.[23]

Figs, Love Apples, and Secret Gardens

"The fig tree puts forth her green figs . . . Arise, my love, my fair one, and come away" (Song of Solomon 2:13). The fig is one of many ancient symbols of sexual fertility that abounds in the Song of Solomon. In some Middle Eastern languages, the word was used to represent the yoni. Open up a purple fig, and in it you see the image of the feminine yoni.

"The mandrakes give forth fragrance, and beside our doors are all choice fruits, new as well as old, which I have laid up for you, O my beloved" (Song of Solomon 7:13). Mandrakes, also known as "love apples," were believed to arouse sexual desire. The Song of Solomon is filled with fruit, symbols of the phallus and yoni—pomegranates, figs, nuts, apples, grapes, and mandrake, all enjoyed in her "garden."

"A garden locked is my sister, my bride, a spring locked, a fountain sealed. Your shoots are an orchard of pomegranates with all choicest fruits, henna with nard, and saffron, calamus, and cinnamon, with all trees of frankincense, myrrh, and aloes, with all choice spices—a garden fountain, a well of living water, and flowing streams from Lebanon. Awake, O north wind, and come, O south wind! Blow upon my garden, let its spices flow. Let my beloved come to his garden, and eat its choicest fruits" (Song of Solomon 4:12–16).

The lover is invited into the garden of the woman's wetness. There is a great feast as he enters the hot embrace of her secret garden. "I entered your garden and plucked your pomegranates . . ." With the lover, the reader enters the garden engulfed by the fragrance of myrrh, aloes, cinnamon, and frankincense—spices used to perfume a bed in preparation for lovemaking.

Honey, Wine, and Lilies

"I have perfumed my bed with myrrh, aloes, and cinnamon. Come, let us take our fill of love until the morning" (Proverbs 7:17–18). The spouse says: "Until the daybreak, and the shadows flee away, I will get me to the mountain of myrrh, and to the hill of frankincense" (Song of Solomon 4:6). The mountain of myrrh refers to the clitoris, the raised area above the secret garden (vagina), covered with gentle hair, a reference to the mons veneris, the sacred mound.

"I am come into my garden, my sister, my spouse: I have gathered my myrrh with my spice; I have eaten my honeycomb with my honey; I have drunk my wine with my milk" (Song of Solomon 5:1). In describing the sexual act as "eating honey" and "drinking milk and wine," the text affirms the utter goodness of Eros.

"My beloved is mine, and I am his: he feeds among the lilies. Until the daybreak and the shadows flee away, turn, my beloved, and be thou like a roe or a young hart upon the mountains of Bether" (Song of Solomon 2:16, 17). A lily approximates an alluring image of the yoni. He feeds upon the lilies. The image is clear, compelling, and arousing. But what are the "mountains of Bether"? One translator reads this passage as "play like a roe or a hart on my perfumed slopes." Slopes are descriptive of mounds, the "mountains of Bether," or "mountains of division," through which runs a very lush and moist "valley."

"As an apple tree among the trees of the forest, so is my beloved among the young men. With great delight I sat in his shadow, and his fruit was sweet to my taste. He brought me to the banqueting house, and his banner over me was love" (Song of Solomon 2:3–4).

You feel the delight of feminine desire in the text. "His banner" refers to the spouse's phallus. Sex is love in the body. The image again is clear, compelling, and arousing.

The Fire between Them

"All the books are holy; the Song of Solomon is the Holy of Holies." After reading the text in some depth, one realizes the full audacity of Akiva's claim. To say the Song of Solomon is the Holy of Holies clearly rejects the sex-neutral and sex-negative narratives. But it also displays the triteness of the sex-positive narrative. The sexual Song of Solomon, as the Holy of Holies, points to something far more potent and profound than a merely sex-positive outlook.

But even the narrative of sex sacred (sex being sacred because it creates children) does not capture the sexual vision of the Song of Solomon, because the sexual so exquisitely described in it is not related to procreation. The images evoke the sexual as a radical practice of delight, quite independent of any procreative intent. The Song of Solomon is rather Solomon's great poem of temple consciousness. The sexual is the source of all wisdom. The sexual models the erotic. The erotic and the sacred are one.

We conclude this section with a final teaching from Akiva. He points to the Hebrew words for man and woman: I-Y-SH (איש) and I-SH-A (אשה). They are made up of two sets of letters. The first set of common letters (I-SH) appears in both Hebrew words. These two letters together, comprised of the Hebrew letters *aleph* (א) and *shin* (ש), form the word *eish* (אש), meaning "fire." Fire represents sex, Eros, and passion. The Y (י) and AH (ה) that appear respectively in the Hebrew words for man and woman are in Hebrew *yud* and *hei* (יה). These are the letters of the name of God.

איש = man
אשה = woman
אש = fire
יה = Yah, the name of God

Akiva taught that when a man and a woman come together in sacred union, God is a third partner in their intercourse. It is not merely sex sacred because they participate in the potential creation of new life below in the visible world; rather, the sexual is always creating new life above, in the divine. The partners not only fulfill themselves in Eros, but they also fulfill God. In Akiva's language, when lovers are aroused in the rawness of passion, "the Shechinah dwells between them." Akiva is daring to suggest that the Shechinah, which dwells between the cherubs in the temple, dwells between man and woman in sexual union. Sexual union, in the Kabbalistic tradition of the Secret of the Cherubs, is the great mystical act that heals all the worlds above and below. The Hebrew mystics of the Kabbalah write of man and woman in these words:

> They should prepare themselves to be of one desire and one intent so that when they join they become one in body and soul; they become one in soul by aligning their wills in cleaving; when they unite in sexual union they become one in body and soul . . . It is then that God dwells between them in unified oneness.[24]

Eros, we now begin to understand, is the primal desire from which the world springs into being. God's Eros created the world. Our lack of Eros could destroy the world. Love or die. The mystics of every religion—those who lived on the inside—understand that this is not mere metaphor. Every act of union causes and participates in divine union. The human being participates in the divine love affair, even as God participates in the human love affair. For beneath the veil of illusion and separation, all really is one.*

---

* This is the truth of the science of enlightenment in every great tradition. This truth is now being validated again by systems science, general dynamics theory, chaos and complexity theory, and zero point field theory emergence science.

CHAPTER TEN

THE EXILE OF THE EROTIC AND THE BOUNDARY-BREAKING SEXUAL

Many years ago I had the questionable privilege of babysitting a twelve-month-old baby named Maya, who was, in the classical sense of the term, quite cherubic. The cherub mystery in this case was that Maya was inexplicably wailing at top decibels. She wanted something, and I could not for the life of me figure out what it was. All I knew was that she kept on crying out, "Nana. Nana." Now, "nana" I knew. It means banana, the essential tool of babysitting. So I kept trying to stuff bananas into Maya's clenched hands, which she would repeatedly thrust away as if I were some illiterate idiot who understood nothing about baby talk.

Finally, I distracted her with my vast repertoire of ridiculous baby faces and spoonfuls of every soft food available. Nothing availed until a spoonful of smashed peas suddenly, mysteriously, quieted her down. When Maya's dad got home I told him, "We had a hard half hour there.

Maya kept screaming out for 'nanas.' So I tried to give her bananas, which she adamantly refused."

"So you gave her the smashed peas, eh?" Brad replied nonchalantly.

I blinked. "How did you know!?"

Dad explained. "When Maya started eating real food, her favorite thing in the world was bananas. She thinks 'nanas' are the yummiest things around. But over time the word 'nana' has sort of transcended being about bananas and has just become a general appellation for anything that falls under the category of 'really yummy.' So when she wants something yummy, like peas or sweet potatoes, she just calls out 'nana.' And since I gave her some peas this morning, it figures that is what she would have had on her mind."

I was floored! The mystery was revealed! What a feat of linguistic brilliance! Not only is Maya cherubic, but she is also a genius. So what if it wasn't my amazing repertoire of baby faces that had so amused her. This infant had brought me to satori, enlightenment! I suddenly understood the whole conundrum of Eros that had been sifting through my mind. Eros and "nanas" are the same thing! We have a little taste of sex—it's inordinately "yummy." It is called Eros. But then we get a taste of cross-country skiing. It, too, is inordinately yummy. It, too, is Eros. And what about writing that vivid haiku the other day? Erotic! Or the photograph you took of a flock of starlings forming a breathtaking spectacle at sunset? Erotic! Perhaps you listened to that old song you love so much, the one that stirs your deepest longing and has you singing out loud with wild abandon? Eros!

Just as I thought Maya was talking about bananas when she said "nana," most of us think we are talking about sex when we say "Eros." Yes, Eros is sexual, but it also transcends the sexual. Eros actually means all the places where I am fully present, on the inside, yearning, and connected. Eros is the experience of being radically alive in my life. Eros takes the sexual and lets it stand as the model for all that fills our deep desire. We are all crying out for Eros, but instead of feeding us on the sweet divine stuff our soul craves, society is trying to sate our deepest desires with sex, which is like trying to stuff a baby with bananas when she really wants peas! Give bananas to a baby who needs peas, and she will continue crying, her hunger unabated. Our society is in need of Eros. So being fed only sex leaves us hungry, desperate, and crying out. We are calling out for Eros. Not sex, but Eros.[25]

EXILED INTO THE SEXUAL

Now let's go back to our lost Ark and its cherubs situated in the inner sanctum of the temple. The Ark in particular and the temple in general are the mythic symbols of the Shechinah, that is, of the erotic experience. That is precisely what the mystery texts mean when they say the Shechinah dwells between the cherubs atop the Ark. The fall of the temple is thus not a mere historical event. In myth, it represents the fall of Eros, the exile of the erotic. This experience is called by the Kabbalistic masters the exile of the Shechinah.

But where did it go? To where was Eros exiled? The answer is that the exile of the Shechinah is the exile of the erotic into the sexual. The holy Eros of the cosmos that takes place at every level of reality is exiled to the small eros of the sexual. That is to say, when the only place we access the core qualities of Eros is in the sexual, then Eros, or the Shechinah, is in exile. When the only time you feel that you are on the inside is during great sex, then the Shechinah is in exile. When intense desire is a feeling you touch only before exploding in orgasm, then your life is poor indeed. When you only participate in the yearning force of being alive while having sex, Eros has fallen. When you only feel the wholeness and interconnectivity of the all during a sexual experience, then Eros is in exile.

The Secret of the Cherubs is that sex is our spiritual guide. Later chapters of this book will outline the twelve faces of Eros, showing how each one is modeled in the sexual. These are the essential qualities needed to live a life of wonder in body, mind, and spirit. However, we have lost our access to them. These qualities wind up not only being modeled by the sexual but also, tragically, being accessed in our lives virtually only in the sexual. As a result, much of our life feels drab and vacant, a pale reflection of what we once dreamed life could be. Our work; our friendships; our relationship to nature, knowledge, the spirit, and to our families, neighborhoods, and communities—all of these have been disenchanted and de-eroticized. We need to return to Eros.

We cannot live in a nonerotic world, so unconsciously we seek compensation. We look to get our erotic fix in the sexual. But this doesn't work. For when you de-eroticize the entire world except for sex, then the sexual collapses as well. You see, we all have erotic needs. These needs require attention in all aspects of our lives, but if we ignore them in most aspects, then we demand that the sexual fulfill all of our erotic needs. And so sexuality shrugs, collapsing under the weight of a burden it cannot bear. When we ask sex to be the sole source of funding our erotic bank, sex has little choice but to default. Sex collapses under the weight of an impossible demand. When sex implodes because it is our sole source of Eros, it begins a cascading domino effect of collapsing ethics all across every arena of our lives and every sector of society.

So as you can now see, the fall of Eros brings in its wake the collapse of sex as well. The modern zeitgeist has slain all the gods save Aphrodite, the goddess of sexual love. Yet she cannot survive alone. We wonder why she has abandoned us. We ask ourselves incessantly, why is sex not working? French philosopher Michel Foucault in *The History of Sexuality* suggests mockingly that we vaunt sex as our great secret and yet talk about it incessantly. Behind all our talk about sexuality we are all frantically asking, "Why has sex not redeemed me? I finally got some, and I am just as depressed, lonely, and confused as I was yesterday."

It is something like the biblical story about Balaam and his donkey, on their way to curse the wandering Hebrews. The donkey is unable to proceed on the path because an angel is blocking his way. Balaam, the great magical seer of the ancient world, is unable to see this angel. So he blames the ass and starts to beat it. The donkey surprisingly speaks up, "I've only done good for you. Why do you beat me up when things don't go right?" The reason, of course, is because Balaam wants something more than the donkey can give. He wants the donkey to take him where he wants to go, so he blames the donkey when the journey fails.

We are much the same way with the donkey of sex. We think the problem is with sex. It refuses to take us where we need to go. But in actuality, the adamant refusal of sex to take us forward is simply symptomatic of the larger malfunction. The erotic endeavor has been betrayed. But with all our information and sophistication, we still cannot see. So we invest all our energy in sex, little realizing that what we crave is not "mere sex," but an experience of genuine and sustained Eros.

EXILE WITHIN AN EXILE

In the language of the Kabbalists, we are now in an exile within an exile. The first exile of the Shechinah is the exile of the erotic into the sexual. The second is the exile of the erotic *within* the sexual. In this second exile, the erotic is banished to a very limited domain within the sexual. We can no longer find the erotic in most of the arenas of the sexual. In order to touch the intense desire that makes us feel alive, lost and found in the infinity of the moment, many people need a sexuality that breaks the boundaries of their own authentic story. In the second exile we only experience the raw pulsation of Eros' pleasure during sex that violates rules and breaks boundaries—transgressive or illicit sexuality.

In order to find Eros after the first wave of arousal has begun to fade, we either upgrade or downgrade sex. The first, the idealized upgrade of sex, often expresses itself in the search for sex in the form of the ideal true love. It is, of course, so ideal that it is inaccessible, leaving us forever fantasizing about the perfect lover or reading endless varieties of the same sexy romance novel.

The expression of the second, the downgrade of sex, appears in a couple of ways. It sometimes appears as degrading forms of pornography and varieties of sexual abuse. Sexual abuse includes all its tragic classical expressions, plus a variety of new forms that have emerged in our culture. These new forms include false charges of sexual abuse by people who claim to be victims. Their complaints may distort the memory of a genuine sexual encounter, or they may be fabricated to serve vindictive or political purposes. Internet smear campaigns are becoming a feature of everyday living. It is doubtful whether Martin Luther King Jr.'s personal life would have survived the takedown culture that dominates the internet today. When J. Edgar Hoover attempted to destroy King by outing his extramarital affairs, the only tools he had available were pre-internet. Hoover would almost certainly have used the internet to attack King for clergy sex abuse, had he been able to. One can imagine that Hoover would have presented himself as rescuer of victims. This kind of perpetration under the guise of a noble cause has been termed "sexual McCarthyism." Such new forms of abuse are degradations of the sexual.

The second expression of the downgrade of sex—played out in order to reclaim some of the rawness of Eros lost—is in boundary-breaking sexuality, particularly where you break the boundaries of your own authentic story or values.

The fall of the temple is the mythic expression of the exile of the erotic not only into the sexual but specifically into boundary-breaking sexuality. Listen in on a strange and fascinating Talmudic discussion.[26]

A man is struck by the beauty of a particular woman. His heart becomes sick. He falls deathly ill. Doctors are consulted.

Their response: "He cannot be healed unless he has sexual intercourse with her."

The sages' succinct reply: "Let him die and not sleep with her!"

"So let her stand naked before him," urge the doctors.

"Let him die, and she should not stand naked before him!" the sages reply.

"Let her talk to him from behind a fence [erotic conversation]," press the doctors.

"Let him die and not be engaged by her in erotic conversation," answer the sages.

This striking case becomes a *locus classicus* in the debates of the academy for many generations to come. One of the central issues debated and recorded in the Talmud was the identity of the beautiful woman. One school held that she was married; a second school held that she was single. According to the first school, it was understandable why there would be opposition to a sexual encounter between a lovesick man and a married woman.

"And if she were single?" queries a voice in the Talmud. "Surely we should allow her to save his life through some sort of minimal sexual engagement—verbal, visual, or otherwise?"

"No!" roars a second voice from the pages. "For if we did so, it would undermine the personal integrity of women."

"Well, then," offers a third voice. "If she is single and he is single . . . let them marry!"

"No, for if he married her," responds the same voice to its own query, "she would not settle his spirit [she would not satisfy his erotic need], for it is written, 'Stolen waters are sweet.'"

"Stolen waters are sweet." This terse epigram means quite simply that after a man is married, his sexual excitement will recede and he will not be fulfilled. Only in the context of "stolen waters"—the thrill of boundary-breaking sex—can the man in the story be sated. He is only interested in the woman as an already married or unavailable partner. Once she is available, his lust will quickly subside.

We should not view this as the peculiar weakness of the man in the story. Rather, the man is a symbol of the times. And here we get to the essence of the text, where the wisdom masters draw a most provocative conclusion: "From the day the temple was destroyed, the taste of sex has been taken away and given to sinners." That is to say, once the temple has fallen, once Eros is lost, the "taste of sex" is experienced only in boundary-breaking sexual relationship! On the face of it, the passage makes little sense. What could the fall of the Jerusalem Temple possibly have to do with varieties of sexual satisfaction?

Once we understand the nature of the text, however, it begins to open itself up to interpretation. The "taste of sex" is another term for Eros. The temple was seen as the seat of Eros. The fall of the temple symbolizes a mythic shift in the erotic psyche of the world, the exile of the Shechinah not just into the sexual but more precisely into the transgressively sexual. In this passage, adultery is the paradigm of boundary-breaking sex. But boundary-breaking sex can also mean looking for superficial novelty to elicit any sense of erotic thrill. This is pseudo Eros.

The text suggests that in the tragic, post-temple world of fallen Eros, men felt they could find erotic satisfaction only in the sexual—and then only if it was the boundary-breaking sexual. It is not by accident that a thousand years later the great Western love story sung by the troubadours was that of Tristan and Iseult. These lovers personify the sweet and mad passion of romantic love. Of course, Iseult is betrothed to another man when she and Tristan meet. Stolen waters. A modern reincarnation of this scenario is a movie called *Unfaithful*. In its lead advertisement, it asks this question: "Would you risk everything in a moment of passion?" Of course, the premise is that the moment of passion, the "taste of sex," could only be available in the context of being "unfaithful." Marketing executives are our highest-paid and often best psychologists. Even if not all of us yearn for that unfaithful moment, most of us understand all too well the hole that it is desperately trying to fill. We are desperately searching for Eros in all the wrong places.

The yearning for a rebuilt temple is not a carpenter's fantasy. Rather, it is the dream of a world in which raw Eros—which today has been exiled to boundary-breaking, illicit sexuality—will be accessed in the context of committed relationships. This text suggests that at least one of the goals of temple consciousness is *to commit adultery . . . with your wife*. Or with your committed partner. Commitment can mean many things in many contexts. The goal is to move beyond the need for stolen waters and to be able to access the full power and passion of the sensual within the context of your own highest story, where your own waters are satisfying and sweet.

THE LIBERATION OF EROS: RECLAIMING SACRED BOUNDARY BREAKING

What needs to happen before we can access the full power and passion of the sensual in our committed relationships and not only in boundary-breaking sex? We need to liberate Eros from its exile. Remember, it is a double exile: not only is Eros exiled in the sexual, but it is also exiled in the "sinful sexual," the transgressive sexual. To liberate Eros means to access its core qualities not only in great sex but also in all dimensions of life. Where sex is concerned, liberating Eros means accessing its raw power not in transgressive sex but through boundary breaking within our chosen, committed relationships.

To understand what the Liberation of Eros requires we need to enter the Secret of the Cherubs even more deeply.

As we will see in subsequent chapters, the core qualities of Eros, all of its primary faces, are about different forms of authentic boundary breaking. Eros is always boundary breaking. That is its nature. Its quality of wholeness and interconnectivity breaks through the walls that make us see ourselves as isolated and separate—an alienated part—that make us act in ways discordant with all life and damaging to others and to ourselves.

Eros yearns to break all artificial boundaries of contracted identity. It yearns to break through old patterns in a relationship to reveal authentic levels of goodness, beauty, depth, and delight. Reaching for interior depth in all realms of life requires the boundary breaking of limited beliefs and old labels that shackle us. It often means breaking through the sham of conventional politeness and showing up with a radical fullness of presence.

Finding newness in the old is key to the authentic boundary breaking that is part of the elemental essence of Eros. This is true in terms of both our relationships and our core sense of self. Breaking through to a new depth in relationships is wildly sexy. Breaking through to a new creative insight is incredibly erotic. But breaking through to an entirely new identity is the most wildy erotic move of all. Moving from the limited identity of separate self to the full erotic glory of unique and evolutionary self is the penultimate in boundary breaking.

In the tradition of the Secret of the Cherubs, when the temple falls, the Shechinah goes into exile. Her exile is the exile of Eros. Where does Eros go in its exile? Into the sexual—in particular, into the "sinful sexual." What that means is that the quality of authentic boundary breaking that is so core to true Eros is exiled in the sexual. When we no longer break boundaries for real—boundaries of false or limited identity, of superficiality, of old patterns in relationship—then the only place we have left to break boundaries in is sex.

When we no longer find newness, new depth in the old, then we look for superficial novelty to fill our erotic needs. Because we have exiled the erotic into the sexual we look to the sexual to fill all of our erotic need for boundary breaking. The result is devastating. Sex begins to only provide a thrill for us when it is boundary breaking. We need some new technique, some new person, or some new form of degradation, to elicit any sense of erotic thrill. This, however, is not Eros but pseudo Eros. Pseudo Eros can never fill the emptiness in any kind of profound or sustained manner. Just like in all forms of pseudo erotic addiction, we need to keep upping the ante in order to get any thrill.

None of this speaks against new forms of play in the sexual. New forms of sexual play and pleasure, be they soft or wild, or by mutual agreement more rough and raw, are all potentially sacred and awesome. In fact, learning how to break boundaries in the sexual is precisely what can inspire us to break boundaries in all the dimensions of our nonsexual lives. That is precisely what we mean when we say that the sexual models the erotic. The sexual points the way to the necessary boundary breaking in every domain of life. But what keeps us from breaking these boundaries? Quite simply, it is fear.

But when Eros is in exile, then instead of the sexual modeling the erotic, the erotic is exiled in the sexual. The sexual then becomes the only place that boundaries are broken. Eros then devolves to pseudo Eros. This is what the ancient text meant when it said, "From the day the temple was destroyed, the taste of sex (the genuine erotic thrill of raw pleasure and delight) was given over only to sinners (to illicit, transgressive sexuality)."

The text means that when we lose temple consciousness—that is to say, when Eros is exiled into the sexual and the sexual is asked to meet all our erotic needs—then sexuality collapses under an erotic burden it cannot bear. The nature of the collapse is precisely that sex with our committed partners is no longer erotically charged. Eros devolves to pseudo Eros. Sex no longer works in our lives unless it is breaking a boundary. This is not authentic boundary breaking but pseudo boundary breaking. It does not take much transformational work to introduce a new form of sexual degradation or a new form of sexual risk.

BREAKING THE BOUNDARY OF FEAR

All true gnosis requires transformation. Without doing the work of transformation, there is no new knowing. "Knowing," remember, in the original Hebrew, means erotic knowledge. It is only in your willingness to break the boundary of your contraction that you are able to transcend your own corruption. That is the only way that authentic consciousness is born.

The universe wants our fullest, most potent pleasure, expression, wholeness, and aliveness. And the structure of the universe is such that if we don't earn it—if we don't participate in our own transformation—we don't get the pleasure. It doesn't become integrated into us. If it's just a free gift, it doesn't become who we are.

If I'm having a moment of emptiness, I can try to fill it with pseudo Eros. Or I can choose to just sit with the emptiness. When I sit for just fifteen minutes, I'm filled with the Eros of reality. What rises up is the fullness of my unique being. This gives me pleasure that's beyond whatever the hit of pseudo Eros might have been. Life is what we do with our emptiness.

To stay in the emptiness, we must break the boundary of our fear: the fear that, deep inside, we are nothing but empty. We cover up the emptiness with hits of pseudo Eros because we are afraid that we are not enough. Knowing that we deserve to be loved, feeling that we deserve to be loved, requires breaking the boundary of our ego's contraction into separateness and exploding into the gnosis that we are a son or daughter of God. When you are willing to stay in the emptiness, you reveal yourself to you. Your Eros arises in the experience of sitting in your own identity, in your radical uniqueness, in the depth of your own story.

WHY WE HAVE AFFAIRS: THE BETRAYAL OF SELF

To really get the full potency of Erotic realization that we have just pointed toward, let's jump ahead for a moment. In chapter seventeen we will talk about the fifth face of Eros, Uniqueness. We will see that to live the erotic life is to undergo a series of transformations of identity—from separate self to true self to unique self to evolutionary unique self. Each transformation requires breaking the boundary of the old limited identity, expanding our sense of self, and living into a greater erotic vision of who we truly are. That is where the real erotic boundary breaking takes place. We talked above about the story of the man who only wants to have an affair with the woman when she is married because "stolen waters are sweet." It is in the transgressive movement—the boundary breaking, the stolen waters—that Eros lives. People have an affair not because they want to betray their partner.* We have affairs because we feel that we have betrayed ourselves. We have lost our own core sense of aliveness. We have fallen out of our erotic life. Remember, Eros is the experience of being radically alive. We have an affair to reclaim our aliveness, to find our lost Eros. This, however, is the exile of the erotic. Having an affair bypasses the genuine source of our erotic predicament. The betrayal of all our beloveds is always rooted in a prior betrayal of self. A hidden affair is pseudo Eros. Authentic Eros can only be liberated from within.

To liberate Eros we must transgress our smaller selves. We must break the boundaries of our limited identity—from separate self to true self to unique self to evolutionary unique self. We must commit to have an affair with a newer version of ourselves. We must commit adultery with a memory of our future self. That is the liberation of Eros.

---

* To be clear, we think that hidden affairs are suboptimal because they involve the betrayal of a partner. They may, however, not be the only or even the primary betrayal in the relationship. The fate of an affair might end the relationship. Or it might be turned into the destiny of a new beginning. It might open the couple to a deeper, more erotic, more ethical, and more authentic partnership. But there are no easy dogmas here. Sometimes, at this moment in our evolution, that which is hidden allows the marriage and all of the good it holds to thrive. But ultimately we need to evolve love. We need a culture which can hold broader erotic possibility with integrity and not demand that people make impossibly anguished choices or else pay a corrupt social price of shaming and condemnation.

PART TWO

THE SEXUAL MODELS THE EROTIC

CHAPTER ELEVEN

FROM SEXUAL ETHICS TO SEXUAL ETHOS

ON EROS, SUBVERSIVE OR TRANSGRESSIVE

We recently had dinner with a colleague who has written some significant work on Eros. It is far more nuanced than virtually anything else out there. In general, we think her work is studded with insight, and we are delighted to recommend it. However, we believe she makes two important mistakes that need to be addressed in the spirit of public debate because they are so impactful in terms of how we experience our lives.

First, she collapses the sexual and the erotic. For her, Eros is a term that for the most part refers to the sexual. She is talking, however, not about banal sex but about what is often called great sex. By Eros she means sex that is, at least on some level, hot and deep. She then makes a very dramatic claim: that Eros by its very nature is transgressive. With this we take exception. The nature of the erotic (including the sexual) is subversive but not transgressive. The difference between these two positions is vast.

Transgressive means to violate an appropriate value or boundary. Subversive implies the intentional subverting of cultural values or boundaries for the sake of a higher vision. Transgressive undermines that which should not be undermined. Subversive is revolutionary, undermining that which needs to be overthrown. The difference is subtle but highly significant.

Our colleague is somewhat of a sexual anthropologist. She looks at the practice of sexuality and finds that what is most alive in people's sexual lives involves transgression—by which she means transgression of the cultural mores held by society or even by the people themselves. Of course, that is exactly the point we were making in the previous chapter. But we would argue that transgression is not the ideal state of the sexual but what one might call the unconscious or shadow expression of the sexual. It is descriptive of the fall of Eros. The goal is to move from the unconscious to the conscious, from shadow to light. When we liberate Eros, we are able to access the aliveness of transgressive sex in the context of our committed relationships of whatever nature they might be. The way to do so is to restore temple consciousness—that is to say, a world in which sex is not transgressive but subversive.

Sex is subversive in that it points to an order of being beyond the conventional. Ordinary reality involves pragmatic surface relationships in which each person looks out for his or her own self-interest. The basic social contract of society is built on precisely such notions of individual self-interest and civil interaction. Sexuality models the possibility of breaking the boundary of the superficial to enter the deep. Sex, in its ideal form, subverts the "normal" order of society.

Let's look at one example. In conventional life, a person is either giving or receiving. You are either making money, and therefore receiving money, or you are losing money—that is, you are giving money away. That distinction between giving and receiving is elemental in our economics, politics, relationships, and just about everything else. The place where this axiomatic relationship between giving and receiving breaks down is in the sexual. We all know that to be a great lover is not merely to give pleasure. The great lover also has a well-developed erotic capacity to receive pleasure.

But it is even more than that. In great sex, the entire split between giving and receiving is effaced. Giving and receiving collapse into one. The giver of pleasure is also the receiver. The giver receives the pleasure of having his erotic gift received. The receiving of pleasure is giving the gift of receiving. The entire conventional split between giver and receiver breaks down in the delightful chaos of Eros.

It in this precise sense that sex is subversive. Sex subverts the conventional order of reality and opens up the possibility of a higher and deeper order of being. As we will see in later chapters, all twelve faces of Eros are subversive relative to the conventional functioning of society. Sex, as the model for Eros, is revolutionary at its very core, opening up the possibility of a politics of love.

FROM SEXUAL ETHICS TO SEXUAL ETHOS

Sexual ethics is vital. One of the great evolutions of consciousness in our generation is sexual ethics. We need to have zero tolerance for all forms of sexual harassment and abuse. This includes domestic violence, date rape, sexual harassment or abuse, false complaints about sexual harassment or abuse, internet abuse, and all the other violations of our sexual integrity. There can be no new sexual conversation without sexual ethics. We must all stand together on the side of the victims, even as we must be careful to discern who the real perpetrators are and who the real victims are. In a classic victim triangle, sometimes the perpetrator disguises him or herself as either a victim or a rescuer.

But while sexual ethics is a prerequisite for any new sexual narrative, it is not the story itself. We need not only sexual ethics but also a sexual ethos. A new sexual ethos transcends and includes ethics. A new sexual ethos includes a new sexual story, what we have called in this book a new sexual narrative. The articulation of the new sexual ethos is precisely the intention of this writing. What must emerge from this new ethos, however, is much more than simply sexual ethics. When we really understand that reality/God is Eros, and that the sexual models the erotic, then the door opens to a possibility far more shocking than externally imposed sexual ethics. What emerges is a new sexual ethos—not only sexual ethics—but that sex *is* ethics. The text of ethics is written in the body sacred. That is the implication of the new sexual ethos.

In the previous chapter, we talked about the relationship between the erotic and the ethical. We saw how all failures in Eros lead to a breakdown of ethics. When we are not filled with the aliveness of Eros, we try to fill up the emptiness with pseudo Eros. Pseudo Eros expresses itself as all forms of addiction or acting out—the moves we make to cover up the void. But the principle that sex is ethics is a momentous leap in understanding, even beyond the intimate nexus between the erotic and the ethical.

Let us say it again: The text of ethics is written in the body sacred. That is the mantra of the new sexual narrative. Sex is ethics means that the quivering tenderness of the sexual contains within it a complete human bill of rights. Sex is ethics means our moral code is enfleshed in our bodies. Sex is ethics means that the ecstatic urgency of the sexual contains within it all principles of virtue and integrity.

Sex implies human rights. The exquisite beauty of the moist feminine open to penetration, the rawness of desire, the yearning to touch and be touched, to ravish and be ravished, to hold and be held—all are radical affirmation of our irreducible dignity and intrinsic worthiness.

In the sexual we are divinity in motion, screaming the name of God. In that divinity our dignity is disclosed. All interpersonal ethics are inscribed in our flesh. That is what the author of the book of Job meant when he exclaimed, "Through my body, I vision God."[27]

Sex implies human rights in another crucial way as well. The radical pleasure and beauty of throbbing phallus and dripping yoni are democratized pleasures. These erotic capacities are not limited to the wealthy or the aristocratic. Every human being is personally addressed by an intensity of pleasure that cries out in affirmation of our infinite worth and dignity. The bill of rights is encrypted in the goodness of sexual pleasure. The democratization of dignity has its source in the democratization of desire. But like all that is democratized, sex can be degraded and taken for granted. To access the radical affirmation of human rights implicit in the texts of sex, wisdom and training are required—rigorous training and practiced attention to become a good citizen in the sexual polis. But with that training, it starts to become self-evident that sex is the seat of all wisdom, sex is ethics. Once we are planted firmly in sexual ethics we can take the momentous leap to the next level of consciousness. It is not only that we need sexual ethics, but rather that sex is ethics.

Let us now turn to some of the specific ethical precepts engraved in our flesh so that we may understand more fully the meaning of "sex is ethics."

LOYALTY TO VULNERABILITY

In sexuality we are all vulnerable. To be a great lover in the sexual, technique is woefully insufficient. Genuine sexual Tantra has nothing to do with circulating the energy up your spine through practiced breathing. Genuine sexual Tantra is about making love with an unguarded heart. This requires radical vulnerability. Authentic sexual Tantra is about merging your heart with your yoni and phallus. Yoni and phallus are not merely exterior forms of genitalia. They are qualities of being that live in every man and woman. It is only from that place that you can be vulnerable enough to risk being ultimately fierce and ultimately tender. It is only from that place that you can risk sexing your partner open to God or letting your partner sex you open to God.

Both of these wonders require your total surrender. The ethics of the sexual is the ethics of vulnerability. You have to be willing to let your partner witness both the surrender of your power and your surrender to your power. Your small self and contracted ego disappear in erotic sex. In sex Eros, we bypass ego and access our most sacred, scared, and secret selves.

SEXUAL HUMANISM

A new vision of human possibility emerges from our vulnerability. "Sex is ethics" means that we are radically loyal to the vulnerability aroused by our sexing. We are loyal even after the ego rushes back in, eager to reassert its dominion. Loyalty means that we do not—years later—tell a different story in which we negatively revise our experience of the sexual. Sex that was beautiful, mutual, and vulnerable cannot ethically be recast as predatory or abusive. Regret is not rape, just as arousal is not consent. That is a violation of the Holy of Holies. Remember the two teachings of Akiva: "All the [biblical] books are holy" and "The Song of Solomon is the Holy of Holies." The sexual love song is the Holy of Holies. To falsely narrate a sexual experience or to break sexual boundaries without invitation is to violate the Holy of Holies.

"Sex is ethics" is also what Akiva meant in his second statement, cited above. "If the Torah would not have been given, then all of the Torah could have been learned from the Song of Solomon," he said. Torah is the book of ethics. Ethics can be learned from the Song of Solomon, the song of the sexual. This is not because the Song of Solomon directly engages any ethical issues. It does not. Rather, what Akiva is saying is that sex in its pure erotic form is naturally ethical. This is the vision of the Secret of the Cherubs, which forms the heart of the Wisdom of Solomon. We might call this teaching by the term "sexual humanism." Just like all ethics live in the rapture of the sexual, evil and pathology result from the collapse of the sexual.

The ethics of the sexual emerge from the moral body. Sexual ethics are not transgressive at all: quite the opposite. Sex is subversive. Sex subverts and elevates ordinary ethics. Sex subverts conventional ethics and holds out for a higher ethical vision. This is true in myriad ways. In sex we are aroused to an ethics of devotion. The great lover is the devotee. Delight births devotion, and devotion demands delight. This need not be written in any legal code. This is the law inscribed in the text of the body.

Our bodies are afraid to surrender. We associate surrender with submission, which we reject, rightly being unwilling to suspend the appropriate boundaries of our personal integrity. The body, however, knows a distinction that the legal codes do not. The body speaks the language of devotional surrender. For sex is nothing if it is not devotion of the body to the body. It is from a place of devotional surrender that our hearts unguard and we begin to be lived as love.

We are used to thinking of the body as the temple of the soul. The soul is the source of ethics, which are needed to overcome the narcissism of the body. But sex is ethics points to a more utopian possibility, in which the naked eroticized body is not the temple of the soul but the soul itself. This is the reason why every Hebrew utopian movement, from the mystical messianism of Shabtai Tzvi in the seventeenth century to the twentieth-century Israeli kibbutz movement, tried to articulate a new sexual vision and a new ethics of embodiment.

BEYOND THE OLD SPLIT

The old split between body and soul that lies at the heart of Western civilization has not healed or transformed our world. There is a better way to live. Imagine a world in which we called the courtesan a sacred intimate, and the great enlightenment implicit in the sacred secrets of the body became known to every man and woman, young and old. What if a new sexual humanism began to teach us what it means to live in Eros in all dimensions of our lives?

The principle we just articulated—that all failures of ethics have their source in a breakdown in Eros—reminds us just how vital a return to Eros is. There is only one choice at this crucial juncture in history: love or die. Love outrageously, or die. It is not enough merely to love one's family. We must participate in the evolution of love. This happens when we realize that love is not an ego strategy for comfort. Real love is outrageous, not merely sweet human sentiment but the very essence of existence itself. Outrageous love is the evolutionary love that animates and drives the self-organizing universe. Outrageous love is Eros, suffusing and driving all reality.

LOVE IN THE BODY

Sex is but love in the body. In Hebrew Tantra, the body is not merely a vessel to hold the light. Rather, it is the highest form of light. In the image of Hebrew Tantra, at the moment of the world's inception (called "cosmogenesis"), a divine shaft penetrates the divine circle, and vessels are formed that hold light. The light is too intense for the vessels. In a defining primordial event, the vessels shatter. Some of the light from the vessels returns to its original source in the Godhead. Some of the light descends downward, where it becomes trapped in the shards of the broken vessels. This is taken to mean that hidden in our physical world of embodiment—which is a world of broken vessels and broken hearts—there is light that can be liberated by the one who has attained mastery.

This is a primary image of Hebrew Tantra. But now comes the seductive secret. In the inner texts of Tantra based on the deepest mystical realization, accessible only by the highest initiates, it is written: "Higher is the root of the vessels than the root of the lights." What might this mean? Here is the shocking teaching. There is actually no such thing as vessels. Vessels are, in fact, but configurations of light. But not just any configurations of light. In the realization of Hebrew Tantra, what appear to be vessels are the highest form of light. "Greater is the light in the vessels than the light itself" is another way of translating this teaching. Simply put, that means that the body is not only a temple for the soul—the body being the vessel and the soul and the light—rather, the body is itself a higher form of soul than even what we usually refer to as the soul.

Embodiment is everything. It is not—as religion has always taught—that the vessels, our bodies, hold the light, hold the spirit. Rather, the vessels are the light. Our bodies are the spirit.

Said differently, the body is the light. The truth of this mystical position finds expression in contemporary science. We now understand that matter is but condensed energy, or what is sometimes called condensed light. The body is the ethical text. Sex is ethics. It is for this reason that the sexual models the erotic. The sexual is the body. The body teaches Eros. The body at its root is a higher form of the sacred than even the soul, which is normally called sacred. That is what we mean when we say the sexual models the erotic and the erotic and the holy are one.

There is a beautiful Hebrew Tantric text commenting on the biblical Genesis story, in which God commands Abraham to sacrifice his son Isaac. In the popular reading, Abraham is faithful and goes to offer his son up as a sacrifice on Mount Moriah. There he hears the voice of God again, speaking through an angel. This time the voice says, "Do not stretch forth your hand against the boy." Abraham hears the voice and spares his son, again in obedience to the divine command.

The mystical interpretation, however, reads the Genesis story quite differently. In the Tantric reading of the text, the voice of God telling Abraham not to harm his son is none other than the voice of Abraham's body. Remember the text we cited above: "Through my body, I vision God." Abraham's body becomes a text of revelation. It tells him that he misheard the original command. His body tells him that to kill his son as a sacrifice to God, which was the custom of his day, is a horrific ethical violation. This is the beginning of the body humanism that is the hidden central motif of Hebrew Tantra. The eroticized person—whole-body Eros, not merely genital Eros—is the new human.

Echoes of Hebrew Tantra also show up in the writings of Herbert Marcuse, Wilhelm Reich, and Norman O. Brown. For Reich, when the sexual energy is blocked in the body, Eros stops flowing. The repression of sexual energy, of life energy in the body, creates a blockage of the natural divine force that flows through you. The repression of life energy creates neurosis and even psychosis, both in the body and in the body politic. Freud talked about the need to repress the sexual impulse in order to create the ethical goods of civilization. That is a slippery slope that leads to the murder of Eros. The connection of fundamentalism to sexual repression is not incidental. Brown correctly takes umbrage at Freud and seeks to re-eroticize not merely the yoni and phallus but the entire body. His vision of a polymorphously perverse erotic body was foundational to the "make love not war" ethics of the 1960s. As we are sexually, so we are emotionally and ethically. There can be no split among body, mind, and heart.

And yet Brown's vision, rooted in a rereading of psychoanalytic theory, as well as Marcuse's vision before him, rooted in a liberal neo-Marxism, are woefully insufficient matrices for the emergence of the new human or the new society. We need a new vision of Eros beyond Marcuse and Brown. The reductionist materialism of both Marx and psychoanalysis are ultimately too pallid and weak to spark a new social or personal politics of Eros. That is why the new-human story of the 1960s collapsed on itself. It lacked the authentic depth needed for the emergence of a new erotic worldview.

In this writing, we articulate a new vision of Eros. This new erotic possibility is not rooted in psychoanalysis or neo-Marxism but rather in the scientific-mystical-evolutionary context of a new universe story. The universe is a love story—not an ordinary love story, but an outrageous love story. And outrageous love is Eros.

We are the erotic mystics infused with the magic to affect the force. We are irreducibly unique expressions of the love-beauty and love-intelligence that are the imitating and animating Eros of all that is. We are outrageous lovers, all costarring in the great love story that is the dramatic thread of the universe. It is only by taking off our body armor and embracing the natural, ethical rapture of the body that we can act in love but be lived as love.

When you really inhabit your body, you become wise in the ways of love. The body becomes the seat of wisdom. Sex invites us to the body. We must say yes to the invitation. In superficial sexing, we can be in sex but not in the body. When we deeply enter the body, we can hear the murmurings of the sacred. Sex is love in the body.

THE LAW OF THE BODY

Let us give two very simple examples of the body's knowing: diets and sexual partners. New diet books proliferate, with dozens of them being published every year. Every new diet claims to have cracked the code to easy weight loss. The well-known fact, however, is that diet books have a minimal impact on people. People cannot regulate the most visceral function of the body—eating—based on external rules. The truth is that we do not need diet books. The law of the body always knows when you have had enough to eat and what kinds of foods you should be eating. But when the wisdom of the body is drowned out in the din of our busy lives, we turn to diet books. The diet books almost inevitably fail us if we do not first reconnect to the erotic ethics of the body.

To hear the voice of the body, we need to become proficient in our discernment between Eros and pseudo Eros. Let's say we feel hurt by some event in our lives. We fall into the hole. We are afraid to stay in the hole, so we seek to fill the emptiness with pseudo Eros. We reach for a Baby Ruth candy bar. We get an immediate rush of sugar. It is damaging to virtually every system in our body. Our consumption of sugar violates our Eros. Candy bars are pseudo Eros. But you do not need a diet book to tell you that. Just feel the experience in your body after one, two, and then three candy bars. When we deny the truths of the body, we begin to read diet books, in all the arenas of our lives. Our Eros becomes blocked, and we lose access to the living divine presence that flows through us.

In the second example, we consider our sexual partners. With whom should we have sexual relations? There are many relationship and religious books that answer this question. But actually, in order to know whom to have sex with, we need only to access the truth of our bodies. Our bodies know perfectly the distinction between sex that is an expression of our vitality and sex that is a violation of our vitality. Relationship books or laws governing sex will not get you there.

THE REJECTION OF BODY ABSOLUTISM

But that does not mean that diet books or ethical books are unnecessary. Akiva writes, "If the Torah would not have been given, we would have learned all wisdom from the Song of Solomon." We have cited this Tantric teaching several times in order to open up the radical wisdom of the body. But that does not in any sense imply that we want to revert to the body as our sole source of ethics. The Secret of the Cherubs rejects a kind of body absolutism in which the body becomes the sole Holy Grail. This rejection of naive body absolutism is essential for three primary reasons:

1. In the body there are states of profound expansion that yield great
    wisdom. This is the natural state of the body when the character
    armor is shed and the force of the divine flows unobstructed.
    But the body also has regressive states where it is hijacked by
    undiscriminating lust, psychological trauma, or emotions like rage
    or jealousy, all of which live in our physicality. The body itself does
    not speak in one voice. We need to take into account the regressive
    and contracted voices of the body. These voices are geniuses at
    self-deception. Reich would, of course, respond that his therapeutic
    processes, which aim to divest the body of its contracted character
    armor, are precisely the method through which we access the
    authentic voice of the divine body. That may be true, although it is far
    from clear how effective or even how available such processes are to
    the average person.

2. We are not merely body. We are body, heart, and mind. Virtually
    all of the body absolutists invite us in one way or another to revert
    to the body wisdom of the animal. We have gotten away from our
    natural animal state, they each say. If we would but re-eroticize the
    entire body, then we would be home. The body is crucial. It is true
    that the texts of ethics are written in the body. Indeed, that is what we
    meant when we said earlier that sex is ethics. But the texts of ethics
    are also written in the heart and mind. The human being developed
    a neocortex, enabling capabilities like reasoning, speech, and control
    of social behavior. That is not an accident of history. Our neocortex—
    that is to say, our evolution of consciousness—gave us access to both
    discernment of the heart and wisdom of the mind.

    Tragically, the wisdoms of heart and mind often became alienated
    from the body. We lost the voice of the body sacred, without which
    no accurate or authentic vision of Eros and ethics is possible. We
    need to reclaim the text of the body, but not at the expense of the
    distinctions of heart and mind. We seek a holy trinity of body, heart,
    and mind erotically inter-included with each other.

3. The wisdom of the body state, when clarified and divested of the
    contraction of character armor, is a vital source of inspiration and
    ethics. The body itself is the holy temple. But its texts are always

interpreted through the level of consciousness of the mind and heart. Said simply, sex is a state of consciousness. A state of consciousness is a temporary alteration of consciousness. There might be a drunken state or a mystical state. It might be an expanded state of wisdom or a state of rage. In each of these states, ordinary consciousness shifts and something extraordinary is born. All our states of consciousness are interpreted through the prism of our level of consciousness. Our level of consciousness includes our sense of identity, psychological maturity, vision of purpose, ethical refinement, and much more.

Let's give a simple example. Enlightenment is a state of consciousness. Let's posit that you are experiencing an enlightened state of consciousness. Your state will be interpreted through the prism of your level of consciousness. If your level of consciousness is ethnocentric—that is to say, you have a felt sense of love and caring only for your family and your country, tribe, or religion—then you will experience your enlightenment as telling you that your people are the chosen people. You might hear a calling to a mission to support your tribe. But if you have the same enlightened state of consciousness, resulting from the same spiritual practice, and you have world-centric consciousness—a felt sense of love and concern for every human being—then your enlightened state will deepen your love for the entire world and not just your tribe. You might hear a calling to do something to end world hunger instead of being called to only serve your people. Your enlightened experience is a state. Your level of consciousness—in this example, either ethnocentric or world-centric—is a prism through which your state experience is interpreted.

In a similar sense, sex is a state of consciousness. Your sexual body state has its own revelation just like an enlightened state has its revelation. That state experience, however, is interpreted by you through the prism of your emotional, ethical, and psychological level of consciousness. That is why body absolutism is as dangerous and naive as either heart or mind absolutism. It is only mind, heart, and body in right relationship that yield a revelation we can trust. A true Eros for the new human requires this holy trinity. It includes not only the neo-paganism of the romantics and their successors but also the ethics of the erotically God-intoxicated prophets as well as the rational ethics of Western freedom. In that holy trinity, we can find erotic and ethical liberation. Eros and ethos fuse into one.

Until now, the revelation of the body has been left out of our sacred texts. We need to reclaim the text of the body in order to re-eroticize our lives and transform our world. The body sacred adds a new ethical text, the text of the body, to our sacred canon[28]—not just sexual ethics but sex is ethics.

Without reclaiming the erotic force of the living body, we become stunted and distorted. The armoring of the body actually allows us to perpetuate violence on each other. We lose access to the full divinity that is imprinted on the body. This is what allows for what Reich called "the murder of Christ." By "Christ" he meant Eros or life force. The more disconnected we are from the living presence of our bodies, the more we want to murder someone who incarnates that life force. This is the source of an enormous amount of both physical and social violence. We need to bring together our pelvis, heart, and mind—and our reason, will, and emotion—to create an inspired life. Platonic friendship, animated by shared purpose and passion, needs to merge with erotic sensuality to create the new human, the new relationship, and the new society.

We will explore in upcoming chapters the twelve faces of Eros. Each of these is fundamentally subversive of the conventional context of identity, relationship, and social structure. Eros modeled by the sexual points us toward playing a larger game with our lives and a fundamentally better way to live.

CHAPTER TWELVE

THE SEXUAL MODELS THE EROTIC

HEALING THE SPLIT

The Shechinah is exiled whenever sex and Eros are split. As an example, Jake, age thirty-seven, works as a claims adjuster in an insurance firm. Often he works well into the night. He feels oppressed by the routine and drabness of his work. On days when he comes home feeling particularly empty, he flips on some pornography. His work is not erotic, so he looks for his erotic charge in sex. The devastating truth is that even erotic sex in the context of a powerful and committed relationship would not fulfill him. Nothing can substitute for his very real need for Eros at work. Certainly most forms of pornography, which are essentially de-eroticized sex, cannot fill his erotic needs. So he winds up with a hangover, the kind you get from drinking too much cheap wine. And work the next morning feels all that much more dead and depressing. The Shechinah is in exile.

HARLOTS AND PRETENDING

One of the most famous images of the Shechinah in exile laced through-out the Zohar (the Kabbalah's chief text) is the prostitute. The problem with prostitution is not primarily ethical. Ethical prostitutes can have far more moral decency than the ostensible pillars of the community. Images of wise and good harlots abound in literature, from Rahab the harlot who marries Joshua in the Bible, to Mary Magdalene, to *The Best Little Whorehouse* in Texas.

The problem with prostitution is the depersonalizing of sex. Eros is about being on the inside, which implies intense personalization. The prostitute is faceless and nameless. Emotionally, the client is always on the outside. There is no intimacy. Ultimately, this erotic failure becomes an ethical failure. The person goes to the prostitute because he is lonely. He is Eros-starved, not sex-starved. The only place he knows he can get an erotic fix is in sex. The Shechinah, the erotic, is exiled in the sexual. All too often—through no fault of the prostitute—the man feels emptier after sex than he did before. He will usually ejaculate but will rarely achieve fulfillment.

The highest-paid courtesan, of course, at least in the ideal of the archetype, is the one who heals the split between sex and Eros. For at least that evening, she is not only sexually available but also fully engaged, present, and loving. Generally, however, the Eros is not real. The myth of romantic love for only one tells the courtesan that it is simply impossible to be truly available and present to so many people, day after day. So the best-case scenario is an unspoken agreement. She will pretend and he will pretend, and the pretense will be sufficient, for that is all there is.

Now, the moralist will be quick to say, "See, that's right! Sex isn't the answer!" Yet we, as teachers and as human beings, do not go with the moralists. That is precisely the point of the Secret of the Cherubs. Sex is the answer.

THE TANTRIC PILGRIMS

Three times a year, pilgrims would gather in Jerusalem from all over Israel. The hidden mystical intention of the pilgrimage was no less than healing the split between the erotic and the sexual. These gatherings were called the Holidays of Vision (*Chag HaReiya*). A careful reconstruction of the sources reveals that on these days the adept pilgrims practiced visualizations, chanting, meditations, and a host of other spiritual techniques.

They would also, according to some veiled references, practice the sacred Tantric arts. The entire pilgrimage revolved around one climatic moment, the only one of its kind. The Holy of Holies in the temple—access to which was permitted only to the high priest himself, and then only once a year—was opened for all to see. The central vision, according to the secret tradition, was the sexually entwined cherubs above the Ark. This vision transmitted the unspeakable Secret of the Cherubs—Reality is Allurement—to all the gathered pilgrims.

Again, this had nothing to do with sexual promiscuity, although the danger of mistranslation was real. The texts speak in depth of the thickly pulsating sexual tension, which models the holy and which characterized the pilgrimage. The pilgrimage was not that of silent monks meditating on the mysteries of church. In the description of the old Aramaic texts, it was more like an explosion of energy. Eros and ecstasy came together in a festival of joy. At the heart of the festival was the Secret of the Cherubs. It was not merely Dionysian explosion of abandon but rather a prophetic explosion of erotic ethics and sensual joy committed to a vision of a transformed world in which peace and justice fill the land.

The Song of Solomon is referred to by the masters as "the Holy of Holies." This is not merely a literary turn of phrase to emphasize its absolute centrality in Hebrew spirituality. It is also a veiled reference to the cherubs in the temple's Holy of Holies who stand as symbols of the Hebrew Tantric mystery.

Hebrew Tantra rooted in the Temple in Jerusalem seeds both Eastern and Western Tantric schools all over the world. There are, however, two enormous differences between Hebrew and Eastern Tantras in their classical sources. First, in much of Eastern Tantra, it is the avoidance of sexual release that allows the adept to rechannel the sexual energy inward and upward instead of outward. In Hebrew Tantra, it is the natural flow of sexual expression—including release—that models the lover's path in all arenas of living.

Second, in Eastern Tantra, the partner is almost a sacred object. Sacred, but an object nonetheless. She is a symbol of the feminine principle, but by being the symbol, she is fully depersonalized—a kind of nameless yogini who is a necessary aid in the spiritual Tantric journey of the male adept.

By contrast, in Hebrew Tantra, the partner is both a Shechinah incarnation and fully personalized at the same time. The sexual, existential fulfillment and pleasure of one's partner is the primary ethical and erotic obligation of the Hebrew adept. The spiritual Tantric journey is only sacred within that highly personalized intimate context.

Moreover, in the Hebrew Tantric path, the partners must share a committed relationship of some form, beyond the sexual. Naturally, then, there is no danger of splitting sex from Eros in all facets of life. In the Hindu Tantric model, there was no committed relationship between the man and woman. For the Hebrew mystic, such depersonalization represents the exile of the Shechinah. Classic Eastern Tantra (not its Western offshoots) limited Eros to the realm of spiritualized sex, effectively divorcing it from all other facets of living. Sex risked becoming a limited spiritual activity that did not spill over into day-to-day partnership and lifelong commitment.

IT'S ALL ART

Whenever we keep Eros confined to one narrow frame of being while de-eroticizing the rest of the picture, the Shechinah remains in exile. But sex is only one of the places where we exile the erotic. There is a wonderful Balinese saying that goes something like this: "We do not have art—we do everything as beautifully as we can." When we build ugly cities where beauty is abused and people are depersonalized and then build a beautiful art museum, the Shechinah is in exile. We exile the Eros of beauty to the constricted precincts of formal art.

The same is true of music. Music is not limited to symphonies or rock concerts. We are all musicians, and life is overflowing with music. Remember the Broadway show *Stomp*? There was no dialogue; it was all music and dance. The catch was that no musical instruments were used. The "instruments" were adapted from the fabric of everyday living: pots, pans, brooms, sinks, faucets, garbage can lids, bottles, bags, newspapers, hands, feet, virtually every part of the body—all of these were used to make music. The implication is stunning: We usually limit art to formal work by people we call artists, just as we limit music to formal instruments and musicians. Formal music and art need to model the erotics of sound and beauty in all of our lives and not just in restricted, narrow provinces. Music and art need to pervade all of living. Every moment is a canvas and is possessed of its own melody. Rumi wisely instructs us:

> Let the beauty we love be what we do.
> There are hundreds of ways to kneel and kiss the ground.

So too with falling in love. Just as it is nonerotic for art to exist only in a museum, so too it is nonerotic for love to exist only in a small circle of people. When we fall in love with one woman or one man to the exclusion of all other people, the Shechinah is in exile. When you are truly erotically engaged, then through the love of one comes the love of all. For true love partakes in the essential connectivity of being. Unity is not divisible; it is holographic: in every moment of love are all the lovers and all the love in the world.

Too often love is merely a synonym for a radically narrowed sphere of caring. We let only the smallest possible group—sometimes only one person—inside our Holy of Holies. We feel alienated, deceitful, or apathetic about the rest of our lives. The Shechinah is in exile.

EROTIC WEDDINGS

In Hebrew Tantra, a wedding is meant to expand and not narrow the circle of Eros. If through the lover each is able to love the world more than before, it is considered a good marriage. If the result of their love is a narrowing in which the world is shut out, then it is not a good marriage.

There is a wonderful mystical teaching that seeks to explain why, according to Hebrew wisdom, one fasts on the day of one's wedding. The answer given is that the day of the wedding is a personal Yom Kippur for the bride and groom. Yom Kippur, also called the Day of Atonement (at-one-ment), is considered the holiest day of the year. It is a time when all sins are forgiven. It is also an Eros day; it was the only time when the high priest entered the Holy of Holies to perform the mystery rite.

Why, ask the mystics, do the bride and groom require a personal Yom Kippur on the day of their wedding? Because the wedding is about love and Eros. Love and Eros cannot coexist with hate. The only reason most people hate someone is because they themselves did something wrong. Master Nachman of Bratslav says, "Each time you do something wrong, you hate one person." Whenever we do something wrong, we project our anger at ourselves onto someone else and hate him or her for it. On Yom Kippur, however, all of our sins are forgiven. All wrongs are erased. Therefore, there is nothing left to project outward and no one left to hate. This allows you to truly open your heart to love on the day of your wedding. When the wedding fast is over, all forgiveness made, the wedding begins.

One of the most poignant moments of the Hebrew wedding is the mythic rite of the groom's placing of a veil over the face of the bride. In doing this, he recognizes that so much of her is still hidden from him, and he commits his life to coming to know her. At this point the community blesses the bride. The officiant invokes the memory of the ancestor Jacob. Jacob is the one who sees Rachel for the first time at the well, falls in love with her instantly, kisses her, and cries. We evoke this story at the wedding because it has some important wisdom to whisper in our ear.

Why does he cry at his first kiss, that moment of ecstasy? They are tears of joy, to be sure. But the mystics add another dimension. They say he cried because at that moment he saw that the Temple in Jerusalem would be destroyed and that the cause of its destruction would be the petty hatred between people. The temple, the symbol of Eros and love, can withstand any attack except that of pettiness and baseless hatred.

What, however, moved the Holy Spirit in Jacob to have that vision and to cry at precisely the moment he loved and kissed Rachel? Because, explain the masters, once you love one person, once you engage one person in true Eros, through that person you love the entire world. Once you are a lover of even one person, you can no longer understand how there could be such pettiness and hatred in the world. You weep at the thought that hatred could destroy the temple of Eros.

So Jacob loved Rachel, and in doing so touched true Eros. In that moment when his lips met hers, Jacob experienced love, longing, intense desire, and connection with the entire world. The kiss aroused his heart and opened it wide to all of being. To be in love is not to be in love with her but to be in love with life by way of her. That is precisely the distinction between ordinary and outrageous love. Had Jacob's love for Rachel closed his heart to the entire world except for her, the Shechinah would have been in exile. Because Jacob was able to love the world through Rachel, we invoke their story as the model of true love for all generations.

AN EROTIC HERO, THE FALAFEL PRIEST

Once—and I will never forget it—I unexpectedly stepped into the Holy of Holies at a falafel stand. We were returning from visiting my sons Eitan and Yair in summer camp near the town of Hadera in Israel. As we were leaving, my partner spotted a falafel stand. Now, falafel is a fried Middle Eastern food that I am less than fond of, and I hadn't eaten one in years. But she insisted, so I went along. Surprisingly, though, as we stepped up to the simple falafel shack, there was something about the shopkeeper that made me want to order a falafel.

I took one bite of the falafel, and I swear to you, it must have been made in the Garden of Eden. I looked up and I was bathed in pure love. The shopkeeper beamed at my pleasure. When we went to pay, he asked for six shekels. My jaw dropped—everyone knows a falafel costs at least fifteen shekels. And his was so unbelievably good. How could he only take six shekels? So I asked him. To which he responded gently, "Because that's what I need." That, my sweetest and most wonderful friends, is Eros pure and simple.

To be erotically engaged at work requires only that you fully enter the inside of whatever you might be doing. When you do—whatever your work may be—worlds open up, opportunity knocks at your door, the angels sing, and you are filled with joy. So full are you with joy that the delight has no choice but to spill over—into your fried falafel, into the person who stands before you, into the very earth at your feet. Joy joins joy, the earth brims with a new peace. This man did not leave Eros in his bedroom; he brought it with him to work every day. Somehow, with this, he made his falafel stand a Holy of Holies.

DOSTOYEVSKY'S DAD

Freud, of course, would have relegated both Jacob and the falafel king to his couch in no time. Freud's understandings, which have so colored our own unconscious view of the world, are the precise opposite of the Secret of the Cherubs. For Freud, everything is a metaphor for sex. For the Kabbalists, sex is a metaphor for everything. Freud was interested in reduction, in bringing everything down. He lived in an era that was still in rebellion against seventeen hundred years of church domination that had crippled science, freedom, and beauty. As a result, like most of the intelligentsia of his age, Freud automatically rejected spirit as a serious force. So Freud reduced everything in the world to sex.

The mystical project, however, is not about reduction; rather, it seeks to raise up all the scattered sparks of light and return them to their source. To the Kabbalist, all the processes in the world, including sex, are erotic at their core. For the Kabbalist, sex points to the erotic. This underscores an even deeper distinction between Freud and the Kabbalah. For Freud, sex was a human release valve that allowed for the discharge of tension and therefore assured more effective functioning. For the Kabbalists, effective spiritual living is facilitated not by releasing tension but by holding Eros. A perfect world for Freud would be one in which everything was desexualized; then sex itself could perform its natural biological release-valve function without creating neuroses and complexes. For the Kabbalists, the ideal world would be one in which the sexual modeling of the erotic is made conscious, thereby eroticizing all of reality.

Certainly Freud was important in moving us to look at ourselves and pay attention to our inner lives. Yet his insight blurs because he cannot free himself from a deep, inner need to reduce everything to the sexual. This becomes especially striking whenever Freud moves to understand the "higher" aspects of mankind—what we would call the erotic or the holy. A striking example is his reduction of a mother's love for her child to sublimated sexuality. In doing so, not only does he violate common sense and our deepest intuition, but he also violates all that is sublime.

Freud said, after reading Dostoyevsky, "Here, psychoanalysis must lay down its arms"—so overwhelmed was he by the sublime and erotic power of what he read. And yet Freud, unable to resist, soon returned to Dostoyevsky trying to locate the power of his presence somewhere in the recesses of his relationship with his father. Freud missed the point. The notion of a core spiritual erotic energy coursing through life was simply too much for his materialist mind to absorb. Life is not sublimated sex. It is Eros itself. Freud's theories remain a great symbol of the Shechinah's exile.

Similarly, Kinsey, the great sex researcher who, in documenting the sexual habits of Americans, took much of sexuality out of the closet, nevertheless radically split sex from Eros. Admittedly, he did so with much less sophistication than Freud. For him, sex was a simple and happy affair not much different than the mating of animals he had observed in his zoological training. Yet, while for Kinsey sex remains a bland, zoological kind of function, and for Freud a more dark and deterministic kind of force, for both of them the sexual remains uninspired and unerotic. Both Kinsey's and Freud's views ignore the soul of sex. To split sex from Eros so dramatically is to exile the Shechinah. Both of these thinkers are seminal expressions of our society's disenchantment.

SUPERMODELS

The Shechinah's exile is all too apparent even in *Webster's* dictionary. *Webster's* defines *erotic* as "tending to arouse sexual love or desire." The sentence would be perfect without the word *sexual*. In the Secret of the Cherubs, sex always points beyond itself. Sex is a kind of meditative practice for the common person. It is the area of our lives that most clearly points beyond itself to something higher.

Paradoxically, the place that understands this erotic secret well is the world of advertising. Even when television is bland and insipid, advertising is often erotic. We all realized long ago that advertising uses the sexual as a primary tool in its campaigns. Somehow we are meant to associate the beautiful woman and the sleek car. Moralists often accuse advertisers of a great ethical wrong in this kind of advertising. After all, it seems to falsely suggest that we will somehow get the girl if we buy the car. I think we have all figured out that the girl does not come with the car. Rather, the implication is far more subtle. On some level, this kind of advertisement actually intuits the Secret of the Cherubs. The profound implication of the girl/car nexus is that the sexual Eros expressed by the girl is a model of the kind of Eros the driver wants in his means of transportation. This profound and true idea drives much of advertising.

It is perhaps more than a telling coincidence of language that these glamorous women are called "models"—an obvious shoo-in for our theme! For essentially, they are illustrators of the metaphysical (and physical) fact that sex models the erotic. Their sexual allure is used to pull at the erotic strings of our soul. When we buy into the ad, we are chasing not the sex it displays but the Eros modeled there, the Eros we so deeply, if subconsciously, quest after. Models, then, become a handy visual and linguistic reminder of the fact that all I am really after is some good Eros.

MIND THE GAP

A few years back the Gap's ad campaign showed alluring young women with a caption underneath that said, "My First Love." The reader/gazer/

consumer expects some sexually provocative image or story to follow. Then comes the wonderful twist that makes this ad stand out. We see a picture of a woman with a book, "My first love—Anaïs Nin" . . . or with a tape, "My first love—the Ramones" . . . or a photo, "My mom." What the Gap ads effectively did is suggest an expansion of the erotic beyond the sexual to include art, music, and personal nonsexual relationships. The ad plays off the Western mind, which expects a sultry story to fill in the blank of what is "love" or what is erotic! The Gap is ever so subtly suggesting that the Shechinah needs to be liberated from the mere sexual. You can live erotically in all areas of life.

While we give kudos to the Gap for intelligent, soul-broadening advertising, it is undeniable that all too often Madison Avenue goes wrong by manipulating Eros rather than serving Eros. That is to say, erotic manipulation is used to sell us products we don't need or want. Madison Avenue feeds on our Eros-starved souls purely for the sake of uninhibited profit. Rather than exiling the Shechinah, Madison Avenue seems intent on pimping out the Shechinah—making her a prostitute, selling her wares to support "The Man."

FIGHTING FUNDAMENTALISM WITH EROS

Whenever we divorce sex from the overarching frameworks of Eros, we vastly diminish sex's power. If we either strip it of Eros or alternatively make it the exclusive focus of our erotic desire, then we exile the Shechinah. The result is a crisis of emptiness of overwhelming proportions both within the sexual and in the rest of our lives. When we allow sex to rise to its natural place, modeling Eros, sex responds by allowing us to step out of separation and into the erotic love affair that courses through all reality.

Sexuality has a natural affinity with freedom: the Eros and dignity of liberty. This is why sexual repression so often goes together with repressive and fundamentalist regimes. One of the first things the Taliban did in Afghanistan when taking power was to de-eroticize the country. Not only sexuality but also all music, art, bright colors, and so many other things that express our essential aliveness were outlawed. The true job of religion (re-*ligare*) is to reconnect that which has been rent asunder. Instead, the Taliban responded to the West's divorcing of sex and love by attempting to crush the sexual and fully de-eroticize the public sphere. In doing so, they created the kind of nonerotic, distorted, and disconnected worldview that could produce evil in the name of God.

The Taliban, however, were not the first to attempt the repression of liberty through the crushing of the erotic and the sexual. There is an absolutely wonderful ancient tradition about Eros and liberty. It describes how the Hebrew slaves managed to attain freedom in the great chronicle of the Exodus.

When the Israelites were enslaved in harsh labor in Egypt, Pharaoh decreed that they not sleep at home nor have sexual relations with their wives. What did the daughters of Israel do? They would go down and draw water from the river, and God would provide for them little fish in their buckets. They would cook them, sell them, and buy wine with the money. They would then go to the fields and feed their husbands.

After they had eaten and drunk together, the women would take out mirrors and look at themselves and their men in the mirror. Teasing them, they would say, "I am more beautiful than you." In this way, they would open their husbands up again to desire.

The story understands that the eroticism of desire is the dynamic that arouses the impulse to freedom and human dignity. Slavery is about the deadening of Eros and desire. A slave, of course, can have a great job, be highly successful financially, and sleep with many sexual partners. But this enslaved individual, whom we moderns recognize so well, has lost touch with the erotics of desire. The wonder of being on the inside—the sense of yearning that goes beyond fleeting sexual need, the sense of the erotic sexual that softens the harsh dividing lines of existence and allows us to feel the interconnectivity of being—all these are virtually lost to modern men and women.

So the story invites us back into desire as a way of counteracting Pharaoh's decree. Raw lust is not foreign to the experience of the slave. But the playful desire that arouses union between committed partners—that is the mark of freedom.

The Hebrew word for "decree" is *gazar*. It has a double meaning: decree, and cutting or ripping away. Pharaoh's decree rips people from the erotic womb of being. The women in the story, symbolizing the dual eroticism of both the womb and passion, reconnect us to our sense of dignity and the possibility of possibility, which we have all but forgotten. The sexual in this story models the Eros of freedom.

MIRRORS OF DESIRE

Later, in a great epilogue to the story, Moses is building the tabernacle in the desert. The tabernacle is essentially the first temple, replete with the Ark, cherubs, and Holy of Holies. Everyone is to bring his or her own special contribution toward the building of the tabernacle. The women bring the mirrors of desire that they used to arouse their partners. Moses is furious! Why are the women bringing sex toys for the building of the temple?

A divine voice intervenes: "Moses, these mirrors you would reject—take them and build the tabernacle with them."

In this story, Moses plays the moralist who is afraid of the subversive power of the sexual. He sees families ruined, loyalties betrayed, and lives unhinged. This Moses voice has an important place in the texts of our lives. Ultimately, however, the divine voice must triumph. The temple where God dwells is the home of Eros. It is the temple with sexually intertwined cherubs at its epicenter. It invites us to embrace the sexual as our spiritual guide—modeling for us the erotic in every area.

A COSMIC LOVE AFFAIR

A young man walks in on Master Baruch and his wife in the midst of a heated argument. Startled, he quickly turns away. Baruch responds with a wink. "You don't understand. You have just witnessed a discussion between God and the Shechinah."

To really touch on what the ancient mystics meant when they so deeply linked the sexual, the erotic, and the sacred, we need to go one final step further. The Holy of Holies is understood as the marriage bed, while the Ark and its tablets respectively represent the male and female sexual organs. Well, whose marriage bed is it anyway? And to whom does all this sexual anatomy belong? To human beings or God—whatever that might mean?

The texts intentionally blur the lines on this issue, for the point is that human beings and God actually share the same bed. That is to say, the cherubs are the symbol of the great marriage between the divine masculine and the divine feminine. Between Shiva and Shakti in Hindu lore, between Kudshah Brik Hu and Shechinah in the Kabbalistic storehouse of symbolism. Kudshah Brik Hu is the masculine divine energy and Shechinah the feminine divine energy. When the Shechinah dwells "between the cherubs," the divine masculine and feminine meet in erotic union. But here is the major new teaching of the mystics. That union is not only modeled by but is actually initiated by human sexual merging.

When the relationship is real, when there is commitment and mutuality and love, then human sexual union not only models the erotic in all facets of life; it also participates in and affects union in the universe. It becomes an agent for healing and oneness, even and especially within God. It is in this regard that the great lover and mystic Akiva says that when man and woman join in sacred union, then "the Shechinah dwells between them."

This is the same phrase the biblical text uses to describe the Shechinah that "dwells between the cherubs." Between the cherubs and between the human lovers is the same place! For the mystics, then, those cherubs symbolize the masculine and feminine, both in the human and in the divine realm. At the apex of sexuality, humankind touches, participates in, and heals divinity. This is the potential for world healing implicit in the sexual, which models the erotic and the holy.

EROS EXPANDED

Erotic fulfillment is reached when you expand the realm of Eros beyond the sexual to embrace all of your existence. Indeed, the root of the Sanskrit word *tantra—tan*—means "expansion." True Tantric energy expands into all realms of life. This expansion is the goal of Kabbalistic Tantra.

The Zohar weaves this esoteric teaching into a seemingly innocent passage. The original quotation is so striking that I decided to leave it virtually intact. Read it slowly, almost as a Tantric meditation.

> Every person must find himself in sexual union [of male and female] . . . For in that way the Shechinah never parts from him. And if you will say that for one who travels [and is separated from his partner and therefore separated from sexual union] the Shechinah departs from him, come and see. Before a person begins his journey, he should organize his prayer—from a place where he is in sexual union—in order to draw the Shechinah down on him before he sets out on his path. Once he has learned the order of prayer and the Shechinah dwells in him through his sexual union, he should set out on his way, for the Shechinah can now remain with him . . . in the city or in the field.
>
> As long as he is on the way, he needs to be mindful of his path in order that the higher union, the Shechinah, not part from him. Even when he is not in sexual union . . . this higher union does not leave. When he arrives home, he should rejoice [be sexual] with his partner . . . for she is the one through whom he accessed the higher union with the Shechinah.

This passage, part of the cherub mystery tradition, makes the merging with the Shechinah dependent on sexual union. Clearly, then, they are not the same thing. The goal is "higher union with the Shechinah." The higher union takes place when one has been able to move beyond the bedroom to transpose the sexual to that person's broader world—to greet the Divine at every doorstep, every crossroad, in every sparrow along the way. When the traveler returns, he is instructed to make love with his partner again in order to recast his life once more in the model of the sexual. In this way, sex leads him to the Shechinah.

It is in the move through the sexual to the erotic that we achieve the ultimate goal of the spirit: higher union with the Shechinah, erotic fulfillment in every arena of living. As the poet Rainer Maria Rilke aptly wrote of the ability of love to travel with us: "Believe in a love that is being preserved for you like a heritage, and trust that in this love there is a strength and a blessing which you are not bound to leave behind you though you may travel far!"[29]

SENSUOUS STUDY AND THE EROTIC TEXT

The Baal Shem Tov, founder of the eighteenth-century Hebrew mystical movement called Hasidism, writes that the ecstatic swaying motion characteristic of Hebrew prayer is the swaying and rocking of a couple in lovemaking. The Zohar writes that when one prays he must be aroused and become the feminine waters of the Shechinah. Again, the requirement is not for men or women to be sexually aroused when they pray; rather, that the qualities of the erotic modeled in the sexual find expression in prayer. It's about Eros, not sex! Prayer is erotic.

We are used to thinking of intellectual pursuits as being somewhat dry. And even if ideas excite us, it is clear that the mind is the primary faculty engaged in the pursuit of intellectual depth. Well, as you might expect at this point, the story masters of Jerusalem had a markedly different idea. For them, the engagement with wisdom was not dry, but a passionate and erotic endeavor.

Source after source uses sexual analogies as a way of describing the erotic nature of study. Elijah of Vilna, the founder of a great Kabbalistic school in the latter part of the eighteenth century, writes that one can study only if one has an *ever chai*, a throbbing phallus. Clearly, the sage of Vilna did not mean that one has to have an erection when one studies. Rather, he meant an erotically throbbing phallus, not a sexually throbbing phallus. It's about Eros, not sex! What he was suggesting is what we refer to as the textualization of Eros. That is, after the fall of the temple, the study of sacred text became for the Hebrew masters one of the primary places for erotic expression. So textual study became the place where one experienced the fullness of Eros.

THE TEXTUALIZATION OF EROS

When the temple was destroyed, the masters knew that the holy writ of biblical myth needed to be expanded and deepened. The temple—the archetypal object of erotic desire in biblical writings—was no more. Where was holy Eros to be found? The ingenious and revolutionary answer for the masters, whispered to them from within the folds of the tradition itself, was the textualization of Eros. The sacred text itself became the Holy of Holies in the temple. Every student was potentially the high priest. The text itself was regarded as a living organism whose soul could be erotically penetrated by all who loved her sufficiently. From the inside of the text, the word of God could be heard and a new Torah channeled.

The model for Eros is virtually always the sexual. Mystical sources abound with the ritualized eroticism in the synagogue service. Here is one image that unpacks itself from several Zoharic passages. The Torah scroll is taken out of the Ark for public reading and study. She is undressed. Her lavish coverings are removed, revealing a scroll of bare animal skin. She is then laid on the altar-like reading table and spread open. The reader places a phallic-like pointer on the spread parchment between the two scrolled sides and begins to chant the text aloud. The esoteric erotic mysteries are hidden in the most open of places.

In a tour de force, the Zohar describes a process of study in much the way the twelfth-century troubadours a hundred years before described their flirtation with their loves. In the troubadours' romantic ideal of courtly love, though, the beloved remained forever beyond reach. In the more hopeful image of the Zohar, the lover ultimately merges erotically with his beloved. The following text, like most medieval texts, is written from a male perspective. New mystical texts need to be written today by women manifesting the Goddess.

> The Torah is like a beautiful woman, who is hidden in a
> secluded chamber of her palace and who has a secret lover,
> unknown to all others. For love of her, he keeps passing the gate
> of her house, looking this way and that in search of her. She

knows that her lover haunts the gate of her house. What does she do? She opens the door of her hidden chamber but a crack and for a moment reveals her face to her lover, and then hides it again immediately.

Were anyone with her lover, he would see nothing and perceive nothing. He alone sees it, and he is drawn to her with his heart and soul and his whole being. He knows that for love of him she disclosed herself to him for one moment, aflame with love for him. So it is with the word of the Torah, which reveals herself only to those who love her. The Torah knows that the mystic (the wise of heart) haunts the gate of her house. What does she do? From within her hidden palace she discloses her face and beckons to him and returns forthwith to her place and hides. Thus the Torah reveals herself and hides; she goes out in love to her lover and arouses love in him.

Only then, when he has gradually come to know her, does she reveal herself to him face-to-face and speak to him of all her hidden secrets and all her hidden ways, which have been in her heart from the beginning. Such a man is then termed perfect, a "master," that is to say, a "bridegroom of the Torah" in the strictest sense, the master of the house, to whom she discloses all her secrets, concealing nothing.

The image in this text is erotic, not sexual. The sexual is not only a metaphor but also a model for the fully erotic. To say that the Zohar's description is accurate is superfluous to anyone who has ever engaged a text in the serious and exciting business of holy amorous play.

COURTING THE SACRED

When I (Marc) sit down to prepare a teaching, the process goes something like this. First is the attraction. I generally teach only that which attracts me. I must have an almost unquenchable longing to explore the subject. Second, I must be fully present in the impassioned pursuit, in the investment of energy and attention, in learning its contours and plumbing its secrets. Finally, on the good days, there is the ecstatic merging with the wisdom, when all the disparate pieces fall together in an elegantly interconnected whole.

I once had such a romance when preparing a series of talks on the topic of laughter. I had decided to give a lecture series on laughter, a topic that had always fascinated me. To prepare, I gathered my ancient texts, bringing them into a friend's apartment in the old city of Jerusalem. I barely emerged from the apartment for three days. I read source after source, but somehow it did not make any sense to me. Ancient sources are very different from the modern essay. The modern essay is too often "a lot that holds a little." The ancient Hebrew wisdom sources are koan-like in their quality and are usually "a little that holds a lot." Moreover, you can understand them only if they decide to let you inside. So I danced with them and flirted. They teased me, led me on, but then demurred and withdrew. Somehow it wasn't clicking.

Finally, one night I arrived at the apartment at two in the morning, very tired and about ready to give up. "No, not just yet—one more time," I said to myself, "and if there's no breakthrough, I'm through with this topic." And as I slowly, gently read the text for the last time, it was as though light—a soft white light—illuminated the room. The words seemed to read themselves, and a single elegant sentence offered herself to me. And then, thunder and lightning and wild erotic ecstasy as the text dropped veil after veil until she stood naked before me in all of her sensual splendor. I was on the inside of laughter. All the sources organized themselves in an instant and unfolded beautifully, as two distinct forms of laughter distinguished themselves in my soul and mind. Knotty issues that had troubled me gently untied themselves. And then, not more than six or seven minutes later, it was over. I was spent but happy.

But the story is not quite over yet. Exhausted, I gathered my books, and after sitting for a while, I walked to the old walls of the city to find a cab back to my own apartment. I got into the cab and the driver, whose name was Ari, wanted to talk. Truthfully, a quiet ride would have worked just fine for me, but such was not what the universe had in mind.

"So what are all those books about?" Ari asked. I knew I could not share with him the whole story, so I nonchalantly said, "Just books I was studying."

Undeterred, he pressed on. "Well, what were you studying?"

Having little choice, I answered, "I was trying to unpack the ontological and existential essence of laughter."

Now usually that would be a conversation stopper. But Ari was undeterred. He went right on. "Laughter—the essence of laughter. That's easy. My grandmother told me about that."

At this point, I was both bemused and interested: bemused because I had just spent three days in intense erotic encounter with this idea, and if he thought he could just throw out a few words about such a profound topic, well . . . And yet interested, because I know that grandmothers are often wise and almost always worth listening to.

To my chagrin, even as I half expected it, he did it. He articulated in different words, in his grandmother's name, that great sentence of illumination that I had experienced but an hour before. Tears gently rolled down my cheek. It was much more than the affirmation of an idea. I knew that God was in me. I felt completely loved and embraced by the universe.

Everything I have described to you has nothing to do, and yet everything to do, with sex. I promise you that during this entire story, the sexual was absolutely the furthest thing from my mind. And yet the process of study was no less than a loving courtship leading to intimacy. Sex models the erotic, but it does not begin to exhaust the erotic. At least for a few seconds on that night, I was on the inside of God's face in the Holy of Holies between the cherubs.

WHERE YOU LET HIM IN

Erotic experiences are available to us in every facet of our lives. We cannot live without them. To access Eros, we just have to make a decision to live high. This is the teaching of the Master of Kotzk, who once asked his students, "Where is God?" (In our terms, I would reframe the question:

"Where is the sacred—the erotic?") One student pointed to heaven and another to nature and the third to the sacred writings. "Yes," replied the master, "Yes, but where is God?" The students were silent. Answering his own question, the master said, "God is where you let him in."

WHY THIS IS ESSENTIAL NOW

For many years the cherubic mystery tradition was not taught publicly and often not at all in the Hebrew wisdom traditions. This was not accidental. Hebrew Tantra is an inseparable part of the whole Hebrew gestalt. In marked contrast to some of its Indian stepchildren and pagan antecedents, the Hebrew worldview was primarily rooted in a commitment to ethics. At the center of sacred works, ethical action was seen as required. It ranked far above any other dimension of spiritual practice. So for the past two millennia after the temple's fall, the major focus of spiritual work has been making ethics an integral part of human life. As Marc's grandfather used to say, "The most important thing is to be a *mensch* (Yiddish for "a person with integrity"). For him and for the tradition that produced him, ethics always trumped all other cards. The problem is that once we have incorporated ethics into the fabric of our lives, we find that it is not enough. We have still not filled the emptiness.

In modernity, as the poet Yeats said in his classic critique, "The best lack all conviction while the worst are full of passionate intensity." If we do not reclaim the erotic for the spirit and the good, then its shadow will seduce us and our world to the worst of places.

Fundamentalism is on the rise in the world because it offers a pseudo-erotic experience of community coupled with a pseudo-erotic worldview. Particularly, sacred fellowship, with all of its passion and interconnectivity, is a key feature of the fundamentalist experience. Whether it is the community of mosque, church, or synagogue, the Eros of communal belonging and caring is intoxicating. Communal ritual with its participatory song and drama, together with an all-embracing worldview that seems to explain away alienation and uncertainty, is undeniably seductive.

But fundamentalism is only pseudo Eros because ultimately it denies true interconnectivity. Too many all-embracing worldviews are built on excluding the "unredeemed" from their embrace. Fundamentalism in both its secular and its religious varieties offers salvation only to the elite group that subscribes to its set of dogmas. Everyone else is an outsider and usually damned to eternal perdition of some variety. This is a violation of the core quality of Eros: interiority, being on the inside. But being an insider often only by making someone else an outsider means there is no interiority and no true Eros. This is precisely what we have termed pseudo Eros. In your need to fill the emptiness, the other person is degraded in order for you to attain the erotic feeling of being on the inside.

Another type of fundamentalist fellowship is seen in the communities of greed and accumulation. Materialism moves people because when the center doesn't hold, the pseudo Eros of money seems the easiest means to fill the emptiness. Paradoxically, more enlightened communities and individuals often seem weak and insipid, leaving us unmoved and uninspired.

If we do not reclaim the erotic for the spirit and the good, then its shadow will seduce us and our world to the worst of places.

We return to Yeats, who wrote in "The Second Coming":

The best lack all conviction, while the worst
Are full of passionate intensity.
Surely some revelation is at hand.

The revelation at hand, that which we yearn for, is the Secret of the Cherubs—how to transform sexuality from a force to be controlled or a mere indulgence into the spiritual master that teaches us how to live erotically in all of the nonsexual dimensions of our lives. The old suspicious approach to sexuality is insufficient to create a world that is holy.

Imagine that a great sage from the twelfth century is resurrected. He rises from his grave and hears that there is a terrible war raging. He says, "I'll help you win this war. Hand me my sword and I can fight off a hundred people!" People would say to him, "Are you crazy? These are not the weapons of today. Today we have more sophisticated weapons. You push a button, and you kill millions in one second." The potential for destruction is greater today than it ever was. Eros is the creative force of contact, construction, and creativity that stands against alienation, destruction, and dissolution. We need a new erotic equal to our new power. Never have people felt so empty, rootless, and estranged, both from themselves and from the world. The old, staid conventions are not enough. We need to return to the wine of ancient teachings in the evolved flasks of these contemporary times. We need the Secret of the Cherubs in an evolutionary context. It is not merely about Eros, it is about evolutionary Eros.

It is time for the secret to be revealed and the wine to be drunk. It is time for a holy Dionysus to emerge and claim his place alongside the cherubs in the Holy of Holies. We've had enough of the sexual pathologies that poison our society—the violent fundamentalism, the abusive sexuality of the church, the vicious McCarthy-like witch hunts that falsely accuse, and the desperately empty sexuality of the everyday. These are all pathologies of the spirit that haunt our world. It is time to heal the split and reclaim the sexual as the master who can teach us how to access the erotic in all of life.

PART THREE

THE FIVE
ESSENTIAL
FACES OF EROS

CHAPTER THIRTEEN

THE FIRST FACE

INTERIORITY:
LIVING ON THE INSIDE

Let's take a few moments to review what we've discovered so far. Sex and Eros are different but essentially related. The relation is that sex models the erotic. Within the sexual are the most important hints of Eros. From the nature of the sexual, we learn what it means to live erotically.

Sex is neither our enemy nor our playmate, though it is sometimes both. Primarily, sex is our teacher, always hinting at the way. Sex models Eros because reality is allurement, the very structure of reality all the way up and all the way down. Sex at its best models what it means to live erotically in all the nonsexual dimensions of our lives.

When sex becomes virtually the only arena in which we experience erotic fulfillment, then the Shechinah is in exile. The exile of the Shechinah is the exile of the erotic into the sexual. The redemption of the

Shechinah is therefore the re-expansion of Eros from the narrow confines of the sexual back into the broad vastness of living. The goal of life
is to live erotically in all facets of our being.

Sex models the erotic, but it does not exhaust the erotic. Sex at its best
can fill our sexual needs, but it can never fill our erotic needs. When sex
tries to do what is beyond its power to accomplish, sexuality implodes
on itself. We begin to find fulfillment only in boundary-breaking sexuality, which becomes the only way that we experience Eros. This is
the Shechinah in exile. The redemption of the Shechinah is manifested
when Eros once again becomes part of the fabric of all the dimensions
of our lives.

Eros is the invitation to be a lover: to be a great lover in every fiber
of your being, in every facet of your life. To be a lover is to be radically
alive and aflame with passion in every dimension of life. To be erotically
engaged is to be holy, to be on the inside, to experience the yearning force
of being—the intense desire that connects us with our aliveness. It is to
feel the fullness of being totally present, and the radical interconnectivity
of the entire web of life.

WHERE WE GO FROM HERE

"Okay," you say, "I want to live erotically. So what are the specific qualities
of the erotic, of being a lover, that the sexual models? What are the faces
of Eros that chart the path to living an erotic life? Break it down for me
and make it real in my journey. How do I become a great lover in every
dimension of my life?"

Beginning with this chapter, we will be exploring the answer to these
questions in the twelve paths of Hebrew Tantra, which we like to call "the
twelve faces of Eros." In each of these paths the starting point will be the
sexual. We will identify a unique quality of the sexual, in that particular
face of Eros, that models the erotic.

The twelve faces of Eros are manifested in our world most powerfully
in the sexual arena. Sex tells us that these qualities are a genuine option in
our lives. Once we know they are possible—for we have experienced their

potent presence in our sexuality—we can begin to realize them in other aspects of our lives. We need to be lovers beyond the bedroom, even as the sexual hints at the way. This is the redemption of the Shechinah, the end of the exile.

Now we are ready to enter into the faces of Eros themselves. The faces are:

First Face: Interiority: Inside the Inside
Second Face: Fullness of Presence
Third Face: Yearning and Desire
Fourth Face: Wholeness and Interconnectivity
Fifth Face: Uniqueness and Identity
Sixth Face: Imagination
Seventh Face: Perception
Eighth Face: Giving and Receiving
Ninth Face: Surrender
Tenth Face: Play and Lishmah
Eleventh Face: Creativity
Twelfth Face: Pleasure and Delight

All of these qualities are essential to great erotic sex. But they are not exhausted by sex. Rather, these qualities are modeled in sex. Experiencing these qualities in sex models what it might mean to live erotically—through these very faces of Eros—in every arena of life.

The faces of Eros, when taken together, form the essence of the Shechinah experience. The first five faces are primary. They are the very stuff of Eros. Each face, besides being a quality of Eros, is a practice and a path to Eros as well. The faces are Eros even as they lead us to Eros. There is no split between means and ends. In fact, as we will see, the collapse of the distinction between path and destination is one of the core features of the erotic.

THE FIRST FACE OF
EROS: INTERIORITY

"What lies behind us and what lies before us are tiny matters compared to what lies within us," Ralph Waldo Emerson pointed out. He was speaking of interiority, the first face of Eros. Interiority is the experience of being and feeling like we are on the inside—on the inside of life, the inside of where it's all happening, the inside of love, the inside of Eros.

In the magical mystery of temple myth, the sexually intertwisted cherubs were not stationary fixtures. No, the statues were expressive and emotive. They moved. When integrity and goodness ruled the land, the cherubs were placed face-to-face. In such times the focal point of Shechinah energy rested erotically, ecstatically, between the cherubs. When discord and evil held sway in the kingdom, the cherubs were turned from each other, appearing back-to-back. In that position, they announced that the world was amiss, alienated, ruptured. Face-to-face, the world was harmonized, hopeful, and embraced. Thus, in biblical text, face-to-face is the most highly desirable state. It is the gemstone state of being, the jeweled summit of all creation. Face-to-face is the state of Eros.

Face-to-face means, first and foremost, being on the inside. Indeed, the God force (the Shechinah) said to rest between the cherubs in the Holy of Holies is no less than the radically profound experience of being on the inside. Eros is aroused whenever we move so deeply into what we do, who we are with, or where we are that it stirs our heart, passion, and imagination.

THE SEXUAL MODELS THE
EROTIC: INTERIORITY

"Being on the inside" means not on the inside of your sexual partner, for that is limited to the masculine sexual experience. Rather, it is about being on the inside of the experience itself. Sex models Eros because in great sex you enter the inside of the inside. In great sex time stands still, concerns of the exterior world fall away as we enter into the secret garden. The external gives way to the eternal. Novelist Roman Payne gives visceral expression to the experience of entering the inside through the sexual body:

> When I touched her body, I believed she was God. In the curves
> of her form I found the birth of Man, the creation of the world,
> and the origin of all life.

Sex is a portal to being on the inside. Sex models Eros; however, it does not exhaust Eros. But being on the inside is not limited to sex. It is modeled by sex. Sex reminds us that we long for the inside places.

THE EROS OF INTERIORITY

Being on the inside is not about a geographical place, but about a soul terrain, a place inside ourselves. Socrates writes at the end of the *Phaedrus*, "Beloved Pan and all ye other gods that haunt this place, give me beauty in the inward soul, and may the inward and outward man be at one."

For the temple mystics, exile occurs when one's inside and outside are not connected in day-to-day living. Exile is nonerotic living. The first, although by no means only, problem with exile is that it is extraordinarily difficult. When I am not living from the inside, I am not living naturally. My choices, reactions, and responses do not emerge spontaneously from what Spanish mystic Teresa of Avila called one's "interior castle." I am not in the flow of my own life. Eros is to be in the flow of the fountain, what the Zohar calls in its oft-repeated evocative mantra, "The River of Light that flows from Eden."

Here's an analogy: Once there were two mountain climbers. The first, old and slightly bent, slowly made his way up the mountain. The second, young and in good shape, bounded past him, racing confidently toward the summit. In late afternoon they met again. The older man still climbed carefully, step after step, toward the top of the mountain. The younger man lay exhausted, unable to move, at the side of the path. As the one passed the other, the younger climber cried out, "I don't understand.

What do you know that I don't?" Responded the old man, eyes twinkling with compassion and laughter, "The difference between us is simple. You come to conquer the mountain, but the mountain is stronger than you, so you are conquered. I come to merge with the mountain, so the mountain loves me and lifts me to her summit."

This old Zen story depicts what we mean about living on the inside of Eros. The younger climber felt himself separate from the mountain. To him it was something he had to conquer. The older climber felt himself to be part of the mountain. To him it was an aspect of himself. The mountain, which represents Eros, did not support the efforts of the younger climber but "lifted up" the older climber to her summit, which represents the interior of Eros, the deepest, most intimate part. The younger man was an outsider; the older man, an insider to the mystery that is Eros.

The older climber's goal was "to merge with the mountain." To merge is to traverse the chasm that separates object and subject. It is to become one with your reality, to be on the inside of the experience of life. Erotic living is living on the inside. The opposite of Eros, therefore, is alienation. To be alienated is always to feel that you are an outsider with no safe place to call home.

The result of nonerotic living is always bad choices, betrayals, and pain. When I am not in the flow, I wind up always having to watch my back. I am on the outside, exiled from my inner castle. I have lost face. The world feels hostile to me, and I must battle obstacles and enemies to make my way toward my goals. By contrast, when I am in the flow, I am like the lover who sees harmony and goodness everywhere. The world serendipitously supports my every endeavor. I am always in the right place at the right time. I feel the love of the universe, the presence of God, as something near and personal to me, closer and more intimate even than my breath. I feel as if I am moving inside God, inside the love of the universe. It feels as if I am being lived as love.

There is a tale told of the master Nahman Kossover. His mystical practice was to meditate on the divine name. It is said that when he taught, he could actually see, reflected back to him, the divine name on the faces of his listeners. At some point Nahman fell on rough times and was forced to leave teaching and become a merchant. He was greatly saddened because he found it very difficult to fully concentrate on the divine name amidst the chaotic atmosphere of the market. Until he hit upon a solution. He hired a beloved student to be his assistant and travel with him, with no other task than to be present. Each time Nahman looked at the face of his beloved assistant, he would be reconnected with the name of God. Was the assistant particularly beautiful? I doubt it. The assistant was every man and every woman. You and me. As soon as he saw the divine name on the face of his beloved assistant he was immediately able to see the divine name in the faces of every man and woman in the marketplace.*

The Sufi poet Rumi puts it this way:

> *The real orchards and fruits are inside the heart; the*
>   *reflection of their beauty is falling upon this water and*
>   *earth* [the external world] . . .
> *All the deceived ones come to gaze on this reflection in the*
>   *opinion that this is the place of Paradise.*
> *They are fleeing from the origins of the orchards; they are*
>   *making merry over a phantom.*

What Rumi is saying is that the Eros of beauty dwells within us. All the exterior beauty in the world is just a reflection of that. People who do not understand Eros think paradise can be attained by immersing themselves in the beauty of external objects. But in chasing material pleasures for their own sake, they actually turn away from the source of those pleasures, which is the Eros within. They pursue a phantom, an echo of Eros, instead of Eros itself. They are on the outside, exiled from Eros. Those who know "the real orchards and fruits are inside the heart" are on the inside, intimate with Eros.

---

* In ordinary love the face of the beloved closes you to all faces other than his or hers. In outrageous love, the face of the beloved opens you to the name of God that lives in every face.

THE SPELL OF SPELLING

In the Hebrew mystical tradition, language is not the mere random designation of sounds and letters in a particular pattern. For the mystic, words are vital portals to meaning. Language is the spiritual DNA of reality. Thus, when one root word is used for seemingly disparate ideas, you can rest assured that these different ideas are in fact integrally related. So let's watch for a moment as the magic of languages dances before us.

The esoteric Hebrew term for the Holy of Holies is *Lifnai Lifnim*. Literally rendered into English, this means "the inside of the inside." The term was not meant to reflect the fact that the Holy of Holies was the innermost point of the temple. Rather, the reverse was true: the Holy of Holies was intentionally situated in the innermost point in order to model the interiority of Eros.

In another architectural expression of this idea, the temples of the Masonic Order have doors that open only from the inside. To enter, you must insert your hand through an opening in the door to grasp the inside handle. The point is that in order to open the portals to mystery, one must approach from the inside. What's more, this opening is shaped like a heart. Eros—the yearning for the inside—is the essence of love. The Masonic Order springs from the Templars, a monastic order of Christian mystics in Jerusalem who fell in love with and understood deeply the Eros of the temple.

That, however, is just for starters. Hold on, for the magic of language, the spell of spelling, has just begun. The Hebrew word for "inside" is *panim*, but it has two other meanings as well. The first, not surprisingly, is "face." The face is the place where my insides are revealed. There are forty-five muscles in the face. From a biological standpoint, most of them are unnecessary. Their major purpose, it would seem, is to express emotional depth and nuance. They are the muscles of the soul. Every muscle of the face reflects another nuance of depth and interiority. When I say, "I need to speak-face-to face," I am in erotic need of an inside conversation. At this point all of the cell phones and sophisticated internet hook-ups won't give me what I need, for while amazingly efficient and effective, they are nonerotic. True erotic conversations rarely happen on the internet.

The spell continues. There is a third meaning to the Hebrew word *panim*. In a slightly modified form, it means "before," in the sense of appearing before God. The biblical text in Leviticus tells that on Yom Kippur, the Day of At-one-ment, the temple's high priest appears *lifnei Hashem*: "before God."

Read in the English, this appears similar to a summons to appear "before" a judging court, generally not a joyous occasion. For the Hebrew mystics, however, rooted as they are in the magic and spells of language, it is an entirely different affair. Remember that all three English words—inside, face, and before—share the same Hebrew root. The essence, then, of the Day of At-one-ment is not a commandment to appear "before God" in the magistrate sense. It is rather an invitation to live on the inside of God's face. Once the journey to God is finished, the infinite journey in God begins.

EVERYMAN'S EROS

The Eros experience is the province of mystics, artists, and scholars. But not only them. It awaits all of us in all our endeavors.

Have you ever gone jogging? You get up not at all enthusiastic about running but somehow feeling obligated. You reluctantly get dressed and begin your route. Slowly the discomfort fades, and you begin to enjoy yourself. You find yourself in the rhythm. And then, on good days, at some point you break through an invisible barrier and begin to fly. Ecstatic, you lose yourself in the wind. Your body, the earth, the wind, the rhythms of your pace, and the sound of your feet all merge into one. It is no longer accurate, even for the briefest of moments, to say, "I am running." Rather, you are the wind, you are the running.

IN EVERY STITCH

It was the middle of the nineteenth century. Heaven was joyous, hell was in an uproar, for it seemed that one Hanoch the shoemaker was about to usher in the Messiah. The Master of Rishin tells the story to his disciples something like this.

> Hanoch the shoemaker used to sit every day intent on the stitching of his leather shoes. It was known that with every stitch Hanoch was *meyached yichudim elyonim*. That is, he was unifying higher unities. Now *yichudim*, my holy disciples, in Kabbalah always means *zivug* (coupling). [*Zivug* is an ultimate erotic term. It refers not to the sexual person, but to the cosmic love affair between the masculine God presence and the feminine Shechinah presence. It is a love affair brought about by human action.]
>
> Now, the strange secret of the story, my holy community, is that Hanoch wasn't doing anything that should have caused such ecstatic *yichudim*. He wasn't fulfilling any religious commandment; he was engaged in no ritual or pious act.
>
> "Perhaps," said one of the disciples, "he was meditating on a passage of Zohar as he stitched."
>
> Another chimed in, "Perhaps he was doing the spiritual exercises of Luria's Kabbalah, which cause pleasure above?"
>
> "No, nothing of the sort," replied the master.
>
> "Then what was he doing while he stitched?" pressed the disciples.
>
> "Nothing!" responded the master with a slight smile. "Hanoch was doing nothing . . . nothing other than being fully inside in every single stitch."
>
> "Fully inside in every stitch?!" Duly impressed, the eager disciples now had another confusion. "So then, Master, why is it that the Messiah has not yet announced his arrival?"
>
> The Master of Rishin sighed and said, "The force of evil discovered the cause and countered it. Sadly, he seems to have gotten the best of our holy shoemaker."
>
> "But how?" the crestfallen disciples asked.
>
> The reply: "With plenty of good business."

And so it was, rushing to fulfill his flood of orders, Hanoch became the busiest and most prosperous cobbler in the region, mindlessly producing shoe after cookie-cutter shoe, and the Messiah still has not yet come.

POET, PROPHET, AND PRIESTESS

Eros is the birthright of every man and every woman. Though we may search long and hard for priests and prophets who can guide and counsel us, in the end we must return time and again to our own inner sanctum. There the poet, prophet, and priest we seek sleep in our depths, waiting to be stirred and finally awoken.

In our deepest erotic longings, so many of us do want to be God's poets, prophets, and priests. Yet we are ashamed to admit it, sometimes even to ourselves. We fear appearing ridiculous or grandiose even in our own eyes. Yet the story of Hanoch the shoemaker insists that we are all potential priests and prophets. We all can enter the Holy of Holies, for it is within us. In contrast to the priestly class and prophetic elites of the ancient Near East, the Hebraic sacred text speaks of a kingdom of priests and a people who are all prophets.

Life itself is the only real temple of the spirit. Eros is everywhere. Churches and synagogues are a pallid, even if sometimes important, compromise for our disenchanted age. Eros is available everywhere. Eros lives in everyone. Eros invites the democratization of greatness.

The Zohar teaches that every erotic inside experience is a Shechinah experience of the Holy of Holies. It occurs when we become one with the way, when we have moved from the outside to the inside. It is in this sense that the temple is called in Hebrew the *bayit*, which means, quite simply, "home." The holiest place in the world . . . is home. Eros is about coming home. Most of us live split off from ourselves. All too often we feel like imposters in our own lives, wearing masks and wondering when, and if, we will ever start to feel at home with ourselves. That is what it means to live on the outside.

COMING HOME

Once a year in a spine-tingling mystery rite, the priest would enter the Holy of Holies. On this day, every person was forgiven. On this day, people were to reexperience themselves in the depths of their own true innocence. For on the inside, we are all innocent. This day is called in biblical tradition Yom Kippur, the Day of Atonement (at-one-ment).

The core erotic idea of the *bayit*, the temple, was that every person could and needs to access the Shechinah experience. Every human being needs to live erotically in all facets of being. Every human has a primary erotic need to move beyond the imposter into his or her own deepest place of oneness, a oneness not only with the self but also with others, and ultimately with all existence. The Zohar refers to the exile from one's deepest self as *alma depiruda*, the world of separation. The most tragic separation is not from the mother, not from the community, but from the self. The journey of a lifetime is to move from *alma depiruda* to *alma deyichuda*, from separation to oneness—at-one-ment. Love is the path back home. We are not talking about superficial love, not merely sexual love, but erotic love.

The litmus of an erotic lover is this: does this person lead you back to your inner self? Are you able to share with him or her your most vulnerable, fledgling, faltering dreams? Every person has a Holy of Holies that, in those most intimate of times, we let another enter as the priest to worship at our altar. And in the gorgeous paradox of the spirit, by letting a lover enter we ourselves are let in as well. For when the temple door is open and the lover enters, we ourselves trail behind. We gain uncommon access to our inner selves, a place that we alone are often unable to reach. The true lover always takes you home. As poet Emily Dickinson observes:

> EDEN is that old-fashioned House
> We dwell in every day,
> Without suspecting our abode
> Until we drive away.[30]

Love lets us realize the Eden we are dwelling in every day. That is what it means to feel at home in your life, the greatest feeling in the world.

LEFT OUTSIDE

Much of modernity militates against the Eros of being on the inside. Indeed, the whole psychological stance of fortifying the ego is about keeping people on the outside. Our way of thinking about all this was powerfully influenced by the work of the child psychologist Margaret Mahler. She taught that the primary goal of growing up and out of being a baby is to achieve what she termed "individuation and separation." The healthy human baby's journey must be toward ever-ascending levels of autonomy and separateness.

This is absolutely true. We must first achieve the stable boundary of self in order to be psychologically or spiritually healthy. If we do not individuate as a healthy, separate self, then every form of neurosis and even psychosis lurks at the door of our psyches. Yet once separate selfhood is achieved, it must be transcended. It is not that we leave a separate self or ego behind. What we leave behind is our exclusive identification with ego. We exist as separate selves for sure. But when separate self becomes the summit of our identity, then we achieve every increasing level of separateness and autonomy until we are at the top, all alone. Yes, we do need to reinforce the ego. We need to become a self. But then we need to let limited identity of separate self-ego boundaries drop. It is the only way to let others, and sometimes even ourselves, inside.

Separate self is a critical step in our identity. But then, if we can continue to grow, we must transcend our exclusive identification with ego and realize our deeper identity with the larger contexts of our lives.

When psychology defines a person's real self as the completely separate ego, then we begin to view the breakdown of ego as a breakdown in normality. We erect our fortress so high and so "healthy" that no one, including ourselves, can get inside. And yet, are not most of the great experiences we seek in life dependent on the ego breaking down? From falling in love to orgasm to spiritual connection, the most sought-after experiences can happen only when the ego boundaries soften to allow entry to these welcome guests. When we spend our lives under the spell of the separate individuate mantra that is core to Western psychology, we block access to the Eros our souls so desperately crave.

We all need others to let us in. They may be lovers, teachers, friends, students, and hopefully parents. No one can survive on the outside.

SIT DOWN

Teachers taught that Zoharic masters can take us home, but only if they teach from the inside. It is reported that Ziv Hirsch of Zhitomir, the charismatic nineteenth-century mystical master, would occasionally, in the middle of his speech, sit down, abruptly ending his address in mid-thought. When pressed for an explanation, he would respond, "My master, the Maggid of Mezritch, taught me, 'If when giving a *sicha* [spiritual lesson] you can hear yourself talking, sit down.'"

In *A Moveable Feast*, Hemingway remarks on the difference between his telling a story and the story telling itself. When he begins to tell the story, he knows it is time to quit for the day. This is a true echo of the temple tradition. Sit down when you can hear yourself speak.

EXPANDING OUR VOCABULARY: EROS AND ZOHAR

The word *eros* entered Western consciousness through Socrates' best student. Plato, in his wonderful dialogue *The Symposium*, calls the inner state that we have been describing "Eros." To be a lover, implies Plato, is to passionately enter the inside of reality. Eros is love, but not in the casual, pallid, and sometimes anemic way we often talk of love. On the inside of things, all is aflame.

In Hebrew, the term for love is *ahavah*, rooted in the word *lahav*, "torch." Similarly, the Hebrew word source for love, *lev* (meaning "heart"), is used in the sense of *labat eish* (heart of fire). For *lev* (origin of the English word *lava*) is expressive of the sometimes volcanic heat that erupts from one's inner depths when erotically engaged in any endeavor. Not ordinary love, but outrageous love.

Thus the Hebrew word *ahava* and the Greek word *eros* enrich our limited Western vocabulary of love. For vocabulary always reflects reality. We don't have an English word for the type of fully expanded Eros we will be revealing in this book, because such expanded Eros is still so foreign to the fabric of our lives. Yet in Hebrew and Greek, there are a plethora of such words.

Kabbalah scholar Yehuda Liebes suggests that the word *Zohar*, the name of the great magnum opus of Hebrew mysticism, is roughly synonymous with the Greek word *eros*. For the authors of the Zohar were not dry medieval scholastics; they were rather men of great passion and depth who believed that by entering the inside of the moment, the text, or the relationship, they could re-create and heal the world. Zohar, like Eros, is powerful, intense, and deep. It is the source of all creativity and pleasure.

Further, the Zohar masters understood Eros to be the essential goal of the spiritual journey. Often in Hebrew mystical texts the erotic is called "a messiah experience." For the masters, the messiah was not a historical happening as much as an inner event. The Hebrew word for "messiah" derives from the root word *siach*. *Siach* means no more and no less than "conversation." The core of the Zohar text is basically a series of sacred conversations. The messiah, they taught, lingers whenever we so fully enter conversation that the boundaries of ego fall away and we are left only with the raw joy of fellowship.

One of the most profound and difficult sections of the Zohar is called the Idra Rabba, the Great Gathering. Similar to *The Symposium* of Plato, it is the story of ten close friends come together for holy fellowship. And like *The Symposium*, it is the passionate conversation and camaraderie of friends reveling in each other's company as they search for depth that infuses the gathering with Eros. Any conversation that is true, authentic, and deep is erotic conversation.

In the Great Gathering of the men of the Zohar, as in *The Symposium*, both the form and the content are about Eros. The value of the gathering is the gathering itself. It need not justify itself in terms of any other standard or value. When one is willing to let go of agendas, stop networking, and enter the depth of conversation, then one is on the inside. When the other person's talk is no longer merely the time to work out what I will say next, when deep listening becomes mutual, when words begin to flow and time stands still, when a few hours seems but a few minutes, then the gods of Zohar and Eros have been invoked.

When Diotima (the old wise woman in *The Symposium*) talks about Eros, and when Shimon Bar Yochai (hero of the Idra) talks about Zohar, neither is referring to the narrow modern sense of sex. Rather, they use these terms to evoke a sense of merging with the flow of the moment, of moving from outside observer to passionate participant. Thus, "Zohar" is not merely the name of the work; it is also an evocative word that seeks to capture glimmerings of Eros. This is the ultimate paradigm of identity between medium and message. Process and content merge in the word. The Zohar experience is the erotic experience. Zohar, like Eros, is powerful, intense, and deep. It is the source of all creativity and pleasure.

Similarly, the temple is an archetype of Eros, and Eros—the Greek term for loving—is the experience of being on the inside. This is the name of the temple's Holy of Holies, *lifnei lifnim*, the inside of the inside. The experience of Shechinah, the sensual divine force that rests between the cherubs in the Holy of Holies, is the erotic experience. In fact, the mystics often use the word *Shechinah* as a synonym for *eros*.

The Hebrew word for "temple" is *mikdash*—literally translated as "holiness." If you put it all together, it is radical, revolutionary, and overwhelmingly relevant to our lives. What it means is that the erotic and the holy are the same thing:

Eros = Shechinah = the Inside = Zohar = Holy

What is the definition of holiness? So many people use the word *holy*, but virtually no one knows what it really means. Ask someone, and you will likely get a fuzzy, nebulous response that will leave you no richer than before. So here, at last, is a definition of holiness. To be holy is to be on the inside. The opposite of holiness is not unholiness or anti-holiness. It is not impurity or demonic possession. The opposite of the holy is the superficial. Eros, holiness, is about depth. Depth is an inside experience.

It has its own unique nuance, texture, and richness. The superficial is bland and common.

Holiness is eroticism. Sin is superficiality.

INTERIORS ARE REAL

Indeed the greatest superficiality is to reduce the world to mere exteriors. Exteriors are no less part of reality than interiors are. The problem is only when you get caught on the outside and can no longer find your way in. Sin is to get caught on the outside. Superficiality is when you can no longer find your way in.

Science has done a vital and stunningly good job at beginning to describe the exterior structure of reality. But all exteriors have interiors. Eros is to enter the inside of reality. Science and its radically amazing descriptions of exteriors are dazzlingly beautiful. But as long as we are only dealing in exteriors, we are still engaged in the superficial. All that we hold most important in life is interior. Values and meaning are interiors. Love, loyalty, and beauty are all interiors. To live an erotic life, we need to be in touch with the inside. The return to Eros begins with the return to the inside.

To get a simple but compelling sense of what we mean by insides and outsides, interiors and exteriors, let's look at the potent example of love. Love is an inside experience. We will talk in more depth about what love means in the chapter on perception, the seventh face of Eros. But for now let's work with the popular understanding of love. Love is a feeling. The feeling of love is interior. But that does not mean that love does not have an exterior. It does. Love expresses itself in the body in objective, exterior terms and not only as a subjective experience. For the first time in history, we are gaining a glimpse into the neuroscience of love. Suffice it to say that love generates a complex cocktail of neurochemicals, creates new neural pathways in the brain, and has a host of other physically measurable effects. Yet we all intuitively understand that love is more than neurochemicals. Love is an inside experience. The interior experience of love expresses itself on the outside through the manufacture of neurochemicals, but it is not reducible to mere neurochemicals.

Human beings have insides and outsides. In fact, the more the sciences advance, the more self-evident it becomes that all of reality—all the way up and all the way down the chain of being—has insides and outsides. But nothing is merely its outside expression, including human beings. The belief that human beings are brain puppets (mere exteriors) is a bizarre, self-contradictory, empty notion. When we say that a human being has heart, we are referring not only to the physical beating heart. We are referring to an interior quality of compassion and courage. When we talk about the thinking capacity of a human being, we likewise refer distinctly to insides and outsides. What we call the "mind" is the inside of the human being, while the brain is the outside.

The most mysterious and exciting new domain in science is perhaps the relationship between interiors and exteriors. The brain is able to reshape the mind, and the mind is able to reshape the brain. The ability of the mind to alter the brain, create new neural pathways, break old conditioning, generate new brain cells, promote well-being, and even direct gene expression forms the true frontier of neuroscience.

We have different faculties of perception for seeing exteriors and interiors. We see exteriors with the eye of the senses. We see interiors with what has been called the eye of the spirit by Christians and Jews and the eye of the heart by Sufis and Kabbalists.

From the perspective of insides, the universe feels. Masters of the interior science from all the great traditions were able to feel the feeling of the universe itself. All of them, living at different places and in different eras with no knowledge of each other—all came to the same conclusion. The universe feels, and the universe feels love. This is not poetry but science. It is science in the sense that an experiment was repeated time and again in double-blind conditions and consistently yielded this same result. The experiments are double blind in the sense that the figures performing the experiments through the milleniums were largely unaware of each other. Different forms of the same experiment were repeated time and again by different figures at different times in different places throughout history, all yielding the same result.

This is how knowledge is produced, both in the classic exterior sciences and in what we call "the interior sciences." The experiments conducted to access the interior face of the cosmos were done with the instruments of the eye of the heart, which include meditation, dance, prayer, ecstasy, and radical amazement at the goodness, truth, and beauty of existence. The interior scientists included not only mystics but also physicists and mathematicians. Exteriors and interiors are literally different sides of the same coin of reality.

My (Marc) longtime friend and colleague, integral theorist Ken Wilber, points out that virtually all the great figures of quantum mechanics trusted the eye of the heart to reveal the interior face of the cosmos that could not be expressed in the exteriors of science. The poor, "uneducated" Indian mathematician Srinivasa Ramanujan, who died at age thirty-two, is reported to have said to his older colleague, the prestigious G. H. Hardy, "An equation has no meaning to me unless it expresses a thought in the mind of God." Hardy's famed collaborator, the great mathematician Edward Collingwood, wrote that "every positive integer is a personal friend of Ramanujan's." Numbers are alive with love. For Ramanujan, the Shakti or Eros of all of reality disclosed a glimmer of herself in mathematics. The conclusion of all of the experiments of the interior sciences is clear: the universe feels, and the universe feels love.

SEXUAL HIJACKING AND THE FOUR QUESTIONS

We began the chapter by saying that the sexual models the erotic state of being on the inside. Let's conclude the chapter with an exercise that deploys the consciousness aroused by entering the inside through the portal of the sexual. In this exercise, we use the clarity that can become available in the altered state of the sexual to accomplish emotional, spiritual, or psychological breakthroughs. At the Tantra school we call this practice "Sexual Hijacking." We hijack the clarity and energy of radical sexual arousal for a purpose beyond the sexual.

One of the ways we do this is through a second exercise called "The Four Questions Practice." The questions are:

1. Do you know you deserve to be loved by me?
2. Do you feel you deserve to be loved by me?
3. Do you want to be loved by me?
4. Do you want to know the meaning of life?

For virtually all the people doing the Four Questions Practice, it is nearly impossible to access the absolute clarity of knowing or feeling that they deserve to be loved by the other person. Accessing self-love is one of the great challenges that every human being faces. Owning the clear desire to be "loved by me" is also difficult. Even if they can express it, it is always with some degree of qualification or deflecting humor. Finally, virtually everyone feels like they want the answer to the perennial question of the meaning of life.

We then instruct the participants to ask themselves the same four questions in the midst of an intensely arousing and loving sexual experience. Their answers are virtually always transformed. They are all able to answer the questions with complete clarity. They answer: "Yes, I deserve to be loved by you. Yes, I feel I deserve to be loved by you. Yes, I want to be loved by you." The last question totally changes as well. The question of the meaning of life becomes irrelevant, not because it has been answered but because it becomes self-evident. In the midst of raw erotic sex with a person you madly love, the question of the meaning of life falls away.

The key point is that the sexual takes us inside to a place of potent interior gnosis and radically evolves our innermost knowing, about both our core identity and our place in the universe. That is what we mean when we say the sexual models the erotic. But it is even more than that. Sex becomes not only a model but also a method to catalyze potent breakthroughs in the most pivotal arenas of our nonsexual lives.

CHAPTER FOURTEEN

THE SECOND FACE

FULLNESS OF PRESENCE

EROS AND PSEUDO EROS

The second face of Eros is presence—or perhaps better said, the fullness of presence. This is not a quality that is distinct and different from the erotic quality of being on the inside. Presence flows naturally with, and even overlaps, interiority. And yet it is not quite the same. Of course, being on the inside requires the fullness of presence. But we can experience full presence even when we have not merged with the moment or crossed over to the inside. Presence is about showing up. You can show up and be fully present in a conversation without necessarily losing yourself in the encounter's flow. Full presence at work can mean you derive joy, satisfaction, and self-worth from your vocation. It means you feel full and not empty. Presence means you are fully showing up right here. You are not anywhere else in this moment.

THE SEXUAL MODELS THE EROTIC: FULLNESS OF PRESENCE

It is in the sexual where—in its ideal expression—we are most fully present to each other. It is in the sexual that we most fully show up. In the sexual we both give and receive rapt attention. Every gesture, fragrance, sigh, and whisper ripples through us as we listen deeply to the erotic instructions that well up from the depth of our soul's body.

Sex models Eros because in great sex you experience a radical fullness of presence. Adrienne Rich, who brought lesbian sexuality into the forefront of poetic discourse, captures the sense of radical presence in the sexual:

Whatever happens with us, your body
will haunt mine—tender, delicate

In the fullness of presence the Eros lives in memory with such clarity that it continues to arouse even decades later.

your lovemaking . . .
the live, insatiate dance of your nipples in my mouth—

Presence never disappears:

your touch on me, firm, protective, searching
me out, your strong tongue and slender fingers
reaching

When we are touched by true erotic arousal the quivering tenderness feels forever. The erotic poetess then takes us home:

where I had been waiting years for you
in my rose-wet cave—whatever happens, this is

Presence is also marked by a sense of radical intensity. Consider what Markus Zusak writes in *Getting the Girl*: "I wanted to drown inside a woman in the feeling and drooling of the love I could give her. I wanted her pulse to crush me with its intensity. That's what I wanted."

THE EROS OF PRESENCE

In our Tantra school we have an extraordinary soul-gazing exercise we call "Panim el Panim," a "face-to-face" living prayer practice. I (Kristina) give simple instructions. Look at the face of your partner as an artist would look at his new subject. Move your fingers—sensually, not sexually—over the contours and crevices of your partner's nose, eyes, cheekbones, and mouth. Now look again at your practice partner, left eye to left eye, without averting your gaze. In the Eros of face tenderly touched and felt, the veil of separation disappears. If you are patient and graced, you actually see Love itself looking back at you.

Have you ever looked, really looked, into another person's face? Have you ever witnessed that moment when the soul comes rushing up from its inner chambers and opens wide the windows of the eyes to see you, seeing the other person? To greet you like the daylight? This is the mystery of love, of the eyes and their Eros. What a magnificent moment of Eros! To live erotically is to be fully present to each other's richness, complexity, and ultimate grandeur. It is to fully wait for the other to appear. The Shechinah in the temple is termed "the indwelling presence." The erotic is always the experience of full presence. The Shechinah, say the mystics, is waiting for us to show up.

The Shechinah is presence waiting for us to be present. She is Eros, standing outside our window, waiting. Waiting for us to feel her presence. Waiting for us to be overwhelmed by her love. Waiting for us to run out and behold with wonder . . . her face.

EMPTINESS AND ADDICTIONS

Eros is about feeling the fullness of being, the opposite of emptiness. Every human being has met emptiness—that feeling we experience in the late night, at home alone, or in the hotel room we return to after a long day's work on a business trip. We enter the room and are often overwhelmed by the intense feelings. We flip on the cable or order up dinner and entertainment—anything not to stay in the emptiness. But that is not the solution to the problem. It is running away from the problem into pseudo Eros.

For many years I, Marc, would begin talks with the sentence, "Life is what you do with your emptiness." In our society, which sadly defines human beings as consumers and not lovers, denial is the primary strategy for coping with emptiness. We are sold fulfillment at every turn and in every guise. We buy, buy, and buy, hoping that one of the hawked elixirs might finally fulfill us. And yet the emptiness lingers.

The way to approach emptiness is not to try to fill it but simply to be mindful of it. To notice the emptiness. The need is to move beyond the void to the fullness of Eros and the Shechinah. Yet, paradoxically, you can access the fullness of being only if you are willing to stay in the emptiness long enough to find your way. The path to Eros is filled with detours to pseudo Eros, but they are all dead ends. When we are so desperate for fullness, when the emptiness hurts too much, these detours seduce us off the path, often spinning us into painful places we never wanted to go.

Addiction is, at its root, the inability to stay in the emptiness. So we rush to fill the emptiness with whatever gives us the quickest hit of pseudo Eros, and pseudo Eros is virtually always addictive. It has many disguises—sex, food, public acclaim, drugs, work. The German writer Goethe was right when he defined addiction as anything you cannot stop doing. We are all addicts.

At our retreats, which are not geared toward drug or alcohol problems, people are thrown for a little bit of a loop by the opening talk that we give at orientation. It usually starts something like this: "I know you are all addicts—but I promise you it will be okay. You can break the habit. Indeed, here at the Tantra school, we insist you let the addiction go." At this point everyone is looking at each other and silently asking, "What is he talking about? We're not addicts. Did we come to the wrong place?" We keep on in this vein for some time until someone is finally fully exasperated and shouts out, "But I'm not an addict!" At which point we suggest that to check that claim, we need to define "addiction."

The definition that emerges is always something like: "Addiction is anything you are incapable of refraining from doing for twenty-four hours that is not essential to your physical health." After that is agreed, we pose the following question: "How many people here believe casual gossip about other people's ostensible shortcomings is essential for your physical health? How many people have succeeded in going twenty-four hours in their lives without talking negatively about someone else?" The place gets very quiet. We realize that almost all of us are addicted to negative gossip. We cannot go twenty-four hours—or much less time—without it! We are addicts!

When you think deeply about it, you realize that talking about other people is one of the easiest ways to engage conversation. Deeper still, it is one of the easiest ways to fill the emptiness. It is a form of pseudo Eros, a shortcut to pseudo fullness.

Watch carefully, and you will see that a millisecond before you are moved to casual slander you touch a moment of emptiness in yourself. Something in the mention of a person's name or in the topic of conversation subtly, almost invisibly, challenges your self-worth, adequacy, or dignity. Imperceptibly, your system moves to fill the emptiness with a quick hit of seeming fullness—gossip—which is only pseudo Eros.

At our Tantra retreats, rather than maintain silence, we invite everyone to mindful speech. Indeed, Kabbalah scholars point out that one of the defining characteristics of the Zohar mystics was that illumination happened not in solitary retreat but in groups engaged in sacred conversation. Fulfillment comes not from escaping but from engaging. It is how we talk to each other rather than how we are silent that defines who we truly are.

CHOCOLATE-COVERED RAISINS

The same thing happens with food every day without our realizing it. Our bodies can be our most blatant teachers. Our bodies are talking, but are we listening?

On a religious fast day a few years ago, I finally realized what fast days are all about. I was sitting at my desk, reading an article. Suddenly, chocolate-covered raisins popped into my mind. I felt very hungry for some. I got up to get a handful. Remembering that it was a fast day, I sat back down. The craving persisted. I thought to myself, "It's only late morning. I've only been fasting a few hours. I shouldn't be this hungry yet." Why did I so desperately desire chocolate-covered raisins?

I pondered the mystery, finally figuring out why. It was the article I was reading. It was written by a colleague of mine about a subject I myself had worked on extensively, but I had not yet published anything about it. Instead of my mind reading the article and screaming, "Jealousy! Emptiness!" it had read the article and blared out, "Chocolate-covered raisins!" Had I not been fasting, I would have proceeded to pop a couple of hundred calories' worth of those chocolate pills into my mouth and would have gone on to the next thing, never truly realizing the cause of my craving.

There's a wonderful short blessing in the Hebrew liturgy that is recited after eating. Strangely, the prayer begins with a unique formula that appears nowhere else in the liturgy: "You created many beings, each with its own unique emptiness." Yet we have just eaten; we are ostensibly feeling well-fed, full, happy, and thankful. So why are we talking about all these creatures having a unique emptiness?

Quite simply, because food and emptiness are the closest of intimates. Food can be used to fill the empty stomach, or it can be used to fill the empty soul. It can be used, and it can be abused. Addictive eating is born from the emptiness. Emptiness is like a shrewd foreign agent who hires food, rather than a beautiful woman, to seduce you. You give in to food's chocolate-covered charm, and as you devour it, the emptiness devours you.

One of the beauties of a spiritual system that invites an occasional fast day is that you can't just jump to devour. Instead, you have to sit there in the hunger, in the emptiness. From there you can observe the moments when you crave, seek out the source of the craving, and then discern whether this is wholesome or unwholesome hunger. Are you feasting or are you being feasted upon? Have you brushed up against the emptiness again? Did you fill it up with a quick fix, or did you take that precious extra moment to pursue the craving's source? That extra moment is the infinite distance between surface and depth. Next time, take the time to search out the source. Erotic presence is about going for the root, rather than snipping at the twigs.

AFTERTASTE

Now, if we are courageous enough to walk one step further, we will see that sex follows the same formula. Every human being engages in two very different forms of sexuality. The first is, by whatever your own inner standard may be, sacred sex, and the second, fallen sex. Everyone's examples will be different, but everyone understands the distinction.

How to tell the difference? Aftertaste. The first leaves you with a wonderful aftertaste; the second leaves you with an uncomfortable feeling, which you try to shrug off as quickly as possible—a minor or major spiritual hangover.

Watch yourself very carefully over an extended period of time (which is really the only path to enlightenment). You will see that shortly before you feel sexual arousal toward what is fallen sex, you somehow brush up against your emptiness. It may be an old tape triggered in your head by some association, perhaps a tape from childhood that says you are not worthy. It could be a feeling of jealousy or incompleteness triggered by a friend's accomplishment or one of a hundred other things. As soon as your system receives that jolt of emptiness, it moves frantically, yet imperceptibly, to send you symptoms of sexual arousal, hoping to fill the void quickly. Next time you find yourself following your arousal, ask yourself whether you are nourishing yourself with sexuality or you are trying to fill up the hole inside of you, desperately trying to avoid the void.

Now, here is a wild idea. Biblical practice suggests that, just as a fast day is helpful in sensitizing you to distinguish between wholesome and desperate eating, regular short periods of voluntary sexual fasting can be ever so enlightening. It is critical in helping you to distinguish between fallen and sacred sex, between the sexually erotic and nonerotic. It is a brilliant spiritual practice for the clarification of desire and the purification of sex. As a side benefit, sexual fasting is also the best practice available for reclaiming passion in a marriage, because anything that is always available, such as marital sex, can soon become terribly boring.

EMPTY WISDOM

The cherubs once again serve as our guide. Remember that the vortex of the Shechinah is no less than atop the Ark in the Holy of Holies, between the cherubs. "Between" is interpreted by the Kabbalists as a word that dances between the emptiness and the fullness.

In the first unpacking, "between," which is *bein* in Hebrew, is understood as the "empty space between the cherubs." *Bein* is the emptiest place in the world, hence the place in which the Shechinah dwells. This is a seeming endorsement of the emptiness. In a second understanding, "between the cherubs" is said to be the place where there is no emptiness. That is the place of the Shechinah—that is to say, of erotic fullness, the radical intensification of presence from which wells up the voice of God. This is a seeming endorsement of the fullness. The meaning underlying these paradoxically different understandings of *bein* ("between") is clear. Only when we can hold the emptiness does it become filled with the divine voice.

Beautifully, the Hebrew word *bein* also means "wisdom"—*binah*. For wisdom comes only when we are willing to stay in the emptiness long enough to hold our center and walk through it. When we try to fill it too quickly, we always wind up shocked and deeply unsettled when the emptiness does not go away. Instead, the void gets deeper, thicker, more palpable, virtually suffocating us.

ECHOES OF EMPTINESS: THE EROTIC AND THE ETHICAL

The arena where emptiness—nonerotic living—is most destructive is in the ethical. Every ethical failure comes from the absence of Eros. It is the inability to stay in the experience of emptiness that moves people to violate their ethics. All crimes are in some sense crimes of passion. But this is actually a misnomer. What we mean is that all crimes are rooted in the fear of passion's loss! We cannot imagine what life would be like without the Eros that we stand to lose.

For example, Joel finds out that his wife is having an affair. The betrayal opens up the void within. Afraid that she will leave if he confronts her, he slowly becomes a workaholic to dull the pain. Work for Joel has become pseudo Eros.

Or take Susan, who was verbally and physically abused by her mother. Never able to claim the dignity of her anger, she became gradually disempowered as a person. As an adult, she is constantly furious at her children, often lashing out brutally at them. She seeks to assure herself that she is still alive and powerful. For Susan, her displaced anger at her children is pseudo Eros.

Here are some more mundane examples. We cheat on income taxes because we think that the extra money will paper over some of the fear of life. Money becomes pseudo Eros. Or we exaggerate our accomplishments because we are afraid that our real story is insufficient to fill the void. Self-aggrandizement is pseudo Eros.

All of our inappropriate behaviors that violate our values are really us crying out, "Pay attention to me—I exist!" All forms of acting out are pseudo Eros. All forms of sexual harassment and abuse have their source in pseudo Eros. When the fullness of presence is violated and the other person becomes an object, not to meet our yearning but to cover over our emptiness, then sex is de-eroticized. Eros devolves into pseudo Eros. Desire is degraded to grasping. When sexual stories are told in ways that they did not happen—false complaints—and the normal hurt in human relationship is weaponized or manipulated as an instrument of malice, then the Eros descends into pseudo Eros. It is only the return to Eros that can move us out of a society that some call a rape culture in which women are violated, and others call a false-complaint culture in which men are socially murdered. Both abuse the sexual. All sexual abuse is pseudo Eros. Pseudo Eros will only be healed when we truly begin living the Erotic life.

Life is about walking through the void. Every time we walk through and not around the void, we come out stronger. Every time we are seduced by pseudo Eros, ethical breakdown is around the corner. There is no ethics without Eros.

The biblical text describes the pit into which Joseph was thrown by his jealous brothers: "The pit was empty; it had not water," reads the story. "But isn't this redundant?" ask the students. "If it had no water, don't we know that it was empty?" The master replies, "This was an emptiness that bred evil. Water it did not have, snakes and scorpions it did!" Emptiness always breeds ethical collapse in its wake.

Of course, the real pit at play in the story is not a pit in the earth. The pit is in Joseph's brothers' ground of being. Their own gaping sense of emptiness makes them envy Joseph so. Their inability to walk through their own pit (void) moves them to project a pit into the world, in which they would cast their brother. The snakes and scorpions come from the unacknowledged emptiness of the brothers.

When we respond to a person viscerally, it virtually always tells us more about ourselves than about the other person. The brothers' own felt emptiness—their pit—moved them to the murderous rage of attempted fratricide. You see, up until this point in the book of Genesis, one son had always been chosen as the inheritor of blessing. Abel was chosen over Cain, Shem over Ham and Yefet, Isaac over Ishmael, and Jacob over Esau. The brothers were convinced that Jacob, their father, was likewise going to choose Joseph over them. Joseph's existence called into question the integrity of the stories they told themselves, and they brushed up against the emptiness. When our old stories are called into question, we are challenged to walk through the void and re-story our lives at our higher level of consciousness. The inability to walk through the inevitable emptiness to the more evolved, deeper fullness on the other side is the source of all ethical collapse.

Ethics without Eros is doomed. Only from a place of fullness of being can we reach out in love to others. The first step to love is always self-love. If you don't fill yourself up with love, then you have precious little to dole out. But as long as your love is not rooted in your erotic matrix, the inside of your fullness, it is doomed to fail. You will have to rely on an ethical source outside yourself, which will always make you view yourself as a sinner. No one is ever able to consistently follow external rules that seem to violate their inner desires.

However, if ethics well up from the inside, if you are at the center, then sin is not disobedience but the violation of human well-being. In the end, all ethical failure is a violation of Eros—your own or someone else's.

CHAPTER FIFTEEN

THE THIRD FACE

YEARNING AND DESIRE

When I am on the inside, when I am fully present, I am able to access the third face of the erotic experience—yearning. Yearning, or desire, is an essential expression of love and Eros. As long as I am on the outside, I can ignore my deepest desires and stifle my longing. But longing is a vital strand in the textured fabric of Eros. It is of the essence of the Holy of Holies. As Rainer Maria Rilke put it so beautifully:

You see, I want a lot.
Perhaps I want everything:
the darkness that comes with every infinite fall
And the shivering blaze of every step up.

So many live on and want nothing,
and are raised to the rank of prince
by the slippery ease of their light judgments.

But what you love to see are faces
That do work and feel thirst.

THE SEXUAL MODELS THE EROTIC: YEARNING AND DESIRE

The yearning for contact is the essence of the sexual. Indeed, the yearning is often thought by poets and psychologists to be more pleasurable and intense than the fulfillment itself. Another word for yearning or longing is desire. Sex and desire are so inextricably bound that the very word *desire* evokes the sexual.

Intense desire means that I yearn for something that I do not have. In many systems of spirit, desire was thought to be the enemy of the sacred. For the cherub mystics, however, the sexual models the erotic and the erotic and the holy are one. It is in the sexual that we access the poignant and potent power of desire.

The sexual models the erotic. Yearning models the desire of reality itself to evolve toward more and more creativity, love, complexity, and consciousness. Yearning is the interior feeling of evolution.

Sex models Eros because in great sex you experience the yearning force of being. Sex models Eros because the same desire that drives us to make sexual contact drives all of reality to make erotic contact. It is precisely this erotic contact at every level of reality—from electromagnetic to cellular to cultural—that drives all of reality.

In living the Erotic life you feel the yearning—the radical desire—for more and more complexity, consciousness, creativity, love, and uniqueness. Thus, at the most essential level, reality is desire. It is in the sexual that we are meant to access both the dignity and demand of desire.

It was perhaps D. H. Lawrence who, more than any other modern writer, captured both desire's demand and its dignity:

And down his mouth comes to my mouth! and down
His bright dark eyes come over me, like a hood
Upon my mind! his lips meet mine, and a flood

Of sweet fire sweeps across me, so I drown
Against him, die, and find death good.[31]

THE EROS OF YEARNING AND DESIRE

We are filled with desires. Everyone has chocolate-covered raisins in their lives. How should we relate to them—as ally or enemy, teachers or tempters? Here again the cherubs hint the way. This is the place to introduce another set of cherubs that appear in biblical myth. The first, of course, are the cherubs above the Ark. The second pair make a dramatic earlier appearance in the biblical book of Genesis as the two cherubs that guard the way to the Garden of Eden. They stand with "a fiery revolving sword, guarding the path to the Tree of Life." The Zohar speaks for much of the mystical tradition when it suggests that the cherubs above the Ark are one and the same as those in the Garden of Eden. The temple in biblical myth is called the Garden of God. The mystics reveal that the Garden of Eden and the temple are in mythical terms on the same plane of consciousness.*

In the Garden of Eden story, Eve, overcome by desire, eats from the forbidden tree and gives Adam a taste of the fruit as well. When confronted by God, Adam blames Eve. Eve blames the serpent. According to the mystic Isaac Luria, had they but waited three more hours, the Tree of Life would have been theirs. Full erotic fulfillment in all the senses of spirit, soul, and body would have been realized. But they could not wait. Unable to stay in the emptiness, they required an immediate hit of pseudo Eros. For their failure to take personal responsibility and for their inability to resist the blandishments of pseudo desire, they are exiled from the garden.

The goal of personal and cosmic history is to return to the garden. The cherubs, however, stand at the entrance to the garden with swirling swords of flame. Anyone who attempts to return to paradise through the

---

*   The mystics were brilliant exegetic readers of sacred text. They pointed to a series
    of textual structures that suggest the Garden of Eden is identical with the temple.

drugs of pseudo Eros is burned by the cherubic sword. The same cherubs stand above the Ark in the Holy of Holies. They give instruction in the path of Hebrew Tantra. If we are willing to do the work, the temple cherubs will ultimately lead us back to Eden. Pseudo Eros will give way to true Eros. Pseudo desire will give way to true desire. For to be in the garden, which is the temple, is to live in quivering desire in every facet of our lives.

THE EYE OF DESIRE

For many of the erotic Hebrew mystics, the symbol of confused desire was Alexander the Great. He conquered almost the entire known world of his day. Yet the cherub mystics of his time insisted that without entering the Garden of Eden and becoming an erotic lover, Alexander would remain empty and desperate.

The ancient Hebrew legend tells of Alexander seeking the Garden of Eden, symbol of erotic fulfillment, on the African continent. Now, the old cherub mystics had a little bit of a soft spot for Alexander. They saw him not only as a confused seeker of desire but also as a seeker of wisdom. So along the way to Eden, Alexander is depicted as growing wiser and slowly divesting the personality of a pure conqueror. He engages in what later erotic Hebrew mystics will call *birur*, or in English, "the clarification of desire."

In one of his adventures on the quest for Eden, Alexander is confronted by an army of women warriors—mythological symbols of Eros and Shechinah. They say to him, "It is not worth your while to attack us. For if we kill you, you will be known as 'the king killed by women,' and if you kill us, you will be known as 'the cruel king who killed women.'" This is his first lesson in the dance with desire. Neither conquest nor submission will do.

Next, Alexander asks these same women for bread to eat. Instead, they serve him loaves of gold. In response to his astonishment, they reply, "You have enough bread in your own city. You came all the way here because bread would not fill you. You needed gold." The second lesson:

the need for clarification of desire. Be honest about what you truly need to fill you.

At this point, Alexander is ready to encounter the Garden of Eden. He eats some fish and recognizes by its scent that the water was from Eden. Smell is considered by the mystics to be the most erotic of the senses. He follows the fragrance to the gates of paradise. He cries out, "Entry!" but is refused access. He is not yet enlightened. Alexander pleads to receive at least some of Eden's wisdom. From behind the gate, a gift is extended. It is an eyeball. Sensing its magical quality, Alexander has the eyeball inspected and weighed. It turns out that this small object weighs more than all the masses of gold and silver he has with him.

"How could this be?" he asks his sages in consternation. They reply that it is a human eyeball—representing desire that can never be satisfied. Human desire is so heavy that it weighs man down. Without a doubt, it weighs more than all the gold and silver that Alexander could carry with him. Unconvinced, Alexander asks the sages for proof. They sprinkle some dust over the eyeball so it can no longer see, and it immediately reverts to its natural weight.

On Alexander's quest for wisdom, he needed to learn the futility of unclear desire. He is empty, as is symbolized in his request for food to fill him. The Shechinah warrior women of Eros teach him to be clear about his desires. Gold and not bread. Do not pretend to be working for your core survival (bread) when it is really gold (honor and glory) that you are after. Know what you want and pursue it.

Finally, know that your desire can never be fully sated, even by all the world's gold and silver. The human eye of acquisition is a black hole of desire, always demanding more. You need to change your essential relationship to the world. Let go of taking, and embrace the law of yearning. In this law, we deepen our relationship to desire. First we clarify our true desire and seek its fulfillment. As Buddha is reported to have said in the original Pali Canon, "Have few desires but have great ones." In part, we are able to achieve our desire. In part, it remains beyond our grasp. It is in this second part that we make our more radical move. Instead of needing to fill our desire, we let the desire itself fill us! This is the hidden teaching on the Eros of desire that the warrior women transmitted to Alexander.

DESIRE IS HOLY

The biblical mystic lovingly counsels us to be with ourselves and gently watch our desires as they come and go. We are invited not to eradicate them, not to get off the wheel of suffering that they are said to create, but to engage in *birur teshuka*, the clarification of desire. To love someone is to wait on his or her desire, to watch it stir, to delight in its presence, to help it crystallize and form.

Eros is to be on the inside, including the inside of your desire. Being on the inside invites you to clarify your desires, yet not transcend them. True desire is attained through the deep meditation in which you access the internal witness. This is a place of detachment, from which you survey with penetrating but loving eyes all of your desires. This place of internal witness allows you to move beyond an addictive attachment to any particular desire. At that point the person engaged in *birur* (clarification) does not abandon desire. Rather, she moves to connect with those desires that are truest to her deepest and most authentic self. It is, as T. S. Eliot once wrote, in the empty space "between the spasm and the desire" that the person is born.

For the biblical mystic, detachment is a strategy, not a goal. In the end, you must not remain a spectator in the drama of your own existence. Rather, you need to become the lead actor on your stage by always living on the inside and never getting lost in the luxury of distance or detachment, so you can fully merge with the part the universe has invited you to play. Longing and desire are good not because we believe that all of our yearning will be fulfilled or realized, but because the yearning itself fulfills us. The desire itself fills the emptiness. When we yearn to grow, when we are alive with desire, we touch fulfillment.

Hasidic lore tells of Hannah who was a walking prayer, constantly calling out to God. People would see her on the streets, carrying her groceries with a light step, all the while with eyes facing upward, a soundless prayer on her lips. Pass by her window, and you would see her by the stove or by the sink, lips lost in prayer, pleading with the heavens for something, for anything, for everything. A neighbor with a jealous eye came to her one day and whispered, "And so why hasn't God answered all your impassioned prayers? You are just wasting your time."

Hannah was shaken. What if this neighbor were right? "When will God answer, and why should I wait?" she asked herself. And so Hannah abandoned her beseeching. She gave up on her yearning. And although the groceries seemed heavier, the stove colder, she refused to pray. Until one night, a divine voice called to Hannah in a dream, "Why have you stopped praying to Me?"

Hannah retorted, "Well, you never answered, so I stopped asking." To which the Divine replied, "Don't you realize, every call of yours is itself my response? Your great yearning is my greatest gift." With this, Hannah's ceaseless prayer came back to her lips. Her burden was again lightened, and her stove was ablaze.

Depression, at its core, is the depression of desire. When we lose touch with our authentic desire, we become listless and apathetic. There is wonderful Eros in desire. It is what connects us most powerfully with our own pulsating aliveness.

'TIS BETTER TO BLEED

In a published dialogue between a well-known Buddhist teacher and me (Marc), the teacher challenged me persistently on this issue of desire. "After all," he said, "if you give up the desire for life, then death will not be horrifying and painful."

"No," I responded. "If I give up the desire for life, I will already be dead." Since the debate took place in a kitchen in Jerusalem, I picked up a knife. "If I took this knife and cut my arm, would it bleed?" I asked.

"Of course."

"Now, what if, with the same knife, I cut my hair? No blood. Why? Because the cells in my hair are dead. And dead cells do not bleed."

Part of the Eros of longing is to experience pain as well as joy. That is why biblical mystics viewed the inability to grieve and weep as a sign of great spiritual illness.

"From the day the temple was destroyed, all the gates are closed; the gates of tears are not closed." So reads a fifth-century Hebrew wisdom text. The Eros of tears, an inevitable corollary of longing and desire, is the way back to the Eros of the temple, to the inside, and to a full sense of your own aliveness. Nachman of Bratslav, an erotic master of the inside, writes, "A human being is like an onion: strip away layer after layer, and all that remains are the tears." To reach the inner recesses of a thing, one must be willing to weep.

THE YEARNING FORCE OF BEING

The mystical tradition tells of time portals, each capable of accessing different regions of our interior castle. The mystical masters understood that the temple of Eros was built not in space but in time. The Sabbath—a temple in time—is patterned in its spiritual blueprint after the temple in Jerusalem. The axis mundi of the Sabbath, its Holy of Holies, takes place near dusk as the Sabbath ebbs away into sunset. In the tradition, this is the time of tears. Not crying in response to personal sorrow but tears that well up from the yearning force of being. This was when the disciples would gather around the master's table and sing songs of longing, often well into the night. Cultural anthropologist Victor Turner called this "liminal time," the time between the cracks when all the gates are open. Here is one of the tradition's tales of Eros:

> It is near dusk as the Sabbath ebbs away. The disciples are gathered. The master Levi Isaac of Berditchev, holiest teacher, rises to speak. He wants to explain to his disciples not the wonder of creation or the mystery of the chariot, but merely that God is the inside of the inside, the erotic life force of the universe, and that therefore every person's life matters.
> He begins his discourse with an elegant teaching from the Talmud demonstrating the reality of God. "Do you understand?" he queries.
> "No," they answer . . . heads hanging.

He then takes them on a dance of light, intricately weaving
the mysteries of the Zohar, which illuminate God's presence in
the world. "Do you understand?" he asks again.

"No," they answer . . . heads low.

In desperation he begins to tell stories, tales revealing great
mysteries. "Now do you understand?" he asks.

"No," they answer, heads still hanging.

So he becomes quiet and begins to sing a melody of
yearning, of longing, of pining. For a few moments he sings
alone, then one and then another joins in, until they become
one voice. Yearning. Pining. Longing. Levi Isaac did not need to
ask again. They raised their heads. They understood.

I YEARN, THEREFORE I AM

It is said that the Great Maggid would convene his inner circle every
night to teach them the sacred texts. All of his greatest students would
gather. The Maggid would begin to speak, "And God said . . ." and Reb
Zushya would leap up, overwhelmed with longing. He would yell out,
"And God said! God said!" He would spin around and around like a leaf
in the wind, and then faint, unconscious for the rest of the teaching.
Every night it was the same thing. The other disciples would tease him.
"Zushya, you're missing all the holy teachings!" This teasing went on for
days and days until finally the master said, "Leave him alone; he's the only
one who gets it."

For the Hebrew mystic, unlike his Buddhist or Greek cousins, desire
and longing are sacred. Eros is the yearning force of being. I yearn, therefore I am. To be cut off from the Eros of yearning is to be left in the cold
of nonexistence. To yearn is to be aflame.

This longing is built into the very fabric of human existence. In the
Hebrew story of the creation of humankind as well as in Plato's myth told
in *The Symposium*, all human beings were initially both male and female.
"Male and female he created them," reads the biblical myth. Then they were
separated from each other. And now they yearn to reunite with each other.

According to the biblical myth recorded in the Zohar, this was the grand design of creation. First, human beings needed to realize that they are essentially interconnected. No human being stands alone. None is essentially alienated, lonely, or separate. Then they must be separated from each other. At this point the longing for reunion begins. That yearning will be the driving force in human growth and spiritual unfolding.

The difference between Plato and the biblical wisdom is that in the latter it is a longing that can essentially be fulfilled. Fulfillment is a genuine option and not an impossible mirage situated over the next hill by a punishing and cruel universe. Yearning is the essential formula of the universe.

INSIDES AND OUTSIDES

This yearning, however, is more than mere myth or metaphor. The interior science of enlightenment teaches us to feel the yearning that lies on the very inside of reality. It is the eye of the heart and the eye of the mind that see and feel the cosmos yearning. All of the longing, desire, and yearning that we have described above participate in the yearning of reality itself. When you yearn, you are an expression of reality's longing. Your desires are a fractal-like expression of the desire of existence itself. As we saw earlier, all of reality has both insides and outsides. Every event, every person, everything has both an interior and an exterior.

The interior experience of being in love is a set of feelings. They may include feelings of mad devotion, ecstasy, delight, gifting, yearning, wholeness, and fullness of presence. The exterior experience of being in love is reflected in the neuroscience of the brain and in a set of concrete actions taken by the person in love. An entire cocktail of love chemicals are secreted in the brain. New neural pathways are formed throughout our brains and bodies as a direct expression of our being in love. We perform concrete actions, which might include buying gifts, moving to a different city, moving in together, sex, writing poetry, and much more. You yearn for more and more contact, mutuality, recognition, union, and embrace. Such is the nature of being in love. There is a constant yearning to deepen, to expand, and to grow together.

This experience of love with its emphasis on yearning has an exterior. It is called evolution. Perhaps this seems surprising. The popular mind, after all, sees evolution as an objective process described by science. But evolution is not only a dry set of scientific theories. It is the greatest spiritual revolution of our time. Evolution tells us that the universe is not merely a fact but a story. A story is going somewhere. The story has plot and direction. The plot line is evolution. That means that reality is a story. Reality is not only eternal, but it is also evolving. The story has a trajectory.

The emerging scientific understanding: Reality is a story with both interior and exteriors. There is a universe story with plot and direction, and you are personally implicated as a major actor in the trajectory of this story.

PLOT LINES IN THE UNIVERSE STORY

Truth be told, the universe story of evolution has at least five core trajectories, or plot lines. Taken together they are the central drama of the cosmos and of our lives.

The first trajectory is the movement of existence to higher and higher forms of complexity. Let's look, for example, at what is often called "the evolutionary chain." The evolutionary chain moves from atom to amoeba (single-celled organisms) to plants to early animals to mammals to early humans walking upright to an awake and enlightened human being. But this is only an exterior description of evolution. What is the interior experience of evolution? The interior of evolution is yearning. If you could feel the inside of evolution, you would feel its yearning.

What does evolution yearn for? Well, just look at its exterior trajectory of evolution and you will know. Atoms to amoebas to plants to animals to mammals to early humans to enlightened humans. What is the trajectory of evolution that we see in this snapshot of the evolutionary chain? We see first that evolution moves from simplicity to complexity. But that is just the outside, objective view. Felt from the inside, we might say that evolution yearns. On the inside, evolution feels yearning. Evolution yearns to evolve from simplicity to complexity.

Remember all of reality, all the way up and all the way down, has interior and exteriors. Seen from the inside then, with the faculty of perception that Integral theory likes to refer to as the eye of the spirit, we can access the felt interior quality of evolution itself. Remember again that we are not separate from evolution. Rather, evolution, when it becomes conscious, awakens as us in person. That is precisely what we mean by conscious evolution. That means that we can access the interior of evolution's longing through our own deepest yearnings.

To see what evolution yearns for we need only to see the trajectories of evolution.

Let's look for a moment at four more trajectories. One of these trajectories is the movement to more and more consciousness. This is easy to see in our snapshot of the evolutionary chain. The more complex a life form is, the more conscious it is. For example, an amoeba is more conscious than an atom, a plant is more conscious than an amoeba; a dog is more conscious than a plant, and a human is more conscious than an animal. Finally, an enlightened human is more conscious than an ordinary human, who goes about life asleep to her true nature and true situation. Felt from the inside, we might say that evolution yearns for more and more consciousness.

The third trajectory of evolution is the movement to more and more creativity. A dog is more creative than an amoeba, and a human being is more creative than a dog. Felt from the inside, we might say that evolution yearns for more and more creativity.

The fourth trajectory is the movement toward more and more uniqueness. An atom is unique. An amoeba, however, is more differentiated and unique than an amoeba. This is a natural truth because an amoeba has an atomic structure—that is, it is made up of atoms—but it also has a more advanced property of uniqueness, which is called "cells." Cells add a level of differentiation and uniqueness to atoms. A dog is more complex and more uniquely differentiated than an atom. A human being is more complex and uniquely differentiated than a dog. A spiritually awake human being, living consciously and focused on sharing his unique gifts, is more complex and differentiated than a person who is unconscious and spiritually asleep. Felt from the inside, we might say that evolution yearns for more and more uniqueness.

The fifth trajectory of evolution is toward deeper and higher levels of love. By love we mean not merely ordinary love, but outrageous love. Ordinary love is often a human strategy to get more security and comfort. Outrageous love is the movement of all of reality—including human beings—to more and more contact, more and more care, more and more union, and more and more embrace. Romantic love, at the human level of reality, is absolutely love. But it does not live alone in the universe. Romantic love is the human expression of the outrageous love that permeates the universe.

Let's look at just a snippet from the evolutionary chain—how a plant displays more love than an amoeba. We have an enormous amount of literature today on the love life of plants, as we saw in our discussion of the cosmo-erotic universe. A dog shows more love than a plant. A human being is capable of more love than a dog. Now, dog lovers always object to this sentence. I am madly in love with dogs, but the sentence stands. Dogs do not build hospitals to care for disadvantaged dogs. That is a human capacity of love that does not exist in the animal kingdom.

Humans don't just build hospitals because they have the cognitive ability to do so, which is lacking in dogs. Rather, humans have the capacity to love and care for those who are not their kin or master and to whom they have no relation of any kind whatsoever other than their common humanity. Advanced humans with this kind of evolved world-centric consciousness are regularly willing to sacrifice everything for their fellow humans. Neither animals nor mammals have yet to demonstrate this consistent quality of love for other animals or mammals to whom they have no relation. Felt from the inside, we might say that evolution yearns for more and more love. Rumi referred to this longing when he said, "I never knew that God, too, desires us."

THE EVOLUTION OF LOVE

How do you feel the yearning that is the interior experience of evolution? You trace your own desire back to its source. You realize that your yearnings are not small or petty or pathetic. Rather, your pathos is the pathos of existence itself. Your pathos and Eros participate in—they are not apart from—the cosmos. Your longings are not rooted only in your personal psyche. Rather, your pathos participates in the Eros of reality itself.

Evolution is not an objective process happening out there. It is happening in you. When you evolve, then evolution happens in you as an individual. When you realize your personal yearning is part of the yearning of cosmic evolution—of which your personal evolution is a fractal—then evolution awakens to itself as you in person. Evolution becomes conscious of itself through you. This is the great movement from unconscious to conscious evolution. Your yearning participates in the yearning of evolution itself. Trace your yearning back to its source and you will know that this is true.

Another way to talk about yearning is to call it telos. This Greek word means that something has direction. It is a yearning to go somewhere, to get closer, to be more, to go deeper, and to feel more. All of these directions are part of the telos of reality. Yearning, then, expresses both the Eros and the telos of reality. If you put the words Eros and telos together, you get what our beloved colleague Barbara Marx Hubbard calls teleros. We live not just in an erotic universe but in a telerotic universe. Eros in its true nature is always teleros.

Thus, the third face of Eros is the yearning force of being. Said differently, the third face of Eros is to participate in the telerotic nature of reality. To live an erotic life is to know that you are personally implicated in evolution. It is not a process out there but the nature of reality awakening in you and as you. To live an erotic life is to realize that your personal transformation is but a form of evolution taking place within you. Your drives for contact in sexuality, for innovation, and ultimately for transformation are all expressions of the evolutionary impulse of all that is awakening as you. The evolutionary impulse is but another expression of what we have called Eros. It is the heart of existence itself.

CHAPTER SIXTEEN

THE FOURTH FACE

WHOLENESS AND INTERCONNECTIVITY: ON THE INTIMATE UNIVERSE, REALITY AS ALLUREMENT

Longing, desire, and tears remind us of the fourth strand in the erotic weave. They whisper to us that we are all interconnected within a greater wholeness. No life stands alone. The feeling of standing alone is experienced as a violation of the very nature of reality. Reality is a larger whole in which all is interconnected. Everything is connected to everything else. Everything yearns for ever-deeper contact. We are all parts of a larger whole.

THE SEXUAL MODELS THE EROTIC:WHOLENESS AND INTERCONNECTIVITY

Wholeness and interconnectivity are nowhere more clearly manifested than in the sexual drive. We are born with an urge to merge. We do not feel whole unto ourselves. We feel like we are part of a larger whole. It is the sexual drive that never lets us forget that we are not whole merely unto ourselves. The sexual reminds us constantly that we yearn for connection and wholeness beyond our separate selves. In great sex you feel the urge to connect, to make the deepest possible contact, to be the most intimate that you can possibly be. In that contact, in that connection, in that intimacy, you become more whole. The Chilean poet Pablo Neruda is direct in his understated declaration of this drive for connection that animates all of reality:

> *I want*
> *to do with you what spring does with the cherry trees.*[32]

Musician Bruce Springsteen, in his Jersey-shore kind of way, is even more unvarnished in singing about the erotic drive for any sliver of intimate connection, as his song "Human Touch" attests:

> *Baby, in a world without pity*
> *Do you think what I'm askin's too much*

A world without pity is a world which feels random, haphazard, and fundamentally disconnected. Everything is apart from everything else. The yearning is for wholeness, for connection. One doesn't require metaphysics to move from loneliness to loving and from alienation to connection. All that is required is the erotic mystical magic of human touch.

> *I just want to feel you in my arms*
> *Share a little of that human touch*

Sex models Eros because the drive for connection, for great whole-ness, that moves the sexual is the same drive for wholeness and connec-tivity that motivates all of our social, cultural, and creative endeavors. But the sexual model of the erotic in this face of interconnectivity and wholeness is even more fundamental than that. For classical mystics like Plato, sex models Eros because in the sexual we are drawn to merge with the prior unity, the original wholeness, that inexorably calls us home. For the evolutionary cherub mystics, sex models Eros because the experience of wholeness promised by the sexual is the strange attractor that moves the entire evolutionary process forward.

THE EROS OF WHOLENESS AND INTERCONNECTIVITY

In the movie *Castaway*, Chuck Noland (Tom Hanks) is a FedEx employee who survives a cargo plane crash, only to be stranded on an isolated island. He somehow learns to survive but is overcome with loneliness. One of the FedEx cargo packages that has washed up contains a Wilson volleyball. Using his blood, Chuck paints a face on the volleyball and names it "Wilson." Wilson becomes his companion, and he talks to the ball as if it were a person. After several years, however, although his sur-vival seems assured, he cannot stay on the island. He risks his life to leave. There is something far more elemental than survival that pulls him to set out on the ocean in a handmade raft. When we cannot make contact with the interior of another person, life becomes not worth living. Chuck Noland desperately needs contact with another human being—not just with one of the animals on the island or even the majestic beauty of nature. He needs a person who shares not only a parallel exterior but also an interior that is similar to his own inner form.

The drive for contact is the essential nature of existence, not some fringe level of reality. Contact is, literally, a survival need—so funda-mental that it overrides everything else. Chuck Noland prefers to take the precarious raft and cast himself into the open sea with only a small chance of physically surviving rather than remain isolated on the island without interior contact with another similar being.

This is what the ancient mystics meant when they said in the book of Genesis, "It is not good for the human to be alone." The word *good* is the key refrain in chapter one of Genesis. After every stage of the world's emergence, the text reads, "God saw that it was good." Then in chapter two, the text suddenly exclaims, "*Lo tov heyot ha'adam levado*" ("It is not good for the human to be alone"—or better translated from the Hebrew, "to be lonely"). All of the good of creation is "not good" if we are lonely. To be lonely is not merely a human neurotic condition—it is in violation of the essential nature of life, which is interconnected and whole. To be lonely is to be cut off from the interior of another, isolated in surface existence. Living on the outside, by yourself, is nonerotic, no matter how successful you are or how many people you are surrounded by.

To be lonely is to be apart and not *a part of*. The truth is that everything is part of the great whole. The world is not in a natural state of war but in a natural state of Eros. Everything is fundamentally interconnected. No part is apart from the larger wholeness. All parts are an inextricable part of the whole. Indeed, the very fabric of reality is parts and wholes. Every part is both a whole unto itself and part of a larger reality. This is the nature of existence all the way up and all the way down the chain of being. Nothing stands apart. All is interconnected as part of the great whole of the universe.

As evidence, we need only look at the building blocks of nature. A quark is a subatomic particle. From one limited perspective, it stands alone as a whole unto itself. From a wider perspective, it's imminently clear that the quark is interconnected with other quarks. It is part of a larger subatomic whole. The subatomic particles then come together to form a new emergent, a new deeper whole called an atom. An atom is a new whole that has depth. It has both subatomic and atomic particles. The atom, however, is not separate from other atoms. Rather, it has myriad lines of interconnectivity with the surrounding atomic structures. So an atom (like a quark) is both a part unto itself and part of a larger whole. The atoms then form molecules, which then evolve into complex molecules, which at some point awaken as cells, which much later evolve into multicellular creatures, and so on. Each level is a new, unique emergent that transcends and includes all the previous levels. This is the nature of evolution on every level of and in every facet of existence. We are all wholes unto ourselves and parts of larger wholes at the same time. In this sense, the entire world is interconnected. Interconnection is everything and everywhere.

As we mentioned earlier, the word *religion* traces its source to the Latin root *ligare*, which, similar to "ligament," is about connectivity. Religion's goal is to re-*ligare*—to reconnect us. Religion's original intention was to take us to that inside place where we could indeed experience the essential interconnectivity of all reality. All of existence is one great quilt of being, and we are all patches in its magnificent multifaceted pattern.

Eros is what allows us to move past the feeling of isolation and separation and experience ourselves as part of the quilt. To sunder our connection to Eros is therefore to sin. Not only would we lose the source of life's greatest pleasure, but we would also undermine the building blocks of connection without which the world would ultimately collapse.

At this point, then, it should not surprise us that in the temple myth, the Holy of Holies is the place of the *Even Shetiya*, the foundation stone of the world. It is that stone, a symbol of Eros, that holds the world together. Eros is the interconnectivity of reality. Eros, wrote the great poet Emerson, is "an ascendancy of the soul." Its place could be nowhere other than the Holy of Holies.

In the Kabbalistic myth, the great sin that caused what is called "the shattering of the vessels" was the sin of separation. Each divine force—*sefira*—held itself apart, autonomous and independent, free of any dependency on the other *sefirot* (plural of *sefira*). The result was that each independent *sefira* was unable to hold its light and ultimately shattered, causing great cosmic disarray. The *tikkun*—the fixing of the shattering—is experiencing every point of existence in connection, as part of the quilt of being.

In this sense, mystics were often also magicians. Ecstasy and magic are in the end inextricably bound up. Both seek to access the myriad lines of connection that undergird the wondrous web of existence. A child intuitively understands this magic. Psychology dismissively refers to childlike intuition as "magical thinking" and sees maturity as the triumph of the rational mind over the imagination. Yet the mystic insists that the child is at least partially right. It is not for naught that the magical Harry Potter books swept the world with such speed. Children who had never read before were suddenly reading hundreds of pages—volume after volume. Children felt that they were finally given something that was true to their spirit. The sacred child in us understands that the world is filled with magic. The world is filled with invisible lines of connection.

Eros is another word for magic and enchantment, the knowledge that everything is alive and intertextured—interwoven and filled with meaning. The experience of sin is the feeling that things, and you, are not holding together, that you are falling apart. Eros is the drive to wholeness and thus to healing and health.

LOVE KNOWS NO DISTANCE: THE NONLOCAL UNIVERSE

The interconnectivity of being is neither doctrine nor dogma. Rather, it is the fully accessible nature of reality if we just take the time to notice. Being enmeshed in a web of connection is the essential erotic experience of mystics throughout the ages. But the rest of us catch glimpses of it as well. We have all known those moments of seemingly inexplicable coincidences—a mother having a piercing pain in her chest precisely when her daughter two thousand miles away has been in a car accident, or that time when you thought of an old friend only to come home to a message from that person on your answering machine. These subtle synchronicities are all part of our daily reality. They are the faint yet persistent whisperings of the universe saying, "You are not alone. Love knows no distance." The all is connected to the all.

In the last twenty-five years, an enormous amount of serious scientific investigation has been done into what is called "nonlocal distance healing." It involves the ability of a person at great distances to effect healing. The results of such healing have been verified through many scientifically sound experiments that measure indicators of health, ranging from protecting red blood cells to lowering blood pressure and much more. What is critical is that these experiments reveal that we are not discrete units but rather interconnected indiscrete "unities." Like a network of rivers that interweave along their way back to the sea, we are beings fully woven into each other and thus able to traverse all the frontiers of separateness, including space and even time.

Physics has for years been speaking about a nonlocal universe. One of the recent leaders in this work is Irish physicist John Stewart Bell. Bell showed that if distant objects have once been in contact, a change in one causes an immediate change in the other. It is irrelevant how far apart they are. Even if they are later at opposite ends of the universe, the connection is not broken. We have known forever that there is a deeper level of consciousness available when we allow ourselves to let go of our separateness even as we maintain the individual integrity so necessary for responsibility and ethical action in the world.

Similarly, the worlds of music, dance, and, most of all, orgasm, allow us glimpses of our higher reality. Here again the sexual models the erotic—the experience of being on the inside of reality where all of being yearns for connection and every living thing knows it has a patch called home that is part of the great quilt of the universe. Outrageous love is the Eros of connection—the underlying interdependence of things, the bond between all living things, the emotional ether in which we all live.

LOVE LETTERS AND LOVE NUMBERS

In biblical mysticism, love and oneness are identical. In Hebrew, there is a mystical technique called *gematria* in which each letter, and thus each word, has a numerical value. The Hebrew word for "love," *ahava*, has a numerical value of thirteen. *Echad*, meaning "one," also has a numerical value of thirteen. To the Kabbalistic mind, this is more than just a coincidence. It is as if a mystical law has been encoded into the letters of these words. Love is oneness, and oneness is love. "One" is but another word for the erotic interconnectivity of all being.

But the pattern of mystical meaning continues, for these two words added together equal twenty-six. Twenty-six is a central number in Hebrew mysticism because it is the numerical value of God's four-letter name: Yud-Hei-Vav-Hei, the divine name of healing and love. Thus, God is one is love. Love is the universe's way of embracing us and telling us that we are not alone. We have a home, a *bayit*. We are connected. One + One = One.

THE WATER-DRAWING RITUAL

The biblical Yom Kippur Day of At-one-ment ceremony—in which the high priest enters the secret garden, the Holy of Holies—is actually part one of a two-part ritual. It begins on Yom Kippur as the priest immerses himself five times in the living waters. The second part takes place in the temple courtyard only a few days later and is called the "Ceremony of the Water Drawing." The primary ritual act is simply the pouring of water. The ceremony is accompanied by a festival of Eros, described in great detail in the sources. It is an ecstatic event of dance, music, song, and prayer. All of the mystics and masters fully participate, mixing with the masses in holy revelry and passion.

Regarding this event, Hillel the Elder, who was wont to whirl in ecstasy throughout the festival, is reported to have said, "If I am here, all is here." The Zohar elliptically comments that "I am here" means "the Shechinah that is called 'I.'" This is the place where Hillel and everyone present transcended separation, re-*ligaring* with the river of being, dissolving all boundaries between human and God. "I" and "all" were, in Hillel's experience, ultimately interwoven. Eros—Shechinah—reigned supreme. Hillel incarnated the erotic life.

AN INTIMATE UNIVERSE

The interwoven universe is the interconnected universe. Interconnectivity takes place in wholeness, the fourth face of Eros. Interconnectivity is the exterior face of wholeness. The interior of wholeness is intimacy. Or, said differently, the interior of interconnectivity is intimacy.

Eros makes one grand proclamation about the nature of reality. We live in an intimate universe. That is what we mean when we say that reality is Eros. Existence is interconnection, and that means that the universe feels. The universe feels intimate. To be non-intimate is to be out of integrity, for integrity means to be integrated, to be connected with, to be interwoven in the larger fabric of being. We might say that intimacy is integral. Anything that is not integral is not intimate, or not erotic. Integral means that the parts are connected and intimate with each other.

To cite but one example, the field of integral thought is intimate and interconnected. In integral thought, science must be connected to spirit. Biology must be connected to physics. Economics must be connected to ethics. Technology must be connected to beauty. The beautiful must be connected to the good. An intimate universe is an integral universe. To be integral is to be intimate. To be integral is to be erotic. To say that reality is erotic is to say that reality is intimate. Interconnectivity is the structural nature of the universe. Intimacy is the feel of the universe. The universe feels, and the universe feels love.

Have you ever fallen in love? If the answer is yes, then you know the truth of the next sentence. When you are in love you feel most at home in the universe. Why should this be so? Because being in love is the nature of reality.* All of existence is in love with all of existence. That is not poetic flight of fancy. Rather, it is the truest expression of reality in its scientific exteriors and its subjective interiors. The reason we feel at home in the universe when we are in love is because that is when we are most

---

* Survival of the fittest begins to mean what Darwin originally intuited, and not what his teachings were distorted by neo-Darwinists to mean. Survival of the fittest means that what survives is what fits with all dimensions of reality—interiors and exteriors. To survive (as leading-edge, evolutionary psychologists rebelling against the old reductionisms in their field have pointed out) is to fit with both insides and outsides. That means that to survive is to be connected to the most beauty, the most love, the deepest values of collaboration, and the highest vision of community, as well as to the most efficient emergent technologies of food gathering and protection.

aligned with the essential nature of existence. It is in the wild nights when true love awakens as sex that finds us home. As Emily Dickinson wrote:

> *Wild Nights—Wild Nights!*
> *Were I with thee*
> *Wild Nights should be*
> *Our luxury!*
>
> *Futile—the Winds—*
> *To a Heart in port—*
> *Done with the Compass—*
> *Done with the Chart!*
>
> *Rowing in Eden—*
> *Ah, the Sea!*
> *Might I but moor—tonight—*
> *In Thee!*

REALITY IS ALLUREMENT

When we are in love, we have two fundamental experiences. The first is belonging; the second is allurement. When we are in love, we are attracted. We are drawn to make contact.

So let's—in an erotic act—weave the strands together. There are three ways of speaking about the fourth face of Eros, wholeness. First, we live in an interconnected universe. Second, we live in an intimate universe. Third, we live in an alluring universe. Existence is allurement. Allurement is a quality of interconnectivity and intimacy. To be intimate is not only to be close but also to be allured. To be in love is to be attracted, not merely to be connected. Love is not only to rest in the eternity of being but is also the quality of presence.

Usually when we access the interior of reality (the first face of Eros), we feel into being. This is the experience of spacious eternity. We feel the quality of resting in the presence. Presence is, of course, the second face of Eros. We feel into the unchanging and undying nature of eternity. This is what we are alluding to when we say that love is eternal. We are pointing toward this quality of being that we feel on the inside—an infinitely sweet quality of forever presence, which is the nature of being itself.

The Russian-American novelist Vladimir Nabokov writes beautifully of this sense of intimacy with all of being:

> Here, I became aware of the world's tenderness, the profound
> beneficence of all that surrounded me, the blissful bond
> between me and all of creation, and I realized that the joy I
> sought in you was not only secreted within you, but breathed
> around me everywhere, in the spreading street sounds, in the
> hem of a comically lifted skirt, in the metallic yet tender drone
> of the wind, in the autumn clouds bloated with rain. I realized
> that the world does not involve a struggle at all, or a predaceous
> sequence of chance events, but the shimmering bliss, beneficent
> trepidation, a gift bestowed upon us and unappreciated.[33]

But Nabokov only tells part of the story, not the story of the whole nature of reality. Ignorance is a partial relationship to reality, which thinks that it is a whole. This feeling of eternal being and spacious presence is but one taste of reality. The interior face of the cosmos has a second taste. That is the taste of becoming. Becoming is the third face of Eros, the face of longing, desire, and yearning. Eros is not just resting in being—it yearns to be something more. It is not just whole unto itself. It is the longing for greater wholeness.

Wholeness, remember, is the fourth face of Eros, which we are now discussing. Wholeness is the reality of an interconnected universe where no strand is ultimately separate from the seamless coat of the cosmos. In that sense, all of reality is intimate. But the wholeness of reality is not merely a static interconnectivity; it is also a dynamic intimacy. Wholeness is intimate. Intimacy is to be allured. Intimacy is to be attracted. Intimacy yearns. Intimacy yearns for more wholeness. Parts are attracted and seek intimacy with other parts in order to form deeper and wider wholes. In this sense, the third face of Eros (yearning) and the fourth face of Eros (wholeness) are inter-included within each other.

Reality evolves. Evolution means that existence is going somewhere. Evolution means that reality is not merely an eternal fact but also a dynamic story that is always changing. This is the scientific truth of reality, but it is an exterior truth. The interior of evolution is yearning. Evolution yearns, as we saw, for more and more complexity, more and more consciousness, more and more aliveness, more and more creativity, more and more uniqueness, and finally more and more love. This yearning of reality has a name. It is called, in science, "a self-organizing universe." That is the term of choice in contemporary evolutionary science to describe the wildly wondrous, dazzling nature of existence that evolves from subatomic particles to the vastly intricate and complex processes of human DNA, even before a human brain was in existence. Reality is allured to higher and deeper versions of itself.

Reality is self-evidently intelligent. Any other claim is self-evidently nonintelligent and nonerotic. The universe is filled with Eros, aliveness, intelligence, telos, direction, purpose, and allurement. The universe is not merely a fact but a story, both an alluring story and a story of allurement. Reality is going somewhere. And as we shall see in the next chapter, to live an erotic life is to know that you are personally implicated—and even desperately needed—in that story. This is the core erotic realization of the Unique Self.

All these aspects of yearning are inter-included qualities of aliveness, inter-included qualities of the erotic. That is why our experience of being in love requires us not only to rest in each other but also to be allured to each other. Imagine how tragically truncated your experience of reality would be if the sum total of your allurement was only of the sexual or romantic variety, and that with only one person.

Allurement is made manifest and obvious in the sexual and in the first phases of love, which we call falling in love. That is why these experiences are so central to our lives. For so many of us, without the possibility of falling in love and without the sexual, life can seem hardly worth living. We equate living the erotic life with the sexual and with the early, ecstatic experience of being in love, which appears for most people in the early stages of relationship. But this is to exile the erotic into these two beautiful but limited domains.

We long to return to Eros. That means we want to live erotically in all the dimensions of our life. These pivotal experiences of allurement and attraction—in the sexual and in falling in love—are pointing out instructions for the rest of our lives. To live an erotic life is to be aflame with allurement and attraction in every quadrant of your being. You want to be always allured and attracted to new depths in yourself, to new and deeper experiences of reality, to new people, to new depths with the people you already know, to new ideas or new depths in the ideas you already have, and on and on. Allurement is not merely being but also becoming. Allurement is not static but dynamic. It feels not like eternal rest but like ecstatic urgency.

Now the contours of reality are becoming clearer. We are connecting the dots, engaging erotically in the process of describing Eros. Reality is Eros. The fourth face of Eros is wholeness. The exterior of wholeness is interconnectivity. The interior of wholeness is intimacy. Intimacy is both being and becoming, both presence and yearning. All the first three faces of Eros come together in its fourth face, wholeness.

To be awake is to know reality. To know reality is to know that we live in an intimate universe. To be intimate is to rest in being and to yearn for becoming. To be intimate is to fall in love. To fall in love means to fall into what is already the true nature of reality's eternal being. But love is not only falling in love but also rising in love. To rise in love is to evolve and emerge, to become more and yearn for more. To rise in love is to be allured and attracted. To be in love, therefore, is to fall in love and to rise in love, to be and become, to rest and to be constantly allured. We dare not exile falling in love to the merely sexual or the merely romantic.

To be in love is to be at home in a universe whose nature is to be in love—to fall in love and rise in love at every level of reality—all the way up and all the way down. In our lives we fall in love all the time, with new people, with new depths of people we know, with new experiences, ideas, and places and with new depths of old experiences, ideas, and places. When you stop falling in love, you die. Love or die: that is our only real choice. To be in love, falling and rising in love, resting in being and charged with the ecstatic urgency of becoming—that is what it means to live an erotic life.

INTERCONNECTIVITY AND INTIMACY RELOADED

From this point on we will use the terms *interconnectivity* and *intimacy* interchangeably. They are but the interior and exterior aspects of the same picture. They are the core qualities of wholeness, the fourth face of Eros. Intimacy is the realization that I am because we are. Everything is the context for anything existing. Try to think of any one thing without the rest of everything, and it does not exist at all. Eros means there is no fundamental separateness in reality.

It is not that boundaries are not real. They are. Separation exists in the mind of God. Separation is both real and necessary. If a baby does not go through separation individuation, but remains fused with her mother, she is likely to be mentally broken in significant ways. The inability to separate from union with the mother is a recipe for psychosis. And yet, ultimately we grow into the realization that all boundaries are soft boundaries. On all levels of reality, interior and exterior, information and energy are being constantly exchanged. Ultimately, all systems are open systems, subject to change in which even minor fluctuations have the capacity to alter the trajectory of the entire system. That is the nature of an intimate universe.

The mystical realization of what Buddhists call "nothingness" is no less than the most accurate understanding of existence. There is no thing in the universe in the sense that there is no separate or isolated thing. There is no thing that is ultimately separate or apart from anything. There is no thing that is not part of everything. And yet there are still boundaries and features.

Intimacy is not fusion but the realization of union. Union is always new emergence that is brought about by the allurement between distinct entities, whether they are persons or particles. Union is only possible, however, because at the deepest level—at what we might call the level of prior unity—everything already participates in the same oneness. This will become clearer in the next chapter when we evoke the fifth face of Eros, uniqueness, which is very different from separateness.

Reality is intimate and yearns for more intimacy, allurement, all the way up and all the way down the chain of being. At the most fundamental physical level, we have the subatomic world. The subatomic world is driven by allurement, which is formally called "electromagnetic attraction." From the first nanoseconds of the big bang, subatomic particles are swept into an intimate dance of relationship. The great philosopher of science Alfred North Whitehead correctly pointed out that this sense of allurement exists even in atoms. He called it by the fancy name of prehension. This allurement is both the animating and the driving force of reality. All newness, all creativity, and all emergence flow from the dance of allurement.

This used to be most obviously apparent on the human level. The allurement of early courtship might well lead, after many steps, to the creation of a baby. We now realize that this principle is true on every level of existence, all the way up and all the way down the evolutionary chain. On the human level we not only join genes but also join genius.[34] This is the allurement that attracts us not only to be soul mates but also whole mates. Attraction and allurement in a dialectical dance with autonomy are the motivating methods of the inherent ceaseless creativity of the cosmos that drives the whole evolutionary process. Said simply, that means that parts do not fuse with other parts and disappear; rather, parts merge with other parts in order to emerge as more complex and conscious wholes, without ceasing to also be parts.

Said even more simply, a dog is a new whole that emerges from many eons of evolution. That evolution begins with subatomic particles and then goes on to cells and multicellular structures, followed by organelles and organs and more and more complex biological systems. The dog is a larger whole that includes all of these parts. For example, the dog has quarks, atoms, molecules, cells, etc. All of these parts maintain their integrity even as they form unions with each other to create larger wholes. Integrity of the parts is a structural prerequisite of intimacy.

On the celestial level, the same force of allurement is at work. We call this force "gravity." But that is just a scientific term we have assigned to this cosmic property of allurement. We think that there is some set of laws underneath it all that explains gravity. There is not. Gravity is but another word for allurement, which is the fundamental axiom of reality, we know not why. Reality is attraction. That's just the way it is. The interior of attraction, which leads to interconnection, is intimacy. Allurement is such a great word because it captures both the exterior of attraction and the interior of intimacy.

A DEEPER CUT OF WHOLENESS: EROS AND SYNERGY

Synergy is a core property of the erotic. Particularly, it is a property of the fourth face of Eros. Wholeness is not only a static description of reality in which all parts are interconnected in a larger whole. Wholeness itself has a dynamic or catalytic quality. Wholeness is a quality of being that overflows, always attracting parts together to create more wholeness. This is because wholeness is intrinsically alluring. It might be said that the allurement of intimacy drives existence to create new wholes from disparate parts. Intimacy is the strange, erotic attractor that pulls forward the entire evolutionary process. So wholeness is not only a static descriptor but also a dynamic attractor.*

---

*   One of the qualities of Eros that we have seen is the yearning for ever greater contact. This yearning is the longing within parts to create new wholes. Yearning is a quality of becoming. Wholeness also allures, but it is a quality of being. Wholeness is the allurement within being that moves being to ever deeper levels of creativity and wholeness. The very beingness of the whole overflows into more wholeness. In the great paradox of reality, perfect wholeness seeks ever greater wholeness by its very nature. In truth, of course, yearning and wholeness are inter-inclusive qualities of the same essence. There is only one. But yearning emphasizes the ecstatic urgency of the part seeking the whole, while wholeness places the emphasis on the whole, which, by its nature, allures, attracts, and overflows as larger wholes. Wholeness is the gestalt that always creates newness. Newness is created by contact. The deeper the contact between different wholes, which are all also parts, the more emergence or newness is created.

Emergence of new wholes is the natural result of synergy, two parts coming together to form a greater whole. On the physical level, contact of a particular form, which we call sex, creates babies. But contact on all levels of reality and in all forms generates new "babies" of sorts—new wholes, or what we call new "emergents." On the level of ideas, for example, we have what social philosopher Matt Ridley calls "idea sex." This is the simple truth that when ideas come into contact with each other, new ideas—often deeper and better ideas—are born. This is self-evidently true in every field of knowledge. New ideas are actually old ideas that come together, creating something new in a moment of creative grace. But the same thing is true when a hydrogen molecule and an oxygen molecule come together in a particular configuration. That new emergent is what we call water.

Evolution is the advancement to higher and higher wholes—or, in scientific language, to greater and greater synergies. Creation of a whole greater than the sum of its parts is the essence of relationship at all levels of reality. Synergy, the intimate contact between parts, always creates a new emergent. Synergy is a core quality of Eros.

JOINING GENES TO JOINING GENIUS: ROLE MATES, SOUL MATES, AND WHOLE MATES

The emergence of a new whole that is more than the sum of its parts is a core feature of erotic synergy. This is true on all levels of reality—including, of course, human relationships. Let's now turn to see how this erotic property of synergy plays out in our human world of relationship. On the human level as well, we are attracted to form relationships by the allurement of becoming more whole. We are allured by wholeness. That is the evolutionary dynamic at play in relationship.

The evolution of relationship is an expression of the evolution of Eros, or what we might call the evolution of intimacy. The drive to not only join genes but to join hearts and ultimately to join genius is the trajectory of the evolution of Eros in human relationship. "Role mate" is about joining genes, "soul mate" is about joining hearts, and "whole mate" is about joining genius.* Intimacy evolves from role mate to soul mate to whole mate. At each level, a new whole is created.

On the physical level, we are moved to join genes and create babies. The relationship that defines couples that come together to join genes and create family is what we will refer to as role mates. A "role mate" means simply that each party in the relationship is responsible for a specific set of roles. Historically, men virtually always played the role of protector and provider while women played the role of nurturer and homemaker. The natural upper-body strength of men and the simple fact that women bear children and make milk for breastfeeding had at least something to do with this historical arrangement. The goal of the role-mate relationship was survival and continuity.

These are both very big deals. Survival of the individual, the family, and the species are not flatland evolutionary mechanisms that can be explained by science. Rather, the drive to survive at all levels is an erotic interior. It is not in any way a scientific given that all beings do everything in their power to survive. This is rather an interior aspect of Eros that is a natural expression of the erotic universe. From amoebas to human beings, all of existence is utterly committed, with all of its energy, to survival.

In many texts of science, however, a creeping dogma is evident that reduces survival to a natural mechanism of a materialist universe. Interior dimensions of reality are regularly dismissed as evolutionarily insignificant because they do not have what is called "survival value." For example, interiors like beauty, music, values, and the search for meaning are regularly dismissed by science as insignificant in guiding evolution because they are not thought to contribute to physical survival.

This is a strange and wrong assumption on two levels. First, these interiors absolutely contribute to survival. But let's focus on the second wrong assumption, which is that survival is an exterior function that is a given in a materialist flatland universe. It is not. The desire to survive

---

*   We are delighted to share that there is a major forthcoming opus on this topic, a
     two-volume work by Marc Gafni and Barbara Marx Hubbard, titled *From Role
     Mate to Soul Mate to Whole Mate: The Next Level in the Evolution of Relationships*.

is just that—an interior desire that is built into the deepest fabric of reality, all the way up and all the way down. The human desire to survive is not an expression of our brute nature but of something far more noble, allusive, and refined. It is an expression of self-love. Self-love is the deep knowing that my existence is worthy and therefore worth fighting for, at almost all costs. Survival may then be seen as the exterior expression of a deeper erotic interior. This expression of love is then extended to one's partner and family and eventually to one's clan, tribe, or people. This is the evolution of love. Role mates come together to ensure that survival. Role mates create a whole that is more than the sum of their parts: they create a family.

A new level of relationship is born when there is a soul-mate connection. Working together for survival and continuity is an insufficient basis for this relationship. Tevye sings to Goldie in the 1963 Broadway musical *Fiddler on the Roof*, "Do you love me?" She does not understand the question. She responds, "For twenty-five years I've washed your clothes, I've darned your socks . . ." She goes through the litany of her role-mate actions. Is that not love, she asks? But in the mid-1960s, the evolution of intimacy went from role mate to soul mate. Love evolved, and love began to mean communication and intimacy. Best-selling books were written about different love languages, differences between men's and women's communication styles, and practices to "get the love you want." Soul mates were focused not on shared survival but on looking deeply into each other's eyes. Emotional intimacy, radical sharing of wounds, healing, and mutual personal fulfillment are the hallmarks of soul-mate relationships. The classic expression of the soul-mate relationship in culture was the 1970 hit movie *Love Story*. It represented the evolutionary movement from role mate to soul mate. The protagonists, Jenny and Oliver, come together, not merely to survive but also to heal each other's wounds. In that healing, there is a new wholeness.

The goal of role-mate relationship is to survive, which, as we have seen, is a form of self-love, which extends to partner and family. The goal of soul-mate relationship is to transcend loneliness through radical joining with the emotional heart of another. The evolution from role mate to soul mate is the move from joining genes to joining hearts. Soul mates create a deeper whole than role mates do because the soul-mate relationship includes a new depth of communication and intimacy.

The great poet of soul-mate relationships is Rumi. He speaks of heart:

> *I have come to drag you out of your self*
> *   and take you in my heart.*
> *I have come to bring out the beauty*
> *   you never knew you had*
> *and lift you like a prayer to the sky.*

Clearly, Eros never wants to leave the soul-mate relationship behind. But soul mates, in all of their splendor, are not the summit of relationship evolution. There is yet another level—what we believe to be the next level of relationship in the story of the evolution of Eros. This new level of relationship is the evolutionary movement from soul mate to whole mate. Whole-mate relationships include and transcend the best of role-mate and soul-mate relationships. We call it "whole mate" because it is the deepest possible relational whole that one can aspire to at this moment in history.

At some point—for many couples at the leading edge of innovation and transformation—personal fulfillment as the attractor in relationships was no longer satisfying. Soul-mate relationship in its classic form remained a necessary prerequisite for relationship, but it was found to be no longer sufficient. Couples wanted not only to join genes and hearts but also to join genius. They wanted not only to look deeply into each other's eyes but also to look together at a shared horizon. Shared purpose became central in these relationships. Relationships felt nonerotic without shared vision and values that could be better fulfilled together than apart. This is a new form of love, a new whole, to which previous relationship levels have been leading. In whole-mate relationships, couples seek to join genius to serve the larger whole. The more that love is evolved in the couple, the wider the whole that they seek to serve. In its highest expression, a whole-mate relationship becomes an evolutionary relationship, a relationship in which both parties are living in an evolutionary context. They experience their relationship as serving the healing and transformation of all that is.

The classic image of this evolutionary whole-mate relationship is Neo and Trinity in the cult movie *The Matrix*. They are deep soul mates. At the moment of her death, being held by Neo, Trinity remembers the depth of their kiss. And yet they are also whole mates. Unlike Jenny and Oliver in *Love Story*, Neo and Trinity have great shared purpose. They are evolutionary partners. In the deathbed scene of *Love Story*, Jenny demands that Oliver not feel guilty about her not seeing Paris. Personal wounds, trauma, and emotion remain the center of their relationship. In marked contrast, in the moment of Trinity's death, after poignantly speaking of the quivering beauty of Neo's kiss as central to her life, she demands that Neo go forward and fulfill the shared quest that has been the great Eros of their life together. For Trinity, the soul-mate relationship is not left behind, but it is not the end of the story. Whole-mate relationship includes and transcends soul mates.

SOCIAL SYNERGY: NEW CULTURAL WHOLES

Erotic synergy not only creates new wholes in the personal realm, but it also creates new social wholes. Social synergy is but another form of Eros or intimacy. It is the impetus to bring together co-creators worldwide who are each at the forefront of innovation and transformation.

Barbara Marx Hubbard has developed a method to catalyze the Eros of social synergy that she calls the "wheel of co-creation." Barbara's wheel focuses not on what is broken in the world but on what is working. The wheel incudes all the major sectors of society, from education to science to technology to spirituality and everything in between. In an exquisitely designed exercise, leaders locate themselves in different sectors of the wheel and proclaim their unique innovations. They are then invited to present what they might need from the other sectors in order to succeed. The isolation and fragmentation among society's different sectors is overcome in this exercise. A new form of intimacy, social synergy, is born.

New possibilities emerge. New wholes are formed. Cultivating the contexts of allurement, the social incubators where these new wholes might be formed, is an essential evolutionary need.

Paradoxically, it is only through focusing on what is working best, and then creating new strategies of transformation through social synergies, that we can hope to heal what is broken. A reality that is not shattered and fragmented into isolated sectors is more whole, and therefore more erotically potent in its ability to transform and to heal.

THE INTIMATE UNIVERSE

Reality is Eros. We live in an intimate universe. These are two ways of saying the same thing. But since, as author Tom Robbins reminds us, there are no true synonyms, each field of language—each phrase—gives us greater access to the vision and felt sense of reality. A third way of saying the same thing is that there exists a meta meme, which includes all other memes. The meta meme is a larger whole, incorporating many sub-memes into its whole-world vision.

Evolution means that the universe is not a fact but a story. The universe is not an ordinary love story but an outrageous love story. At this point we understand that by outrageous love we mean Eros. Ordinary love is when persons living nonerotic lives believe they are separate from all that is; they love each other in order to gain advantages of security and comfort. This is a legitimate form of love. Ordinary love, however, is highly limited in its pleasure, potency, and sustainability. Outrageous love is the Eros that animates and drives all reality, all the way up and all the way down the chain of being. The universe is an outrageous love story.

When outrageous love awakens on the human level, when we awaken to our true identity as outrageous lovers, the pleasure, potency, and sustaining power of the love relationship are virtually infinite. That the universe is a love story is not a metaphor. It is a fact. Calling it that is the best explanation of reality, culling all the information we have from all quadrants of knowledge at this moment in history. "The universe is a love story" is the most accurate worldview available to us at this moment in time. Generating new realities from within this erotic worldview will alleviate more suffering and effect more healing than any other single social movement or scientific technology. The realization of this worldview is the core of the return to Eros, which is so urgently needed and yearned for at this pivotal moment in the arc of time.

NOT A CHASTE LOVE STORY

The realization that the universe is a love story births a new form of Eros and intimacy.

The love story of the universe is not chaste. We live in a sexual universe, sexing all the way up and all the way down. Said differently, reality is allurement all the way up and all the way down.

From the microcosm of subatomic particles to the macrocosm of celestial attraction between planets, the universe is making love. Between the micro and the macro is the plant world where the birds and the bees are symbolic of the great pollination dance.[35] From fish to early animals, then mammals, and into the human realm, erotic allurement defines and guides reality. We live in a cosmo-erotic universe. The universe is driven by evolutionary Eros, the desire for contact in order to form ever deeper and ever greater wholes. The point is not just that everything is connected. It is that everything is allured to everything else. Everything is moved, driven, and passionately drawn to make contact. The interconnected universe could be a static given. It is not. It is a dynamic, cosmo-erotic reality.

EVOLUTIONARY INTIMACY

The realization that this is the nature of reality awakens us to the possibility of what we like to call "evolutionary intimacy." On the outside, this is the enlightened realization that everything is interconnected and everything affects everything else. Systems theory, chaos theory, and complexity theory all talk about the radical interconnectivity of all things. This is a scientific realization at a depth that was not even vaguely approximated in any previous generation.

Yet that is but the exterior expression of reality. The interior of interconnectivity is intimacy. It is for this reason that the great Buddhist teacher Master Dogen defined enlightenment as "intimacy with all things." A universe of mutually interdependent beings, co-arising, is an intimate universe. Enlightenment is but the realization of the true erotic nature of reality.

Enlightenment, Eros, and intimacy all turn out to mean the same thing. Eros means that no one is left out of the circle. No one is grasping for pseudo Eros by pushing someone else outside—an action that in Appendix B we call "the murder of Eros." Enlightenment means that nothing and no one is left outside.

It is not at all inaccurate to say that Eros is simply another word for enlightenment. Enlightenment is not some esoteric Eastern meditative practice. Enlightenment is sanity. Sanity is simply knowing the true nature of reality. Reality is allurement—allurement to form the highest possible wholes.

Reality is intimate. We live in an erotic, intimate universe. Therefore, we can fairly say the following: enlightenment means there are no externalities. There is nothing we can simply commodify, claiming its value is purely its ability to serve as a means to someone else's end. Whales are not simply whale oil, and humans are not merely disposable soldiers in the games of pseudo Eros played by corrupt elites.

Everything and everyone is in the circle. Nothing and no one is outside the circle. Nothing and no one is unloved. We need to love our way to enlightenment. That is not a sweet, spiritual idea but simply what it means to return to Eros and align with the true, erotic nature of reality.

ANYTHING LESS THAN EROS

Anything less than this erotic experience may well destroy our planet. We abuse each other personally. Nations mass-murder other nations. We rape the environment and allow twenty million people to die of hunger or related diseases each year.

The simple and essential cause is a lack of Eros. We desperately need to feel like we are on the inside, but we don't. So we settle for pseudo Eros. We pretend like we are in the inside by placing others on the outside. We do not feel embraced in the real Eros of love, so we grasp for the pseudo Eros of fear, war, and obsessive consumption. We have only two choices: Eros or death. Love or die. Let's choose to be outrageous lovers living the erotic life.

DO YOU KNOW WHAT I NEED?

Isaac Luria, the great Kabbalist writing in sixteenth-century Safed, taught: "All evil is a failure of love and Eros. I can hurt you only if I feel that you are not connected to me. Would the hand stab the foot to take revenge?" For Luria, love in its very essence is the erotic re-*ligaring* with all of being.

It always starts, however, not with all of being, but with a friend whom you already know:

> The master Moshe Leib of Sassov said he never knew what it
> meant to be a lover until he learned it from a drunkard. It hap-
> pened that the master was in a tavern and overheard a dialogue
> between two men deep in their drink. One was professing how
> much he loved the other, but the other argued that it was not so.
>
> "Ivan," Igor cried, "believe me when I tell you, I love you
> more dearly than anything in the world."
>
> "Not so, Igor," Ivan replied. "You don't really love me at all."
>
> Igor gulped down a glass of vodka. The tears streamed down
> his face. "I swear, Ivan, I love you with all my heart," he wept.
>
> Ivan shook his head. "Igor, if you really do love me, tell me
> why I am not satisfied in my life. If you really loved me, you
> would know what I desire."
>
> With this, Igor was silent. This time Ivan was the one who
> cried.

All the four faces of Eros we've studied so far show themselves in this tale: wholeness, yearning, interiority, and presence. If you really love me, then we are deeply connected. If you are truly not whole without me, then you will hear the deepest desires of my soul because their melodies resonate in your soul as well. You learn to hear my soul's music by being fully present in our encounters. Moreover, you are radically empathetic to my needs. Radical empathy comes when the fullness of presence engenders a great yearning to move beyond the alienation that separates us. There is a sense of devotion between us. Devotion is an intimate sister of yearning. The yearning to move beyond the loneliness of the separate self is what propels us to shatter the ego boundaries that alienate us and enter the inside of another's story. Then we are each other's erotic lover.

CHAPTER SEVENTEEN

THE FIFTH FACE

THE EROTICS OF UNIQUENESS
AND IDENTITY

H is name was Zushia of Onipol. He was one of the great, spiritually incorrect masters of Hebrew Tantra, and he was on his deathbed. Devoted disciples surrounded him. It is difficult to describe the depth of enlightenment that Zushia incarnated. He was utterly devoted to the erotic merger with the Shechinah, the union with the Goddess divine. No human suffering or hurt could sway his devotion to Eros. Because his erotic life was strong, he was ethical beyond what any of us can even imagine. He lived the teaching that the erotic and the ethical are completely interdependent. Because he lived the erotic life with such abandon and ecstasy, there was never a reason for him to act out or collapse his ethics.

As he lay on his deathbed, however, he was crying—sobbing almost uncontrollably. The disciples were troubled, but not only because their master was dying. They also did not understand why he was crying. After all, Zushia was the great master of oneness and union. Life, he taught, was about piercing the veil of separation. Separation in his teaching meant losing connection with the Shechinah. The idea that any human being was separate from the larger whole was for Zushia the very opposite of erotic and holy. He taught that, upon death, we are held accountable for our deeds, and if we have merit, we return to the arms of the Shechinah.

His philosophy was not dissimilar to what in the East is called the Tao. Seen from this perspective, death is a great liberation, particularly if one's life has been well lived. If all this were so, reasoned the students, why was Zushia crying? After all, he was the great master who had lived a life beyond reproach. If he was weeping uncontrollably on his deathbed, because, they assumed, of the impending judgment, what hope was there for the rest of them? So they turned, somewhat shamefacedly, toward their master and said, "Please give us a final teaching before you pass from the world. Let us ask you a final question."

"Yes," he said. "Ask and I will answer."

"Rebbe, master," they implored, "why are you crying?"

The master answered, "When I pass I will come before the heavenly tribunal of judgment, before which all human beings are held accountable. If they ask me, 'Zushia, why were you not like the lawgiver Moses?' I will have good answers. I did not have Moses' gifts of intellect or mind. If they ask me, 'Why were you not like the high priest Aaron?' for that, too, I will have a good answer. I lacked the natural overflowing love of humanity that made Aaron such a great priest. If they ask me, 'Why were you not wise like Solomon?' for that I also will have an answer. I did not possess his mind or his kingly grace. But I know that the heavenly court will ask me none of these questions. There will be only one question: 'Zushia, why were you not Zushia?' And for that question, I will have no answer. It is for that reason that I weep."

Zushia, the master of oneness, at the moment of his death transmitted the great teaching of Unique Self. All his life he had taught that at the deepest level of reality, we are all the same. Zushia's core teaching was the dharma of sameness. Differences are only superficial. Separation is a lie. It is a misperception that we are cut off from the flow of life; separation is simply a misperception. The separate self is, as Albert Einstein famously reminded us, an optical illusion of consciousness. It is an illusion that we exist as separate selves, divorced from each other and from the Eros of existence that lives in, and as, all of us.

Both the modern science of systems theory and the interior science of enlightenment taught by Zushia have shown us that this is simply false. Zushia had been a classic mystic, teaching his disciples to move beyond their stories of separateness and difference and to rest together in, and as, one. Difference, he taught, is a seduction of the ego. We are all part of the same True Self. True Self is a singular that has no plural. It means Eros, the cosmic radical aliveness. True Self is our cosmic self, our innermost consciousness, the place within where we are one with all that is.

But Zushia realized on his deathbed that he had overemphasized this teaching of oneness. The Eros of oneness, of non-separation—in which all are interconnected as part of the great whole—that is just part of the story. We are also, Zushia realized in the intensity of his mystical perception right before death, wonderfully and radically unique. Each person is an individual, different from every other. And our uniqueness is not an accident of nature that should be overcome. It is not a property of the ego to be transcended. Uniqueness is a quality of Eros and essence. Uniqueness is erotic. We are not merely True Self or what we sometimes call cosmic self. We are also Unique Self. Only the experience of our radical uniqueness can truly fulfill us. Only the realization that we are Unique Selves opens the door to living the erotic life. Living our Unique Self is an essential portal in our return to Eros. Eros is rooted in personal identity. When our core identity collapses, our Eros fails, and we fall out of the erotic life.

Your identity is not a complex equation. It is rather the direct answer to the great question that must guide every life. That question is: Who are you? The answer is that you are both a True Self and a Unique Self. There is no True Self without Unique Self. By True Self we mean your essential consciousness, which is indivisible from the larger field of consciousness. Your True Self is the singular that has no plural. The total number of True Selves in the world is one. Your True Self, however, has an irreducibly unique perspective and an irreducibly unique quality of intimacy. It can be expressed in the following equation:

True Self + Unique Perspective + Unique Quality of Intimacy = Unique Self

As a person, you are not merely True Self (sometimes called No Self) as the great Eastern traditions claimed. You are also an irreducibly unique expression of the love intelligence and love beauty of all that is. The love intelligence and love beauty that drives all reality lives in you, as you, and through you. There is no one like you that ever was, is, or will be. You are your True Self, and you are also your gorgeous and irreplaceable Unique Self.* It took existence nearly fourteen billion years of complex and dazzlingly precise synchronicities to produce you. Your cellular signature is the unique dance of seventy-five trillion unique cells—unlike any others that ever were, are, or will be—in unique symphonic relationship.

Imagine that you could see your immune system. You would be blown wide open by the dazzling complexity, intricacy, and beauty of it. Once the sheer wonder receded, you would discern that, on the one hand, everyone's immune system appears to share the same core features and structures. And, indeed, they do. On the other hand—and herein lies the magic—you would also see that each person's immune system is wildly and fabulously unique. Our radical uniqueness, just in this one feature of our bodies, is the equivalent of a magnificent piece of art, the likes of which would be unrivaled by the greatest artists of all time.

Uniqueness, you see, is an objective structure that expresses itself physically. But it is also an interior quality. Each of us has an irreducibly unique essence. Each of our unique perspectives, tastes, and qualities of intimacy are expressions of our unique interior qualities. Our unique interiors are our immutable birthrights even as they evolve through the mythic tales of our sacred autobiographies. Every single person in the world has the birthright of uniqueness.

---

*   These short pages summarize a series of six volumes that Marc has written on what has come to be called Unique Self Theory. If you want to take a deeper dive into the subject, read *Your Unique Self: The Radical Path to Personal Enlightenment* by Marc Gafni (Integral Publishers, 2011).

THE SEXUAL MODELS THE EROTIC: UNIQUENESS, SAMENESS, AND IDENTITY

Sex models Eros because sex is both radically unique and personal even as it is radically impersonal. In sex we are all unique and in sex we are all the same.

Sex Is Personal

When we have great sex, the personal and unique are at the center of the experience. In that sense, sex is the ultimate form of relationship between two Unique Selves. During an awake sexual experience, we feel ultimately connected to the being of our sexual partner. Intimacy is by its very nature unique. The quality of intimacy between every sexual couple is ultimately unique, unrepeatable, unlike any other. It is Pablo Neruda again who captures the quality of irreducible uniqueness that defines what we have called sex erotic:

> I hunt for a sign of you in all the others,
> In the rapid undulant river of women,

Neruda reminds us of the intensely personal quality of erotic yearning.

> Braids, shyly sinking eyes,
> Light step that slices, sailing through the foam.

The true lover seeks not merely merging but an utterly particular merging with the Beloved.

> Suddenly I think I can make out your nails,
> Oblong, quick, nieces of a cherry:

In true Eros, the Beloved is unlike any other.

Then it's your hair that passes by, and I think
I see your image, a bonfire, burning in the water.

The Beloved is the yearned-for missing puzzle piece. All true erotic intimacy contains a quality of irreducible uniqueness.

I searched, but no one else had your rhythms . . .
Nobody had your tiny ears.

Sex Is Impersonal

At the same time, the sexual impulse that arises in us is an expression of the seemingly impersonal evolutionary Eros of all of reality, incessantly driving all of reality—us included—to more and more contact, creativity, and aliveness. Sex is deeply personal and deeply impersonal. That means that sex is both radically unique between each couple and radically the same between all couples, as it is the same life force that runs through all of us. In this latter sense of sex being an expression of the common life force, we identify sex as an expression of the evolutionary impulse awake in us that drives us, seemingly indiscriminately, to make contact wherever and whenever we can. In this very way sex models what it means to live erotically in all of life. Sex, like all of our erotic lives, is both radically personal and impersonal. We are simultaneously all unique and all the same.

We need to live into our uniqueness and give our unique gifts even as we need to feel into our sameness and know that we are not different from each other and therefore all profoundly connected. We connect through our uniqueness—our puzzle piece that connects us to the larger puzzle—and we connect through our sameness—we are all part of the same puzzle. In this precise fashion the sexual models the fifth face of Eros, our simultaneous sameness and uniqueness.

UNIQUE SELF = YONI + PHALLUS

Remember that reality is Eros has nothing to do with inappropriate sexuality. It has everything to do with loving the moment open and being loved open by the moment. To love the moment open, and be loved open by the moment, requires the erotic energies of both yoni and phallus that live in each of us. To love the moment open is to penetrate so deeply into the Eros of the moment that something new and sacred is born. But that is only half the story. For the moment to birth its gift, you must also so deeply receive the moment that you let the moment love you open. It is in erotic contact between the pregnant person and the pregnant moment that new creation is born.

The erotic energy symbolized by your unique combination of yoni and phallus is none other than your Unique Self. It is with your Unique Self, your unique gift, and your unique quality of intimacy that you make contact with the moment waiting to give its gift. You can only love the moment open through your Unique Self. Sometimes, loving the moment open requires radical rigor and restraint. At other times, loving the moment might require your abandonment to rapture and ecstasy. You can only be loved open by the unique quality of the moment through your Unique Self. But you can only engage the Eros of the moment through the Eros of your Unique Self.

THE EROS OF IDENTITY:
UNIQUENESS AND SAMENESS:
"WHO ARE YOU?" RELOADED

Your Unique Self is your unique perspective. Your unique perspective births your unique insight. Your unique insight is actually reality's unique insight through you. Your unique insight births your unique gift.

Your unique gift has two dimensions. One is the unique quality of intimacy that is beingness lived as you. The universe is having a you experience, and the universe is delighted. Your unique gifts, however, also create your unique capacity. Reality needs your unique gift. Your unique gift is your unique capacity to respond to a unique need in your unique circle of intimacy and influence. You are reality's eyes, hands, feet, and love. You are a unique expression of evolution.

Evolution is love in action. Evolution awakens as you, in person. You have unique gifts to give and a unique life to live, one that is utterly and essentially needed by the whole. You are in relationship to all of reality. Reality needs your service. There is a corner of the world that will remain unloved unless you stand on the abyss of that particular darkness and say, "Let there be light!"

Who are you? You are an irreducibly unique expression of the love intelligence and love beauty that is the animating energy and aliveness of all that is—that lives in you, as you, and through you—that never was, is, or ever will be again, other than through you. You are here to write the poem that only you can write. You are here to sing the song that only you can sing. You are here to be the unique presence of being and becoming in the world that no one else but you can be.

BE IN THE FIELD

All of reality conspires to support you in awakening to your Unique Self. When you genuinely commit to the search, when you genuinely commit to being in harmony with the field of being, the field turns to find you. First you have to get out of the way of the narrow contraction and grasping of the egoic mind. The contraction of your egoic self is, in its own insidious way, always comparing you to everyone else.

Do you wish to directly experience the nature of your Unique Self? Find your own inner rhythm and get quiet. Settle your awareness into the field of being, your True Self. You might find it by watching the ocean. You might find it through music or dance. You might find it by walking. You might find it simply by sitting quietly or meditating. When you are there, let yourself sit in it—resisting the compulsive need to fill it up with busyness or thinking. In this state of quiet, expanded awareness, allow the quality of your Unique Self to arise in you. Access the field, the True Self, the universal consciousness of which we are all made. Then, from the ground of that infinite consciousness, allow the feeling of your Unique Self to arise.

THE FIRST FOUR FACES OF EROS

Eros cannot fill you if it is not in the context of your Unique Self's story. Uniqueness itself is a core quality of Eros. It is the organizing principle for all of the other erotic expressions of your life. Said simply, your Unique Self is the essential key to living the erotic life.

Let's look once again at the four faces of Eros we have discussed so far. The first face is interiority, or what we called living on the inside. In fact, uniqueness and interiority are indivisible. Being on the inside is radically unique. No two interior spaces are the same. Inside space always holds a unique quality of intimacy that is unlike any other. Intimacy is an inside quality, and all intimacy is unique. It is your interior castle. From that place you find the unique flow of your life. That is what it means to live an erotic life as your Unique Self.

The face, with its connotation of "inside," is the clearest expression of a person's Unique Self, and therefore the truest reflection of the erotic. Lucian Freud, the artist, was an erotic master who spent his life painting portraits, seeking to enter "the inside" of faces. Face is Eros. To lose face is to become de-eroticized. In the mystical tradition it is written that when the cherubs atop the Ark in the Holy of Holies are face-to-face, blessing flows in the world. We saw earlier that the Hebrew word for "face," *panim*, means "inside," "face," and also "before." We saw that the Hebrew mystical mantra, to be "before God," *lifnei Hashem*, can more profoundly be translated as being "on the inside of God's face." The inside of God's face is Eros. To be before God is to live in Eros as your Unique Self. It is through your Unique Self that you live the erotic life. It is through your Unique Self that you enter the inside of God.

The second face of Eros that we tasted was the fullness of presence. Presence is always unique. Sit silently with two different friends, and each time you will have a different experience of presence. The fullness of presence that is Shechinah, that is Eros, refers specifically to the fullness of your unique perspective and your unique quality of intimacy, which generate your unique presence.

The third face of Eros that we engaged was yearning, or desire. Yearning, however, is not neutral. Yearning is always unique. Your yearning, like your presence, is an expression of your unique perspective and your unique quality of intimacy. Your longing and desire are not peripheral to the holy. Rather, being utterly unique, they are vital strands in the textured fabric of Eros. The erotic and the holy are one. Remember, reality is allurement. Your Unique Self is your unique set of allurements.

Your allurement, your yearning, your desire is Eros. Your allurement and your desire are holy. Of course you must always clarify, as we saw earlier, between true desire and pseudo desire, true allurement and passing fancy, between depth and surface yearning. This is the distinction that we drew between Eros and pseudo Eros. Desire and allurement must always be distinguished between their authentic and inauthentic forms. But at their core, allurement and longing are holy.

And as we saw in the chapter on the third face of Eros, your yearning is not a function of your separate self. Yearning is not a private affair. The universe yearns. Yearning is the interior quality of evolution itself. And evolution yearns to manifest as you. When you awaken as your Unique Self, you are, in effect, awakening as evolution in person. So living your Unique Self is an expression of the universe's yearning for your Unique Self even as your yearning always leads back to your Unique Self. This is the circle of allurement and desire, which is the erotic circuit of reality itself.

Your deepest desire and greatest pleasure as a human being are to become transparent to the interior face of the cosmos yearning to evolve through you. The yearning of the cosmos to evolve shows up as the evolutionary impulse living in you. Your Unique Self, your unique allurements, is the personal face of the evolutionary impulse—awakening in you, as you, and through you. When you awaken to your Unique Self, and you invite the yearning of the cosmos to singularly fulfill itself through your eyes and your heart and your hands, you are living the erotic life.

We yearn to create life and to be a contribution. We want our lives to matter in the grand scheme of things. We yearn for power and purpose. We may hide our yearning, deny our yearning, or medicate our yearning, but it won't go away.

We often lose ourselves in our external obligations to dull the pain of an unfulfilled dream to live a larger life. We sacrifice ourselves on makeshift altars to false gods. The drive to sacrifice ourselves is universal, existing in every culture and at every time. In the act of sacrifice, we transcend our small selves, even if for a moment. But if we cannot find a true altar at which to prostrate and offer up our yearning, we choose an alternative path of deadening ourselves to the pain of the smallness of our lives. We lose ourselves in mindless media, we overdose on bad novels, or we work when what we really want is to find in ourselves that drive, that power we've felt in the peak moments of our lives. We ask ourselves: "What would it mean to live that way every day? To live from whatever that source is?" That source from which you desire to live is the erotic yearning of your Unique Self.

The fourth face of Eros is what we call wholeness. Full erotic living wells up from knowing that your unique part is not apart, but a part of—indeed, indivisible from—the whole. It is through your very uniqueness that, like a puzzle piece, you fit into and complete the larger whole. All reality is made of puzzle pieces that are part of a larger puzzle. This is the great knowing of both the old sciences of interior enlightenment and the modern sciences that focus on exteriors. All parts are puzzle pieces that fit into larger wholes. Your Unique Self is your puzzle piece that fits perfectly and is needed desperately by the larger whole. Your Unique Self finds its sense of home—of fitting—by connecting with and completing the larger puzzle. The feeling of fitting just right, completing and yet being held by the surrounding puzzle pieces, is the feeling of Eros. Your Unique Self is your deepest erotic nature through which you join with and complete all that is.

Mature individuality exists only in the context of interconnectivity with the larger whole. The evolutionary impulse to wholeness demands that you live the puzzle-piece nature of your story. That is how you fill the hole in the wholeness of reality that can only be filled by you. It is only

when you respond to this evolutionary invitation, through gifting existence with your unique expression of outrageous love, that you can feel a
sense of wholeness in your individual life.

Interiority plus presence plus yearning plus wholeness plus uniqueness equals holiness. The erotic and the holy are one. The opposite of
holiness, of sacredness, is not impurity or demonic possession. The
opposite of sacredness is superficiality. Sin is superficiality. Holiness is
Eros. With this chapter, we have added one more element (uniqueness)
to the equation for holiness: to be superficial or to sin is to fail to live the
full uniqueness of your story.

THE THREE SELVES

We have talked in these pages about separate self, True Self, and Unique
Self. To really understand the Eros of identity inherent in your Unique
Self, let's compare and contrast the three selves.

Separate self is the experience of being a puzzle piece yearning for the
larger puzzle, only to be told there is no larger whole. You are separate
from others, from nature, and from all that is. Separateness is nonerotic.
In the wake of separate self-consciousness, life wilts and a deadness sets
in. Eros collapses. Every form of pseudo Eros—addiction, acting out, and
violation—seeks to fill the void left by the failure of Eros. Much of this
failure in contemporary society comes from a breakdown in identity. The
individual who is driven to success and prominence, who is disconnected
from his part in the larger whole, loses his Eros. When life becomes
de-eroticized, separated from the larger context, it gradually collapses in
on itself.

True Self is the experience of oneness, of the whole puzzle. But being
only a whole puzzle while denying the existence of the separate puzzle
pieces is to deny reality. Oneness by itself is also nonerotic. When the
yearning for distinction is denied and the natural feeling of being special
is crushed, then life is de-eroticized. Acknowledging the importance of
the True Self without embracing your Unique Self is a form of pseudo
Eros. To acknowledge the value of the one but not the value of the many,

the value of the whole but not the value of the parts, is to divide creation. A so-called "spiritual community" that denies the infinite value and dignity of the irreducibly distinct and special individual loses its Eros and eventually collapses in on itself.

Unique Self is the experience of being the puzzle piece that completes the puzzle. As your Unique Self you are both a distinct puzzle piece while at the same time you are needed by the larger puzzle which is incomplete without you. When you complete the larger puzzle, you fulfill your purpose. You are held in the embrace of the larger puzzle even as you are honored for giving your unique gifts in the form of your unique puzzle piece.

Your Unique Self is the unique expression of your True Self. Remember the equation of identity that we introduced earlier: True Self + Unique Perspective + Unique Quality of Intimacy = Unique Self. As a Unique Self, you realize that you are part of the seamless coat of the universe. At the same time, you realize that reality may be seamless but it is not featureless. You are its unique feature. You are an irreducibly unique expression of the larger field of love intelligence, which is reality. You are a puzzle piece that is uniquely suited to complete the puzzle in a way that no one else ever has or will in quite the same way as you Eros is born only in the paradoxical experience of being radically unique and radically the same. We are all the same, and we are all connected. We share our physicality with all living things, and we all are part of the larger consciousness that permeates the universe. As humans, we all have the same general array of feelings, the same organs, and we all share the same basic experiences of life. In our sameness we feel connected, compassionate, and at home. But at the same time, we are—each of us—distinct. We are each unique, not in an incidental but in an essential way. Our uniqueness is not something trivial—merely a function of our social, psychological, or cultural conditioning, as most enlightenment teachings have argued for centuries. Our uniqueness is, rather, a sacred expression of the essential intention and yearning of the cosmos.

The cosmos has only one question for us. "Zushia, why weren't you Zushia?" This is not about Zushia being a successful separate self. Rather, the cosmos calls Zushia to realize that he is the same as everyone—an indivisible part of the One—and yet radically unique and distinct. Zushia realizes on his deathbed that the core mystical teaching of his life—the demand to surrender one's individuality in deference to joining with the One—was flawed. You must never give up your uniqueness, your personhood. The universe yearns to have a Zushia experience. The universe yearns to have a you experience.

THE FOUR EROTIC TRUTHS

To fully embrace your beautiful Unique Self, you need to realize four erotic truths:

1. Your uniqueness means that you are intended by reality. Being unlike any other, your uniqueness means that you are not "extra." You are the direct result of the successful intention of existence. You are a good child of the universe.
2. Your uniqueness means that you are intended—chosen—by reality. To be reality's intended one is to be chosen. You do not need to wait for a romantic partner to choose you. You are romanced by reality itself. You are chosen, and you are special in your sacred uniqueness.
3. Your uniqueness means that you are loved. To be intended and chosen points to the truth that you are loved. The universe has both exteriors and interiors. It is concrete and physical, but the universe also feels. What it feels is love. Not only an impersonal love, as expressed in the forces that move the planets and stars, but also a personal love directed uniquely at you.
4. Your uniqueness means you are needed by reality. Nothing in existence is incidental or accidental. The impulse of evolution is guided by what science now calls a self-organizing intelligence. This intelligence seeks the evolution of love. You are needed by all that exists for the evolution of love.

To really get this fourth erotic truth, we need to place ourselves once again in the larger context of the new universe story. The underlying meme of our entire conversation is what we might call "The Universe: A Love Story." Let's recap for a moment the major narrative elements.

The universe is not merely a fact; it is a story. It is not an ordinary story; it is a love story. It is not an ordinary love story; it is an outrageous love story. By outrageous love we mean the underlying force of cosmos, the evolutionary Eros that both sources and drives all of reality, interiors and exteriors, from quarks to cells, to plants to animals to mammals, to the most advanced humans all the way to spirit.

To awaken as a human being is to realize your true nature as an outrageous lover. What does an outrageous lover do? She commits outrageous acts of love. But which outrageous acts of love does she commit? After all, there are so many choices and so much that needs doing. The answer: she commits the outrageous acts of love that are a function of her Unique Self. It is your outrageous acts of love that stand at the abyss of darkness and say, "Let there be light" into a corner of the world that—without you—would remain in darkness. There is a patch of reality that will be lost in unlove without your radical commitment to your outrageous acts of love.

Because the plot line of the universe is love, you are an irreplaceable character in the story. You are needed by all that is. Here is the one-line plot summation: Evolution awakens as you in person when you wake up as an outrageous lover committing your outrageous acts of love that are a function of your Unique Self. That is what it means to be personally implicated in evolution. In short, the universe is a love story and each of us is an essentially necessary actor.

In fact, we are all co-directors, co-creators, of the next stage of the universe story. Evolution is waking up as us. We have moved from unconscious to conscious evolution. The evolutionary impulse is awakening as the Unique Self of every human being. We now have the possibility of recognizing ourselves—and every human being—as what we most deeply are: an irreducibly unique expression of the love intelligence and love beauty that is the animating Eros of all that is. We are each leading men and women in the great play of cosmic Eros.

In "Life While You Wait," Polish poet and Nobel Laureate Wislawa Szymborska writes about coming to grips with this sense of the utter necessity of our roles in the great cosmic drama:

I know nothing of the role I play.
I only know it's mine, I can't exchange it . . .

Szymborska writes the truth of destiny in secular prose:

You'd be wrong to think that it's just a slapdash quiz
taken in makeshift accommodations. Oh no.

She restores the gravitas of the personal in language stripped of artifice or dogma.

I'm standing on the set and I see how strong it is.
The props are surprisingly precise.

The intelligent universe is never careless. The realization of that precision is revelation.

The machine rotating the stage has been around even longer.
The farthest galaxies have been turned on.

There is no split between the cosmological and the personal. All is allurement, all is "turned on."

Oh no, there's no question, this must be the premiere.
And whatever I do
will become forever what I've done.

Szymborska captures elegantly the Eros of Unique Self. The "farthest galaxies have been turned on" and wait for you to speak your lines, which are heard everywhere and impact everything. That is the core truth of the interior sciences of enlightenment, the exterior sciences of systems theory and evolutionary emergence, and the essential action required of your role in the universe story. You are needed by all that is. There is little that is more erotic than that realization.

CLOSING THE CIRCLE: THE OLD DANCING MASTER

Eros always returns to the point of origin, and we conclude our conversation about the first five faces of Eros where we began: with the story of the dancing master. The Kung Fu warrior was powerful but ultimately nonerotic. He was a separate self, highly trained and successful, but he had lost touch with Eros. Because of that, his essential power was compromised. He had lost his place in the great dance of being. He had lost access to the Eros of evolution, even though he was an expert in his Kung Fu moves. He had fallen away from his Unique Self and hence had fallen away from Eros.

That is why the young Dalai Lama knew that the old dancing master could best him in combat. The old master had lived the fullness of his unique story. He was carried through life by the dance of being. He was not in a battle with the movement of Eros. The story is about the Kung Fu master's return to Eros. His eyes were opened. The sensuality of his fragrance was released. His yearning was awakened. All those are steps in the return to Eros. Fundamentally, the Kung Fu master was called back to his Unique Self. He became the next dancing master of Tibet. In his recovery of his personhood, his Eros was restored, and the cosmos began to dance in him and as him.

UNIQUE SELF, UNIQUE RISK AND DANGER: A SEX MODELS EROS PRACTICE

In a world where Eros is liberated, appropriate sexual boundary breaking becomes a model for authentic erotic boundary breaking. Consider, for example, the need to take risks. The old dancing master of Tibet risked his life to find his successor. Taking risks is a form of boundary breaking. In order to live your Unique Self there is always a moment where you must take a risk and trust that the net will appear.

This form of risk taking for the sake of realizing your Unique Self is what I (Marc) called a "Unique Risk." Not to take your Unique Risk is mortally dangerous. Paradoxically, the risk of inaction is too high. The dancing master enters the danger of his Unique Risk. When you are not living into your Unique Risk, then you will likely be drawn into the pseudo Eros of risks that are inappropriately dangerous. Appropriate danger is always necessary for true transformation. The master of the Tao, Chuang Tzu, explains it well when he writes, "I come to speak dangerous words, and I ask only that you listen dangerously." But danger and risk are appropriate erotic expression of boundary breaking only when it is your Unique Risk—a risk that is pivotal to living your authentic story. The sexual in its true form is not only raw delight; it is also the great teacher. Sex can model for you appropriate risk taking, boundary breaking, and the courage to flirt with danger as part of the Eros of your larger life.

At our Integral Evolutionary Tantra school, one of our core practices is called "Take-a-Risk Sex." In this practice you might take a risk in being vulnerable around sex. As we are sexually, so we are emotionally and spiritually. The appropriate risk you take in sex often opens the door to the Unique Risk you need to take in life. The goal of your Unique Risk is no less than repatterning your capacity for life. You do this by first stepping out of your old ways of sexual being into new ways of sexual being. This then points you to the new way of being that beckons you in all of your life. These practices are not for sissies. They are potent and powerful. They literally open up new possibilities of relationship and transformation in your life. The sexual models the erotic.

UNIQUE SELF AND UNIQUE GENDER: LINES, CIRCLES, AND LIVING THE EROTIC LIFE

Hieros Gamos, the divine marriage, is the hidden mystical doctrine of God is Eros. It means that at every level of existence, the god and goddess—the initiating and receptive forces of creation that we traditionally have called "male and female"—are making love, constantly giving birth to not only new, but also higher and deeper, orders of existence.

These two forces used to be called masculine and feminine, but we can no longer exclusively identify them with men or women. Borrowing a term from the Renaissance-era erotic mystic Isaac Luria, we like to call them "lines and circles." Luria writes: "Every moment of reality, on all levels and in all worlds, is born from the unique interpenetration of lines and circles that takes place in that moment."

Interestingly, in physics, one branch of string theory postulates that matter, at its deepest level, is made up of strings and loops. A loop is a string that joins end to end with itself, forming a circle, and a string, of course, is a line. Lines and circles are qualities of reality. They include such dual distinctions as allurement and autonomy, attraction and independence, reception and thrusting, centrifugal and centripetal, directional and cyclical—all primary characteristics of the cosmos.

In our own lives, these complementary but opposite forces are expressed through the prism of the Unique Self. Eros is a unique event, happening uniquely in every human being. Understanding that truth is essential if we are to return to Eros. You cannot live an erotic life generically. You must, rather, incarnate the unique Eros that is the texture and invitation of your life.

In the ancient mystical world, the core properties of existence were thought to be masculine and feminine. Men incarnated the masculine principles and women incarnated the feminine principles. Our friend and colleague John Gray captured this vision in his book *Men Are from Mars, Women Are from Venus*. While the book is often thought of as a pop psychology best seller, that is to misunderstand both John and the book. The book is actually a profoundly insightful exploration of how the qualities of masculine and feminine show up in men and women. Books like *The Female Brain* and *The Male Brain*, both by neuropsychiatrist Louann Brizendine, provide powerful scientific structures that validate in significant ways the core intuitions of the Mars and Venus work.

At the same time, John's articulation of Mars and Venus was a major first step in the story but far from the end of the story. It was a critical first step because there are so many ways that most men are different from most women. Failing to notice these differences creates communication nightmares that destroy love. John stepped into a politically correct world that was committed to the denial of differences between men and women and fiercely articulated the Mars and Venus vision in order to restore love.

But today we are at a new crossroads. We are at a place where men and women are no longer able to locate themselves fully in their identity as either men or women. This quandary destroys self-love because it undermines identity and causes a profound alienation from self, which is the root of all breakdown and suffering. Today we need to move beyond Mars and Venus. Because at a deeper level, Venus and Mars—that is to say, feminine and masculine—exist in every person.

For many of us, Venus and Mars do not express our identities. We are awakening to a new realization that every person is a unique calibration and integration of Venus and Mars qualities. We are realizing that while classic gender distinctions are the beginning of the conversation, they are not the end of the conversation. This new emerging understanding we have termed "Unique Gender." Unique Gender is not the right balance of masculine and feminine in a person. It is rather an entirely new emergent. To bring this evolutionary emergent forward (which is to participate in the evolution of love), we need new language because, as the cherub mystics remind us, language creates reality. The terms "Unique Gender" and "lines and circles" are important first steps.

The terms that we will adopt to move us toward the new emergent of Unique Gender are creatively borrowed from Luria, who writes, for example, "all of reality in all of its parts is made up of lines and circles." We jettison the terms *masculine* and *feminine* and adopt the new terms *lines* and *circles*. Reality is constructed from line and circle qualities.

In a forthcoming book tentatively titled *From Transgender to Unique Gender*, I (Marc) outline ten core qualities of line energy and ten core qualities of circle energy. Each of the qualities directly reflects the geometric shapes of line and circle. Directionality and distinction are line qualities. Inclusion and cyclical movement are circle qualities. Autonomy is a line quality, and communion is a circle quality. Independence is a line quality, and interdependence is a circle quality. But they are no longer merely masculine or feminine qualities; that is just not true. Rather, they are line and circle qualities.

Lines and circles are qualities of reality that live in every person, in every situation, and in every dynamic.* You might say that lines and circles appear as the dynamic erotic contact that connects different people, ideas, particles, and forces of nature. The Eros of lines and circles takes place not only between things and people but within each thing and each person.

So how does Unique Gender relate to Unique Self? Unique Self is the unique calibration of lines and circles that live in every person. This is part of what manifests a person's unique quality of intimacy, unique perspective, unique gifts, and unique insight—that is, the unique constellation of Eros that manifests within each person. Lines and circles merge and calibrate uniquely in each individual. That merging/calibrating is Unique Gender. The implication that "reality is erotic" takes place uniquely within every person. Every Unique Self has a Unique Gender. Lines and circles uniquely interweave in every uniquely gendered being.

Unique Gender is the evolutionary expression of the ancient concept of Hieros Gamos, the divine marriage, the Eros that incarnates in every one of us, symbolized by the two cherubs sexually embraced above the Ark in the Holy of Holies of Solomon's Temple in Jerusalem.

In the philosophy of Unique Gender, we have woven together four strands of wisdom to bring a new fabric of revelation to reality. The first strand is the concept of Hieros Gamos, the divine marriage. In ancient wisdom, this took place between the divine principles of the cosmos, incarnated as god and goddess. The second strand is the notion of lines and circles constituting the core structure of all units of reality. The third strand is the new understanding of identity that we call "Unique Self." The fourth strand is the transgender movement's critique of traditional gender understanding.

---

*   Luria already made this claim, but he was still stuck in a cultural reality in which
        classical line qualities were largely masculine and classical circle qualities were
        largely feminine. Reality and love have evolved, however.

FROM TRANSGENDER TO
UNIQUE GENDER

The transgender movement's critique of the way our culture understands gender poses a critical challenge to our most basic sense of identity. Transgender consciousness says, "My identity is deeper than man or woman or even masculine and feminine. Those are boxes that actually obfuscate and often distort my true identity." When all of the old identities based on religion, nationality, and race had fallen away, gender remained identity's last safe haven. At least we still had some sense of who we are. You are either a man or a woman, and that was at least a point of origin for the all-important identity conversation. Along came the transgender movement and it powerfully challenged this one remaining bastion of identity. The transgender movement's questions intuited a much more profound sense of personal identity underneath the old gender structure of man/woman, masculine/feminine.

Tragically, however, the transgender movement did not offer any deeper sense of identity. It was all questions, with a virtually dogmatic anathema for answers. But the collapse of identity is catastrophic both for a person and for a culture's sanity. Identity is erotic. When identity is lost, then the person or culture is de-eroticized. A de-eroticized person or culture is dead and thus prone to any and all forms of regressive pseudo life that seek to replace or cover up lost forms of Eros that had their source in the old identities.

With the incisive questions of the transgender movement, the last remaining bastion of identity was swept away. This has resulted in myriad forms of breakdown—sexually, personally, and culturally. The transgender movement is the latest expression of the classic postmodern movement: brilliant deconstruction with no reconstruction. The return to Eros may be appropriately seen as part of a larger reconstructive project. Our reconstructive project honors the questions, but then, by integrating all of the leading-edge streams of wisdom available at this moment in time, we point not to dogmatic answers but toward a new vision of meaning, the vision of Unique Gender, which emerged from the ancient enlightenment teachings in a new form.

Paradoxically, the transgender movement's challenge to identity is the same challenge posed by the all of the great schools of enlightenment. The great question of enlightenment inquiry practice is, "Who are you?" The point of the question is to get underneath all of the culturally constructed contexts that are in the way of your most authentic identity. You are not merely boy or girl. You are not merely Christian or Jewish. You are not simply British or French. You are essence, a unique essence. You are a Unique Self. Unique Self is an identity that is underneath gender and all the other superficial structures of self. But Unique Self does not ignore gender. Rather, it says that the core qualities of gender—what we call lines and circles—are qualities of the cosmos.

And these cosmic qualities show up uniquely—in unique integration, texture, and calibration—in you, as you, and through you. You are your Unique Gender. This is not to be confused with the lovely idea that John Gray writes about, the need to have balance between your masculine and feminine sides. While that is certainly true, Unique Gender is not saying that. The philosophy of Unique Gender says that you are a radically new and unique emergent—a unique integration of line and circle qualities in a way that never was, is, or ever will be again. It is not so much that your masculine and feminine are balanced. It is rather that you are something else, something new and precious, which is far deeper than masculine and feminine. It does not leave masculine and feminine behind but transcends and includes them.

Who are you? You are your Unique Self. What is that? It is the unique expression of your Eros. Your Eros is your unique Hieros Gamos. In the ancient world, Hieros Gamos took place only in the realm of the Divine. In the philosophy of Unique Gender, we bring Hieros Gamos to earth. And not only to earth but also to a democratized vision of Hieros Gamos. Every single human is a Unique Self who is a unique integration of the cosmic qualities of lines and circles.

At the leading edge of neuroscience, researchers like Daphna Joel have moved beyond the vision of the male and female brain. Joel writes of what she calls "the intersex brain." The intersex brain is not a concept: it is an anatomical and cellular reality. Every human brain is a unique integration of what we are calling line and circle properties.

Said differently, every human brain is a unique expression of the Eros of the cosmos.

The brain structure is but the exterior expression of an interior reality. Every human being is heart, brain, mind, and body in a unique Hieros Gamos—a unique incarnation of the perpetual Eros of the cosmos, the unique Eros that yearns to occur in every person. It is only by living your unique Eros, in your own interior self, that you can live your erotic life.

Naturally, your Unique Gender will directly affect your sexuality. Attraction is no longer aroused only between male and female or even between masculine and feminine. Attraction is between Unique Genders—that is, between Unique Selves. And that opens up entirely new worlds.

CHAPTER EIGHTEEN

MORE ON THE FIFTH FACE

STORY, VOICE, AND SOUL PRINTS

The path of the fifth face of Eros is the path of living your story, the texture of your Unique Self. No matter how skilled or competent or professional you may be, you cannot experience radical aliveness in a story that is not yours. The failure to realize this truth is a source of every form of depression, acting out, addiction, and suffering. To live your story—whatever the particular circumstances of your life might be—is always a source of power, delight, and aliveness. Your story is your Eros.

"Living your story" is very close to the popular expression "finding your voice." Voice is that unique and infinitely special sound wave that only you can generate in the symphony of the world's voices. As we shall see in the course of our discussion, the unique voice of your story is the wellspring of both your greatest personal creativity and your highest personal pleasure.

THE SEXUAL MODELS THE EROTIC: SEX AND STORY

In the path of story, as in the other paths of Hebrew Tantra, sex models Eros. As in sex, the degree to which Eros imbues every facet of our existence is intimately linked to the degree to which we are living our stories. Sex divorced from story is fragmented, in exile, not sacred. When the sexual is "de-storied," then the erotic Shechinah is exiled into the faceless sexual. When this happens, in the language of the Zohar, the erotic Goddess of Shechinah becomes an *eshet zenunim*, a prostitute. A prostitute is the archetype of the person who splits off her sexuality from her personal story. We never know a prostitute's real name. She is either anonymous or carries an impersonal trade name: Candy, Lola, Sugar. The Shechinah is exiled to anonymity. For to be anonymous is to live with your true name, your unique story, unknown.

Sex is most potent when it is part of a larger story. When sex is alienated, that violates one's story and is called abuse. Sex that is alienated from one's story society calls prostitution. Sex that is connected and committed to a larger story we naturally call holy. The larger story may be long or short, but it is the larger context of shared story that elevates sex from the animal to the human. Sex models Eros. The degree of your aliveness is always connected with the degree to which you embrace and live your story.

The story might be the story of relationship or marriage. But sex can be holy even if the story is a conscious agreement to have sex without a story—that, too, is a story. When two people consciously come together in sex, even if only once, a story is created. They must be committed to the integrity of that story. That includes their full presence during their sexing as well as their commitment to not distort the story after the sexing is over. Rewriting a sexual narrative with false complaints of sexual harassment, for example, is a violation of the integrity of a sexual story, even if the story happened to be short. In that sense, false complaints are an abuse of the sexual, a form of sexual abuse.

There are several people with whom, I (Kristina) have had beautiful one-time sexual experiences. In each experience, the thread and texture of the encounter was very different. The beauty of the sexing was the freedom between us, which emerged precisely because we were not committed to any substantive form of a shared life story. In one particular instance, I had regrets about the encounter the next day. I shared my experience with a friend, who immediately began to demonize him. She had been sexually abused when she was young and seemed to be conflating my experience with hers in a way that related to her own traumatic experience. I had to choose to honor my commitment to the integrity of my "yes" in that moment and not allow it to be hijacked by social pressure or by the old voices of shame and guilt. So while I was not interested in an extended story with that person, I was absolutely committed not to violate—but to indeed honor—the integrity of our time together.

I learned four potent lessons from this experience. First, I understood what it means to take responsibility for my "yes." This was a great liberation for me. Second, I fully claimed my power to choose when I want to be sexual. I am not a woman waiting to be chosen. I get to choose who I want to have sex with and then I take responsibility for my choice. I am not a victim of someone else's sexual power when I have said yes, bodily or verbally. Third, I realized that regret does not mean that I get to rewrite the story from a place of clench or contraction, or even harassment. Regret is just regret. Fourth, I learned to honor the potency of my desire, my sacred "yes," as well as the goodness and wild beauty of our short story together.

In my work with women over the past fourteen years, I have been supporting them in reclaiming the power and dignity of their desire. I have found that self-empowerment, both in taking responsibility for their "yes" and in claiming their desire, has been the single most transformational move a woman can make. When a woman connects to her own pleasure and desire, she reclaims her true power. She can then begin to use her aroused sexual energy for full-bodied orgiastic living, releasing her inner victim and discovering her inner outrageous lover!

THE EROS OF STORY

When you are living your story, even life's difficulties are somehow all right. When you are caught in a story not your own, then even life's successes are never enough. There is no Eros more satisfying or fulfilling than the Eros of living your story. You can only fill the void of emptiness with the stuff of your own sacred tale.

To fully understand the de-storying of life, which expresses itself in the prostitute archetype in all of our lives, we must first reconnect to what it means to live one's story. Another term for Unique Self is "soul print." Soul print is the term I (Marc) coined (and published a book by that name) to refer to your infinite uniqueness, the spiritual DNA of your soul. I used both terms in my first book, *Soul Prints*. (I starting using the term *Unique Self* because it works for scientists, Buddhists, agnostics, and others in a way that the term *soul print* does not.)

Be that as it may, "soul print" is a wonderful expression for our infinite uniqueness, the spiritual DNA that makes us each who we are and no one else. So let's talk about "soul" for a minute. The image used most often in biblical myth to describe the soul is light. In Hebrew, light is *sapir*. The English word *sapphire* is derived from this. A sapphire, with its incomparable blue shine, is a stone of light. A sapphire radiates Eros and aliveness. It should be no surprise that the word meaning "light" is also the luminous root of the word *sipur*: "story." Your story is your unique configuration of light. Your *sipur*, just like a wave of light, is flowing and streaming, the wave of events and emotions you experience in a lifetime. The incidents, details, images, and apparent coincidences of your existence all weave a story unlike that of any other human being on the face of the planet.

The great author and social critic Charles Dickens wrote in *David Copperfield*: "Whether I shall turn out to be the hero of my own life, or whether that station will be held by anybody else, these pages must show." *Sipur* is about being the hero of your own life. Realizing your destiny comes from your ability to follow the outline of your own story. That is why Alzheimer's Disease is far more than the ultimate physical disability it inflicts. What is so infinitely painful is the gradual yet conscious loss of the outline of your story. When you lose your story, you lose access to your own radical aliveness.

Each of us sleeps, eats, loves, rages, works, and speaks. Not one of us, however, does those things in quite the same way. Living your story is about expressing the originality of your commonness. It is about making the ordinary extraordinary. *Sipur* also means "calling," the human experience of being summoned to a specific mission or destiny, a unique destiny. *Sipur* is the unique weave, the blending and melding of all the moments and encounters of a lifetime. For it is your own story, your unique story, that calls you forward, propelling you upon your path.

The soul's story says that you are singled out, unique, one and only, and that therefore you are called to a mission that you alone are charged to fulfill. This is the place of your light, where it shines brightest in the world. When we see people living their story, we feel a great rush of love for them. This is because love at its core is a soul print perception. To love is to perceive the infinite glow and uniqueness of your beloved's story.

In *Love: What Life Is All About*, Leo Buscaglia tells a story of how a teacher drew a green tree on the board and asked the children to copy it. One little girl drew a purple tree.

> "You didn't copy my tree," said the teacher disapprovingly.
> "I know," said the girl. "I painted my tree."
> "But I've never seen a purple tree," said the teacher.
> "Isn't that a shame," said the girl.

The Hebrew myth master Abraham Kook, commenting on this story, adds:

> Along come the learned teachers and focus their gaze on all that is outside. They too distract us from the "I," they add fuel to the fire, giving the thirsty vinegar to drink . . . stuffing the minds with all that is external to them . . . and the "I" is more and more forgotten.[36]

Sometimes our educators, our leaders, our parents, haven't the eyes to read our interior. And so we rewrite our own stories to fit their skewed vision, even if it means a betrayal of our own destiny. Children are all naturally unique until they "try to be." They try to be in order to get us to notice them because we weren't paying attention to them when they were painting purple trees. The job of an educator (and we are all educating one another) is to impart basic skills to the student and to honor her purple tree.

The purple tree is rooted in the part of us that cannot be fully expressed, cannot be narrowed into words, and cannot be subjected to laws. Ultimately, every person is completely free and has her own special salvation. No form of instruction exists; no savior exists to open up the road. No road exists to be opened. The road is you. Your soul story says, "I am more than that." You are the sum of your choices—but you are more than that. You are the sum of all your particular traits and dispositions—but you are more than that. The "more" is your soul story—that is, the unique constellation of loving that is you. The "more than that" is what makes healing and transformation possible. The "more than that" is the unique face of God that is your face.

Try to be anyone else but you, and you will always be second best. But you are the best "you" there will ever be. There is no higher calling than living your story. You are a messenger of God, sent to this earth as God's personal envoy. There is something in this world no one can do but you. Is there any other job that could be more special?

SOUL PRINT HINTS

A word in the Zohar used for souls who are living their story is *lechisah*, meaning "whisper." To live your story is to be able to hear the intimate whisper of divinity erotically caressing your life. We are all recipients of cosmic love notes. Philosopher and theologian Paul Tillich reminds us that we can only hear through the love that listens. Buber captured the spirit of biblical myth when he wrote, "To live means being addressed."

To live one's story is erotic in the resonance of its melody and the fullness of its canvas. The world, when we are in our story, is no longer empty. The soul is not here just to pay back karmic debts. It has a contribution to make from the depth of its infinite specialness. Through making that contribution, a human being feels fulfilled. That is the Eros of living one's story.

When you are in your story, the universe becomes full of what Nachman of Bratslav called *remezie deorayta*—"divine hints." Interestingly, the most important shared feature between lovers and schizophrenics is that they tend to interpret the world as if it is happening for them alone. Plato terms love a form of divine madness. But who is truly insane? Often mild insanity is a refuge for the truly sane, and those of us normal folks marching to the beat of any drummer but our own are the ones who are disconnected from reality.

The universe is full of whispers, and they are talking directly to you. And here is the paradox: the more you act as if you are being addressed, the more you will be. The world is filled with soul print hints. It may be the lyrics of a song, a sign on a building, an old friend you meet after years of not seeing each other, or a book that grabs your attention and demands to be read.

British thinker Adam Phillips, in his wonderful work *The Beast in the Nursery*, understands well the slow and subtle Eros of hints. The artist inside us, he writes, is "all the time on the lookout for material to make a dream with . . . inspiration means being able to take the hint . . . It is not only a tuned responsiveness; it is also an unconscious radar for affinities, for what speaks to one by calling up one's own voice."

The more deeply we enter our own character and story, the more whisperings are heard and hints are detected. Of course, the wink, the subtle gesture, the tilt of the head—all these are the language of lovers; hints and intimations are the hallmark of intimacy. Each person has his unique talent, pleasure, obligation, form of silliness, and pathology. These are all personal soul print hints that direct you toward living your story.*

---

* If this path is particularly compelling to you, then allow me (Marc) to invite you to read my first English-language book, *Soul Prints*, and a later opus that goes well beyond the Soul Prints teaching, *Your Unique Self: The Radical Path to Personal Enlightenment*.

THE STORYING OF SEX

The great biblical affirmation is that for sex to be sacred it must be personal. Personal means connected to story. Impersonal sex may mean sex that is used to weave a false story, or it may refer to sex that is detached from the web of soul print passions and commitments that is your life. It refers as well to sex that we use compulsively to cover up, even from ourselves, the dull throb of emptiness.

The connection between sex and story is hardwired into our spiritual operating system, so much so that we have a universal name for one who separates his or her personal story from the sexual. We call that person a prostitute. The essence of the prostitute archetype in every culture is the de-storying of the sexual.

Of course, the prostitute archetype is not limited to our vision of the single woman soliciting her male client. When we talk of prostitution, we can be referring to any combination of man or woman. More important, it can refer to sexual relations within a marriage or even nonsexual interpersonal relationships. There are many ways to be a whore.

The archetypal prostitute is willing to separate sex from her deeper personal story. The symbol for a person's story is her name. A name is the gateway to the personal and intimate contours of one's life narrative. The prostitute assumes a fake name. The client is a John, and she is an anonymous body. She is the fantasy object of her client—object, not subject. This is their contractual agreement.

The classic expression of the de-storying of intimacy is the archetypal refusal of the prostitute to kiss. The kiss is the time when all distinctions between subject and object melt; the Zohar calls it the merging of spirit in spirit. She refuses because it is too difficult to depersonalize a kiss. She has sold her body, but she is trying to protect her soul. The client has not earned the right to the intimacy of personal contact. And though she may have compromised her Eros by separating her sex from her story, she tries to protect her inner light by placing a screen between her soul and the client. He may enter her physical space, but he is denied entry into her story, which is her spirit.

When the divine Shechinah Goddess achieves union with the divine male God, it is called kissing. The human and the Divine mirror each other in Kabbalistic myth. When there is no kissing, the Shechinah is in exile. She is Eros exiled into the merely sexual. She is Shechinah degraded to being a prostitute.

A prostitute is the opposite of a sacred intimate. A sacred intimate is a critical function that society would do well to recover. A sacred intimate is not your wife, husband, boyfriend, or girlfriend, but someone who dances with you in the realm of sexual energy. The dance is profound, personal, and intimate even as it is sacred and transpersonal. In working with your sacred intimate, you might use sexual theater as a way of working with early wounds. You might do intense spiritual practice in the play of the sexual. You might do work to access your power and the power of your surrender through the play of domination and submission. You might write outrageous love letters—or even outrageous erotic love letters—to each other. Choosing the words with quivering tenderness and raptured intention, you might create a sacred space that is radically safe and appropriately dangerous at the same time.

At leading-edge institutions like the Masters and Johnson Institute in the 1970s and 1980s, sexual surrogates were engaged both for psychological work and to improve sexual competence and function. But the function of sacred intimate is beyond that of sexual surrogate. A sacred intimate is radically committed to the infinite depth of meeting, play, and transformation. The sacred intimate reveals sex to be a form of prayer. Regardless of whether it is sex rooted in the rawness of fuck or in the tender shudder of exquisite lovemaking, sex with a sacred intimate transforms play into pray, lust into longing, and attraction into allurement. The sacred intimate understands that reality is Eros. He or she understands that the sexual Eros that lives in you is a portal to the radical aliveness of the erotic that is the inner core of the cosmos. The sacred intimate is a contemporary troubadour who knows the truth of Solomon's realization: "Its insides are lined with love." It is the mandate of the sacred intimate to sex you open to God.

Of course a sacred intimate can choose—together with his or her partner—whether to work with sexual energy or with direct sexual play.

But to be truly transformative in a way that you are forever changed, the sacred intimate must be in the dharma of Eros; must engage with full heart, mind, and body; and must be willing to fall in love again and again and again. This is because the methodology of the sacred intimate is not sexual technique. The only method must be the method of an unguarded heart, the way of outrageous love.

That society has been unable to draw clear demarcating lines between classic prostitution and sacred intimacy is part of the essential confusion around sex. We need a new sexual narrative in which the potent relationship between the holy trinity of sex, Eros, and love is clearly articulated. This is an edgy distinction but one that needs to be made. When we lose our edge, we lose our aliveness. Life becomes de-eroticized, and every manner of ethical breakdown ensues.

THE IMPERSONAL AND THE TRANSPERSONAL

The prostitute archetype manifests itself in two forms. The first is the classic prostitute with whom sex is non-intimate and impersonal. The second is the temple prostitute, who expresses the sexual as transpersonal and cosmic. The temple prostitute would engage in transpersonal sex with both worshippers and temple priests as part of the erotic service of the Goddess. What both share in common is that the prostitute, whether man or woman, is not related to in personal terms. The prostitute is upgraded to a symbol. Once that happens, degradation is sure to follow eventually.

For the slippery slope between the impersonal and the depersonalized is seductive and steep. Thus, as powerful and even necessary as a transpersonal erotic moment might be, the prophets disallowed the temple prostitute. The prophets recognized that the sexual model of the erotic courses with a powerful energy essential to human fulfillment. However, they insisted on replacing the male and female temple prostitutes with the male and female cherubs. This was their way of ensuring that the transpersonal did not slip into the impersonal, which could slip into the nonpersonal, which could slip into the nonethical, which could slip into evil. Paganism allowed the mutilation and even slaughter and sacrifice of the prostitute as an integral and regular part of the pagan cult. Once the sacrifice of a human being who was seen only as a symbol occurred, all ethics broke down.

The Eros of the prophets insisted on the radical holiness of every individual Unique Self. The individual is of infinite worth and dignity and can never be reduced to a symbol. Indeed, Unique Self is precisely the irreducible dignity of unique personhood. It is this emphasis on infinite value, the personal story of every human being, that is the driving force of prophetic ethics. We see in our own culture just how insightful this prophetic intuition is.

For example, everyday pornography and soft porn may play the role of the temple prostitute and seem innocent enough to be on the counter of respectable newsstands or on the movie channel at the best and most established hotels. But the line—driven by profit and emptiness—between the impersonal and the depersonalized is very, very thin. Eventually, it may lead to the radical depersonalization that lies at the core of all evil. Pornography based on rape and violent abuse is now available all over the world.

EROTIC AND ETHICAL ENTITLEMENT

Personal Eros comes from living your story. But though the prophet is fully identified with Eros, he insists nevertheless on the merger of ethos and Eros. What does it mean to be ethical? The answer: to behave in a way that supports a person's ability to live her story. What is an ethical violation? To behave in a way that undermines someone else's ability to live his story. This could be an active violation, such as theft, deception, false complaints, public smear campaigns, or violence. Or it could be a passive violation—failing to get involved in making the world a place where every human being has the opportunity to live his or her story. Since the primary ethical violation is to desecrate someone's story, the ethical and erotic merge, because the underlying principle of ethics is to affirm and support the erotic integrity of every human being's story.

The only clash, then, between the erotic and the ethical is when my Eros is at the expense of yours. Since every human being is, in Dante's words, a homo *imago dei*—"a divine miniature," then all human beings are equal in their erotic entitlement. Any violation of that equality would be an ethical—and an erotic—violation. So all ethical lapses are really violations of Eros.

As we saw earlier, the inner impulse for all ethical violation is a lack of Eros. When we human beings feel empty, exiled from our stories, we try to feed off other stories. That is the core of every ethical violation: when another person becomes not an end, a story unto themselves, but rather a means to fulfilling your own story.

It now becomes clear that there is no possible distinction between the erotic and the ethical. In fact, the word *ethics* comes from the Greek *ethos*, meaning "the special nature of a person or group"—in other words, their story, which is also the source of the most powerful erotic fulfillment.

The prophets insisted that the erotic sexual affirm the stories of both partners in a relationship. To de-story the sexual destroys intimacy, which leads to the prostitute archetype, the exile of the Shechinah, and the destruction of the temple. Sex models Eros in that it must always emerge from deep within our story line. When it does, then we can embrace the full erotic nature of the sexual as the guiding spiritual model for all of the nonsexual dimensions of our lives.

STOLEN STORY

Remember the story about the man who could be cured of his lust only by sleeping with a particular woman—if she was married. From the day the temple was destroyed, the taste of sex was given to violators of the path. Stolen waters are sweet. This expresses how we have lost the core temple energy, when the erotic was an integral part of a person's story. People in exile feel they need to violate the parameters of their story in order to touch erotic fulfillment. "Stolen waters" refers to something that is not part of your story, and "sweet" means that it gives you a quick pseudo-erotic charge, which allows you to forget the emptiness for a moment. By definition, this must be an illusion, for full Eros is only available to a person who is living her story. Your story is the web of ongoing commitments, promises, and dreams that form the core of your narrative. The reclaiming of temple energy is no more than an expansion of consciousness, allowing a person to realize the full Eros of living his story; the sexual is an organic and holistic expression of all the primal power and passion of that story.

When you are not in your own story, the need for fulfillment becomes obsessive, overwhelming. But when you are living the depths of your story, freely chosen full sexual expression, which is both gentle and wildly erotic, can well up and fill you.

LEAH

Now, lest our dear readers be all too confident that the prostitute lingers only at the outer reaches of society, in red-light districts and on dank street corners, let us share with you a vision of psychological prostitution, the de-storying of Eros, which is far from marginal, and not far from many of our homes.

Who is the biblical myth archetype of the prostitute? Amazingly, the wisdom masters identified Leah—the great matriarch, mother of six tribes of Israel—as an occasional manifestation of this. What makes her a prostitute is that she is disconnected from her story. She has no true home. Her existence is therefore nonerotic, an expression of the Shechinah in exile. And a careful reading of the biblical story reveals that not only Leah but also Jacob, her husband, played the whore on occasion. The very heroes of the biblical narrative wrestle with their prostitution inclinations. Let us briefly reconstruct the narrative.

Jacob comes to his uncle Laban's home. Laban has two daughters: Leah, the elder, and Rachel, the younger. We are told that it has already been decreed by destiny that Leah is to marry Jacob's older brother, Esau, while Rachel is betrothed to the younger brother, Jacob. Leah, however, desperately wants Jacob. She feels that without Jacob her life would be drab, empty, and unbearable. Jacob, on the other hand, wants desperately to marry Rachel. She is the woman for whom he lifted the great rock at the well. She is the woman he kissed and wept over.

But Jacob knows that Laban, the father of these two women, will attempt to deceive him. So the well-prepared Jacob gives Rachel a sign that she should give to him as she is escorted, heavily veiled, to the wedding canopy. She will covertly give him the sign, and he will be assured that he is getting the right bride.

But as is often the case with the best-laid plans, something goes wrong. In his bedchambers after the nuptials, Jacob finds himself with Leah and not Rachel. It was she and not her sister who gave him the coded signs under the canopy. "How can it be?" ask the reader and Jacob in unison. The answer: Leah, who so desperately wanted Jacob, manipulated Rachel into giving her the codes. She cried that she could not survive the humiliation of her younger sister being married before her, the elder. She wept and screamed, perhaps even threatened to do herself harm. In the end, Rachel succumbed to the manipulation and gave her the signs. Rachel will have to wait another seven years to wed Jacob.

On this night, though, it is Leah who marries Jacob. But Leah has violated the destiny of her story, intended as she was for Esau. She has deeply hurt her sister and made Jacob a pawn in her desperate bid to find fulfillment. But she cannot find fulfillment by marrying Jacob in the darkness. We all know that! Have we not all, at one time or another, married Jacob in the darkness?

She may now have Jacob, but she still does not have fulfillment, and so she tries to use their children to win Jacob's love. She has her first child, naming him Reuben, an acronym for "God has seen my affliction." Her second child she names Simeon, the biblical acronym for "God has heard that I am hated." Still, Leah flounders in her darkness. The next son is called Levi, biblical acronym for the pathos-filled "now maybe my husband will take walks with me."* Her fifth son she calls Zebulun: "maybe this time my husband will find me luxuriant and fertile." It is a tragic

---

*   Her fourth son, Judah, breaks this pattern. See my (Marc) Hebrew book *Redefining Certainty* for the story of Leah and Judah and what I have termed "The Judah Moment."

pattern that climaxes in the birth of her sixth son, Issachar. But first, the narrative leading up to Issachar's birth.

Leah's firstborn, Reuben, has brought her mandrake flowers from the field. He brings his mother flowers because, like his brothers, he desperately seeks her love. Reuben, Simeon, and Levi internalize their mother's degradation as the unloved wife of Jacob. They are filled with rage toward their father. They desperately seek to fill their mother's emptiness, an impossible task for any child.

So Reuben brings his mother flowers. Tragically, even in receiving his gift, Leah can still not see Reuben. There is no recorded discussion between them. No "thank you," no embrace. She sees only the flowers, intuiting immediately that they might be a tool in her ongoing bid to win her husband's love. So Leah, still desperate to be filled by Jacob, struts about with her flowers in full view of her barren sister, Rachel, who by now is also married to Jacob. Rachel is desperate for children. These flowers are the double symbol of motherhood. (First, they are mandrakes, powerful fertility plants. Second, they are a son's doting gift to his mother.) "Give me your mandrakes," Rachel pleads with Leah.

Which is precisely what Leah intends for Rachel to do. "Is it not enough that you take my husband—will you also take my son's mandrakes?" cries Leah. Of course, Rachel falls into the manipulative web.

"I don't want Jacob," Rachel answers. "Take him. I will give you my night with him but you must please let me have those beautiful mandrakes from your son." And the tragic exchange between two desperate sisters is done. Jacob comes home that night, thinking to go to his beloved Rachel's bed. But it is Leah who brazenly goes out to greet him. "To me you shall come tonight," she says, "for I have hired you with the mandrakes of my son."

A humiliated but not innocent Jacob for the second time is made to sleep with Leah instead of Rachel. Born of this mandrake-purchased union is Issachar—meaning "he [Jacob] was hired." On that tragic night, Jacob becomes a prostitute. But not only Jacob. Leah "goes out" to greet Jacob. The wisdom masters observe, "Leah, our matriarch, was a whore that night." The interpretive key is "she [Leah] goes out." That is to say, she went out of her story.

But it is not about that night alone. That night is but the symbolic expression of Leah's tragic inability to embrace the fullness of her story. That is precisely the prostitute archetype: the divorcing of the sexual from the fabric of an authentic personal story. The Leah figure of biblical myth is the proto-feminist story of a married woman who attempts to use her husband as her story. Jacob, she is convinced, can fill her emptiness. So painful is her hole, her emptiness, that she hires Jacob—turning him into a prostitute, if only to feel the fleeting libidinal illusion of being filled.

But prostitution occurs not only when we divorce sex from our story. More seriously, if we are sexual in a story not our own, if we use our sexuality to weave a false story, or if our sexuality is not integrated into our story, then we fulfill all too grandly the prostitute archetype.

THE HOME THAT IS HOLY

The symbol of your story is home. The place of the cherubs, symbols of the erotic, is *Beit HaMikdash*. Although usually translated as "the temple," what it really means is the "home that is holy." The Hebrew myth image for the most sacred space—the epicenter of the spirit, the great temple—is the home. In much of Hebrew literature it is not even called the holy; rather, it is referred to as either the *mikdash* or the *bayit*, meaning "the sacred" or "the home"—as if using both appellations would simply be repetitive. The cherubs, sexual symbols of the erotic, are in the *bayit*. This is precisely the notion we have been trying to unpack. The sexual needs to be connected to home and story, not to hotel rooms or hideaways (although at times hotel rooms can also be transformed into sacred homes). Have you ever been ashamed to bring a boyfriend or girlfriend home? This is not a good sign about the depth of the relationship. If it's not a relationship you can "bring home," then it's not a sacred relationship.

The Eros of home and hearth, your story, provides a stable matrix for the full erotic power of the cherubs. The talmudic epigram *Ishto zo beito*—"His woman is his home"—has nothing to do with patriarchy or ownership. Rather, it means his Shechinah (his erotic self) needs to be rooted in his *bayit*, his story. So for woman, so for man. Emily Dickinson continues the idea: "A home is a holy thing / nothing of doubt and distrust / can enter its portals." Home is created by love.

My (Marc) Jerusalem home, where I lived for almost a decade, had two rooms. The only furniture was a double bed, one table, one chair, a closet, and a few thousand books, which lined the walls from floor to ceiling. In that place I first understood what "home" meant. I discovered my interior castle, where the Secret of the Cherubs revealed itself to me. It is where I grew up. It was my temple, and it travels with me on all my paths. I lived in that home, however, as one cherub. It is only when a second cherub appears, who is willing to merge sex with shared story, that the full meaning of home is realized.

That is what it means for a home to be a temple. A beautiful poem by Mary Mackey, "The Kama Sutra of Kindness: Position No. 2," always allures us to the vision of what it means to live as two cherubs. It captures one vision of the intertwisting of sex and story:

> love comes from years
> of breathing
> skin to skin
> tangled in each other's dreams
> until each night
> weaves another thread
> in the same web
> of blood and sleep

There is magic in the embodiment of years of tangled blood and sleep. This is part of the mystery of mature monogamy for which some part of every human being yearns.

THE EROTICS OF VOICE

Sex in its full erotic and sacred context has a story. So our lives, in their full erotic and sacred form, must also have a story. To live in my story is to find my voice. Voice, however, is not only to have a story, but also to find the words to tell my story. Voice is our full emotional range and our ability to be fully present and expressive of our feelings. If the free flow of my story is blocked in the world, then I do not have a voice.

Great and sacred sex is about the free flow of voice. Wonderfully, the Talmudic wisdom masters refer to sex as a form of speech. Perhaps that is why we get so hurt when, during sexual play, our partner says, "Shh! Keep your voice down." Good sex comes from freely flowing emotions. Bad sex is when the emotional flow is blocked—when we are stuck in our throats.

The throat is the narrow passage connecting heart and head. Fascinatingly, the word for "Egypt"—*mitzrayim* in Hebrew—means "the narrow places." So in Kabbalistic myth, to be in Egypt is to be with too many words stuck in your throat, too many sentences and paragraphs edited away in the censorship of life. To be in Egypt is to have a blocked voice. To leave Egypt—Exodus—is to find and claim your voice.

Philosopher and poet Samuel Coleridge had this to say about voice:

Ah! From the soul itself must issue forth
A light, a glory, a fair luminous cloud,
Enveloping the Earth—
And from the soul itself must be there sent
A sweet and potent voice, of its own birth,
Of all sweet sounds the life and element.[37]

VOICING DESIRES

Sex is the place where you give voice to your truest self. It is not a coincidence of biology that the female sex organ has lips and is essentially a mouth. "Mouth" is one of the erotic mystical names given by the Kabbalist for the Shechinah, symbol of Eros in all of our lives, for they are one and the same. Eros in the profoundest sense is about giving voice to our deepest desires, which need to be the ultimate guides in our story. My true voice speaks my deepest desire, which is my soul print. Desire, in psychotherapist Adam Phillips' phrase, is "what speaks to one by calling up one's own voice." For Kabbalist Mordechai Leiner, finding true voice is called *birur*. The equation is simple. *Birur* literally means "the clarification of desire." To identify true desire is to find your voice. To find your voice is to live your story. To live your story is to be free. Freedom, voice, and story are the heart of Eros and love.

The Kabbalist I. L. Peretz, writing at the end of the nineteenth century, tells the story of Bontsche the Silent. It is a tale of disconnection from desire and the exile of voice.

> All the heavens were in an uproar. Bontsche the Silent, the most righteous man, had died. Bontsche, who never complained and always accepted his fate with graceful silence, was coming to heaven—what a day! The angels exuberantly recounted the tales of humility of this silent, saintly man—how he never asked for anything, was always simple, accepting, and sublimely silent! The angels rolled out the reddest celestial carpet they could conjure. The celestial hosts were eager to honor their celebrity.
>
> On his arrival in heaven, Bontsche was granted a meeting with God. This was more than unusual—it was never done—but for holy Bontsche an exception was made. He came before the throne and heard the divine voice say, "Ask for anything. Anything you want is yours."
>
> Never had the celestial hosts heard anything like it. Every ear strained to hear. What would Bontsche say?
>
> Bontsche was a little overwhelmed by all the attention. After all, he viewed himself as a simple man. He replied to God, "It would be wonderful if I could have a roll and butter every day."

When the Buddhists got hold of this story, they went wild. What a satori story, they said, what an example of total detachment and simplicity, the reduction of all expectations, the giving up of desire even when God offers you everything!

Yet from the perspective of biblical myth, this story reads very differently. Hebrew mystics say: "What a shmuck! God offered Bontsche everything, and all he could think to ask for is a roll and butter? If he wanted nothing for himself, then what of a world that suffers so? For them as well he could think of nothing to ask? Was he so absent from himself that he could no longer feel joy or pain—not only his own but not even that of others?"

Biblical mystics look at his life of silence and view it as a tragedy. Bontsche is totally disconnected from his own desires, from his own story. He is called Bontsche the Silent because he has no voice. His silence is a silence of absence.

SIGHTS OF SILENCE

But there is a different kind of silence from which our voices can truly emerge to express our story. In the biblical story of the divine chariot so beloved by Hebrew mystics, the prophet Ezekiel envisions what he calls *chashmal*. *Chas* means "silence" and *mal* means "speech," hence *chashmal* is "speaking silence." Our silence enables the opening revelation of divine speech.

But it is even more than that. Our speech itself has two forms. First, there is speech that comes from speech. It is unconnected to the deep silence. We speak because we cannot tolerate the silence; its emptiness is painful and oppressive. The second kind of speech is *chashmal*—that is, speech that wells up from the silence. We all know the difference between conversing with a person who speaks from speech and a person who speaks from silence. Compare cocktail party chatter and the words of a Zen master. The speech that comes from speech is a desperate attempt to paper over the void. The speech that comes from silence wells up from having stayed long enough in the quiet to hear it become full of sound. In the words of Zen master Dogen, "I have no need for my speech to come [only] from my tongue"—that is, his speech is connected to a higher sound: the sound of silence.

A person who speaks from silence is comfortable with the space between words. Imaginereadingwordswithoutanyspacesbetweenthem— it's not easy to comprehend what is being said, is it? What a jumbled, mumbled world it would be without the empty spaces! Words by their very nature need space; the silence surrounding them is an essential ingredient of their meaning. Someone who speaks from silence allows for space, allows for emptiness.

The scroll of the Torah is black ink written on white parchment. According to the Zohar, the black-inked words represent the speech that comes from silence. The Zohar calls this "black fire." The white spaces between the words are the silence itself, the white fire. Master Levi Isaac of Berditchev teaches that a Torah scroll is deemed invalid—that is, it cannot be used in ritual reading—if the black ink of even one letter spills over into the white space. According to one mystical text, it is because the white fire is the source of the black fire and must always be protected, lest our words turn to ash. In a world overflowing with noise and nonstop words, we need to take great care to protect the spaces of our silence.

Some teachers have taught that the revelation heard long ago at Mount Sinai when God spoke to human beings was an event that occurred only once in the lifetime of the universe, calling it, according to its biblical phrasing, "A great voice which did not continue." The mystics insist that another reading is possible. In the original Hebrew, the phrase "did not continue" can paradoxically be read as "did not cease." The voice of Sinai is accessible, even after the echoes of the original revelation are long since lost in the wind. The voice of revelation has never ended.

So if the voice still continues, in what form does it live on? It thrives in the voice of the human being who speaks from the silence. This is what we have termed "silence of presence." When we listen deeply, we are able to uncover the God-voice within us. We become present in the silence. We are called by the presence, the God-voice within us, that wells up from the silence.

LEARNING THE LANGUAGE OF GOD

When you attain voice and realize your soul print, fully becoming your name, you become one with God. When Moses did this, he found his voice. Moses is the ultimate contrast to Bontsche the Silent. In the beginning of the book of Exodus, Moses is described as stuttering, unable to speak clearly. He asks God, "Who am I to go to Pharaoh? I am not a man of words." And yet by the end of the five books, Moses gives great and powerful speeches to Pharaoh, to the people, and even to God.

The beginning of the last biblical book of the Torah, called Deuteronomy (which in Hebrew is *Devarim*, meaning "words"), opens with the sentence: "And these are the words that Moses spoke." The transformation is easy to miss for the untrained reader. But when you catch it, it is simply breathtaking. Moses, who in the book of Exodus says, "I am not a man of words," has become the ultimate man of words. He now speaks the word of God. When we find our voice, when we connect with our inner soul print, then divine energy courses through us and we are able, each in our own way, to speak the word of God.

All of a sudden, the intent of biblical and Kabbalistic myth becomes clear. Moses is the one of whom the Zohar says, "The Shechinah speaks from his throat." Not surprisingly, then, it is Moses who finds his voice and is called to lead the Hebrew slaves out of Egypt, for what is Egypt if not the narrow place, the throat? And what is a slave if not a person who has no voice, whose voice is usurped by his master? Any human being who has lost the courage to speak her unique story is a slave. Moses is the biblical hero because he dares to claim his voice and live his story.

For the Hebrew mystics, however, Moses is not merely a person. He is also a mythic archetype. Anyone who attains full voice participates in the Moses archetype. The artist, writer, creator, businessman, doctor, gardener—anyone can tell you that when they feel merged with their calling, when they're no longer standing on the outside performing a task but standing on the inside, flowing with their action, then something higher is speaking through them. Remember what photographer extraordinaire Ansel Adams said? "Sometimes I get to places just when God's ready to have somebody click the shutter." Great teachers say they often get lost, and feel the words flowing by themselves, shaping and forming sentences almost magically before them. It is in such moments that we access our soul print and realize fully our unique voice in this world. In these moments of actualized soul print, we have learned to speak the language of God.

EROS AND VOICE

Now we have come full circle to the erotic and the sexual, for in a series of stunning passages Moses is described by the Hebrew mystics as being *Ish HaElohim*, "God's man." For them, that is an erotic term in all of its full power. Moses attains the ultimate mystical level referred to as *zivug* with the Shechinah, erotic union with the feminine Divine. So Moses, who attains ultimate voice—so much so that his voice merges with God's voice—is also the highest expression of erotic fulfillment, *zivug* with the Shechinah. "When Moses comes, voice comes," says the Zohar in one passage. In a second passage: "The Shechinah speaks through the voice of Moses." In a third passage, Moses is "the man of the Shechinah." That is to say, Moses is pictured as erotically merged with the feminine Divine.

CHAPTER NINETEEN

THE HARLOT BY THE SEA, A FIFTH-FACE STORY

All the themes of the previous chapters on voice and Unique Self come into sharp focus in a fabulous but little-known myth told by the third-century Babylonian wisdom masters.

In the style of the Talmudic study hall, we first will tell the story. Then we will raise a series of literary queries that highlight what is strange and needs to be explained in the tale. Finally, we will unpack its underlying erotic themes.

> Once there was a man who was very careful in his fulfillment of the law of ritual fringes. (Ritual fringes are items of clothing recommended by the Torah to help preserve purity.) This man heard about a certain harlot by the sea who accepted four hundred gold coins as her wage. He sent her four hundred gold coins and fixed a time for their encounter. When the day arrived, he came and waited at her entrance. Her maid went to the woman and told her, "That man who sent you four hundred gold coins is here and waiting at your door."

To which she replied, "Let him enter."

When he came in, she prepared for him seven beds, six of silver and one of gold, and between one bed and the other there were steps of silver, but the last steps were of gold. She went up to the top bed and lay down on it naked. He also went up after her to sit naked, facing her.

At that very moment, his ritual fringes ascended the stairs by themselves and slapped him in the face, whereupon he slipped off the bed and sat on the ground. She also slipped off and sat on the ground. She said, "I will not leave you alone until you tell me what blemish you saw in me."

He swore, "Never have I seen a woman as beautiful as you. But there is a commandment called 'ritual fringes,' and the ritual fringes have appeared to me. They represent to me a higher order of value. I cannot sleep with you."

She said, "I will not leave you until you tell me your name, the name of your village, the name of your teacher, and the name of the academy in which you study Torah." He wrote it all down and placed it in her hand. She then arose and divided her wealth into three parts. A third she used to pay taxes, a third she gave to the poor, and a third she retained. However, the beautiful bed sheets she had used on her harlot's bed she kept with her.

She then came to the study hall of Master Hiyya (the man's teacher). "Give me instructions," she said, "so that I may convert."

"My daughter," replied the master, "perhaps you have set your eyes upon one of my students." (In which case, her desire to convert may have been insincere and thus legally invalid.)

She took out the paper on which the man had written his name and the name of his village, master, and school. Upon seeing the note, Master Hiyya agreed to convert her. "Go," he said, "and enjoy your acquisition. [You may marry him.]"

The very sheets she spread for the man as a harlot she now spread for him as his wife.

A strange and wonderful story, to be sure. In the way of the myth masters, let us reread it, this time keeping our eyes and hearts open for *remezie deorayta* ("glimmering of light") and *lechisah* ("whispers of meaning").

We have here a man who is very careful about the Hebrew commandment of ritual fringes. The Hebrew word for "careful" is *zahir*, which means both "careful" and "illuminated" or "shining." Remember that the image for one's story is light. The word *zahir* derives from the word *zohar*, which, as we have seen, also means "Eros" or "fullness." Your story is always the source of your fullness and Eros.

In a different passage, the Talmud asks a wonderful question about one of the spiritual teachers. "In what was the master most *zahir*?" Literally, "In what spiritual practice was the master most careful? What was the source of his illumination?" Or in our language, "What was his soul print?" Our passage is playing off this set of allusions when it says, "He is *zahir*—he shined—in the mitzvah of ritual fringes." This indicates to us that his soul print, his special calling, perhaps even his particular struggle, was somehow connected to ritual fringes.

Biblical law speaks of a spiritual practice in which one places specifically designed ritual fringes on all four corners of a garment. The reason given for the injunction is "in order that you not stray after your hearts and eyes, which you tend to stray after." The word in Hebrew for "stray," *zonim*, plays with the Hebrew word *zonah*, meaning "harlot." Thus, ritual fringes are in some measure designed as a countermeasure to unredeemed sexuality. It is certainly not a thematic accident that the protagonist in our story, uniquely engaged in ritual fringes designed to prevent *zonim* (sexual straying), is on his way to see a *zonah*, a harlot.

The soul print of our hero is clearly bound up with his struggle with emptiness. He is going to a harlot not because he is overcome with natural sexual desire. He is not one who passes by a brothel or accesses an internet site and is temporarily overcome by lust. This harlot lives far away by the sea. She takes four hundred coins as her wage. Four hundred in biblical myth means an enormous amount. She is the highest-paid courtesan in the land. He makes an appointment with her months in advance. He is looking for a peak experience, something that "will take him there," that will break through the emptiness that plagues his days. "If only I could have that experience, whatever 'that' may be, perhaps then I would be satisfied."

He has heard of this harlot by the sea. The sea (water) is virtually always in myth the symbol of overwhelming passion. At this moment of intensity in his mundane, landlocked world, a visit to the harlot by the sea seems to be his only way out. He makes an appointment, and he waits with great anticipation for the meeting. Desire and yearning fill him, and at least temporarily his emptiness abates.

This is an encounter with shadow to be sure. It is a meeting with the most primal of energies. He has paid not just with coins, but with gold coins. "In the shadow is the gold," writes depth psychologist Carl Jung. Jung draws from alchemy and biblical myth that says gold always represents shadow. When the children of Israel leave Egyptian slavery and begin their journey to the Promised Land—the mythic journey from sickness and fragmentation to wholeness and health—they carry with them from Egypt vessels of gold and silver, vessels they have received or perhaps even stolen from the Egyptians—definitive shadow symbols. That shadow will erupt in the flames of the golden calf, formed from those very vessels. In the end, the journey can only be successful if that same gold can be melted down and re-smelted as the gold of the temple, the gold of the Ark, and the two cherubs. These are the three stages in the journey of gold/shadow in biblical myth. So the gold in our story evokes images of primal energy and shadow work—the alchemical process of turning darkness into light, shadow into spirit.

But who is she, our harlot woman? At this point, she is an archetype. She is the sexual incarnate. Relationship, depth, and commitment are not her trade. She deals in fantasy, filling up men's emptiness with peak experiences that crash the next morning. In the image of the Zohar, she is the Shechinah in exile, the lost princess.

The week of the appointment arrives. The man has been telling himself for weeks that he should not go, but when the time draws near, he simply cannot resist. His legs carry him almost magically to the village of the harlot by the sea. He knocks on her door. In the Hebrew text, it reads,

"He comes and sits at her opening." A liminal place. A pivoting point. Surely a sexual image.

"Let him enter," says the harlot. She—master of her trade—sets up seven beds, gold and silver, with ladders between each one of gold and silver, which evoke in us the shadow images we remember all too well from the Exodus story. Seductively, she climbs the ladder naked, inviting him to follow. He does, and she sits *kenegdo*, facing him, or more literally, opposite him. And yet the climb was not easy. The Hebrew text speaks of the ladder being *bein* ("between") the beds. *Bein* is a word we are familiar with from the mystery of the cherubs. God rests in the space "between the cherubs," in the empty space there. Only by walking through the emptiness between the cherubs can one touch the Divine. This is the emptiness that the Buddhist masters yearn toward and that the Kabbalists call *ayin*. Our protagonist climbs the space "between" the beds, reaching, yearning, struggling, hoping. Life is what you do with your emptiness.

The story is about to reach its natural climax. But then something magically strange and unexpected happens. The man's ritual fringes somehow follow him, ascending the ladder through the emptiness. And as he stretches his hand to caress her cheek, the fringes slap his face.

He recoils. She draws back. Almost in unison, they flee from the elevated bed and sit on the ground, facing each other, still naked. She does not understand. For the first time, they speak to each other. Voice is introduced.

"Am I not pleasing to you?"

"No, that is not it," he responds gently. "You are more beautiful than I could have ever imagined. And your face is kind. But I cannot be with you. If I cannot be with you fully in the world, then I do not want you like this."

She is at first confused and then, when she realizes his intention, overwhelmed.

For the first time in all her years, during which her body has been exposed in all of its intimacies to so many men, for the first time she feels seen.

She says to him, "What is your name? The name of your master? Your village? Your school?"

A cacophony of questions about names spills from her throat and heart. Up until this point, the text used only pronouns and nouns to describe the subjects—the man, the harlot, the maid, that man, she, he . . . no names. A desperate encounter—faceless, nameless, anonymous, and sad. His ritual fringes interrupt them in the midst of it all. The biblical verse describing the function of the fringes is, "And you shall see, and you shall remember, and you will not stray." To see is to perceive. Sexual seeing models love, but love goes deeper. Love is seeing with God's eyes, such as taking in a kind face or eyes that have suffered.

"What is your name?" she asks. The word in Hebrew is *lishmah*, meaning "for the sake of the name." The whole encounter turns around. Prostitution we defined as sex without a story. The prostitute whose name you do not know, to whose dreams and vulnerabilities you are impervious, is the archetype of the impersonal. She is de-storied. She lives in a world of pronouns. She is never "there" (*sham*). She has no name (*shem*). Both she and the man who seeks her services exemplify the prostitute archetype. The harlot in the Zohar's imagery is thus the Shechinah in exile. And in the tale's beginning, both the woman and the man manifest the prostitute archetype. Their redemption is when they move out of their anonymity and begin to weave the strands of shared story. The impersonal becomes personal.

It is not that the biblical myth masters did not recognize the power of the impersonal and even the cosmic erotic. They did. In the philosophy of Luria, the world is recreated every moment, as cosmic circles and lines erotically penetrate one another, and existence is brought forth anew. Ecstasy, dance, music, prayer, study, and meditation were all part of the prophetic service. They were all practiced in a way that would allow the initiate to access the coursing Eros of being as it washed and revitalized his soul.

So, impersonal cosmic Eros was vitally important to the prophets. However, it was the prophets who replaced the ancient cult of the temple prostitutes with the cherubs. Though the cherubs themselves are explicitly sexual figures, they are not personal. That is to say, the cherubs are not human beings who are depersonalized and transformed into symbols of cosmic Eros, which had been the case with the temple prostitutes. It was the dehumanization that troubled the prophets.

Before being replaced by the cherubs, the temple prostitute was thought to represent and even embody the Ashera goddess. Ashera and her prostitute were both commonly referred to as "my lady of the sea." Ashera temples and their prostitutes were usually found in towns by the ocean. It is very likely, then, that our passage about "a harlot who lived in a town by the sea" is precisely the Ashera temple prostitute archetype. She is the manifestation of the powerful, impersonal erotic force—but in abased, depersonalized form. This depersonalized Eros is what the prophets fiercely opposed.

In asking for the names, our harlot invites a story. By engaging a story, she is transformed from a prostitute into the Shechinah. The merely sexual becomes erotic. "What is your name, the name of your village, the name of your master, the name of your school?" Four questions. With each one, a hundred gold coins of shadow are transformed into a hundred gold coins from which the temple may be built.

Remember that the Holy of Holies in the temple, in the image of the wisdom masters, is no less than the erotic, divine marriage bed. It is that bed—the bed with a story—rooted in commitment and depth that the woman seeks. She has left the faceless world of the void and has entered the world of the name.

The harlot, who is transforming before our eyes, asks for all of the man's names. She says, in a literal translation of the Hebrew: "I will not be comforted until you tell me . . . your name." Her comfort zone has been pierced. She has lived her life being invisible even when she was in full view. She did not know anything else was possible. When he flees her bed because he wants her in a much deeper way, she is shaken to her very core. All of the compromises on which she had based her life no longer seem necessary. She knows she can never return to her old way of living.

So she breaks her one great rule to which she has held fast all these years. She asks his name. In that moment she is no longer a harlot and he is no longer a client. They become authentic, fragile, hopeful, scared, vulnerable . . . and real. Not naked of body, but naked of soul.

He does not respond to her request in spoken words. Language cannot hold in its weak and paltry vessels what he feels at this moment. His is not a silence of absence. It is a silence of presence, pure and simple. "He writes and puts it in her hand." This is the very verse in the Bible used to establish the requirement of *lishmah* in issues of marriage and divorce. *Lishmah*, "for the sake of the name." He writes in silence and gives her all of the four names that she requests—his name, his village, his master, his school. In writing, the essential self is given over.

It is an act of trust and vulnerability. His writing identifies him. The harlot could use it against him. She could sully his name, the name of his teacher, and the name of his school. He goes on his way. There are no words of parting. Silence again. She closes her business, liquidates her worldly possessions, pays taxes, and gives a large amount to the poor. Even at its height, the erotic must never obscure the ethical.

The harlot travels to the village written on the piece of paper, to the school, and to the master. The man is a disciple of Master Hiyya, one of the great teachers of the day. It is not every day that a woman of so much beauty and worldliness shows up at the study hall asking for lessons in conversion. Conversion in this story is not concerned with the dogmas of religion but with personal transformation. The legal requirement for conversion is that it be *leshem shamayim*, "for the sake of heaven." Translated more literally, *leshem shamayim* means *lishmah*, "for the sake of the name." God's name. Master Hiyya doubts the woman's intentions are "for the sake of the name alone." Perhaps she is interested merely in the advantages of marriage. He questions her. Again, silence. She does not have words that suffice to hold her truth. She takes out her slip of paper. It is filled with names. The name of the student—one of his best—of the village, of the school, and his own name, Master Hiyya.

From the scrap of paper, the master understands everything. He smiles to himself. He is a true master. Yes, this conversion is *lishmah*, for the sake of the name. He performs the conversion and perhaps officiates at their wedding as well. Marriage, like conversion, is an act *lishmah*—for the name's sake. The master understands that this conversion is the woman's claiming of her deepest name.

Until this point in the narrative, she remains anonymous. She is the harlot. She lacks a sense of personal story or name. She is first awakened to personhood by the man's last-minute refusal to engage her sexually. He is totally ready, throbbing with passion and desire. She is ready to receive him. And just then his ritual fringes, symbols of his inner story and commitments, step in. When they prevent him from acting sexually at the height of passion, she realizes there is something in his personal story more powerful than her most potent allurement. When she sits on the ground with him, she feels seen for the very first time.

Part of what moves her toward conversion and transformation is the wondrous experience of being seen. To be seen is to be loved. Love is perception. This provokes for the first time her desire to see, to know her client's name, to be a lover, to connect sex and story. She blurts out her song of names. Yet he cannot call her by name. For in a conceptual sense, she does not yet have a name in the story. The entire narrative is about her moving toward name. The word *lishmah* is most literally translated from the Hebrew as "toward her name."

The story crescendos in her conversion. On the outside, her conversion seems not to be "for the sake of God's name." After all, she wanted to marry Master Hiyya's student. On the inside, however, it was fully for the sake of God's name, for it is the encounter with Hiyya's disciple that prompts her journey toward the claiming of her name. In this deeper sense, the conversion can be said to be for the sake of God's name, for we manifest God's name when we live our unique stories.

The tale is almost over. One critical point remains to be told: the satin sheets she used as a harlot. Those she did not sell. She remained the same seductive woman she had been. Her sexual allure and the magic of her body were not lost in her spiritual transformation. "The same sheets she spread for him as a harlot she now spread for him as his wife."

In an earlier story, we met a man smitten by a woman he could only remain attracted to if she was unavailable. "Stolen waters are sweet." Sexual intoxication quickly evaporates at the thought of a "licit" sexual encounter because the fall of the temple is the exile of the erotic into the sexual. In the image of the Zohar, the Shechinah becomes a prostitute. But in this story of the harlot by the sea, it is different. Here, the attraction of the man is fueled by Eros, transcending the desire to paper over his emptiness with pseudo Eros. For that reason, he yearns no longer for illicit sex but for a rich, erotic, and spiritual relationship, with texture, intimacy, and commitment. With the help of the ritual fringes, he has moved from exile back into Eros, and has taken the harlot with him.

The myth we just explored together now becomes clear. It is the story of the Shechinah's redemption. It is the liberation of Eros. The prostitute becomes the Shechinah once again. Erotic union is achieved. The seductive thrill of the forbidden is rejected. Sexual fulfillment in all its raw and primal power is delayed. He wants her. She wants him. But only if they can share their individual stories with each other will they share their bed. The sheets of forbidden sex are now spread as sheets of erotic love.

The transformation has been made. No longer are stolen waters sweet. These two have broken the boundaries of contraction and reached for depths that had been previously inaccessible to them. They each have broken the boundaries of their limiting beliefs about what was possible for their lives. Their Eros is not transgressive but subversive. The taste of sex is returned to the *bayit*, the home and hearth of depth and commitment. In this story that means marriage. In another story it might mean something else. Depth and commitment come in many shapes and sizes. In this sacred tale, the full, erotic, sexual intoxication the man waited for on the day he sought the prostitute is fulfilled as husband and wife meeting on the marriage bed, the Holy of Holies where the Shechinah dwells. The Shechinah has been redeemed.

With all this in mind, we understand the calling out of the name, which is our ultimate cry, both at times of intense pleasure and at times of great pain. In both pleasure and pain we cry out, "Oh, God!" Many times we reach for the Shechinah, seeking comfort and wanting to be embraced, but ultimately we participate in God, for this is the ultimate comfort and the only embrace. We are part of divinity, and are held in this deep and intimate knowledge. We know that God is the force for healing and transformation in the world, that eventually good will triumph, that in the end we will know that it has always been good. We trust the name. We are part of the name.

PART FOUR

MORE FACES OF EROS

CHAPTER TWENTY

THE SIXTH FACE

IMAGINATION

S ex models the erotic, but it does not exhaust the erotic. One of the core qualities of the erotic is imagination. The Zohar, the magnum opus of Hebrew mysticism, says explicitly in many places, "Shechinah is imagination."

In common usage "imagination" is implicitly considered to mean "unreal." Indeed, "unreal" and "imaginary" are virtual synonyms. To undermine the validity of an antagonist's claim, we say it is "a figment of his imagination." In marked contrast, the Hebrew mystics held imagination to be very real. Indeed, it would not be unfair to say that they considered imagination to be "realer than real."

IMAGINATION

The power of imagination is its ability to give form to the deep truths and visions of the inner divine realm. Imagination gives expression to the higher visions of reality that derive from our divine selves. Language and rational thinking are generally unable to access this higher truth. But the imagination is our prophet, bringing us the world of the Infinite, which speaks both through us and from beyond us. This is what the biblical mystic Hosea meant when he exclaimed that God said, "By the hands of my prophets, I am imagined."

But who are these prophets who so handily imagine God? Why don't we all have access to the experience of prophecy? "Because the Shechinah is in exile," respond the mystics. The erotics of imagination have been exiled into the sexual. The sexual is the one place where virtually everyone is able to access the full power of imagination. This means that the core erotic quality of imagination no longer plays in all the arenas of our lives, where it is so desperately needed. For it is imagination that allows us to access the wisdom and vision we need to re-chart our lives.

THE SEXUAL MODELS THE EROTIC: IMAGINATION

One of the core qualities of the sexual is fantasy. To be sexual is to fantasize. Virtually every man and woman has sexual fantasies. To fantasize means simply to imagine. Fantasy is a quality of imagination. Sex models Eros because in the sexual we learn the power of fantasy. The sexual models Eros when it teaches us how to access the potency of imagination in every realm of our lives. What would it mean to fantasize about a world without hunger and sexual abuse? What would it mean to fantasize about a world in which every person's unique gift was received and honored? It is the power of fantasy and imagination that arouse us in the sexual. We require the power of fantasy and imagination to arouse us in the personal and the political as well. That is what it means for the sexual to model the erotic. When we only access the full power of imagination and fantasy in the sexual, then the Shechinah, Eros, is in exile.*

But it is in the sexual that we practice the art of imagination. The modern erotic classic *Vox* by Nicholson Baker takes place in a series of conversations between Jim and Abby. They never actually touch each other. All of their contact takes place in the realm of imagination. In this drama, their imagination is aroused in a series of phone conversations on an erotic phone line. It is precisely in the sexual where we are able to access the power of imagination. Jim evokes Abby's imagination in the sacred text of his erotic description.

> . . . I run my fingers just down the long place where the insides of your thighs touch, all the way to your knees, and then I'd let go of your legs, and they'd fall slightly apart, and as my hands started to move up inside them, with my fingers splayed wide, they'd move farther and farther apart, and then I'd lift your knees and hook them over the arms of the armchair, so that you were wide open for me, and in the darkness your bush would still be indistinct, and I'd look up at you, and I'd move on my knees so I'm closer, so I could slide my cock in you if I wanted, and I touch your shoulders with my hands, and pass my fingertips all the way down over your breasts and over your stomach and just lightly over your bush, just to feel the hair, and then I say, "I'm going to lick you now . . ."[38]

The Eros of imagination is exiled to the sexual. The liberation of Eros, which is the liberation of the Shechinah, will take place when the power of erotic imagination becomes available as a potent technology in personal, political, and social imagination. This liberation happens when the sexual becomes our guide—when the sexual models the erotic—and teaches us how to access the power of imagination in every dimension of our lives.

---

* There are different forms of fantasy, some which emerge from early childhood dynamics and others that emerge from the gorgeousness of our desire. We hope to publish a full volume focused entirely on the dynamics of sexual fantasy.

This exile of the erotic Shechinah's power of imagination is reflected both in our language as well as in our most intimate experiences. Our English word *fantasy* derives from the Greek word *phantasia*, which derived from a verb that meant "to make visible, to reveal." For the Greeks, fantasizing had nothing to do with sex. It meant "a making visible (through imagining) the world of the gods," the realm of pure spirit and forms.

So why in modern usage does the word *fantasy* first and foremost conjure up images of the sexual? We very rarely talk about economic, political, or social fantasies. We don't even talk about food fantasies. But we do talk about sexual fantasy . . . all the time. Just like the adjective *erotic*, the verb *fantasize* has found itself relegated to the narrow confines of the merely sexual. The reason is clear. In modernity, we have lost much of our ability to make visible—to imagine—the deeper visions of the spirit. It is mainly only in sex where we use imagination to conjure up images of that which is hidden.

THE EXILE OF IMAGINATION

A year ago, at a workshop on arousal and Eros, I (Kristina) was attempting to teach an important idea about the erotics of imagination. I wanted to give the students a deep embodied experience of how we have exiled imagination to the sexual. I began with a classic visualization script and instruction "take a moment to relax your body, take a deep breath in, breathe out . . . and continue to breathe slowly, deeply. Imagine there is a protective white light shining, glowing around your body . . . Feel how relaxed and calm and safe you feel as this light surrounds you . . ." I continued on for another fifteen minutes or so, saying, "Imagine being protected head to toe by this light," and then I proceeded to go through every part of the body asking them to imagine the light filling each and every body part. I ended with "feel a shield of protective light" and then asked people to share, asking, "How many of you had a clear experience?" Almost every single hand went up. I then, somewhat cheekily, challenged their claim and accused my surprised audience of being perhaps a bit dishonest. After a funny and impassioned dialogue, most of the crowd confessed to having much less of a clear visionary experience than they had initially claimed. We realized together that the New Age, with all of its good qualities, also fosters spiritual inferiority complexes: "What do you mean you can't see the colors of my aura? No high sense perception at all? You can't see my guides or angels? I'm sorry, but this just isn't going to work."

I decided to try again, but this time I was going to go all the way. I began again with another trajectory for an exercise in imagination. Without being totally raw and explicit, I invited them to imagine a sexual scene. "Imagine that your perfect lover, passionate, burning hot, and wildly sexy, has you pressed up against a wall, holding your hands firmly above your head. They whisper hungrily into your open lips, 'Your mouth tastes like a rare Cabernet . . . and I know other parts of you that taste even better.' They begin to trace the outline of your mouth with their tongue; quivering, you swallow your hesitation and respond, 'Are you going to find out?' They answer back, 'You bet your ass I am, in more ways than you can count. The very first moment I saw you, I wanted to rip your clothes off and both tenderly make love to you and ravish you deep and hard, watching as you scream the name of God!'" I continued on in graphic detail, aroused and flushed myself by my own internal thoughts! At the end of this process, I asserted with complete certainty that virtually every single person in the crowd was able to feel and sense in graphic detail the complete sexual visualization for most, if not all, of the time. We all laughed out loud. Slowly everyone realized that we had just grasped the point we were struggling with in the previous visualization. Imagination, that gorgeous erotic quality, has been exiled into the sexual.

The simplest evidence of this is that we all have no problem accessing the power of imagination when it comes to sex. As we just saw in the erotic novel *Vox*, Jim and Abby, two ordinary people, are masters of imagination in the realm of the sexual. But we have enormous difficulty accessing that same faculty of erotic imagination not only in a nonsexual visualization but also in all aspects of our nonsexual lives. The Shechinah—Eros, incarnate in imagination—has been exiled into the sexual.

THE EROS OF IMAGINATION

Mirrors of Desire

Eros and imagination hold the keys to many gates, not the least of which is the gateway to our freedom. We saw in the mirrors story of an earlier chapter how the erotic imagination of the Hebrew women in Egypt set into motion the process of the Jews' liberation from slavery. Pharaoh had insisted that the male slaves sleep in the fields separated from their wives. In defiance of the decree, women visited their men in the fields, teasing them with mirrors. Their men, wilting under the oppression of slavery, had lost their potency, but the women, in response, found tools to evoke their men's desire. With these mirrors, they engaged the men's imagination, even when their bodies would not respond. The mirrors are a symbol of the women's erotic play, which resulted in the men of Israel reclaiming their potency.

Throughout the ages, sex play has often involved using strategically placed mirrors. The mirror can amplify the quality of imagination. The mirror offers us an image, allowing us to see in a way that was previously hidden. If you hold a mirror in front of you, you can suddenly see behind you. A rearview mirror is so helpful precisely because it shows you something your normal eyes cannot see. Or position a mirror at a sharp curve in a road, and you can suddenly see around the bend, catching a glimpse of something to come that would otherwise have been hidden.

In the women's mirrors of imagination, the men were able to reclaim vision, to see the lost images of their women's sexual beauty, which the oppressive burden of slavery had rendered invisible. It was, however, not primarily the women's bodies that were made visible by the mirrors: it was the men's. The women taunted them to see their own beauty. "Look, I am more beautiful than you." Mirrors are a tool of imagination because they allow us to see images of ourselves that would otherwise be inaccessible. To see oneself making love reveals a whole other image of the erotic self.

According to one biblical tradition, this erotic play was itself the beginning of the liberation. In erotic play, the imagination is engaged.

Once the men were able to re-access their imaginations, the images of freedom were not long in following. The Exodus from slavery became just a matter of time. Sexually erotic imagination was then the model and catalyst for politically erotic imagination. About this the Talmud writes, "In the merit of the righteous women of the generation, the Hebrews were redeemed from Egypt!" When we think of typical "righteous" women, we rarely imagine troops of women with sex toys going to seduce their men in the fields. But that is the precise righteous act to which the tradition is referring. The fact that our idea of righteousness is at odds with the sexual is yet another sad example of the Shechinah in exile.

CRISIS OF IMAGINATION

The greatest crisis of our lives is not economic, intellectual, or even what we usually call religious. It is a crisis of imagination. We get stuck on our path because we are unable to reimagine our lives differently from what they are right now. We hold on desperately to the status quo, afraid that if we let go, we will be swept away by the torrential undercurrents of our emptiness.

The most important thing in the world, implies wisdom master Nachman of Bratslav, is to be willing to give up who you are for who you might become. He calls this process the giving up of *pnimi* to reach for *makkif*. *Pnimi*, for Master Nachman, means the old familiar things that you hold on to even when they no longer serve you on your journey. *Makkif* is that which is beyond you, which you can reach only if you are willing to take a leap into the abyss.

Find your risk, and you will find yourself. Sometimes that means leaving your home, your father's house, and your birthplace, and traveling to strange lands. Both the biblical Abraham and the Buddha did this. But for the Kabbalist, the true journey does not require dramatic breaks with past and home. It is, rather, a journey of the imagination.

In the simple and literal meaning of the biblical text, Abraham's command from God is *lech lecha*—"Go forth from your land, your birthplace, and your father's house." Interpreted by the Zohar, it is taken to mean not "go forth" but "go to yourself." For the Kabbalist, this means more than the mere quieting of the mind. The journey is inward, and the vehicle is imagination. Imagination is the tool that allows us to visualize a future radically different from the past or even the present. That is exactly what Abraham was called to do—to leave behind all of the yesterdays and todays and to leap into an unknown tomorrow.

It is only in the fantasy of reimagining that we can change our reality. It is only from this inside place that we can truly change our outside. The path of true wisdom is not necessarily to quit your job, leave your home, and travel across the country. Often, such a radical break indicates a failure rather than a fulfillment of imagination. True wisdom is to change your life from where you are, through the power of imagination.

THINK "COOKIES!"

Virtually every crisis, at its core, is a failure of imagination. Some years back, I (Marc) took off three years from "spiritual teaching" to get a sense of what the world tasted like as a householder. I took a job at a high-tech company, and from that relatively undemanding perch began to rethink my life and beliefs.

During this period, I did a bit of consulting with Israeli high-tech start-up firms. Truth is, I had little good advice to offer, but some of the high-tech entrepreneurs who had been my students would call me anyway. At one point, I received a call from a small start-up firm in Ramat Gan, Israel. The problem: They were almost out of venture capital, their market window seemed to be rapidly closing, and their research and development team was simply not keeping pace with their need for solutions.

Apparently, the problem lay with the elevator. The company was on the top floor of an old warehouse. The elevator was small, hot, and inordinately pungent. By the time the R&D teams would get through the daily morning gauntlet of the elevator, they had lost some of their creative sparkle. The president was convinced that this experience dulled their edge just enough to slow down the speed and elegance of their solutions. What to do? I have to confess that I hadn't the slightest idea. Our meeting was on a Friday. As was my custom, I went home for the Sabbath and met with my own private consultant, my then-eight-year-old son, Eitan. When I asked him what I should tell the company, he laughed and said somewhat mockingly, "It's simple, Dad—cookies." I did not find this particularly funny. I raised this subject with him several times, but he would only respond, with maddening gravitas, "Cookies."

Finally, I gave up on him. Several days later I went to tell the president I had found no solution. I was going up the same malodorous elevator when in a blinding flash I realized what Eitan meant. Cookies! Of course! We had all been focused on elaborate ways to fix the elevator or to move locations. Eitan—with the simple brilliance of a child—reminded me of the true issue at stake. The crux of the matter was not the elevator; it was how the R&D team felt when they left the elevator. So what to do? Cookies. We set up a table with juices, fruit, and healthy cookies right outside the elevator. So even though the ride up the elevator was terrible, people would spend the whole ride eagerly anticipating the goodies that awaited them. No one else could envision Eitan's simple yet elegant solution because their imagination was "stuck in the elevator." A simple paradigm shift was inspired by reimagining.

Just as we fear so many of Eros' expressions, we fear imagination, for imagination holds out the image of a different life. It challenges our accommodation to the status quo. It suggests that all of the compromises upon which we have based our lives might not have been necessary. Our fear of imagination is our fear of our own greatness. So we work hard to kill it. We tell children to grow out of it. "It's only your imagination," we tell them, as if this were somehow an indication that "it" was therefore less real.

It was Albert Einstein's gift of imagination that allowed him to formulate the concept of relativity. Einstein imagined what it would be like to travel on a beam of light. What would things look like? What would another traveler, on another beam of light going in the opposite direction, look like to him? Without leaps of imagination, no growth is possible, and the spirit petrifies in its old frozen masks.

DREAM TO BE FREE

Erotic imagination is about the ability to see beyond the status quo. This is the deep intent of a second group of wisdom masters, who, like those we met earlier in the chapter, also credit the liberation from Egypt to the power of imagination. The great Exodus began with a man who had a dream. He was a man by the name of Nun, a Hebrew slave under Egyptian rule. One morning he awoke, stunned by his night imaginings. He had dreamed what seemed to be the unimaginable: he saw a time when the Hebrews were free! More than free—they were courageous warriors responsible for the dignity of their own destiny. News of the dream spread. It is said that the hope inflamed by this vision unleashed the dynamics of revolution, which ultimately led to freedom.

Although it would take many years for it to become real, this dream was the true beginning of the Exodus. Slavery ends when we can reimagine ourselves as a free people. Nun was none other than the father of Joshua, successor to Moses, who led the people into the Promised Land. All freedom begins with our willingness to stand and say, "I have a dream!" And even if we don't get to the Promised Land, we may well set into motion currents of redemption that will eventually heal our world. If we don't get there, perhaps our children will. Nun's entire generation died before reaching Canaan. Yet all of his grandchildren grew up in the Promised Land.

THE POSSIBILITY OF POSSIBILITY

Nikos Kazantzakis, a prophet of imagination, writes, "You have your brush and your colors, paint paradise, and in you go." This is a near-perfect description of the spirit that animates the biblical ritual that yearly celebrates the Exodus from Egypt. Every year on the anniversary of the Hebrew Exodus, people gather for Passover. Unlike the Fourth of July or other freedom anniversaries, it revolves around not commemoration but imagination.

The guiding principle of the holiday is: every person is obligated to see himself as if he had left Egypt. This Talmudic epigram, the guiding mantra of the ritual, is explained by the Kabbalists as an invitation to make a personal reimagining of the most fantastic kind. You are in Egypt—your own personal Egypt. The word *Egypt*, *Mitzrayim* in Hebrew, means "the narrow places," the constricted passageway of our life's flow. Egypt, which Kabbalistically is said to incarnate the throat, symbolizes all the words that remain stuck in our throats, the words we never speak, and the stories of our lives that remain unlived, unsung, unimagined.

We are slaves. Slavery for the Kabbalist is primarily a crisis of imagination. Consequently, healing slavery is a ritual of imagination. For an entire evening, we become dramatists, choreographers, and inspired actors. Our first step on our path to freedom is to reimagine our lives. As playwright George Bernard Shaw reminds us, "Imagination is the beginning of creation. You imagine what you desire; you will what you imagine; and at last you create what you will."[39]

God is the possibility of possibility—limitless imagination. The first of the Ten Commandments begins, "I am God." When this God is asked to identify himself, He responds, "I will be what I will be." That is, "You cannot capture me in the frozen image of any time or place. To do so would be to destroy me." It would violate the second commandment against idolatry. Idolatry is the freezing of God in a static image. To freeze God in an image is to violate the invitation of the imagination. It is to limit possibility.

HOMO IMAGINUS

French philosopher Gaston Bachelard was right when he wrote of imagination, "More than any other power it is what distinguishes the human psyche."[40] Or listen to Norman O. Brown, the twentieth-century prophet of Eros: "Man makes himself, his own body, in the symbolic freedom of the imagination. The eternal body of man is the imagination." We turn to the Hebrew mystical master Nachman of Bratslav: "It is for this reason that man was called Adam: He is formed of *adamah*, the dust of the physical, yet he can ascend above the material world through the use of his imagination and reach the level of prophecy. The Hebrew word for 'I will imagine' is *adameh*."

For Nachman, the core human movement that gives birth to our spirit is the evolution (within the same root structure) from *adamah* to *adameh*. *Adamah* is ground, earth, Gaia. Yet it can also be read as *adameh*, "I will imagine." Man emerges from nature to live what philosopher Joseph Soloveitchik called "a fantasy-aroused existence."

Imagination is neither a detail of our lives nor merely a methodological tool. It is the very essence of who we are. We generally regard ourselves as thinking animals, Homo sapiens. French philosopher René Descartes' "I think, therefore I am" is hardwired into our cultural genes. Yet biblical myth offers an alternative understanding of the concept of humanness. The closest Hebrew word to "human," or the Latin *homo*, is *adam*. The word *adam* derives from the Hebrew root meaning "imagination" (*de'mayon*). The stunning implication is that the human being is not primarily Homo sapiens but what we will call Homo imaginus.

Man is described as being created in the divine image. "Divine image" does not mean a fixed and idolatrous copy of divinity. God has no fixed form. Instead, God is the possibility of possibility. We saw how the biblical opposition to graven images was grounded in the refusal to limit God to the confines of an image. Consequently, the statement that human beings were created in the divine image should be understood in two ways. First, humankind is not so much "made in God's image" as we are "made in God's imagination"—we are a product of the divine fantasy. Second, human beings actually participate in the divine imagination—we are Homo imaginus.

How different this understanding is from the bleak depression of modern existential thinking! Our longing for the good is dismissed by existentialist philosopher Jean-Paul Sartre as a "useless passion." Human imagining, writes Albert Camus, yet another existentialist philosopher, condemns us to misery, for it is absurd. To him, we long for goodness, beauty, and kindness in a world perpetually marred by evil, ugliness, and injustice.

But for the biblical mystic, our erotic imaginings of a world of justice and peace are the immanence of God in our lives. Our creative discontent, which drives us to imagine an alternative reality, is the image/imagination of God beating in our breast. The cosmos is pregnant with hints that guide our imaginings. We are called to heal the world in the image of our most beautiful flights of fancy. The Eros of imagination is the elixir of God running through the universe.

Imagination is powerful. Very powerful. "Think good and it will be good," wrote Menachem Mendel Schneerson, the last master of Chabad mysticism. This is true not merely because of the psychological power of positive thinking, but also because every imagining gives birth to something real that eventually manifests itself in the universe.

Imagination is transformative not only on the human plane; it has a powerful effect on the divine scale as well. Kabbalists teach that each dimension of divinity, known as a *sefira* in Kabbalah, has a color that incarnates it. By ecstatically imagining the colors of the *sefirot* and combining them according to the appropriate mystical instructions, one can actually have an impact on the inner workings of the divine force. The Zohar is even more audacious, portraying man creating God in *his* image—that is to say, in man's imagination. Unlike for the philosopher Ludwig Feuerbach, who called human imaginings of God mere projection, for the Zohar such imagination simply reinforces the substantive reality of God. While there is a limited truth in saying that God is a figment of human imagination, we need to remember that imagination is a figment of God.

For the Kabbalist, imagination is not childish. It is the spiritual reality called forth by the sacred child within. The God we do not create doesn't exist. Yes, there is a divine force that exists beyond us. Yet there is also a powerfully manifest current of divinity that is nourished by our being. The act of nourishing, sustaining, and even creating divinity is called "theurgy" by scholars of mysticism. The term expresses the human ability to dramatically impact and even grow God. One of the great tools of theurgy is imagination. In fact, theurgic imagination is the medium and message of a Kabbalistic rereading of "In the beginning . . ." This first string of letters in the Bible, *bereshit bara Elohim*, can be reread as *b'roshit bara Elohim*—"in my mind God is created."

A PILGRIMAGE BEYOND ROUTINE

If imagination can change God, then it is certainly a sacred path and vital tool in our everyday lives. Remember that the path of imagination is the path of the prophet. "By my prophets I am imagined."[41] The prophet symbolizes the divine energy of transformation that reminds us that the status quo is not holy. What is, is not necessarily what needs to be.

One wisdom text from the Hebrew Passover Seder reads: "Had God not taken us out from there, we, our children, and grandchildren would still be slaves to Pharaoh in Egypt." Clearly this is not a reasonable claim to make for the descendant of a Hebrew slave. After all, the Pharaohs are long gone, leaving behind only their pyramids to be remembered by. Rather, it is a statement about the tyranny of inertia, the idolatry of the status quo: "This is the way things have always been, son . . . don't rock the boat." It is divine imagination that breaks the status quo, freeing us from our Egypts.

The prophetic imagination, with which we are all potentially gifted, insists that things can be different and better. Three times a year, taught the biblical myth masters, at least one member of every Hebrew family should make a pilgrimage to Jerusalem. The purpose of the pilgrimage was to access the temple energy of Eros, in which imagination played an essential part. In the ecstasy of the temple service, particularly during the autumn Feast of Tabernacles (Sukkot), nearly all of the participants flirted with their prophet selves. The Hebrew word for these triannual temple pilgrimages is *aliyah le'regel*. This means something close to "going up, ascending, by foot." Walking—going by foot—is our most automatic activity. Hence the Hebrew word for "routine," a virtual synonym for the status quo, is *hergel*—deriving from the Hebrew root *regel*, which also means "foot." Just so, our English word *regular* is a direct and obvious descendant of *regel*. And so a better translation of the Hebrew term for temple pilgrimage—*aliyah le'regel*—might be "transcending routine, going beyond the regular, the status quo." How? By accessing the prophet archetype within, and with that prophetic strength reimagining life beyond its ruts and routines.

In the areas surrounding the temple, there were imagination chambers designated for prayer, meditation, and visualization. There the temple mystics would chart their journeys into the depths of imagination and soul, where God is found. Yet we are beyond the days when the spirit of imagination was reserved for spiritual elites. In our divine core, we are all prophets, architects of our own temples. Remember that Bezalel, artisan of the mini-temple in the desert, was a master of imagination. The very word *bezal-el* is a play on an earlier biblical phrase, *b'tzelem Elohim*, meaning "in the image of God."

In our interpretation, human beings participate in divine imagination and are thus invited to be the artisans of their lives. The raw materials, colors, and dimensions of your life's canvas are a given. How you mix the colors, weave the material, even choose the picture to draw on the canvas, is your artistic privilege and obligation. To be the artist of our own life—to be our own creator—is both the highest level of the sacred and the most profound expression of our glorious, our wondrous, humanity.

In a paradoxical set of mystical texts, Bezalel, the master craftsman of the book of Exodus, receives no clear blueprint from God or Moses on how to build the tabernacle. And yet he builds it in accordance with "God's will." For the Kabbalists, this is a hidden allusion to the power of holy imagination to intuit cosmic truth. When the mystics suggest that Bezalel is "taught by God," they speak in code. The artist is "wise of heart," "filled with the spirit of wisdom, intuition, and intimate understanding." All of these draw their inspiration from the breath of divine imagination.

TEMPLES OF IMAGINATION

In the mystical tradition, God shows Bezalel a vision of a tabernacle of flames. This apparition fires Bezalel's imagination and guides him in erecting the desert temple. The careful reader of the Exodus story cannot help but notice the other image of gold that emerges from the fire, namely the golden calf.

The golden calf emerges from the fire of uncertainty. The tradition tells us that Moses is to come down the mountain toward evening on an appointed day. He has scheduled a rendezvous with the people. Moses is the parent figure. He is security and comfort for the newly freed slaves. But Moses is late. The biblical commentators tell us there has been a miscommunication. Moses thought they had set the time for one evening; the people thought it was for the previous evening. They enter a twenty-four-hour limbo. What happens in this crisis of uncertainty? Can the slaves reimagine themselves as free people without Moses?

Their anxiety as they wait for Moses to come down the mountain is a test of their freedom. Will they be able to hold the center in the emptiness of their uncertainty? The answer is no. The people are not yet free. They are overwhelmed by the prospect of being free, yet responsible, actors in their own drama.

So they build an idol, the golden calf. An idol, you recall, is a "graven image." An engraved fixed image is a false certainty, a failure of imagination. In the language of the mystic Tzadok—the priest who expresses a theme that runs throughout Hebrew mysticism—they fixate on the face of the ox. The ox is only one of four images that, according to the prophet Ezekiel, are engraved on the cosmic vehicle, God's chariot. The others are the faces of an eagle, a lion, and a man. The chariot is the ultimate Hebrew mandala image. It is the locus of mystical meditation on the Divine.

Tradition has it that during the theophany of mystical encounter at Mount Sinai, the people were gifted with this precise vision of the Divine. They actually saw the four faces on the chariot. The only problem is that later they chose to focus on only one of the images—the face of the ox. The golden calf is a manifestation of the ox face. It is precisely such exclusive focus on only one image that short-circuits the imagination. "Getting stuck" is often caused not by imagination's absence but by the overbearing presence of one image. The Zohar teaches that the sin of the golden calf was that the people became so transfixed by one image that all other possibilities were blocked. This narrowness of vision is the unifying theme in the story. Initially the Hebrews' fixation was on Moses; they could not imagine life without him. When Moses disappeared, they were unable to wait for his return and transposed their Moses fixation onto the calf.

WHAT ARE YOU WAITING FOR?

There is much in our lives that evokes images of waiting. We are not fully realized—we await some future that we believe holds the secrets of our transformation and healing. But that future is fully available to us in the present. The secret is in how we wait.

One image of nonerotic waiting was given to us by playwright Samuel Beckett in *Waiting for Godot.* The play captures the all-pervading sense of ennui, despair, and hopelessness that comes when one loses all sense of present and presence, waiting instead for a fantasy messiah. This is the shadow of imagination: the inability to heal and repair the world because we are paralyzed by imaginary redeemers upon whom we wait, hoping they will finally make everything all right.

It is easy to get stuck in imagination. I am reminded of the story of a meditation teacher who gave an assignment to his students to sit in isolation and imagine themselves as something radically different from what they had ever imagined themselves to be. When the time came for the students to emerge from their meditation, one student didn't appear. Hours passed. The ashram was searched. Finally, finding the young initiate in a broom closet, they invited him to come out and join the group. He said he could not emerge, for he had imagined himself as a bull. His horns were simply too wide to fit through the door, and so he sat. Every facet of Eros has its own shadow. We must be careful not to get lost in imagination. On the contrary, imagination needs to be the place where we "get found."

An alternative image of waiting is supplied by the biblical mystics. This is not the passive and resigned waiting for Godot, but waiting for the Messiah, not as some future event that will make it all better, but as a reality, available in the full presence of the present. Messiah waiting is a process of active imagination that brings in its wake the social and spiritual activism of *tikkun*, the healing and transformation of the planet. In "waiting for the Messiah," we give birth to the first level of the existence of a better world. This is erotic waiting, as opposed to nonerotic waiting.

The act of imagination is transformative. For as the contemporary biblical mystic Abraham Isaac Kook wrote in the early twentieth century,

"Whatever you imagine exists." Your imagination discloses the way things could be and, on an inner level, the way they already are.

IN-FANCY

Little Jane comes to us in tears. "I wished Tommy would get hurt, and he did. But I didn't mean it." We comfort little Jane, wanting her to know that she is not responsible for the accident that happened to Tommy. And we are partially right, but only partially. The essential intuition of the child needs to be validated and not explained away. Our kids need to know that they are powerful. They can reimagine the world—for good or for evil, to hurt or to heal. Imagination is an essential part of responsibility.

We intuitively look for our children to create a better tomorrow for all of us. Hebrew tradition interprets the word *banim* to mean both "children" and "builders." Children are always building imaginary realms and constructing fortresses and castles with such exquisite aptitude. Children are always dashing around as superheroes, saving banks from robbers, and creating elaborate family scenarios with a few dolls. We need to nurture infancy, in-fancy, to encourage its power rather than undermine it with scoffing and ridicule.

We have long since forgotten our true nature as agents of transformation. We have forgotten that we are superheroes. At the backs of our closets and eaten away by moths, our magical capes are long neglected. Birds don't fly because they have wings; they have wings because they fly. We are what we imagine ourselves to be. The wings always come in good time. We need to reclaim our capes of holy imagination and heal our fear of flying.

THE CAPACITY TO BE

One favorite—if occasionally frightening—television show of kids in the 1960s was *The Twilight Zone.* Once there was an episode about a boxer who loses a fight as his young son watches the contest at home on television. The son believes what the father does not, namely, that Dad really can win. So with his passion, his conviction, and the great love of a son for his father, he summons up all his inner concentration and tries to reimagine the fight. Lo and behold, we see the fight being replayed on the TV screen, and this time Dad wins.

When Dad comes home a few hours later, the son tells him what happened. Dad, of course, thinks this is sweet but childish nonsense. "No!" his son says desperately. "You've got to believe. You've got to believe." The father ultimately cannot bring himself to believe—in himself, in his son, or in the power of imagination. For the third time we see the fight replayed on the screen before the father and son. The father loses as his son cries.

When raising a child, the parent often has to teach the distinction between the real and the illusory. And yet the child also must raise the parent, reminding him that imagination is real and possibility is infinite. Such is the deep wisdom of the following wonderful story told by the mystical master Nachman of Bratslav:

> The king's young son seemed to have gone mad. He sat, stark naked, underneath the king's table, claiming he was a turkey. There he sat making soft gobbles, taking his meals, and sleeping. He sat stark naked because, as he explained, nobody ever saw a turkey in human clothes. All the king's analysts and all the king's therapists couldn't put his son back together again.
>
> Finally, a wise old man, who was very young in spirit, came and offered to heal the prince. No one had heard of this old man, but the king, being rather desperate, consented to his offer. The old man promptly went and, much to everyone's consternation, sat under the table, stark naked, with the boy.
>
> "What are you doing here?" asked the very confused and surprised prince.
>
> "Why, I am a turkey," responded the old man.
>
> "Well . . . I guess that's okay."
>
> And the two became friends, as only turkeys can. Some days went by and the old man put on a shirt.

"What are you doing?" cried out the boy. "I thought you were a turkey."

"Why, I am," said the man, "but is there any reason a turkey cannot wear a shirt?"

The boy thought, and truthfully, although it did seem a bit improper, he could think of no substantive reason why a turkey could not wear a shirt. And if a turkey could wear a shirt, well, it was a bit chilly, so he put on a shirt as well. And so the process continued to pants, shoes, and eventually to sitting at a table, until the prince was fully healed.

Often a child seeks to compensate for the pathologies of society. The kingdom suffers from a lack of imagination. A lack of imagination is a lack of soul. So the child rebels and seeks healing through an increase of imagination. Yet it does not always hold that an increase of imagination is an increase of soul. Sometimes we overdose and lose ourselves in the very imaginings that were to be our healing. Often such overdosing is the key to the psychological reality maps of children. The child can be made whole only if we enter with her into the world of imagination. Our healing can flow only from that inner place. The underlying therapeutic principle can be summed up in two words: empathetic imagination, which is essential not only to psychological healing but also to all authentic relationships.

Next time you are in an argument with someone you love, step out of the circle of conflict and imagine yourself as that person. Try to experience the argument through his or her psyche. The Kabbalists say God is radically empathetic to the suffering of every individual. To be a lover is to be like God—to enter into the space of your beloved so you can receive the full depth of her story, including her loves and triumphs, but especially her hurts, fears, and vulnerabilities. For the mystic, this is the essence of our relationship to the Divine, both within and beyond. To feel the pain of the Shechinah in exile is to exercise imagination; it is to enter divine space and feel what God feels.

Whenever they see their beloved children arguing, parents are greatly pained. Imagine through your parenting experience how God must feel when his children kill each other. In doing so, we participate in the pain of the Shechinah in exile.

Just so in joy. When our children love each other, we are delighted beyond words. Imagine how God must feel when we are good to one another. In kindness, we touch ecstasy. We participate in the rapture of the Shechinah redeemed.

CHAPTER
TWENTY-ONE

THE SEVENTH FACE

PERCEPTION

The Tantric Secret of the Cherubs teaches that love and Eros are skills that are modeled by the sexual. Sex is our teacher. Those very qualities are what teach us—in all aspects of our nonsexual lives—how to be great lovers. We rise in love when we learn the art of Eros.

We do not need to wait for love to happen to us. We can choose to be lovers. The reason we can choose is because love is not an emotion, at least not in the sense we are used to thinking about emotions. We are taught that an emotion is something that happens. We are love-struck. Blinded by rage. We fall in love. We experience emotions, negative and positive, as external forces with which we have to contend; we are victims of their venom or recipients of their nectar. We are plagued by emotion, wracked by guilt, paralyzed by fear, heartbroken, carried away, and smitten. We are wounded by Cupid's arrow, poisoned by bitterness, or driven insane.

THE SEXUAL MODELS THE EROTIC: PERCEPTION

The first great truth of Hebrew Tantra is that love at its core is not an emotion. It is a perception of another person—a perception that often arouses in its wake great and powerful emotion. Love and Eros are modeled by sexuality. The sexual always begins with a perception, usually external in nature. It is often an external perception of beauty or power. It might be the perceptive faculty of sight that arouses sexual attraction. But it could just as well be touch, hearing, smell, or taste. Any of these may arouse an emotional, intellectual, or even chemical attraction.

As with sex, so with love and Eros. Love is also initiated by perception, albeit an internal perception. It is the ability to see, to intuit, to sense the infinite divine specialness, the divine point, in the beloved. Sex models love and Eros in that attraction is aroused by perception.

Perception, as we noted, is often that of physical beauty. If wonder at the sight of beauty does not seem unusual to us, then we have lost touch with its counterintuitive and almost mystical quality. One of the original poets who grasped the counterintuitive nature of the erotic perception of beauty was John Donne:

> *If ever any beauty I did see*
> *Which I desired, and got, 'twas but a dream of thee.*
> *And now good-morrow to our waking souls,*
> *Which watch not one another out of fear;*
> *For love, all love of other sights controls,*
> *And makes one little room an everywhere.*[42]

Donne points out the perception of "beauty I did see" that arouses love is diametrically opposed to our usual "watch[ing] . . . one another out of fear." The perception of beauty that arouses love has the power to override all of our more contracted watching out of fear. That is Donne's intent with the words "for love, all love of other sights controls," meaning the perception of love triumphs over the perception of fear.

Donne's poem bridges us naturally from the perception of beauty to the deeper perception of love. The cherub mystics took it one step further. They taught that there is a deeper form of sexual arousal that is provoked not by the perception of physical beauty but by the perception of love. This is somewhat more common in women than men but relatively rare in both. Imagine how the world would change if men were aroused to sex by the perception of love. The entire structure of reality and relationships—and with that, politics, power, and everything else—would radically change. It would be a world moved by Eros rather than pseudo Eros.

THE EROS OF PERCEPTION

The Path of Hebrew Tantra

The mystics understood that sight—the core perceptive faculty of the sexual—models and can even lead to the more profound perception of love.

The great myth master the Maggid of Mezritch was very young and had just begun his teaching path. He was sitting one day minding his own business when a "loose woman" came walking by, provocatively dressed in a way that was simply impossible to miss. Apparently, the master had a momentary sexual response, a fact that agonized his soul. A great revulsion began to rise in him, so he started visualizing the lowly, physical origin of the woman, reminding himself that from the earth she was made and to the earth she would return. He repeated the mantra "from dust to dust," frantically conjuring up images of formation and decomposition until with this visualization he broke through the sexual attraction. He even started throwing up in utter disgust.

Clearly, at this stage in his life, the sexual was for the master—as for the Buddha, Jesus, and virtually all the saints at some point in their path—a trap to be avoided at all costs. The good news is that this is not the end of the story.

Many years later, after the master had deepened greatly in his service, he taught a very different teaching about our relation to the sexual. He tells the story of Akiva, the master who witnessed the destruction of the temple.

Akiva was at the time a well-known teacher who often represented his community to the Roman powers. One of the Roman leaders, Turnus Rufus, returned home one day greatly distressed. "I just debated Akiva," he told his wife, "and as usual he made a fool of me."

"Let me deal with him, my dear," coolly replied his wife.

So Mrs. Turnus Rufus—one of the ravishing beauties of the time—invited Akiva for a meeting. She alone was present. The candles burned seductively low. The most arousing and intoxicating incense was lit. The finest wine to drug the senses was served. The wife of Turnus Rufus was dressed in the most elegant yet revealing of clothing, the curves of her body more sexually alluring than one could ever dare imagine.

Akiva saw her. He spit, he laughed with joy, and he cried.

Akiva spits to avoid being seduced only by the Roman woman's allure. He laughs with joy and pleasure because her sensual beauty opens the door for him to see her inner gorgeousness. He cries because her beauty moves him in the very core of his soul.

The Maggid wrote, "In beholding her great beauty, Akiva saw how this beauty was but a reflection of the greater beauty of the Shechinah—the feminine Divine."

The feminine Divine to which the Maggid referred is not Venus or Aphrodite sitting on Olympus, nor is it merely the platonic "form" of beauty. Rather, by seeing her sexual beauty, Akiva was moved to a deeper kind of perception. He saw her body in all of its immense beauty, and then he looked in her eyes and there he saw . . . Shechinah. He saw not merely the dust that the woman was composed of and the dust to which she would return, but rather the Divine with which she was suffused and the Divine to which she would return.

With this interpretation of Akiva's ancient story, we see that the Maggid has done a one hundred eighty-degree turn. In the first story, sexual seeing was a trap to be avoided at all costs. In the second story, with Akiva as his teacher, the Maggid recognized that sexual seeing is a door of perception, which, when cleansed, opens us up to the infinite perception of love. When done consciously, sexual gazing leads to a lover's deeper perception. Love is the perception of the Shechinah in the other.

All this and more is understood by the Maggid later in his life. In a parallel source he makes a religiously radical suggestion: "The spiritual initiate should seek out sexual beauty in the marketplaces." Why? In order to practice the cherubic mystery that transposes sexual seeing to the soul's perception. Sexual seeing can be avoided, neurotically crushed, or expanded as a door to the higher seeing of love. In picking which path to walk you must employ common sense. Clearly, there are times for avoidance and discipline. Yet in the higher world for which we strive, it is only the path of expansion that will lead us back to love.

"All Eros from the sexual to pure love is of the same essence," wrote the nineteenth-century mystical master Nahum of Chernobyl. It is therefore possible to transpose sexual looking into the wondrous perception of love. The sexual models the erotic; this is the Secret of the Cherubs.

RECEIVING THE SHECHINAH

A strange teaching of the wisdom masters is: "If you are in the middle of meditation—rapturously receiving the Divine Presence—and guests that need greeting beckon at the door, first greet your guests and then finish the meditation." Why? Because the wisdom teaching instructs: "Greater is receiving guests than receiving the face of the Shechinah."

Now let's suggest a deeper reading. Greater is receiving the Shechinah in the face of your guest than receiving the Shechinah in meditation. Receiving the Shechinah, suggests the teaching, is perceiving and receiving the divine point of beauty that dwells in each person. Eros and ethics become one.

Now back to Akiva. The master Akiva is one of the important sources of our great understanding that sex models Eros and love. He teaches a simple if elegant truism.

If sexual perception is so powerful, then it must insinuate something greater. It must model love. Love, teaches Akiva, is not merely an emotion that happens to you; love is also a perception that allows you to see the inner gorgeousness—the Shechinah—in the other.

In this passage we are not told of the outcome of the meeting between Mrs. Turnus Rufus and the master Akiva. In a different passage, however, we are told that they fall in love and Akiva marries a second time. Isaac Luria explicitly implies that this is a bond that grows out of the power of sexual seeing transmuted into pure and deep love. He makes the radical assertion that Mrs. Turnus Rufus is an incarnation of Lilith, the provocatively sexual first lady of ancient Hebrew myth. In her encounter with Akiva, both she and the master are transformed. Akiva is powerfully moved by the potent divine spark that burns in the woman's Eros. He sees her. She feels seen. Mrs. Turnus Rufus becomes Mrs. Akiva. Leaving Rufus and the pomp of Rome behind, she marries Akiva, the first man who really "sees" her.

CELEBRATORY SEEING

One of our good friends, Lesley, tells us that, in high school, her friends said one of the things they loved about hanging out with their African American male comrades was that "they knew how to look at a woman." Now Lesley did not mean that they were ogling or rude, or that they looked at women in an inappropriate sexual manner. What she did mean is that when she and her friends were with this group, they felt seen and appreciated in a special way. They didn't just pay attention to girls most guys would think were good-looking. They knew every woman was beautiful, and were more than happy to let her, and anyone else around, know it as well.

Allan Bloom, in his erudite work *Love & Friendship*, is correct in critiquing a society that has lost its natural Eros. We have lost our ability to distinguish between celebratory looking and inappropriate, invasive looking. This fall of Eros, in Bloom's phrase, cuts us off from the natural and sacred vitality that is one of the essential passageways to love.

The Babylonian wisdom masters speak of a blessing that one would recite upon encountering a beautiful person. And it is worth remembering that a person's beauty and virtue are not determined by the artificial impositions of a centerfold culture; it is determined as beauty must always be—in the sacred eye of the beholder.

CIRCUS CLOWNS AND COUNTY FAIRS

Love is a perception; to be loved is to be seen. When I (Marc) was a kid, I was little, scrawny, not worth a moment's notice by anyone or anything—or so I thought. I was at the county fair in Columbus, Ohio, with my parents and brothers, who were otherwise occupied. I had wandered off, as kids do, seeking amusement or at least distraction. And there Distraction stood, draped in a long suit of glitter: a six-foot-tall circus clown. He was amusing a crowd of candy-sucking, entertainment-hungry fairgoers. Being small, I squeezed my way toward the front and crouched down so I could look up at the glittery spectacle from between people's legs. And from that position I watched and whooped with laughter along with everyone else.

When the show had reached its finale and the clown was about to quit his stage, he looked down. His eyes locked with mine and lit up with a great warm smile. Perhaps I amused him—a scrawny thing crouched on the ground. Perhaps he pitied me, or perhaps this was just part of the act. Or just maybe it was spontaneous, real, and loving. Whatever the case, he held out his shimmering arm and motioned for me to stand up and join him. Surprised, terrified, and delighted, I stumbled out into the center of the circle. With a great extravagant gesture, he pulled out a large red envelope and handed it to me. I opened it and read: "Free Ice Cream—All You Can Eat." I was sure it was either magic or a miracle. "For me?" I asked dumbfounded. "For you, and no one but you," the clown said, grinning into my bedazzled eyes.

I bounded back to my family to show off my newly won ticket to ice cream paradise. So what if the three double-scoop cones left me sick in the morning? I had been seen! By a jumbo circus clown, no less, who had looked out into the crowd and seen me. From then on, I had a habit of lingering around fairgrounds, hoping to duplicate that magical encounter. Well, it never happened again. But it had happened once, and that was enough.

It's the kind of moment that makes a person want to go to clown school, just so that somewhere along the way you could change some little kid's self-perception. But we need not don a clown suit to peer into a crowd of faces and perceive the divinity of a person's uniquely gorgeous soul. We don't need to give out free ice cream on the street, but we do need to give out all the love and attention our eyes can muster. We do need to become lovers, masters of erotic perception.

It is not by accident that the common term for dating is "seeing someone," or that the outdated but expressive term for trying to pick someone up is to "make eyes" at him. Our language reveals that being seen is essential. It is really what being loved is all about. Love is a perception. A great lover is one who trains, refines, and excels in the art of perception. When a lover is with you, you have the wonderful sense of having been truly seen.

THE NEED FOR PIETY

Many years ago, when I was nineteen, I broke up a relationship with a woman whom I loved with all my heart. Though not yet a rabbi, nor even a teacher, I felt powerfully called to the spirit. I believed, as I had been taught, that only a full curbing of sexuality would allow me to be sufficiently pure to answer my spiritual calling. My teachers at the seminary reinforced my desire for piety and "purity" and lauded my decision. I broke off the relationship abruptly, honestly citing my need for purity as my primary motive.

Although I was completely unaware of it then, this was, in retrospect, probably the greatest sin of my life. Paradoxically, it was the fear of what I thought to be sin that brought about the greatest sin—the inability to see one I loved and who loved me.

About six months after we broke up, I received a letter from her that had apparently been written six months earlier and gotten lost in the mail. It was a beautiful note. I cried for two hours after I read it. I did not cry again for twelve years, when I was thirty-one.

At that time I was married and needed to make a decision about getting divorced. I went to the person who had been my primary teacher for many years. The first words out of his mouth, before he really had a chance to think, were, "But you will ruin your career." It was the first in a series of moments of clarity that set me off in search of a deeper truth. I decided to reject the counsel of my teacher and follow my heart into the unknown.

I understood then that a teacher who is not a lover, who cannot see his students but only the students' "careers," is not a real teacher. I knew that I needed to leave such teachers behind.

DISAPPEARING-SPOUSE SYNDROME

There is a wonderful pre-marriage ceremony in biblical myth called *tenaim*. It represents the mystical merging of the two souls that occurs even before the wedding. It is a spiritual prenuptial agreement in which we read a bill of mutual commitment where both sides commit "not to run away and not to disappear." It seems redundant—if you do not run away, then, of course, you will not disappear! That is, unless you remain physically present yet are not available. Or worse, if you cause your partner to disappear. You do everything you are supposed to do—in the kitchen, in the bedroom, and in the family room—but your partner has long since disappeared from your consciousness.

There is a fantastic story by Ray Bradbury that captures beautifully the Disappearing-Spouse Syndrome. It is set in the year 2500. Robotics has developed into a fine art. A woman wants out of her marriage but doesn't want to hurt her spouse, so she contrives the perfect escape plan. She will have a robotic replica of herself made, substitute it for herself, and be free. There is just one small difficulty with robot replicas. Humans have a heartbeat, but robots give off a sixty-cycle hum. When her husband gets close, he will hear the hum and know the robot spouse is a fake.

The woman has a brilliant idea. She programs the robot's first action to be to record her husband's heartbeat and incorporate it into the robot's own system. It's an ingenious idea, ensuring that her husband will never know the difference. All is prepared. The robot goes to the husband and takes the necessary recording of the heartbeat . . . only to find out that the husband himself gives off a sixty-cycle hum!

A chillingly comic tale to be sure, and all the more potent in its twisted irony. It is the modern tragedy of the "disappearing spouse," who, although present in person, has long ago fled in spirit. A dearth of perception is bound to turn any healthy heartbeat into a sixty-cycle hum.

Our all-too-well-founded fear of being replaced by robots is no less than a fear of a world robbed of erotic perception, of the ability to be seen for ourselves, instead of being seen as interchangeable cogs in the world machine. But we can re-eroticize even the most sterile of modernities. As Bradbury hints, it begins with the heartbeat, with hearing and perceiving the unique rhythm of the person who stands beside us. This is Eros, no robots necessary.

YADA, YADA, YADA

To fully ground our point that love is a perception, we need to summon up the evocative English phrase "carnal knowledge." It is an idiom that is rooted in the translation of the biblical word *yada*, which in Hebrew means "perception" and "knowledge." Yet it is used in biblical myth first to describe sexual knowing—carnal knowledge, as in "Adam knew Eve, his wife"—and only later to describe noncarnal, erotic perception.

The first biblical text says, "Adam knew Eve, his wife." Carnal erotic knowledge. Only later does the text say, "You shall know God with all your heart." Noncarnal erotic knowledge. This is because sex is the first level of seeing. It models the perception of loving. It is often the most potent realm in which we access perception. Thus, sexual seeing can guide us to a much deeper form of perception.

William Blake wrote:

LOVE to faults is always blind:
Always is to joy inclin'd,
Lawless, wing'd, and unconfin'd,
And breaks all chains from every mind.[43]

Martha Beck, on the other hand, said in her book *Expecting Adam*: "Whoever said love is blind is dead wrong. Love is the only thing that lets us see each other with the remotest accuracy."

Beck is right, and Blake is wrong. Love is not blind! Infatuation is blind. Love is in the details. Not in the sense of the petty particulars, but more as twentieth-century Hebrew mystic Abraham Isaac Kook writes, "Love is 'the great art of the spirit.'" Art is where each magnified detail is part of a harmonized whole. An artist is a master at perceiving.

What is so special about the artist's eye? It is always open to the new, the never-before-noticed. The poet Emily Dickinson describes this kind of perception as having "unfurnished eyes." What a beautiful phrase! We don't need to wait for Godot, an external God who will redeem us with a great new vision of truth and beauty. We merely need to unfurnish our eyes. Our eyes are furnished with old trauma, competition, greed, and jealousy that color our perception and prevent us from seeing the world clearly. But love removes that blindness. Love is like a magnifying glass. We notice more about the beloved than we notice about anyone else, for good and for bad.

Of course, criticism can certainly be the shadow side of perception. Every great quality of the spirit has its own unique shadow. We all know that the second we decide to love someone, we start noticing virtually every detail of his dress, habits, idiosyncrasies, all the wonderful and the not so wonderful. But love is much more than just a magnifying system for small particulars. The artist's eye, the lover's eye, is unfurnished, and the unfurnished eye sees true. It is not blinded with the opaque trappings of preconceptions and misconceptions. Eros calls us to have unfurnished eyes—not only in the very narrow realm of personal relationships but also in every arena of our lives.

For this reason we often equate the lover and the poet. Indeed, it is love that moves all of us to be poets. Who has not at some time picked up a pen to write poetry for his or her beloved? And if you haven't yet, you should now. Poetry and love are intimately related because poetry, like love, is an art of perception.

Poet Allen Ginsberg is in the tradition of the great lovers when he reminds us of the need for "clear seeing and direct perception." We always begin talks on poetry by quoting Ginsberg: "Don't treat an object indirectly or symbolically. Rather, look directly at it and choose the aspect most immediately striking . . . and then write."

Love and poetry are about noticing the details. Charles Baudelaire, who precipitated the shift in poetry's focus from the ethereal to the concrete, understood this well. All of a sudden, the poetic consciousness of the nineteenth century started to include the city, real estate, carriages, and machinery. It was the great lover Walt Whitman who said, "Bring the muse into the kitchen."

To be a lover, writes Chögyam Trungpa, a Zen master, is to know that "things are symbols of themselves." What Trungpa means is that if you perceive a thing directly, it's completely there, completely revelatory of the eternal universe that's in it. In the lover's vision, perception is first narrowed, concretized, and then expanded into the realization that in the ordinary resides all of the extraordinary. The lover's eye is open, ready to receive the Divine in all it sees.

REVEALERS OF THE DIVINE

Weddings . . . they can be pretty beautiful. There is a moment when the bride and groom walk down the aisle or look at each other for the first time under the wedding canopy, where you just gasp and quietly say, "Oh my God—this is magnificent!" Such moments help us understand the enigmatic Kabbalistic koan: "The bride and the groom are revealers of the Divine." We all know that special and wonderful feeling we have as we witness the vows of the bride and groom on their wedding day.

Something different, something divine, is in the air. God, holiness, the force, the numinous—all of these become felt presences at a wedding.

You may ask, what is so special about the bride and the groom that their hearts are able to uniquely reveal the divine forces of beauty and goodness in the world? The Kabbalists explain: On their wedding day, the bride and groom reveal God by revealing the Divine in each other. The bride sees something in the groom—a glimpse of his infinite specialness, his divinity—that no one has previously been privileged to witness. And the groom likewise perceives something in the infinite specialness of his bride, something that no one—not her parents, not her best friends—have been able to grasp fully. We stand moved, humbled, and quietly ecstatic as we witness the revelation of divinity, of the God who walks among us. The highest truth and the highest potential in each other are revealed through the prism of love's light that is the nuptials.

To say, then, for example, that the bride loves the groom is consequently to say that the bride perceives the infinite specialness, the divinity, in the groom. In that perceptive experience, she is pleasured and feels the grand rapture and beauty of loving. All lovers are revealers of the Divine in each other. They are God seeing God.

"All love is the love of God," wrote Menahem Recanati, a Renaissance mystic. Love is to perceive another person unmasked, in the pristine beauty of his spiritual and emotional nakedness. Love is the pleasure produced by such a perception, when our loving awareness strips the beloved of all outer coatings until she stands fully revealed before the perceiving mind. Love is a perception of the full divine wonder that is your beloved.

It is like Dante's description of his first sighting of Beatrice: "Something like the glory of God walking towards him." Or for those of us who don't speak in the bombastic language of "the glory of God," we turn in *Anna Karenina* to the more personal existential description of Tolstoy's Levin on the night his wife, Kitty, gives birth to their child:

> Levin . . . jumped out of bed, hardly conscious of himself and
> without taking his eyes off her for a moment, put on his dressing
> gown and stood still gazing at her. He had to go but he was

unable to move, so struck was he by the look on her face . . .
her flushed face, with soft hair escaping from under her night
cap, was radiant with joy and dissolution. Little as there was of
artificiality and the conventionalist in Kitty's character, Levin
was still astonished at what was laid bare to him now when every
veil had been removed and the kernel of her soul shone through
her eyes. And in this simplicity and in this baring of her soul he
could see her, the woman he loved, more clearly than ever.

Tolstoy understood that love is the perception of the soul's nakedness. To love someone is to see her in all the rawness of her authenticity,
that is to say, in her divinity. As the novelist D. H. Lawrence said in *Pan-
sies*, "What's the good of man unless there's a glimpse of a God in him? . . .
And what's the good of woman unless she's a glimpse of a Goddess of
some sort?" To love is to perceive the God and the Goddess in the other.
And the desire to be loved is the great desire for that God or Goddess to
be seen.

INSIDE, INSIGHT

Love is all about insight, or rather, in-sight. It is the ability to see into
the inside of the inside, into the Holy of Holies that is your lover. Eros
is being on the inside. Thus, love is an erotic perception of the highest
order. Naturally, you have to move way beyond sexual seeing. Sex only
models Eros. To be an erotic lover you have to understand that "what is
essential is invisible to the eye," as Antoine de Saint-Exupéry reminds us
in *The Little Prince*.

When something is far from you, you have to open your eyes really
wide to see it. As it gets closer, you squint your eyes; when it gets really,
really close, you close your eyes. Seeing with closed eyes is when we perceive way beyond seeing. The adjective *close* and the verb *close* are the
same word. Closeness, intimacy, higher vision—all of these happen when
we close our eyes. We move beyond sight and invite the other faculties of

perception to guide us. Smell, sound, touch, and taste all become alive in a deeper way when we cloak our eyes.

The central mantra of Hebrew tradition is a daily meditation on the unity of God. It is called the *Shema*, the listening prayer. Tradition requires that it be recited with hands covering the eyes, because it is only with eyes closed that we no longer see the world of distinctions and differences. Only then do we appreciate the fact that the boundaries between us are but illusions. For we are one and all is one. This is the meaning of the universal religious epigram "God is One." We close our eyes in order to let drop the screens that so distort our perception.

It is also why, when making love, in the moment of rapture that moves us beyond sexual seeing to lovers' union, we close our eyes. In the Zohar, *Shema* is the lover's prayer. Its goal is to achieve erotic union with Being precisely in the same way sexual love achieves erotic union with the beloved. The highest perception of loving is the realization that you are part of God.

TRAILING CLOUDS OF GLORY

A number of years ago I (Marc) was teaching at a spiritual retreat center in California. Teaching was beautiful. Yet I was also in the midst of what I would call a "deepening" in my relationship with two good friends there, Ronit and Gil, the married couple who were organizing the seminars. As in every authentic relationship, there are pivotal moments where it either deepens and blossoms or wilts away. Well, we were at such a point, and I was having a hard time fully appreciating their point of view. That is, until orientation the second week, which, as always, was being masterfully led by Ronit.

In the midst of this evening, I caught Gil watching Ronit as she was talking to the group. A little later I glimpsed a momentary expression on Ronit's face as she watched Gil doing his presentation. Both displayed expressions of such utter love that I was jealous. Clearly, they saw in each other a light and a divinity that, much as I loved them both, I was not able to see on the same level. I prayed to be open to seeing just a fraction of what they each—in the private images of lovers—saw in each other.

Wonder of wonders, my prayer was granted. Even if but for a moment, I was actually able to enter Ronit's love and get a glimpse of how she saw Gil. Conversely, for a millisecond, I was privileged to see Ronit as a flash of light reflecting off Gil's eyes. What a glory it was to behold! The verse that found its way to my mind was Wordsworth talking about how we all, as newborn babes, enter the world:

> . . . *not in utter nakedness,*
> *But trailing clouds of glory do we come*
> *From God who is our home.*[44]

We are born so beautiful, and the beauty never fades. Our eyes just get tired, and we stop looking. It is this wisdom of love that psychologist philosopher R. D. Laing, one of our favorite modern thinkers, understood so well:

> *What we think is less than what we know;*
> *What we know is less than what we love;*
> *What we love is so much less than there is.*
> *And to that precise extent we are much less than what we are.*[45]

ON IN-LAWS AND LOVE

In the end, we all want so desperately, so deservedly, to see and be seen. This is one of the best reasons to get married: to reveal and be revealed. Much of the tension in a family between the newlyweds and each set of in-laws is based on this dynamic of perception as well. The parent who so loves her child is convinced that she sees him or her like no one else could. "Then along comes this young woman—who did not give birth to him; nurse him on sleepless nights; worry, weep, and wonder over him for twenty-five arduous years—and she knows how to love him? She sees him, knows him, in a whole different way than I do? Unfathomable!" And yet it's true. The mother and father intuitively know that the lover of their child perceives their child in myriad ways that they cannot.

Listen to this Hasidic story of perception:

The Malach was in search of a wife. They called him the Malach, the Angel, for his appearance was so stunning, his wisdom so immeasurable, he seemed a divine presence among common men. Word spread throughout the *shtetls* and cities, and the search for a wife began.

The representative of the Malach came to the town of Shalom Shachnah, a great master in his own right, who was famous for his intense study. He would sit before stacks of books, consumed in the words, sweating with concentration, moving for nary a bowl of soup or a stoke of the fire. Shalom had a daughter who, rumor had it, had inherited more than a little of her father's intensity.

The Angel had found his partner—the *shidduch* (match) was made. A buzz went out far and wide: the Angel was marrying the daughter of Shalom Shachnah.

Crowds gathered for the celebration. Everyone was there. A great host of people. But the host of the party? The father of the bride—where was he? He simply did not show up. Indeed, back at home, he had not stirred from his study, engrossed as he was in his great stack of books.

The wedding went on without him—and how it went on! It was ecstatic, enlightening, with dance and drink canopied as if by a bow of divine light, as befit the joining of the Angel and his bride.

After the wedding, the mother of the bride went home to her book-bound husband and screamed, "Where were you?! Do you know what you just missed? A wedding like you wouldn't believe! Your own daughter's wedding . . . and she was wedded to an absolute angel, a celestial soul! And you, you honored your books over your own blood! I refuse to speak to you until you go to their house in Mezritch for a proper Sabbath to give them the respect they deserve."

And what is a man to do when his wife protests so? He set out the next week for the three days' travel to Mezritch. He arrived for the Sabbath. The Sabbath prayers commenced. The Angel started to sing. His voice rose and riveted each soul in the room—a voice unparalleled in earthly and heavenly spheres. A light filled the prayer hall, a light so enormous and magnetic that Shalom was overcome by its brilliance and fainted. The song finished, and Shalom awoke.

The Angel approached him and asked, "Tell us, Shalom, what did you see?" Shalom answered in an awed whisper. "I saw your angels. I saw all of your surrounding angels dancing about your shoulders! They were exquisite, amazing sights to behold! It was too much to bear. I passed out."

The Angel, shaking his head, replied, "Dear father-in-law, it is a good thing that you passed out when you did. For if you had beheld your daughter, you would have perceived an even mightier and more majestic host of angels surrounding her. Their brilliance would have so overwhelmed you that you might not have woken up at all."

An incredible tale. At first glance, Shalom seems tragic; but in the final analysis, he is redeemed. Quite simply, Shalom, with all his study of the sublime, could not perceive the sublime nature that sat before him in the form of his own daughter. But that's okay, because the Malach could. The Malach—with his acclaimed celestial radiance—saw in his wife an exquisiteness even greater than his own. And this beauty was not for her father, who would not have been able to bear it, to perceive. Indeed, it was not meant for him to bear. Parents, with all their immense love, are privy to a different perception than what the lover beholds.

This story relates what the Hindus call *bhakti*—truly seeing the other bathed in his or her divine radiance. "Love your neighbor as yourself," cries the famous line in the biblical book of Leviticus. But loving your neighbor is not the whole story. That quotation is three words too short.

What all too often gets left out of the passage are the three last, and perhaps most crucial, words. For the complete verse reads: "Love your neighbor as yourself—I am God." To love your neighbor is to know that the "I"—the essential self—is God. To love your neighbor is to reveal, to disclose, their ultimate divinity.

A PERCEPTION-IDENTIFICATION COMPLEX

Even when we say that love is perception, we do not mean it is merely perception. The beloved not only perceives the Divine, the soul print of her lover, but she also identifies him with that divinity. She understands that as his essence. She sees and identifies her beloved with his infinite specialness. This stage in the art of loving I have termed "the perception-identification complex."

This notion of perception identification is most clear in reference to parents and children. I love my kids. The neighbor's kids, however—well, they are just so incredibly rambunctious, annoying, and immature. At the same time, I recognize that there may really be no appreciable difference between my kids and the neighbor's kids. Why, then, do I love my children and not the neighbor's? Not merely because they're my children—but rather, because I am invested in them. This investment causes me to focus on them more intensely than on other kids. The result: I am able to perceive them in ways other people are simply unable to do. I perceive my children's beauty in a way that no one else can.

But perception of beauty is not enough. If I am a good parent, I know my child also has faults, and those shortcomings are real. They need to be addressed forthrightly and never swept under the rug. Because love is not blind. Love is a microscope. Parents should be madly in love with their kids, but they should never be infatuated with them. Infatuation—that's what is blind.

Having said this, how is it that I love my children even after I know their long laundry list of faults? The answer is the second step in the formula: identification. I perceive both my children's goodness and their not-yet-such-goodness, but I identify their goodness as the core of who they are. All the rest I will deal with in whatever way necessary, but I know that at their core the trailing clouds of glory are the essence of my children, and I love them for that. With kids not our own, what we often (wrongly) tend to do is to identify the children with their failings or acting out instead of with their infinite specialness and grandeur.

MIRARI

Have any of your friends ever gotten engaged and everybody's response was something like, "I can't believe it. She is going to marry him? We don't understand what she sees in him." But see in him she does. She perceives him, sees him, and discloses him, in a way that we are unable to access. Our eyes are too "furnished" to see the miraculous, infinitely unique glory that is her beloved.

But let there be no mistake about it: glorious he is. To her, the man is a miracle. The word *miracle* comes from the Latin *mirari*, meaning "to behold with rapt attention." She has beheld the wonder of her betrothed and found him to be divine. She has seen his soul essence, that, like a snowflake, is unique among billions. To love is to witness the miracle of your beloved.

PARENTS' LOVE

And yet parents are our first lovers in this world. When that love is missing, then we spend the rest of our lives searching for it. "Three partners are there in creation," read the wisdom texts, "mother, father, and God." Just because parents aren't privy to the same perception of us as our lovers, they nevertheless take center stage in our love lives for many crucial years. A parent's obligation to a child is, above all, to love.

"What does one do with a child who has fallen under negative influence?" a parent asked Master Israel of the Good Name. "Love him more," the master responded.

Love is not an abstract emotion with which parents are automatically endowed upon a child's birth. Love is about the work of revealing the infinite specialness and beauty of the child. The audience for this revelation is not, as is commonly assumed, the world. The father who carries around baby pictures to show to anyone who will look is sweet, but this offers no evidence of his being engaged in real parenting.

Real parenting is realizing that the one who needs to see the picture most is the child herself. The sacred task of the parent is to reveal the unique beauty of the child to the child. Not to flash her picture to the world, declaring her beauty in broad boasting statements, but to reflect her wondrousness back to her in a loving gaze or in quiet words of confirmation. The parent's ultimate mission is that the child comes to know—beyond a shadow of a doubt—that he is infinitely special, that his ray of light is unique and precious to the planet. The parent needs to be a prism that refracts to the child the infinite love that God feels for him.

Parents and lovers can't and don't need to make us beautiful, but they can and must remind us that we already are. And in so reminding us, they move us—through the supremely motivating power of love—to express our beauty in our every step, in every second of the day. They give us the confidence to follow our dreams, to trust the whisperings of our souls, to talk to God, and to be ourselves.

Years back, I (Marc) gave a talk at a summer camp in one of the wealthier enclaves of Long Island. The kids at the camp were between ages five and twelve. After my official talk, I had some extra time, so I asked if I could perhaps have a casual talk with the kids alone. The camp director, being more creative and flexible than most, on the spot canceled that afternoon's activity and brought the kids together for a *kumzits*, a chat/singing session with the teacher. I sang with them, horsed around; I thought I was outrageously funny, but I wasn't getting the kind of gut response I wanted. Laughter, participation, yes, but real presence—soul sharing—wasn't happening.

Out of nowhere, I asked them, "When was the last time someone told you that you were beautiful?" Silence. "We need a first volunteer," I said, pushing them. So one brave nine-year-old gets up and, with a flutter of hesitation, says, "My mother told me on Saturday that I was the ugliest little girl she knew." Silence. This time the quiet was worlds sadder but somehow more real. Then a little boy, looking not more than ten, raised his hand and said, "My mother was in the Holocaust. And she says that if she had known that I would be her son, she wouldn't have worked so hard to survive."

And then the stories came tumbling out. Of parents, so many parents, who weren't lovers, who didn't know how beautiful their children were. Stories of so many parents who broke the commandment to love. My heart broke.

Right now, before you do anything else, before you go on to the next page, before you turn on the TV . . . turn to your child, call up your friend, call out to your lover, and tell them just how beautiful they are. Let your eyes mirror their splendor; let your mouth remind them of what wonders they already are.

AS YOU LOVE YOURSELF

Of course, to remind another of her full beauty, you have to be fully aware of your own. The Master of the Good Name has a wonderful teaching on the biblical mandate to "love your neighbor as you love yourself." He points out that the mandate is, actually, a statement of fact: you love your neighbor precisely as much as you love yourself. For in the end, you can perceive another's greatness only if you have glimpsed and believe in your own. Self-love is self-perception.

If this is so, then a powerful question arises. How do you love yourself when you know all of your foibles, pathologies, and blemishes? Isn't self-love self-perception? And does not honest perception yield forth all of the reasons why we are not lovable?

And yet most of us manage, at least to some degree, to love ourselves. Is it just self-deception? No, not at all. Love is not merely perception; it is a perception-identification complex. Self-perception means that although you are aware of the full complexity of your persona—the good, the bad, and the ugly—you identify the essence of who you are with your good—your loving, giving, creative, and generous self.

That does not mean that you deny your beast. It is, of course, critical to integrate all of you into your self-picture. But the essence, the core of who you are, remains your goodness, virtue, and beauty. To love yourself is to identify yourself as part of the Shechinah. Writes the Master of the Good Name: "To love yourself is to love the Shechinah." Not to love yourself is to send the Shechinah into exile. So proclaim the Kabbalists, to which Rumi adds:

> *By God, when you see your beauty*
> *You will be the idol of yourself.*[46]

In your deepest nature, you must know that you are the hero of your story. In your deepest nature, you are love and grace and strength and splendor. Now you must decide to identify with your deepest nature. Do you focus on your innocence or your guilt? Do you focus on your ever-inevitably dirty hands, or on your ever-eternally pure soul? To love yourself or anyone else, you need to know that your innocence is your essence. That you always remain worthy of love. That your innocence is never lost.

THE DEEPEST OF THE DEEP

Biblical myth consciousness teaches us that we have three faces. The first face is the social you. It is called, in the Zohar, "the revealed world." The second face is the secret you. This is the primal raging of the subconscious. The Zohar calls this "the hidden world." Neither is your truest face. Your truest face is your third face, what the Kabbalists call *umka de umka*, "the deepest of the deep." In the language of Abraham Isaac Kook, the twentieth-century mystical philosopher, "The truth of your essence reveals itself in your moments of greatness." It is those moments of greatness that set the standard that defines you. Who you really are is you at your best.

Marc shares a story:

During my first year as a rabbi in Palm Beach, Florida, there was one bar mitzvah boy I will never forget. Louis was his name, and he was the first child to become a bar mitzvah during my tenure. He and his parents came to my office just a few weeks after I arrived. It turned out to be quite a disturbing meeting. You see, Louis was not a happy kid. He was over-weight, awkward, and socially ill at ease. These traits were not easy for a twelve-year-old who was trapped in the superficiality of a culture that idolized body, grace, and cool.

But to add to the taunts of his peers, his parents seemed to be doing their fair share of damage to Louis' self-esteem. They informed me that Louis was not the brightest kid, and that he probably would not be able to read the usual portion from Prophets read by other bar mitzvah boys. They figured that it would be enough for him to recite the blessings and be done with it. In their infinite wisdom, they said this in half-veiled sentences with him in the room. When they left my office, I was bewildered, angry, and near tears. Perhaps it was his parents' insensitivity, or perhaps his awkwardness reminded me of myself at his age, but I resolved to do something.

In the ensuing six months, I met with Louis approximately three times, as often as I would have met with any other bar mitzvah boy. To my extreme delight, I found that Louis had a beautiful singing voice and would have no problem reciting the usual bar mitzvah requirements. But I also believed that he could do more. Thus we prepared for not only the standard reading but also the entire biblical portion for the week, no mean feat for a twelve-year-old by any standard. He practiced and practiced and practiced.

On the morning of the bar mitzvah, it seemed that angels carried his every word. Louis shined! He glowed! The room and the heavens stood still in awe and wonder at the beauty and grace that was Louis. I got up to give the speech that I had prepared, but only one thought filled my mind. I had to speak directly to Louis. I had to make sure he realized the full magnificence—and significance—of that moment. The whole congregation seemed to disappear as I turned to Louis and let the words flow from my mouth. "Louis, this morning you met your real self. This is who you are. You are good, graceful, talented, and smart. Whatever people told you yesterday, and Louis, whatever happens tomorrow, promise me one thing. Remember . . . this is you. Remember, and don't ever lose it."

Several months after his bar mitzvah, Louis' family moved away, and I lost track of him. But two years ago, I received a letter from Louis. He had just graduated from an Ivy League university, was beginning medical school in the fall, and was engaged to be married. The letter was short. It read, "High school was a nightmare. Sometimes I didn't think I would make it through. But I kept my promise: I always remembered my bar mitzvah morning when you said that this is who I am. For this, I thank you."

The essence of who you are is you at your best. Do not desire to be someone else. Embrace your own personal greatness. Here is a simple yet powerful practice for developing self-love that we would like to share:

Close your eyes. Imagine going to a land where the things most highly prized are the very qualities that you happen to possess. For instance, if you are short, then in this land, shortness is the most ideal size. If you have red hair, then red hair is considered the most beautiful of colors. If you are a dreamer, then dreamers stand at the top of the social and economic ladder. If you are a runner, then running is the most acclaimed activity. Now soak in the sensation of being absolutely accepted, appreciated, and admired. This is the land for you. Realize that you carry that land inside of you. Whoever you are, you can always find inside of you the best of you. Now visualize, inch by inch, that your inner land starts stretching, spreading, and seeping out from within you until it completely surrounds you and it becomes the real world as well. Open your eyes and believe it, and it will be.

SELF-LOVE OR NARCISSISM

Whenever we talk to people about self-love—which is, after all, according to most authorities, the most important injunction and the goal of the entire biblical project—there is always a group that gets upset. It sounds narcissistic, they claim, or it will lead to selfishness.

So let's take a moment to make two clear distinctions. Narcissism is to be in love with your external self, your mask. This is not a good idea because sooner or later masks fall off, and then you are left loveless. Self-love is to love your internal self, your Holy of Holies.

Selfishness is to narrow your circle of caring until it includes only yourself and perhaps those who directly affect your well-being. Selfishness is then a narrowing of your identity. It stems from the failure to see your interconnectivity with circles beyond yourself and ultimately with all of being. That is definitive nonerotic thinking. Self-love, by contrast, is not self-centered at all; rather, it is ultimately expansive.

Self-love is radically erotic in that it is the experience of being interwoven within the great fabric of being. It is the deep intuition that the world is a unified, loving consciousness in which you participate. The only true sin, from which all else flows, is to deny your greatness. Ultimately, the answer to who I am is "I am part of God." It is the only humble answer to the question you can give. To think you are not lovable is the ultimate arrogance because it assumes that you are independent of God.

THE CREATIVE GAZE

The Kabbalists were often referred to as *mistaklim* or *chozim*, roughly translated as "the lookers" or "seers." To get a handle on what that might mean, just imagine how we feel when someone looks at us with erotic, loving eyes. We feel energized, uplifted, and embraced. We become more vibrant, audacious, and alive. We feel safer in the world. The sense of alienation, separateness, and loneliness of our empty days and painful nights seems to lift.

The steadier the loving gaze is, the more we can locate ourselves and chart our direction and purpose on the path of being. It begins with the loving eyes of mother and father—our first lovers—and continues throughout our lives. Love's eyes sustain us, nourish us, and connect us to the essential aliveness that courses through the universe. Being seen makes us alove and alive. The same is true of God. The gaze of the mystic sustains and even "creates" God.

Once a few years back, my (Marc's) son Yair walked into the room, sat down, and started playing with his Game Boy. I began looking at him, but really looking—perceiving him, loving him, with all my heart pouring out through my eyes. I was seeing every beautiful detail of his being as he sat there innocently playing. Suddenly he started singing. Yair singing? A rarity. Could it have been from my love pouring out in his direction? He got up and sort of danced his way out of the room. Yair dancing?

Well, proper scientific data it is not. But it was enough for me. It was exhilarating! Since then I have done this practice in a thousand different places—in streets, lecture halls, pubs, churches, libraries, and synagogues. As a result, the world has been much fuller of singing and dancing. I realized that a loving gaze can transform reality. We call this in formal theology *imitatio dei*, the imitation of the divine force. Just as God looked lovingly into the darkness and there was light, just as God's gaze made it good, so too can our loving perception transform darkness into light and chaos into harmony. Try it!

THE FESTIVAL OF SEEING

We return now full circle to the cherubic mystery of love. When the pilgrims came to the Temple in Jerusalem three times a year, the biblical verse tells us that they came to "see and be seen." The festivals were great gatherings of Eros and vision. Ecstatic dance, camaraderie, overflowing joy, and temple ritual characterized these great convocations. If you can imagine a rock concert or a sports event held with sacred intention and ritual, then you can approximate at least something of the erotic energy that pulsed through these events.

The grammar in the biblical text is unclear: "the holiday of seeing." But who is seeing whom? The deep, inside understanding is that two different mystical processes are happening at the same time. In an erotic circular loop, one feeds into the other. On the first level, the pilgrim comes to be seen by God. To be seen is to be loved. When the pilgrim would make his entrance into the temple, one of the priestly greeters would call out, "So-and-so has arrived from village such-and-such to bring the appointed offering." His name would echo through the temple. Perceived upon entry!

In the ecstasy of the festival, the pilgrim reached the consciousness that moved him to cry out, "If I am here, all is here." The Zohar explains that if I who am the Shechinah is here, then all is here. The description is one of virtual *unio mystica*. A shift in perception takes place in which the individual leaves his isolating identity behind and imagines himself as part of the divine body. This results not in a loss of self but in the total reinvigoration of self as an infinitely unique reflection of God's face. When the pilgrim felt seen and loved, he was then able to open his heart and let it overflow in joy. He himself became a lover. That joy and love, writes the medieval sage Maimonides, had to express itself in acts of kindness and love, which the pilgrim did for others.

The pilgrim became a lover once again. He was able to love himself, God, the world, and most importantly, his community and family. That is the essence of the Holy of Holies: to become a lover and a seer. To love is to become God's verb. To love is to see with God's eyes.

FEASTING ON THE VISION

The model of love's perception remains the cherubs sexually intertwined atop the Ark in the Holy of Holies. The cherubs were not only in the Holy of Holies. As we have noted, they adorned the curtains, walls, and vessels of most of the temple. At every turn they confronted the eye.

Part of the spiritual work of the temple priest involved erotic gazing and its transformation into love. The priest envisioned, through both meditation and visualization, the sexual merging of the divine masculine and feminine. This spiritual practice was fraught with danger. One could get caught in the intense erotic pleasure of the sensual and not know how to translate it into loving and ethical action. In biblical myth, this is the failing of the sons of Aaron, Nadav and Avihu, who are described as *zanu einehem min ha Shechinah*. Usually this is translated as "they feasted on the vision of the Shechinah." It could also be legitimately translated as "they were harlots with the Shechinah," as feasting and harlotry share the same Hebrew root.

The point is that Nadav and Avihu, driven by their erotic desire to love, attempted the practice of the cherubs and failed. Nadav and Avihu, the text relates, were consumed by the fire of the Holy of Holies. They were mythically "burned out" by their erotic drives. Moses, by contrast, is described as "taking pleasure from the rays of Shechinah." Here also the implication is erotic; Moses, however, was able to move from the merely sexual to Eros and love beyond the sexual. Nadav and Avihu remained transfixed by the sexual. They were unable to take that energy and expand it to all of life beyond the sexual realm.

The sexually intertwined cherubs, which so defined the temple energy, clearly invited sacred sexual gazing. Yet great care was taken to ensure that the sexual did not override the love, Eros, and ethics that lay at the temple's core. Only the high priest was permitted to see the cherubs once a year during the mystery of the incense offering on the Day of At-one-ment. Except! Except for the three love festivals. On each of these auspicious gatherings, the curtains guarding the Holy of Holies were gently opened and the people were invited to behold the entwined cherubs. Erotic gazing!

The sexual gaze, so teach the cherubic mysteries of love, is but the model. With it you can only see the outside. Now look deeper. Look on the inside. Become a lover. Learn the art of erotic perception, and you will see beauty and experience pleasure far beyond even your wildest dreams.

CHAPTER TWENTY-TWO

THE EIGHTH FACE

GIVING AND RECEIVING

In his classic work *Love and Will*, humanistic psychologist Rollo May bemoans modernity's overemphasis on performance and technique at the expense of feeling and passion. He tells one story of a patient who used ointment on the tip of his sexual organ because it dulled feeling, thus increasing his ability to perform. May viewed this as a kind of pathology symptomatic of his time, a telling example of the wanton willingness to forfeit feeling for the sake of achievement. And Rollo May may well be right.

But this patient's goals are not necessarily worthy of our contempt. After all, the achievement he is after here is fully based upon giving to another, even at the expense of his own pleasure. How often in life is the standard of success based on how much you give, rather than on how much you get? Imagine if everyone's greatest goal was to give the optimal amount of pleasure to other people. What a radically brighter, more alive world we would live in! So the patient in May's example actually sets the highest standard for what the moral or honorable heights of life might be.

THE SEXUAL MODELS THE EROTIC: GIVING AND RECEIVING

You see, built into the sexual is an enormous desire to give, particularly to give pleasure. In virtually all arenas of living, most of us are perpetually on the prowl for "the best deal." The best deal is always about getting the most while giving the least. The great exception is the sexual. In sex, being a great lover is taken to mean that you give your partner an unbelievable, unforgettable experience. This ability to give pleasure (and the more, the better) is considered a great honor, a virtual badge of merit. As well it should be! Yet we need to expand this desire to give to apply to so much more than just sex. Sex models Eros. It should not exhaust Eros. The erotics of giving must engage every facet of existence.

The Persian poet Hafiz understood this elemental ethic of erotic giving when he spoke of the sun making love to the earth in "The Sun Never Says":

Even
After
All this time
The Sun never says to the earth,

"You Owe
Me."

Look
What happens
With a love like that,

It lights the
Whole
Sky.

THE EROS OF GIVING

Imagine if we brought into every realm of life this standard of giving. Imagine if all of us were willing to forfeit feeling some of our own pleasure, our own comfort, in order to further the pleasure and comfort of another. People who behave this way consistently over long periods of time are called saints; they are the Mother Teresas of the world. Paradoxically, it is in the sexual that the glimmerings of sainthood first appear. For it is in the sexual that the greatest hero is the one who gifts the beloved with the greatest pleasure. The Eros of delight arouses the ethic of devotion.

THE GRADUAL WIDENING OF SELF

It is through the consistent commitment to the growth of the other—expressed through regular and spontaneous acts of giving—that you become a lover. Slowly over time, in a gradual expanding of self, you are able to regain and surpass even the initial ecstasy of falling in love. The ego boundaries dissolve, self is expanded to include the beloved, and the true intimacy of shared identity is achieved.

This is the spiritual dynamic of lovers. The beloved could be a man, woman, child, community, vocation, location, animal, or cause. The principle remains the same. There is no loving without giving. Love always involves the willingness to transcend self for the sake of the growth of another. This is what the romantic philosopher Goethe refers to when he says, "The sum which two married people owe to one another defies calculation. It is an infinite debt, which can only be discharged through all eternity."[47]

For the Hebrew mystic, love is self-transcendence: the ability to break the walls of your narrow persona in order to embrace a wider understanding of self. To love another means to create a new shared identity that is larger than your individual identities. And yet the integrity of each independent "other" is maintained. Love is the great and wonderful paradox of shared identity and powerful individuality. So self-transcendence is the widening of self through consistent giving and commitment to the growth of your beloved.

For the Hebrew mystics, the word for "love" itself expresses this notion of giving, which they so cherished. "Love" in the original Hebrew is *ahava*, derived from the word *hav*. The primary meaning of *hav* is "giving." Wonderfully, in the original Hebrew, "love" and "giving" are the same word.

Every human being is born incomplete. True birth takes place over the course of a lifetime and not at life's inception. There is nothing more tragic than to die before being born. A lover is a midwife. To be a midwife is to be committed to helping your beloved birth his or her highest self. This is the great gift of love.

THE BARON LOVES PIKE

The one proviso for the type of giving that is truly loving is to make sure that your focus is really on the growth of your beloved. Too often giving is but the most sophisticated disguise for taking.

There was once a fisherman who caught a large pike. Seeing what a substantial catch this was, he said out loud, "I won't eat this fish. He is such a great catch that I will take him to the baron. The baron loves pike."

Hearing this, the fish breathed a sigh of relief. "There's some hope for me yet!" he thought.

The pike was brought to the manor house. At the gate, the guard asked, "What do you have?"

"A large pike!"

"Wonderful," responded the guard. "The baron loves pike."

By now the fish was gasping for breath, but he felt relieved. A few more minutes, and he would be safe with the baron who loves pike.

The pike was brought to the kitchen. The baron himself entered with a big smile on his face. "I love pike," said the baron.

As the fish, with its ebbing strength, wiggled around to ask for water, he heard the baron say, "Cut off the tail and head and slice it down the middle."

In his last breath of terrible despair, the fish cried out, "Why did you lie? You don't love pike—you love yourself!"

To love is to be committed to the growth of the other. This always requires at least the temporary ability for self-transcendence. We are divinely hardwired for giving as self-transcendence. God in the meditations of the mystics is revealed as a giver, not a taker. According to the Kabbalah, the very formation of the world is motivated by a divine love expressed in an infinite desire to give. If there is any need in God, it is the need to be a giver. Our own deeply felt need to give is our overwhelming desire to incarnate the God point in our lives. To give is to be like God. It is in radical giving that devotion and delight merge. That is the quality of the Divine.

A LIGHT MOTIF

Usually, when I give you something, it means that you now have it and I do not. Not so in reference to light and love. One candle can light a hundred candles without losing any of its own brilliance. It is for this reason that light was held to be the incarnation of love.

The core intuition of all the great systems of the spirit is that love and Eros are captured best by the image of light. The Kabbalah teaches that the light that fills the vessels of creation is love. The word *torah* itself—an all-encompassing Hebrew term meant to refer to all divine wisdom—means "light." (The root of *torah* is *orah*, which is the Hebrew word for "light" and which is also the basis for the English word *aura*.)

Much like a candle, when you give in love, you are able to illuminate many people without ever losing any of your own luminescence. Giving love only creates more.

SMALL DEEDS OF GREAT LOVE

The paradigmatic biblical myth of love and giving is the story of Abraham, who sits, sick, at the entrance to his tent in the heat of the day. He is greatly saddened, for there are no guests to grace his house on that day. Tradition tells the story of God, who, having compassion for Abraham's suffering in his sickness, made the day especially hot so as not to disturb Abraham with guests. Yet Abraham has a deep need to give. He gets sadder and perhaps sicker because there is no one to serve. Until, lo and behold, in the distance he spies three men.

The narrative describes in great detail how Abraham rushes to greet them and hurries with great alacrity to wash their feet and prepare them food and lodging. In reward for his hospitality, tradition records that Abraham merited many wondrous divine gifts. One contemporary mystical teacher, Chaim Shmuelevitz, dean of the greatest Talmudic academy in Jerusalem, asks a simple but highly provocative question. "Big deal! So Abraham was generous in his hospitality. So am I. So are many other people. What was so special about Abraham that his hospitality earned for him such an abundant divine reward?"

Responding to his own question, Shmuelevitz writes almost the exact same words that are ascribed to Mother Teresa: "There are no great deeds of giving; there are only small deeds performed with great love." When Abraham served his guests, he was doing it from a place of unending and pure love. All of the infinite love in the universe was contracted into his every small deed of hospitality. When the infinite and the finite merge in a small point of goodness, all of the worlds are raised higher. A smile. A good word. Abraham is the master of "small deeds with great love." This is why only Abraham, of all the biblical myth heroes, is called by the text a "lover." For to be a lover is to be a giver.

GIVE FIRST, LOVE FOLLOWS

"Giving is not only the litmus test of love; it also leads to love," teaches the Baal Shem Tov. "If you want to be loved, be a lover."

Raised on the love ethic of Western capitalism, most of us regard feeling love as the necessary prerequisite for caring: only when you love someone will you be ready to really give to her. But for the Hebrew mystics, it is precisely the opposite. Don't wait to be a giver until you are a lover. Be a giver, and you will become a lover. In the act of giving to another, you invest yourself in them. They become, in a small way, part of you. This allows you to focus on them in a far more concentrated and sustained fashion. Remember that love at its core is perception. Care, concern, and giving are inextricably intertwined with passion and ardor. Once you give to a person, you always start to love him. Is there someone you simply do not like at work but have to "put up with" all day? Bring him a present and witness the subtle shift in your own, not to mention his, attitude.

To be a lover, then, means to be there even when the feeling is not, in the good months and the bad months, in the heat of passion and in the cold dreariness of life at its toughest. When you say, "I love you," what you are really saying is that you will stay even on the days when you can't fully access the depth of that passionate love. That is the gift of true love. Eventually, it is only in the dynamic of commitment that the heart opens in a way that outlasts the vagaries of time and the fickleness of human emotion.

WHAT'S YOURS IS OURS

Another Hebrew word used for "giving" is *tzedakah*. Usually mistranslated as meaning "charity," it really means "justice." The difference is enormous. Charity means that the money is mine, and because I'm feeling magnanimous, I give some to you. Justice, the correct translation for *tzedakah*, is understood by the masters to mean that your money is not owned by you at all. In Hebrew law, a portion of your money is in reality owned by the poor in the community. According to one legal school, the Tosafists, the only right you have to the money is to determine which poor person will receive it.

Wow! This law reminds us of the great truth of nondual thought: you are not separate from everyone else. The accumulation of property and possessions in this lifetime is overwhelmingly due to sets of circumstances entirely beyond your control. You may have worked hard, but there are a million people who worked just as hard, and the universe did not allow them to accumulate your level of wealth. Those possessions are not essentially yours. And so, a portion of your possessions, according to Hebrew mystical doctrine codified in law, belongs to those less fortunate than you, not because the government legislated taxes, but because non-separateness is the essential metaphysical truth of reality.

"Charity saves from death" is a koan of the Hebrew wisdom masters. Not to experience the interconnectivity of being is to live a nonerotic, dead existence. I must give not out of charitable altruism but because of the metaphysical fact that you are part of me and I am part of you.

JERUSALEM'S HOLY BEGGARS

In Jerusalem where I (Marc) lived for many years, the streets are filled with beggars, men and women who for all sorts of different reasons make their living by asking passersby to "share the wealth." In almost any other city in the world, these people would be deemed panhandlers and con-signed to the bottom of the social ladder. While I cannot tell you that these people are Jerusalem's elite, there is a strong sense that they are holy people. We invite them to our weddings, we wait on their blessings. We talk to them like they are family. For they are.

The holy beggars of Jerusalem, city of lovers, are an essential part of her spiritual fabric. One has the sense that the beggar is doing the pass-erby a favor. After all, their open hand is affording us the opportunity to give. The ancients taught that when the human being is possessed of a desire to give, the universe will give him wealth so he can fulfill that desire. Such spiritual physics turns our common understanding of the nature of reality on its head.

For many Western tourists coming to Jerusalem, the beggar scene is hard to bear.

Often I was asked by tourists who came to my lectures, "But do we have to give money to people who look like fakes?" An understandable question to be sure, yet it is still based in that possessive part of us that is pained by the thought of parting with something that "belongs to me." I usually gave the startled tourist three different answers: First, you should know that every time you pass a person whose hand is outstretched and you ignore them, something closes in your heart. The love channels in your being begin to clog up. Not only will it become more and more difficult for you to give love, but it will also become increasingly difficult for you to receive love back.

There is a teaching that if you have a hundred different coins, you should give them to a hundred different people. Even though the money will have little real-life impact on the recipient's economic reality, the very act of giving to every hand you meet could have a real impact on your reality. Simply put, giving is at least as much for the giver as it is for the receiver. The rich need the poor more than the poor need the rich. Unfortunately, neither is conscious of this fact.

Second (I say this before my tourist friend can run away), I share a story of the great master Zushia of Onipol:

Zushia had a disciple who would visit him occasionally and donate funds toward his support. It seemed that the more he gave to Zushia, the wealthier he became. At some point, the disciple discovered that Zushia himself had a master whom he would go visit, the Master of Mezritch. The disciple reasoned that surely the master is greater than the student. And with that he stopped visiting and supporting Zushia, switching his allegiance to the other master.

From that point on the disciple's business began to fail, getting worse and worse as time went by. Realizing this was no coincidence, he went to visit his original master, Zushia. "Holy master," he said, "surely even you agree that your teacher from Mezritch is greater than you. So why should I not be allowed to give my support to the higher master?"

Zushia responded with a twinkle in his eye. "You see, my son, God is our shadow. His dealings with us are but an imitation of our dealings with others. As long as you gave without first judging to see if the person was worthy or not, as long as you would support someone as undeserving as Zushia, then the universe imitated you and was willing to support you without checking exactly what you deserved. But once you became selective and began to support only those whom you thought deserved it, the universe also became more selective in choosing where it sends its support."

Third, for those who are still unsatisfied and find it too painful to give indiscriminately, I would ask a simple question: How would you like to be asking for money on the street? Much as we honor the holy beggar, it certainly is not the easiest way to make a living. To be a lover, you have to engage in the spiritual practice of *harchavat hadaat*. Literally translated, this means "the expansion of consciousness." Taught by the nineteenth-century mystical master Nachman of Bratslav, it involves widening your narrow field of vision to incorporate more of the other person's story.

Say that someone smashes into your car from behind. You jump out of the car and furiously race to the door of the offending vehicle. Fuming, you open the door, see the other driver, and exclaim, "Mom!" Your anger cools in an instant because the faceless offender has recovered a personality. It's Mom. She has a story. When you open yourself up to her story, your feelings of love and empathy overcome your anger. You want to give and support her. You have been transformed into a lover.

When you encounter the beggars on the streets of Jerusalem, you have to open yourself to their stories. Imagine them as a relative, a child on their birthday, or a person on their dying day. Envision in a millisecond the imaginary details of their story. Allow them to have a face!

SOCIAL TRANSFORMERS

We have, all of us, an erotic need to give, to contribute in a meaningful way to individuals as well as to our larger communities. We are driven not only to small acts of giving but also to great acts of sacrifice and heroism. We all desperately need to feel that our lives matter, that they are possessed of something essential, meaningful, and valuable. The unheard cry for meaning is always a desire to give. We are hardwired for giving. We long for not so much what we do not have as for what we do not give. We are unable to feel that essential sense of fulfillment that comes from living a life that matters unless we feel we are making some significant contribution to our larger community.

Happiness is not a goal; it is a by-product of a life well lived. That life must include profound loving and giving or it simply cannot satisfy us.

Life cannot be lived without a cause that is larger than life itself. There is a profound human need for sacrificial action for the sake of the larger community. We ignore this need at our own peril. If we do not honor it with creative and ethical expression, then we or our children will be seduced to sacrifice to the manifold pseudo altars of repression, fundamentalism, and extremism.

That does not mean that we all yearn for lives of public service. It does mean that we need to feel that in our corner of the world we are doing our bit for society, above and beyond caring for our immediate circle. We all know, after all, that giving to our immediate circle—who are, in effect, extensions of ourselves—is really but a form of self-preservation. It is important and vital, but insufficient.

We yearn to widen our circle of caring to include at least some broader sense of community. When we are denied the right to serve a higher purpose, or when that essential need is denied or even ridiculed, make no mistake about it, we are being oppressed. We are living in a socially induced denial of our basic humanity. Denial and oppression create a psychological time bomb that sooner or later will explode in our faces.

THE EVOLUTION OF LOVE

The evolution of love is when the causes and people we love extend beyond our own immediate survival circle. Egocentric love is when I experience a felt sense of care and concern for myself and the people I need to survive. Ethnocentric love is when I experience a felt sense of care of concern for my entire people. My people might be my fellow citizens, my coreligionists, or any larger affiliation beyond those that I know directly. This is the evolution of love from egocentric to ethnocentric. Love evolves again to world-centric when I experience a felt sense of care and concern for every human being on the planet. Finally, love evolves yet again when I experience a felt sense of care and concern not only for human beings but for all of reality. This has been called cosmo-centric love.

CIRCLES OF CARING, CIRCLES OF INFLUENCE

The major reason that we stop giving and loving beyond our circle of protection is that it hurts too much. We know that if we open our hearts, they will all too often get trampled and trashed.

We basically feel powerless and that we cannot really change anything. Once that belief is internalized, a self-protective mechanism kicks in. We cannot tolerate a situation in which our circle of caring is far larger than our circle of influence. When we feel that our ability to experience hurt is far greater than our ability to alleviate the pain, then we simply turn off. The dissonance becomes too great to bear. The gap between our perceived ability to be hurt and to help is simply too wide to traverse. So we narrow our circles of caring to only those we feel we have the ability to help. But to do so, especially in a world where graphic images of pain daily invade our lives, we need to shut down our hearts. Powerlessness corrupts. We need to know that each of us by ourselves, and even more powerfully as a community, can make a difference for love.

THE GENESIS FESTIVAL

In the hills of Galilee some years back, I engaged with a ragtag band of seekers in nurturing the seedlings of a new activist mystical movement. We call it Bayit Chadash. Together with wonderful partners, students, friends, and teachers, we are trying to reclaim the holy impulse of both Hebrew mysticism and social activism. We are radically underfunded and understaffed, often to the point of absurdity. Yet we hold to the belief that a future vision of Hebrew thought needs to be reborn from the same hills that birthed the Zohar and Lurianic Kabbalah. We realize how truly silly it is that common folks like us should set about this task, but in the words of the ancient Talmudic sages, "In a place where there is nobody, try to be somebody."

For several years I was invited to lead the opening ceremony of what was called, in Israel, the Genesis Festival. It is a wondrous gathering of some twenty-five thousand people that takes place at the time of the Hebrew New Year. Several years ago we started a custom of blowing one hundred *shofarot* (ram's horns), accompanied by three hundred and sixty drummers, to bid farewell to the past as we usher in the future. In the middle of all this, I gave a short talk, which was always the same.

"On the New Year," I would tell them, "our tradition teaches that those who merit are inscribed in the Book of Life. At this moment, the universe is judging who will live and who will die. Here at the Genesis Festival of love, we will not allow God or his angels that choice. We will not allow judgment to separate us from each other. So I ask each one of you to turn to the person next to you and say: I refuse to be written in the Book of Life . . . without you!"

Thousands of people turn, and with pure love flowing from open hearts, they embrace the person next to them, and we all say together, "I refuse to be inscribed in the Book of Life without you!"

At those moments, I felt like we were in the temple, in the inner sanctum of the Holy of Holies. It is worth being born just to experience these minutes. The people who attend these festivals give me great hope. They are the best in all of us. They remind me that we can transform our world into something more.

THE POSSIBILITY OF POSSIBILITY

We need a politics of love! We need to know love is a practical political possibility. We are taught that what human beings want is money and power. Anyone in close contact with people knows that, at the deepest level, this is not true. At the superficial level, many people do crave money and power, but that is because the Shechinah is in exile. Money and power are pseudo Eros. But in our hearts, beneath the craving for superficial distractions, human beings want to live in a world based on love and caring, awe and radical amazement.

Everyone knows that having more is not being more. The great credo of faith for religion today is not dogmatic assertions about the metaphysical quality of divinity. Rather, it is the belief that God is the power for love, healing, and transformation in the universe. God is the belief in possibility. In fact, it is the possibility of possibility—which is affirmed by lovers everywhere—that ultimately love will win out and we will be able to create a better world. There is a covenant not only between the human being and the Divine, but also a covenant between generations. Each generation commits itself to living so that we can show our children a way that is a little more loving, a little more compassionate.

This is possible because the underlying reality of the universe is relationship and interdependence, not loneliness and alienation. We are born into loving hands. Left alone, we would die. It takes a world of cruelty and greed driven by fear to produce a reality where so many people die alone.

It is possible, as Robert Kennedy reminded us in the 1960s, to change the bottom line. Instead of a gross national product measured in purely economic terms, we could have a bottom line in which loving, human dignity, value, and uniqueness are factored into the equation. In such a scenario, a company that was highly profitable financially but insensitive to human dignity in measurable ways would not be given the same benefits or would be taxed at a higher rate.

At first, this sounds absurd because we have internalized the pathologies of our generation. Philosopher Erich Fromm and psychiatrist Viktor Frankl have pointed out that entire societies, including our own, can be profoundly imbalanced. We need to understand this or else we will experience our generation's pathologies of spirit as our personal failures. If we feel emptiness in the mad drive for success, it is not because we are neurotic but because the success we seek is an empty goal. If we feel powerless and frustrated, it is not because we need treatment. Quite the opposite; because our social norms need to be changed, frustration with life as we know it is often an indication of sanity and inner balance. It means we have not succumbed to the superficial values touted by our society.

We must know that our deep desire to give, to be lovers, is the most profoundly normal human state of being. We cannot have a delusion of grandiosity, for we are, in fact, grand. For the Kabbalists, the natural human condition is to feel wholly dissatisfied unless we feel we are meeting a cosmic need. Meir ibn Gabbai, a Renaissance mystic, teaches, "Only with the knowledge that our gift is needed—that the universe 'needs our service'—can we touch fulfillment." This is what it means to be a lover of God and humans. It is our calling to embody love and giving in our lives.

We are God's language in the polis. *Polis*, in Greek, means "community," and "politics" means "affairs of the community." There is no split between politics and love. Love, Eros, and politics are one. We understand that on the inside we are all interconnected. Politics is usually about protecting our rights, particularly our right to be separate. It needs also to be about obligation and love, *chovah* and *chibah*, which derive from the same root word in Hebrew. Both affirm the erotic interdependence of all life.

We experience an intense yearning and desire to be of service in our communities. Through that loving service, we experience the fullness of being. We need a new politics of Eros, a politics of love.

A SHARED VISION

To move toward a politics of love you do not need to found a new political party or national social movement. You just need a small group of people with a shared vision who are willing to stand together. As the anthropologist Margaret Mead said, "Never doubt that a small group of thoughtful, committed people can change the world. Indeed, it is the only thing that ever has." Political and spiritual lovers should be chosen the same way we choose a spouse: based on shared visions and values.

The philosopher Maimonides, taking his cue from Aristotle, teaches that there are three kinds of friendship communities. First, there are the pragmatic friends that help one another through life. Whether carpooling, giving a hand at the office, or rounding out a doubles game in tennis, these friends make our lives more practically feasible. The second group, more psychological in nature, comprise an empathetic community. This is a place to share our woes, sorrows, triumphs, and victories. The third, and by far the highest kind of fellowship, is one based on shared vision and values. This is what philosopher Abraham Joshua Heschel calls "a community of concern."

If you think that you are only one person in a small band of committed individuals who can't change the world, know that you are the only ones who can. It is the gift of commitment and love between holy friends and communities that can bring healing where there would otherwise be only sickness, and life where there might otherwise be only death.

L'CHAYIM: TO LIFE!

A famous tale is told about the Seer of Lublin, a mystical master who lived in Eastern Europe one hundred and fifty years ago. Everybody knew that the holy man could see from one end of the world to the other. For him, past and future were transparent in the present moment.

One day, Levi, a disciple, came to the seer to be with him for the holiday. However, as soon as Levi came in, the seer said, "I am sorry, but you cannot stay with me this holiday."

"But why?" protested Levi. "I have come so far to be with you!"

"The angel of death surrounds you," said the master. "I see that you are destined to die this holiday. It would be better for you to go to one of the surrounding villages and die quietly there."

You can imagine the shock and despair that overcame the poor disciple. He had only one day to live. He took his belongings, and with tears streaming down his face, began walking out of town toward his death. On the road, Levi saw a coach full of the seer's students traveling toward Lublin. They were singing with great joy, obviously on their way to the seer for the holiday. Spying Levi on the side of the road, they stopped the coach and invited him in.

"Holy friend!" they called out. "Jump in! The holiday is soon, and you are walking the wrong way!"

Levi could barely talk and motioned them to continue on without him. But being mystic initiates in the art of loving, they could not just leave him on the road, so they pressed him for an explanation of his strange behavior. Accordingly, Levi related to them what the seer had told him and how he was going to die in a nearby village. The students glanced wordlessly at one another and then back at Levi. Virtually in unison they responded, "The seer is not always right. You do not have to die alone in a village. Come with us to Lublin; that way, if you do have to die, we can at least make you comfortable and help you in the crossing. Yes," they insisted, "you must come with us, and let us rejoice in the holiday together."

So Levi got in, and they continued on toward Lublin. On the way, they passed a tavern, which prompted one of the students to say to Levi, "Since you will die tomorrow, surely you do not need your money. Why don't you buy us all drinks at the tavern and we can have a preholiday celebration." Levi agreed that this made sense, and they all piled into the tavern.

They bought a great deal of good whiskey. Each time one of the students was about to down a shot, he would turn to Levi (who was, after all, footing the bill) and say, with great passion, "*L'chayim*, Levi! Levi, to life!"

What a time they had! They got higher and higher, and soon Levi got caught up in it all. Each time a student would drink and cry out, "Levi, *l'chayim tovim aruchim!*"—meaning "Levi, a good and long life to you!"—Levi would respond by downing another shot and returning the *l'chayim*. Before long, tomorrow seemed eons away. Round after round, the blessing of *l'chayim* poured forth.

They lost track of time and arrived at the seer's prayer service only minutes before the holiday—happy, more than a little inebriated, and deeply bonded. After the service, which was overflowing with people, Levi, unsteadily but respectfully, edged his way to the seer to wish him a good holiday.

The seer smiled at him with great love and said, "Levi, the angel of death has left you! A master's protection is not as powerful as the love-filled blessings of *l'chayim* that the students give to one another. So Levi," he said, lifting his holiday wineglass, "let me add my blessing to theirs. *L'chayim*! To life!"

When we come together in holy community, when we stand for life together against the forces of fear and greed, we can indeed change the world.

THE MATHEMATICS OF EROS

If you were to enter your bank, ask a teller to withdraw fifty dollars from your account, then ask her to record it as a deposit, she would think you were joking. Then she would think you were crazy. Then she would call her manager, who would escort you out of the bank. And the bank would be right. Everyone knows depositing and withdrawing are opposite actions. To deposit is to give money into your account and to withdraw is to take money out of your account. Giving and taking are opposites, and never the twain shall meet. It's first-grade math: addition and subtraction. Everyone knows this. All the structure of economy politics and our social relations are based on this dichotomy.

Giving and receiving are opposites in nearly every sphere of our lives, yet the lover seeks to infuse this sharp and angular world with the softer curves of intimacy. The lover wants to transcend and transform the rules of first-grade math. The model for the lover? The sexual. In sex, giving and receiving follow very different rules and flow very differently.

THE SEXUAL MODELS THE EROTIC: GIVING AND RECEIVING ARE ONE

Not only is sexual love the model for radical giving, but it also personifies a very particular kind of generosity, one that defies all other giving patterns. In sex, we transcend the world of win-win, common goals, give-and-take, and getting even. The sexual models a different order of reality, where giving and receiving are indistinguishably one.

Sex is at its highest when your partner not only knows how to give you pleasure but is a master at receiving it as well. In your beloved's receiving of pleasure, you are given a great gift. In the sexual, the rigid boundaries between giving and receiving are so dramatically blurred that the two become virtually indistinguishable. Sexuality at its highest collapses the separate spheres of giving and receiving into an undulating, rhythmic flow of union. It is a great leap beyond the give-and-take of business into the virtual identity of giving and receiving within every pleasured gesture.

The sexual models a reality where the giver himself is deeply aware of how, in the very act of giving, he has received. Similarly, the receiver herself feels that in the very act of receiving, she has been privileged to give. In erotic living, withdrawals become your deposits . . . and giving is the greatest gift.

It was Aphra Behn, the first Englishwoman to earn her living by her writing in the mid-seventeenth century, who captured the subversive nature of erotic exchange.

> *I saw 'em kindle with Desire,*
> *While with soft Sighs they blew the Fire;*
> *Saw the Approaches of their Joy,*
> *He growing more fierce and she less coy . . .*
>
> *His panting Breast to hers now joined,*
> *They feast on Raptures unconfined;*
> *Vast and luxuriant! such as prove*
> *The Immortality of Love.*
> *For, who but a Divinity*
> *Could mingle Souls to that Degree;*
> *And melt them into Ecstasy . . .*[48]

Behn's point is that the classical split between giving and receiving could neither "mingle souls to that degree" nor cause "his panting breast to hers now joined." It is only the sexual that models the possibility of a new vision of Eros, in which giving and receiving collapse ecstatically into one.

SCORE SHEETS AND GIFT LISTS

The sexual teaches us how to be lovers in all facets of being. To be a lover, I need to stop keeping score. Who did whom the last favor? Who cares!

When I (Marc) was growing up, I remember how most of the families in my neighborhood had gift lists. This meant that your parents kept a chart that included the names of all the guests invited to your confirmation, bar mitzvah, or wedding. Next to every name, there were three columns. First, did they attend or not? (If they attended, it means you spent money on them and thus expected a commensurate gift in return.) The second column was an estimation of the cash value of any gift they gave. The third column listed what they should be given in return when you got invited to their celebrations. Of course, we would never give in excess of the amount we received, for, God forbid, the generosity might just topple the whole balance of the universe!

The mystery of love, the Kabbalah's Secret of the Cherubs, teaches something else. It teaches us to throw away the gift list, to tear up the score sheets. The total dichotomy between giving and receiving, which guides our economic and political lives, is in the end false. It misses the true Eros of giving and receiving modeled by the sexual. In the erotic, every act is simultaneously invested with both giving and receiving.

When giving and receiving are split, we remain de-eroticized, loveless, and—worse yet—unsatisfied. The reason, of course, is simple. I can be satisfied only when I have received something. Only then can I be fulfilled. But when I take, I have not received anything, so even though I have tried to fill up, I remain on empty. The art of the lover is not only to know how to give pleasure in the world; it is also to know the secret of receiving pleasure and thus being full.

THE BAOBAB TREE

In every act of receiving, there is a gift. Taking, however, is fully distinct from receiving. To take is to acquire without receiving. The spiritual definition of "theft" is taking without being willing to grant the gift of receiving.

In the Eros-exiled world, we seek gratification of all forms without wanting to give of our souls in return. Mutual using has become the norm. Natural trust between people is effaced as everyone seeks to take maximum advantage of the other. Giving and receiving is replaced by taking without receiving. Of course, people get hurt much more than need be in such a world. At a certain point—after repeated emotional battering—our hearts close down, much like the baobab tree in the following tale.[49] When that happens, we simply become less human.

The day was hot, the air was thick, the ground was hard, and the mouth was dry. The hare was making his way home when he came across a baobab tree. "Baobab tree," he called out, "you are old and wise and generous. Please let me rest in your shade."

The tree answered, "Hare, your request is true. Come sit in my shade." The hare sat and thanked the baobab tree. But the air was still thick, and the ground was still hard, and the mouth was still dry.

The hare called once again, "Baobab tree, you are old and wise and generous. Allow me to drink from your sap."

The baobab said, "Hare, your request is true. Please drink from my sap." The hare drank from the sap, was refreshed, and thanked the baobab tree.

Some time went by, and the hare called out once more, "Baobab tree, you are old and wise and generous. Won't you allow me to enter your heart?"

And the tree answered, "Hare, your request is true. Come enter my heart." The tree opened her heart, and the hare entered. Inside he saw unimaginable beauty—lights of all colors, sparkling dewdrops, onyx and emeralds, diamonds and sapphires—all glittering and glowing.

The hare called to the baobab, "You are old and wise and generous. Won't you allow me to take one of your stones to my wife as a present?"

The tree answered, "Your request is true. Won't you take one of my stones?" The hare thankfully took a single crystal, stepped out, and the heart closed behind him.

The hare took the stone to his wife, who placed it on a chain around her neck and walked around town, showing it off to everyone. That night, the wife of the hyena said to her husband, "Go get me a stone from the heart of the baobab tree."

The next morning, the sun was hot, the air was thick, and the ground was hard. The hyena came to the baobab tree and said, "You are old and rich and beautiful. Let me enter your heart." The baobab tree opened her heart. The hyena entered and saw lights of many colors, sparkling dew, and precious stones. He quickly grabbed a diamond, a sapphire, and a ruby. Soon he grabbed more, feeling frantic with greed. Out of control, he took from every corner of the baobab's heart.

The tree, trembling and terrified, called out to him, but the hyena could not hear. So, with a great shudder, the baobab closed her heart, trapping the hyena inside. The hyena died. From that day on, the baobab tree never opened her heart to anyone, even to those whose call was true.

They say that we humans were once like the baobab tree, that all one had to do was call, and immediately we would open our hearts. Is there a hyena trapped in your heart today?

THE SECRET OF THE KISS

The Kabbalists viewed kissing as the highest model of Eros. The teaching, called by initiates *sod haneshika* (meaning "secret of the kiss"), references two modes of communication. The first is speech. Although there are many levels of speech, they all suffer from one weakness: the subject-object dichotomy between giver/receiver and speaker/listener remains in place. The very act of having to speak implies a sharp separation between two souls.

The second mode of communication the teaching identifies is kissing. When the Zohar says that *"nat* [intimacy] is only found in the mouth," it refers not to speech but to the kiss. Kissing is the level of communication speech naturally flows into in the context of a sacred relationship. Kissing is the ideal communion.

In a wonderful rereading of a Talmudic text, one mystic interprets the rabbinic admonition of "you shall not talk too much to women" to mean "don't talk when you should already be kissing." In the kiss, the yawning gap between subject and object, giving and receiving, is bridged. The split dissolves. This is the erotic model of union. Thus the great love epic of biblical myth, the Song of Songs, opens with the fantasy, "Kiss me from the kisses of your mouth, for your love is more wonderful to me than wine."

In the mystical reading of this verse, what is intended is a yearning for erotic union beyond the sexual. There is a longing for the life of the kiss, where the hard and brittle boundaries of ego are softened and smoothed. This happens only in the secret of the kiss, where in every transaction both parties give and receive simultaneously.

TWO RUBLES' WORTH

Yet sometimes it is excruciatingly hard for people to receive. For some—and this is often the case with women—it is more comfortable to give than to receive. This creates an imbalance in a person's life, which at some point always exacts a painful price. For others—often men—having a liability of gratitude hanging over one's head becomes too heavy a burden. Instead of receiving gracefully and graciously, they sometimes strike out violently at the very bestower of the gift. My grandfather used to say to me, "Mutty—you should know, some people don't know how to be *mekabel a tova.*" Roughly translated, it means, "some people who don't know how to receive a favor." Or, as the maxim goes, "No good deed goes unpunished." Hebrew mysticism is called Kabbalah, a word that means "receiving," in recognition of the great spiritual art of love implicit in reception. Sometimes it is exceedingly difficult to receive, and doing so requires both discipline and art, as the following tale demonstrates.

Two men board a train in Krakow to return to their native village of Stanislav. One gentleman has somehow lost his wallet. Having no money, he asks the other, whom he recognizes from the village, for two rubles. The second man gladly obliges. The man who borrowed the money keeps fidgeting around uncomfortably in his seat. Unable to calm him down, the second man takes out a ledger book and writes in bold letters: "On such and such a date, I lent Mr. X two rubles." He requests that the first man sign it.

At this point the first man becomes exceedingly annoyed. "What's your problem? Why are you making it such a big deal? It was only two rubles."

"Ah," responds the man. "That is just my point. You see, I have done you a favor. But I see you do not know how to receive a favor. So I am sure you will try to hurt me eventually. When that happens, I want to be able to remind you that you only have the right to hurt me two rubles' worth."

THE FUTILITY OF TAKING

Stealing breaks the intimate covenant of giving and receiving, violently redrawing the line of separation. It reinforces the illusion that we are separate from one another and that therefore my good can only come at your expense. Stealing is a form of rape.

One of the great biblical tragedies is the story of Amnon and his half-sister Tamar. They are both children of King David. Amnon, smitten with Tamar, feigns sickness in order to lure her to his bedroom. He attempts to seduce her. She rebuffs him, pleading that he ask David for her hand. He cannot wait and rapes her. After the rape, all of his love for her turns to hatred, and he moves to throw her out of his quarters. Again she beseeches him, saying that to be cast out with such disdain is worse even than her rape. He is unmoved and throws her out of the house. In the tragic end to this unhappy story, Tamar's brother Absalom avenges her honor by killing Amnon.

Clearly, Amnon is "taking" Tamar. He is neither giving to her, nor is he receiving anything in return. Yet what is important to notice in the story is not only its immorality. Biblical philosopher Joseph Soloveitchik observes correctly that this greed-driven immoral act doesn't even work. Amnon is not satisfied after taking Tamar. He feels his alienation even more acutely. The very person whom he craved in order to fill his void now becomes the new symbol of his emptiness.

Similarly, the corporation that may have cost thousands of families their jobs seeking to fund a hostile takeover, creating untold despair and pain, does not feel fulfilled by its acquisition. Rather, it prowls on, seeking yet another victim for its insatiable greed.

The sexual again models all of life. To be a lover is to merge giving and receiving. That is erotic living. Anything less, in the final calculation, is not only immoral but also futile.

THE SECRET OF FULFILLMENT

There is a wonderful biblical epigram: "You shall eat, be satisfied, and give blessing." The biblical law professors read this to mean that you only have an obligation to give blessing if you have eaten enough to be full. And then, as legal scholars are wont to do, they go on to argue just how much food you need to have eaten to be "legally" considered full.

The mystical psychologists interpret the text more deeply. "You shall eat, and if you are satisfied with what you ate, that itself is the blessing!" Following this way of reading, it would be fair to say that feeling happiness—truly the greatest blessing—is to be satisfied with what you have. Feeling miserable is to be satisfied only with what you do not have. Happiness, then, is fulfillment—mastery of the lover's art of becoming full, of receiving, and thereby achieving satisfaction.

EVEN AN OLIVE'S WORTH

There is a passage that most stunningly captures this notion and takes it one step further. Recorded in the Babylonian wisdom texts, it is a strange symbolic conversation between God and his angels. "Why," the angels ask God, "do you accord the people of Israel your favor even when they are not deserving?" God responds, "How can I not? After all, in my Torah it says, 'And you shall eat, be satisfied, and give blessing.' And the children of Israel give blessing even if they have only eaten an olive's worth of food."

The exchange refers to the biblical text injunction we just mentioned above, which seems to indicate that one is required to give blessing in thanks for food only if one is fully satisfied. Nonetheless, continues the Talmudic passage, the children of Israel give blessing over food even when they are not satisfied, even when they have only eaten an olive's worth.

Mystical master Aaron of Karlin unpacks the powerful wisdom of the passage. What the text suggests is that if you wait to be satisfied, to be fulfilled until you have everything you desire, you will never be able to give blessing. Moreover, you will never experience your life as a blessing. Spiritual greatness is about being able to experience satisfaction and blessing even when you have only an olive's worth of fulfillment.

The feeling of blessing emerges from the ability to experience the fullness of divine reality in every fraction of goodness. When I fully receive anything, no matter how small, it is enough to make me full. This is the lover's art of receiving and giving blessing. It is the secret of fulfillment.

STORY EXCHANGES

We yearn—in our deepest hearts—not to take but to give, and in that giving to receive deeply. Sexuality is the model for this, because one single act contains within it both giving and receiving. The same is true, however, in all of our relationships. Every interpersonal relationship is an iridescent web of exchange. We each have a piece of each other's story. In a lover's exchange, I invest myself in our relationship sufficiently that over time I share with you the piece of your story that I carry with me, and receive from you the piece of my story that you carry with you. It may be an idea, an experience, a perspective, a song, a moment of intimacy, or a thousand other possibilities. The nature of the world is that every significant meeting we have is choreographed in order to return to us a precious missing piece of our being.

The Baal Shem Tov said to each student, "I am dependent on you; without you a part of my teaching can never be heard in the world." And so it is with us. For we are all teachers and all students. And so it is with God. Every human being is a prism that can uniquely refract a particular color in the spectrum of divine light. We are all God's faces.

God needs us to be revealed in the world. God needs us as we need him. Giving and receiving define our relationship as lovers with the Divine.

God's gift to you is your life. Your gift back to God is what you do with your life. God's gift to us is infinite love. Our gift to God is to receive that love. In our receiving, we love God in return.

OF SOUP AND STRUDEL

Two stories conclude our meditation on the lover's path of giving and receiving:

> A man lies on his deathbed, minutes away from his death. His son says, "Dad, is there anything I can get you . . . anything at all?"
>
> "Yes, my son. I smell your mother's apple strudel in the kitchen. Perhaps you could bring me a bowl."
>
> "Dad, of course. Wait just one second." Two or three minutes go by until the son returns. He has a crestfallen look on his face and no strudel.
>
> "Son, what happened?" asks the father with his last breath.
>
> "Sorry, Dad," mumbles the son. "But Mom said the strudel is for the shiva."

Many times we are so concerned with external forms—with pleasing the mourners, as it were—that too often we lose sight of the true object of our giving. When that happens, our giving is not giving. It is rather a subtle form of taking for ourselves.

Contrast that story with this second tale, one of the great erotic stories of the Hebrew masters:

The master Elimelech from Lizhensk was on his deathbed with only a few weeks left to live. His son asked him, "Father, is there anything I can bring you?"

"There is, my son," he said. "Many years ago I passed a tavern where there was a woman who made the most marvelous soup. It had the taste of the Garden of Eden. I would like to taste that soup again."

Now this was a strange request indeed. Reb Elimelech was from the old school of ascetics who ate little and certainly did not remember women from taverns visited years ago. Yet that was the father's request, and so off went the son in search of the tavern.

He managed to locate it. Sure enough, the same woman still worked there. He asked her to prepare the exact same soup that she prepared for his father years ago. He was sure she would not remember his father, but lo and behold, she did. In fact, she seemed overjoyed at the request.

Unable to resist, the son asked her, "Please tell me what was so special about that soup."

"Well," replied the woman, "this was many, many years ago. When your father entered, I knew immediately he was a very holy man. In fact, I loved him very much the moment I laid eyes on him. I wanted so much to do something for him. But what could I give him? We had just opened the tavern. We served only drinks. We didn't even have any money for food.

"Sensing my despair, he came and asked my name and ordered some soup. 'Put everything you have in it,' he said, 'and it will be wonderful.' But I had nothing. So I boiled water and put in salt and cried and cried as I prepared the soup. So much I wanted for him and so little I had to give. Well, I brought it to him. With the first taste he lit up, jumped up, and began dancing all over the tavern, crying out at the top of his lungs, 'The taste of the Garden of Eden!'

"I thought he was mocking me, but he motioned for me to taste it as well. Without a doubt—I couldn't believe it, but it was the most heavenly soup I had ever tasted. With tears in both our eyes, we thanked each other, and I never saw him again."

As the woman finished the story, both she and the man's son were drenched in tears. Tears for the father and saint who lay on his deathbed, tears for how deep and holy life can be. With these tears they made a pot of soup for the dying man. And the taste . . . well, you can imagine.

The woman in the tavern really had nothing material to give. But she was a lover, and she wanted to give with all of her soul. So she gave her love. Reb Elimelech truly wanted to give. He knew his greatest gift was the ability to receive. And yet there was nothing to receive. But he loved so much that he received anyway. And what a gift it was!

Reb Elimelech, who was from the old school of severe ascetics who would scarcely look at a woman, understood the difference between the sexual and the erotic. This is the story of a great encounter between two lovers. Of course, it has nothing to do with sex. The complete blurring of giving and receiving is but modeled by sex. To be a lover is to leave behind the old and brittle distinction between giving and receiving and claim Eros in all the arenas of our lives—from our soup bowls to our baobab trees, on trains to Krakow, and yes, even on our deathbeds.

CHAPTER TWENTY-THREE

THE NINTH FACE

SURRENDER

Human beings are educated to be in control all the time. Many of the messages we receive, beginning with early childhood, are that we must be in control. The first conflict with our instinctive natures is, for most toddlers, toilet training. We are taught to control our bowel movements. This is but the first step in a lifetime that will constantly demand we be in control. From early on in life we are rewarded for doing this. We get painful disapproval, or worse, when we fail to exercise control. One of the most damaging assessments one can hear about a person is, "He's out of control." The mantra hammered into our psyches is: "Get ahold of yourself. Control yourself!"

While control education could be accomplished a bit more gently, we all recognize its importance. Going with the flow has its limitations. Few of us want to live in a world where people let their bowel movements (or any other impulses) flow naturally without any restraint whatsoever. Civilization is built on the lucid understanding that the world cannot survive without systematic self-control. In the life of the individual, the ability to delay gratification and channel energy and impulses is the key to a richer and deeper life. As all jelly bean devotees know, five jelly beans are delicious. On the other hand, uncontrolled consumption—three hundred jelly beans in one sitting, for example—will make you very sick.

"Who is a hero?" ask the wisdom masters. "He who controls his impulses." In the hero's journey, control and discipline are what create ethical human beings. Moreover, exercising tight control is at least one stretch in the road toward transformation. It is true that, initially, control adds some pressure to our lives. It is worth remembering, though, that coal only becomes a diamond when subjected to significant pressure. Control is and should be part of our understanding of the heroic life. But this is where the popular Western educational myth usually ends, when in truth, this is really just the beginning of the story.

THE SEXUAL MODELS THE EROTIC: SURRENDER

Great sex is about giving up control. Giving up control is not about an unholy submission where you are giving up your power. To submit is to give up the power that is the dignity of your being, invested in you by reality itself. Submission, however, is very different from surrender. In surrender, you give up the artifice of your posturing and claim the power of your authentic self. The sexual models the erotic, for it is in the sexual that we learn the art of holy surrender. Giving up control in sex is holy surrender where the ego is bracketed and you are actually lived as love.

But surrender is not an abdication of power. Quite the opposite. The capacity to surrender is the greatest power that one can possess. The great paradox is that the more powerful you are, the more you refuse to submit and the deeper your surrender. Never submit other than when it is necessary as a momentary strategy; always surrender, for that is your highest sacrament.

It was undoubtedly the Beat poet Allen Ginsberg who captured most provocatively but simply the way in which sexual surrender models Eros.

Please master can I touch your cheek
please master can I kneel at your feet . . .

The poem becomes progressively more raw in its sex:

please master can I gently take down your shorts
please master can I have your thighs bare to my eyes

He moves from the sexual to the erotic:

please master can I take off your clothes below your chair
please master can I kiss your ankles and soul . . .

The Poem moves in the other direction as well, from the erotic to the sexual:

please master, please look into my eyes,
please master order me down on the floor

Ginsberg understands the fluid movement between the erotic to the sexual and then back again.

THE EROS OF SURRENDER

It was the sensual Persian poet Hafiz who understood the full power of erotic surrender in every arena of life. The ecstatic poem "Tripping Over Joy" transmits something about the power of surrender:

What is the difference
Between your experience of Existence
And that of a saint?

The saint knows
That the spiritual path
Is a sublime chess game with God

And that the Beloved
Has just made such a Fantastic Move

That the saint is now continually
Tripping over Joy
And bursting out in Laughter
And saying, "I Surrender!"

Whereas, my dear,
I am afraid you still think
You have a thousand serious moves.

LOOSENING THE REINS

The one master who saw it as his role to reclaim the erotic at the core of life was the Baal Shem Tov, Master of the Good Name. We have already met this master of Eros in this book, and we will encounter him many more times along the way. The Baal Shem Tov was an eighteenth-century magician, mystic, and healer who founded the movement of spiritual renewal, Hasidic Judaism, that swept Eastern Europe in the 1700s. The story is told of a fateful meeting between Jacob Joseph of Polnoye, a well-known religious master of the time, and the Baal Shem.

The master from Polnoye had apparently heard of the Baal Shem before but had refused to join his ecstatic movement. Then Jacob Joseph heard that there was a lone individual in the marketplace telling stories. His stories were preventing people from coming to the prayer house for morning prayers. He had his attendant summon the renegade storyteller with the intention of severely reprimanding him. The Baal Shem came to him, smoking his pipe.

Before Master Jacob could begin his scolding, the Baal Shem managed to say, "Allow me to tell you a story." Jacob's voice caught in his throat. Against his will, he was silenced.

The Baal Shem began. "There was a man who had a fine carriage. It was pulled by four great stallions. Unfortunately, all of the stallions were stuck in the mud. Try as he might, yanking at the reins with all his human strength, he could not get them to move. A farmer passed him traveling in the opposite direction. The farmer called out to him, 'Loosen the reins, loosen the reins!' Do you understand, Jacob Joseph?" asked the Baal Shem.

"Yes," said Jacob Joseph, beginning to cry. He cried and cried. He finally understood.

This is a story about Eros. Jacob Joseph was a religious leader who viewed his job as enforcing the rules. He was angry when people stopped to hear a storyteller in the market and missed morning prayer. He was often angry, and his carriage was going nowhere because his horses were stuck in the mud.

In Plato, in biblical writings, and in much of mythology, horses are symbols of vitality, both erotic and sexual. Our horses are stuck in the mud. To get them out, we need to listen to the farmer, who is a man of simple but elegant wisdom. "Loosen the reins," he tells us, "and let the horses lead the way."

The sexual, as we see throughout this book, is the model for becoming a great lover in all of life. In the sexual, we all know that we need to loosen the reins (yet not let go of them) and let the horses lead.

Now we are ready to unfold the next layer in the mystery of love. To be an erotic lover, we need to know not only how to give but also how to give up. Most specifically, we need to loosen the reins, to give up control. It was to this sense of holy surrender as the mark of the enlightened one that William Blake referred to when he wrote his poem "Losing and Loosening Control":

He who binds to himself a joy
Does the winged life destroy
But he who kisses the joy as it flies
Lives in eternity's sunrise

INVITATION TO VULNERABILITY

Great sex is not about being ethically out of control. The rapist and the abuser are no heroes. Nor is unbridled and uncontrolled promiscuity a cultural ideal. We all agree that for sexuality to be both ethical and sacred, it needs to have limitations.

Yet within the context of ethical sex, letting go of control is the essence and ideal of the experience. The level of passion and intensity of pleasure are directly related to the degree to which the lovers allow themselves to lose control. Great sex cannot be fully experienced without yielding some significant measure of control, not only in orgasm but also in the earlier and more gradual unfolding of desire. Sounds, facial expressions, body movements, and raw emotion are all freed from the tight reins of our internal regulators.

What is unique about sexual love is that lovers not only let go of their internal controls but they also invite their lovers to witness their surrender. In the invitation to the other to both participate and witness, there is a giving up as well as a giving over of some dimension of control to the beloved. To love—in all arenas of living—is to relinquish control but also to grant a measure of control to the other—that is to say, to be utterly and openly vulnerable.

The moment we cross the line into the world of love, we have to let down some of the walls. We can be hurt. We have invited the other into our Holy of Holies in the trust and faith that she will tread gently. The uncertainty (and vulnerability) inherent in giving up control is inseparable from the invitation to love.

MIXED MESSAGES

Control is most often used in the world as a tool of power over others. When we say a person is powerful, we essentially mean that she has direct control over other people's lives. We label a person powerless in modernity when he exerts no obvious control over destinies other than his own, and often not even that.

So we receive mixed messages. On the one hand, we know that to be a lover we need to give up control. On the other hand, we are driven by a society that worships control as the elixir of the gods and the implicit goal of living. Driven by fear, we seek to exercise maximum control and wield maximum power. This ambivalence reflects itself in the comic absurdity of much of therapy. We go to our shrinks to learn how to "let go" and how to "get control of our lives." We want both. We feel constricted, tight, trapped; at the same time, we feel we are losing control.

Deep down, the knower in us understands that love and what society labels as power are two very different, virtually opposite, modes of being. To love is to give up control and to expose our vulnerability. Power is to maintain control and hide vulnerability. In love, my gain is your gain. In power, my gain is your loss. In love, the goal is to serve and the grail is intimacy. In power, the objective is conquest and the trophy is domination. Love is inspired by the desire to give even as you give up control. Power is motivated by the desire to take even as you exert control.

Ultimately, the refusal to retreat—accept limitation and loss of control—is the source of evil. Only the human ability to step back and give up ownership and domination holds out hope for a good, kind, and gentle world. This is what it means to be a lover.

Here again, sex models the spirit. The greatest gift a lover gives to his beloved is to relinquish his vaunted self-control in her presence. To be sexual is consequently to trust in the presence of the beloved. It is so for the lover in all facets of human life.

VICTORIOUS SURRENDER

Lindsey was a bright-eyed eight-year-old. One day at the grocery store, she saw a plastic pearl necklace priced at $2.75. How she wanted that necklace! How she begged her father for it! And what father can refuse the determined enthusiasm of an eight-year-old? Lindsey's pearls became her pride and joy. She wore them, flaunted them, and polished them lovingly.

One night, after reading her a bedtime story, Lindsey's dad leaned over and asked her, "Lindsey, do you love me?"

"Yes, Daddy. You know I love you," the little girl answered.

"Well, then, would you give me your pearls?"

"Oh, Daddy, not my pearls! You can have Missy, my favorite doll. Remember her? You gave her to me last year for my birthday."

"No, darling, that's okay." Her father brushed her cheek with a kiss. "Good night, little one."

A week later, after the bedtime story, her father asked once again, "Lindsey, do you love me?"

"Yes, Daddy. You know I do."

"Well, then, give me your pearls."

"Oh, not my pearls! But you can have Randy, my toy horse."

"No, that's okay," her father said and brushed her cheek again with a kiss. "Sweet dreams, little one."

Several days later, when Lindsey's father came in to read her a story, Lindsey was sitting on her bed, a few tears trickling down her check. "Daddy . . . here," she said, and held out her hand. In it was her beloved pearl necklace.

With one hand her father took the plastic pearls, and with the other he pulled out of his pocket a blue velvet box. He opened the cover, and inside was a string of beautiful, genuine pearls.

He had had them all along. He was just waiting for Lindsey to give up her plastic pearls so he could give her the real thing.

When we first read the story, Lindsey's father seems cruel, even sadistic. Often God appears the same way until we realize that God is waiting for us to give up the imitations in our lives so that we can receive the real thing. We all recognize imitation personalities, imitation happiness, and even imitation loving. Imagine what would happen if we really opened up to the knowledge that there is a force holding things together without our being in control. What if we surrendered to that force and allowed it to guide us in our lives? What if we stopped to realize that the planet is constantly supporting our lives?

The very air we breathe—unless we interfere with our planet's ecosystems—is constantly made available to our lungs by plants and ocean plankton through the remarkable process of photosynthesis. The universe is consciously supporting us and breathing life into our souls at every moment. For the Hebrew mystic, creation is not a one-time event. It is instead a continuous process, hinted at by modern quantum physics, in which the universe recreates itself in love at every second.

This essential giving up of control does not mean that we do not expend enormous effort and energy in trying to chart our destinies and repair the world. It does mean that we need to do so in such a way that we understand that even as we labor mightily, we know that it is simply not all up to us. Knowing that, we consciously invite the universe to be a partner in our efforts, breathing its life and energy into and through us.

The spiritual process of giving up control is called *bittul* by the Hebrew mystics. Usually, this is explained as self-nullification to God. In reality, it means something quite different. Rather than abnegation, it is a way of making ourselves transparent to God. We give up lower self-control because we desire the higher Divine Self to flow through us. This is the experience of Eros modeled on the sexual. We can access it in creativity, prayer, sexuality, study, work, and any other arena of life in which we are willing to be lovers.

AIKIDO AND SURRENDER

One paradigmatic example of giving up control to let a higher force infuse us is the martial art of Aikido. Randori practice in Aikido is a form of free-style training in which the student is attacked by multiple assailants. In this kind of attack—as is so often true in life—there is no way for you to control the outcome through raw power, no matter how skilled you are.

The key to randori is to become an erotic lover of yourself and the universe. The student steps deep inside to access an interior center of calm and balance. Everything slows down, and when it happens, you feel what the Japanese call *ki* and the Hebrew mystics call *shefa* (flow and divine effluence, respectively) gently coursing through you. You do not decide which response or technique to offer your attackers. That would be an attempt to control the situation. Rather, from a deep place, you feel your attackers' energy and you visualize the outcome of the combat before it has even begun. The student is always grounded and centered even when swirling to meet the next attack. The key to randori is paradoxically to give up control, to be a lover. Here is the description by one Western randori practitioner of his black-belt test:

> I bowed to my attackers, giving them the signal to begin. They came rushing in, far faster than I was prepared for, and almost without thinking I dropped to my knees directly in front of my first attacker, destabilizing him enough to completely throw off his balance and attack. When I rose to my feet again, although I knew my attackers were moving very quickly, my perception of time had changed. I discovered I had the space to take a few steps, the leisure to feign a strike to an attacker, the opportunity to pivot and lead an attacker into a fall. Yet during these chaotic moments, I was more deeply attuned to my breath than to my attackers. The sound and rhythm of my breathing filled my ears more than the cries and grunts of my opponents.
>
> Because I spent a fraction of a second too long throwing one of my attackers, two of the other opponents converged upon me, seizing my arms at the same time in an attempt to immobilize me. I knew that they were far stronger than I was, and that if I did not do something, the other attackers would descend upon me in a moment. In a fraction of a second of panic, I discovered that I could not dislodge them with my strength alone. In that moment, my panic subsided and I gave up my ego. I did not even try to struggle with them. I ceased caring whether or not I would emerge successfully from this situation; I stopped caring whether my teachers would promote me or what my friends who were watching would say if I failed. I let go of my sense of self, and for the briefest moment in time, I was happy not to care. I centered myself and exhaled deeply, whirling around, shaking all of the tension and anxiety out of my body like a dog shaking off water after a swim.

I could have said "abracadabra" and the effect would not have been any less magical—my attackers flew off me as though we were magnets whose polarities had suddenly been reversed. In that moment of shock and amazement, my trance ended. I found myself gasping for breath and drenched in sweat. My test was over, and suddenly, everyone in the room was clapping.

This could well be the archetype of the experience of *bittul*—transparency—taught by the Hebrew mystics. The soul longs for loss of control. There is a part of us that wants to give up the charade of constantly thinking, planning, and directing our lives. We sense intuitively that there is some deep part of us that can be revealed only when we "loosen the reins" and give up control.

THE SEXUAL MODELS THE EROTIC: THE PRACTICE OF SURRENDER

Sexual Theater

One way in which the sexual might model the erotic is what we refer to as sexual theater—intentional role-playing in sexuality—as an approach to working with the deeper dynamics in your relationships or life. Sexual theater is also a core practice in our Tantra school.

One of the major forms of sexual theater is in the play of domination and submission in sex. We talk extensively about this form of boundary-breaking sex in our book *Sexually Incorrect*. For now, it is enough to say that playing intentionally with power dynamics through sexual theater can be profoundly transformative in a person's relation to power, both wielding power and surrendering to power, in every other dimension of life. The sexual models the erotic. It is in this play that we access the power of surrender in our bodies. Submission is transformed from a standard S&M practice to the holy surrender of ecstatic devotion and delight.

MUSIC AND HELPMATES

One of the places where we overcome alienation and step inside an act of surrender is in the sacred realm of music. Song and music are erotic. We plunge into our depths even as we surrender ourselves to the sound. Eros cuts through ego and touches essence. We feel alive and totally present in the fullness of our longing.

Mastery in song and music takes place precisely at the point where radical discipline and control are transcended. At the intersection between control and surrender, the singer or musician gives herself up, allowing herself to be played by the universe. It is, of course, not an accident that an essential component of the temple service was music. The text reads, "If you are searching for Shechinah," then come to the temple with its symphony of holy song. Through music from exotic instruments and songs that opened the heart, the people were aroused to the erotics of desire and personal surrender.

It is in the music of relationship, however, that giving up control is most important. As British philosopher Adam Phillips said, "It is only when two people forget themselves in the presence of the other, that they can remember each other."

Man is lonely. In biblical myth, God makes him a helpmate, *kenegdo*, "opposite him," or in some translations, "a helpmate against him." "Now what does that mean, a partner who is against him?" asks virtually all of biblical commentary. The Hebrew word used is *ezer*, a "helper." If she is a helpmate, then how can she also be *kenegdo*, "against him"? Adam is lonely. The only way beyond loneliness is love. Love is the opposite of control. If the relationship is one of domination and control, it will fail on two levels. First, both sides will remain lonely. Second, they will not help each other, for an equal partnership is premised on giving up control. It is only if he respects her *kenegdo*, her opposition, her "no," that there can be love and partnership.

Whenever you insist on control in a love relationship, there are two reasons why you ruin the love. First, because only mutuality can redeem you from loneliness. Second, because love is a perception, and domination always blurs perception. This is why I often refer to our Edenic couple as

"Adam and Even," for the point of Eve being a helpmate "against" is that Adam must view her as even to himself, or the relationship is doomed. When you are not *kenegdo*, when you are not face-to-face at the same level, you simply cannot see each other with clarity.

NAMING, NAKEDNESS, CLEAVING

Sometimes it helps to survey the results of past relationships to understand the deep necessity of giving up control. Before Eve was created, God brought Adam the animals to name. Naming, in this context, was a symbol of control. These were not intimate, affectionate names. The context was similar to the taxonomist naming animals zoologically as an act of classification and control. Rashi, the eleventh-century interpreter of the Talmud, suggests that Adam did not merely name the animals. Mythically, "naming" implies that Adam had sexual relations with all the animals. The image suggested is sexuality as conquest, sexuality without giving up control. The animals, in this reading, become symbols of sex divorced from love and Eros. Adam wanted to know if sexuality by itself was sufficient to redeem him from his loneliness.

The answer? "Man did not find among all the animals an *ezer kenegdo*—a partner opposite." After the sex, Adam merely felt his loneliness all the more acutely. So God caused Adam to fall asleep, a powerful myth image of vulnerability. Then in the first recorded surgery in history, God removed the rib from which Eve would be formed. The point is clear: only by giving up control and being literally opened up and exposed can an authentic relationship develop. What's more, it is only by giving up a part of your being, in this case symbolized by Adam's rib, that you can hope to overcome the infinite ache of loneliness. Only vulnerability and sacrifice can create the connection and lift you out of your loneliness.

Man and woman are described as being "naked and not ashamed." With each other they are able to be totally vulnerable, exposed, and unembarrassed. To be naked means to let go of the need for posturing. By contrast, if someone falls in love with your outer facade, you remain lonely because deep down you know the person your lover adores is not you at all.

"Man cleaved to woman, and they were one flesh," says the text. "One flesh" is an obviously sexual image. "Cleaved," which is a translation of the Hebrew *devekut*, is a word of the spirit connoting Eros and deep love. Once man gives up his striving for domination and control, once he is ready to create a relationship of mutuality where each side challenges the other in love to higher growth, only then is loneliness transcended into union and love. Love is a surrender, a relinquishing of control. Love of God is responding in trust to the loving force of being—the God-flow in the universe. Love of an other is responding in trust to the divinity of the other.

WHERE LOVERS GAZE

Love means mutuality. Neither side can have a controlling vision. We recently heard of a mother whose son very much wanted to be a writer. For years, though, for not fully understandable reasons, he was unable to get it together and write. Finally one day, on the verge of despair, he broke down crying to his mother. He told her that he was going to abandon writing. To his surprise, she said to him, "I have been waiting for you to give up writing all these years. I know it isn't right for you. Indeed, I pray every day that you should not write."

This is a story that sends shivers down our spines. Naturally the poor guy can't get a word out! And his mother, of course, does not love him at all! We are told that Saul, the first king of Israel, loved young David very much. Yet when he tells David, after the latter has slain Goliath, "You shall not return home but shall eat at the king's table," the reader knows that something is amiss. If Saul is attempting to control David, then he cannot love him. Trouble lies ahead. In due course, jealousy emerges, and Saul spends much of his later years in pathetic attempts to have David killed. As soon as the desire to control enters the story, it is only a matter of time until love fails.

In the classic lover's model, the two lovers look deeply into each other's eyes. This lasts for as long as they are still head over heels in love.

But eventually, in ordinary love, the magic fades, and then the struggles for control begin. Looking into each other's eyes changes to staring each other down. The dominant personality in the relationship usually determines the controlling vision that guides them forward.

For true erotic lovers, though, relationship is based on something more than long, melting looks while gazing into each other's eyes. That may work for role mates and soul mates, but more is required for whole mates. Whole mates, as we saw in an earlier chapter, gaze at each other as soul mates do, but they also gaze at the horizon together. They come together based on erotic attraction for each other, but sustain the relationship with the Eros of shared values and vision. Lovers who don't share a higher vision, who don't work toward a common higher purpose, end up in ferocious battles for control.

THE ETROG

Love happens when each side gives up its controlling vision of reality. This allows each side to forge its connection in the raw fires of untainted love. Hebrew mystical initiates like to tell the story of Reb Mikel's *etrog*. An *etrog* is a kind of citrus fruit used in the ecstatic rituals of the biblical harvest festival, Sukkot.

Reb Mikel loved the ecstatic ritual of the *etrog* fruit. As such, he was greatly saddened at not having sufficient funds to purchase a proper *etrog*. He grew even sadder when he heard that there was one beautiful *etrog* available at a very high price in town. He went to see it and was taken by its particular beauty and precise measurements that fit so perfectly the legal requirements of the ritual. But alas, he had debts and obligations. There was no way he would ever have such money.

It so happened that before Sukkot, a wealthy merchant gave Reb Mikel a particularly fat envelope to give to his wife. For some reason, perhaps because of the thickness of the envelope, Reb's curiosity was piqued, and he opened it. Imagine his surprise when he saw a very large amount of money inside. He was overjoyed. Surely this gift was directly from

God. He literally ran into town and used all the contents of the envelope to buy the beautiful *etrog* for Sukkot.

He came home thrilled and showed his wife the wonderful *etrog*. She was silent for a moment. Then, with a voice quivering with rage, she asked him, "Where did you get money for such an *etrog*? We are so poor and have no savings. Where did you get the money?"

Just as she feared, he was oblivious, overjoyed as he was at his *etrog*, and answered gaily, "Why, a wealthy merchant gave me an envelope. You won't believe this, holy wife, but it was filled with money. A gift from God! Isn't that wonderful, my dear?"

His dear, naturally, realized that he had spent all of their charitable food money on his *etrog*. She was both furious and brokenhearted at the same time. She stormed over to the table where the *etrog* sat, picked it up, and hurled it against the wall, where it smashed to bits.

Reb's face went white, and there was dead silence in the room. Brokenness. He then slowly walked over to his wife and said, "Before, we had the money, then we had the *etrog*, now we have only each other. Let us, sweet wife, dance together." They both burst into a mixture of tears and laughter and danced in the bliss of love all through the night.

Truly this is a love story. Both Reb Mikel and his wife had visions of how life should be lived. For years, each had attempted to impose his or her own perception as the controlling vision that guided the relationship. (Mikel was more otherworldly and mystical; his wife was more practical.) Finally, it all came apart as the *etrog* exploded on the wall of their tiny home. Money gone, *etrog* gone. At that point, the partners realized their own inability to impose their vision on the other. It was a Zen moment of turning and illumination. In the same instant, they both, in a fit of despair, gave up control. But once they let go, something opened: the gates of love. For the first time in so many years, they were able to see each other again, to give, to love, to dance, to laugh.

DIVINE MINIATURES

Maybe the most important Kabbalistic teaching on love comes from the realm of cosmology, where the biblical mystics introduce to us a beautiful and important idea that enormously affects how we live our lives. The idea in two sentences: The world does not come into being through divinity stepping forward in a creative gesture. Quite the opposite: God steps back in a movement of sacrificial withdrawal in order to create the world. God creates an empty space, and only then, in that space, can the world emerge from the divine womb of being.

"But how could that be?" we ask the mystics. "Isn't the whole point of the God idea that divinity is infinite and everywhere? How can God just step back?"

"This," respond the biblical mystics, "is precisely the mystery of love."

It can be explained by two images, and the second expands on the first. In the first image, Raphael of Barsad tells of his meeting on the road with eighteenth-century Eastern European mystical master Pinchas of Koretz.

"Please," says Pinchas to Raphael as his coach pulls up alongside where Raphael is walking. "Please get in and ride with me."

"But master, there is no room!" protests Raphael.

Responds Pinchas: "Don't worry. Let us be close friends and there will be enough room."

In the second image, a sacred conversation takes place between fourth-century Babylonian wisdom masters. It is written that God withdraws his presence from the world to dwell in the empty space between the cherubs in the temple. But how could this be so? Is it not also written that all of heaven, indeed all the space in the cosmos, is not enough to contain divinity?

"Ah," says Master Yusi. "It is to be likened to lovers. When they quarrel, even a palatial home is not enough for their needs, but when they love, they can make their bed even on the edge of a sword."

The mystery of creation, of existence itself, is *tzimtzum*, meaning "withdrawal." God creates the world by withdrawing to make space for the world. What is the motivating force of *tzimtzum*? Both of our images give the same answer. The motivating force of *tzimtzum* is love.

Love is the force in the cosmos that allows God to step back and allow room for us. As with God, so with us. We are homo *imago dei* and we participate in the divine image: we are divine miniatures. In order for us to create a world, a relationship, we need to step back and create an empty space in which there is room for other, in which there is a place for the relationship to unfold. "Let us be close friends and there will be room." If I love you, I need to know how to step back and make space for you. *Tzimtzum* is God saying, "You can choose—even if you choose against Me." This is the gift of love.

The teaching of *tzimtzum* is the central realization of renaissance Kabbalah. From a rationalist perspective, the teaching of *tzimtzum* makes no sense. If God is infinitely powerful, then how could it be that God steps back? That is why the rationalists in religion rejected this esoteric teaching. The mystics of the Kabbalah, however, realized that this teaching on divine withdrawal is really about God's surrender. Paradoxically, divine power does not contradict divine surrender. It is just the opposite. It is precisely God's power that allows God to surrender. Surrender in its highest expression is not an act of weakness but the most profound expression of power. Only the powerful can truly surrender.

S-MOTHERING

Just as God steps back and allows us room to be and to choose, even when we choose against him, so a parent needs, at a certain point in the child's development, to step back and allow the child room to choose, even if it is a choice against the parent. The litmus test of love is not only giving but also giving up control. Can you, as a parent, step back to make room for your child's growth, even if it is sometimes growth away from you?

There is something tragic yet beautiful in this moment of love. A mother begins by being bonded to her child. Her primary gift of love in the early months and years is radical presence. It is the presence of the mother that allows the child to become psychologically healthy and spiritually sound. Yet as time passes, it is the mother's job to become more and more absent. This is the nature of Shechinah love.

Remember the biblical story about the two mothers who came before the wise King Solomon? Each claimed the same baby as her own. Solomon offered to cut the baby in half to give part to each mother. One woman protested, "No! Give the baby to her . . . only do not harm him!" Solomon knew immediately that the true mother had spoken. The story is about loving and giving up control. True love gives life while pseudo love smothers and strangles.

In the Bible, we are told that Rebecca loves Jacob. This is the only place in Genesis where we are told of a mother's love for her child. It is also the only place in Genesis where we see a mother sending her child away. Rebecca sends Jacob far away from Canaan, to her brother Laban in Padan Aram. As they part, she promises to bring him back. She never does. Rebecca never sees Jacob again.

She sends him away in part to protect him from his brother Esau, whose birthright Jacob has stolen on Rebecca's instructions. Yet she primarily sends him away so he can begin his hero's journey. For she knows that only if she lets go can her son find his own voice, "the voice of Jacob."

Not only mothers, but also lovers need to give up control, to step back and withdraw their presence to allow room for the beloved. The husband who claims to love his wife cannot refuse her desire to go to school, even if he is afraid that it will allow her to go places where he cannot follow. Love is commitment to the other's growth without controlling the direction and nature of that growth.

PRESENCE IN ABSENCE

Love is the revelation of another person's freedom. The body of the beloved may be penetrated, but on some level you know that your beloved's consciousness can never be fully penetrated. In the biblical wedding, there is a custom where the husband covers his future wife's face with a veil. It is as if to say, "I know that I can never fully know you. Even as I commit to spend my life trying to understand you, I promise always to honor the mystery."

But even when parents, partners, or lovers withdraw their presence, they are still there. They never go away. Even if they are not with you, they are always on your shoulder. Paradoxically, the moments of greatest love are sometimes the moments when we are least obviously present, when we have absented ourselves because we know it is essential for our partner or child's growth.

Mom is teaching her son to walk. She holds on to both of his hands as he takes the first step. She lets go. He takes the first steps on his own. Who among us does not understand that the mother is closer to her son at the moment she lets go than she ever was before? It may take a long time. He falls, rises, walks a few steps, and falls again. Love is a commitment to growth and giving up control even if it takes a very long time.

LETTING GO OF PERFECTION

Perfectionism is but another disguise for control. Self-love then means giving up on your own need to be perfect. Self-love allows room for imperfection and failure. Emerson was right when he wrote, "There is a crack in everything that God has made." It's like the old Japanese tea masters. When they made their utensils, they'd make sure that something, be it the tea scoop or the bowl, would have a flaw. A really nice and well-placed flaw, mind you, but still a flaw. If the thing was flawless, they'd fix that. For as every wisdom master knows, nothing is flawless.

The Baal Shem Tov was asked by his disciples, "After you have gone, how will we know whether another spiritual master is true or false?" The master responded, "If he promises to teach you pure prayer, know that he is a false master." So the first movement of love is to let go of the need for purity, which is really just a cover for total control.

EVEN GOD DIDN'T GET IT RIGHT

A man ordered a suit from an excellent tailor for his upcoming business trip. The day before his departure, he went to collect the suit, but it was not yet ready. Unable to postpone his journey, he traveled, returning after many months. Again he went to collect his suit, but the tailor said, "Sorry, another four days."

Four days later the suit was ready. The man tried it on and was over-joyed. The cloth felt wonderful, and the suit was both beautiful and an incredible fit. Wearing it, the man felt magnificent currents of energy and confidence. But he could not resist asking the tailor, "Why did it take you so long for one suit? After all," he added, "even God only took six days to create the world."

The tailor, not batting an eyelash, replied, "That's true. But look at his world, and look at my suit!"

For the Kabbalist, failure is built into the very fabric of existence. Ultimately, that means that God is both the source and the model of fail-ure. One of the least understood and most radical dimensions of Kabbal-istic teaching is the model of a God who cannot seem to get it right the first time around.

Remember that in Renaissance Kabbalah, the primary image of cre-ation is the God force emanating light into vessels. For whatever reason, these vessels are structurally flawed. "Structurally," of course, is not a physical term but refers to the diagram of the spirit on which the vessels are patterned. The flawed vessels are unable to hold the light streaming into them from the divine emanation. They shatter. Shards of vessels fall and disperse throughout reality. Many of the shards retain sparks of light. The purpose of existence is to gather the sparks of light, called *nitzotzot*, and reintegrate them with their divine source.

What is essential in this Kabbalistic image is the centrality of failure. God tries to create the world. It doesn't work because the vessels shatter. Our whole lives are then spent trying to return to the original pristine state before the vessels shattered, the only difference being that this time when we return, we are humbler, wiser, and able to transcend even the initial perfection with which we began.

An image from Talmudic mysticism is the God "who creates worlds and destroys them." God is dissatisfied with his creation. He is the artist who tears up draft after draft until one spills from his brush that seems right.

We are imitators of divinity. We participate in divinity. Just as God stood on the abyss of darkness and said, "Let there be light," so do we stand on the abyss of darkness and say the same. Just as God failed in his creative gesture yet reached deep within to find the love to create again, so do we.

The human creative gesture is modeled on that of the Divine. The story goes that Thomas Edison tried to invent the light bulb over a thousand times before he finally succeeded. Just before his success, a friend teased him, saying, "Thomas, how does it feel to know you've failed at something over a thousand times?" Edison answered, "I haven't failed. I've simply found over a thousand different ways that a light bulb won't work." Creativity and failure are inextricably linked.

Businesses fall apart, love is on the rocks, theorems and theories are exploded. Yet built into the original design of our being is a special reservoir of inner strength, which allows us to pick ourselves up off the floor and start again. And the second creation—be it an idea, a marriage, or an invention—is always potentially more beautiful and more complete than the first. The question is not did you fail, but rather, did you try again?

Failure is part of the hardwiring of the system. Failure is structurally embedded in both the Divine and in ourselves. There can be no creativity without it. When a business fails, a marriage falls apart, or a dream shatters, we are playing out the primal drama of creation, which repeats itself time and again from the beginning of history to the end of time. But failure is a stepping-stone on the way to ultimate success.

The primary job of the parent is to teach us that we are worthy of love even when we fail. Parental love is distorted in the parental urge to control the child. Often such a distortion is motivated by a genuine desire to save a child from failures that parents have encountered in their own lives; even so, it does not show real love. To love is to give up control and make space for the other. But when we lack an inner center ourselves, it is nearly impossible to make space.

BROKEN TABLETS

Inside the Ark in Solomon's temple were two sets of tablets, each containing the Ten Commandments. In the language of the masters, "tablets and broken tablets rested in the Ark together." The broken tablets were received by Moses at Mount Sinai in his first valiant but failed attempt to bring God's law to the people. When he realized he had failed, Moses smashed the tablets. The second set of tablets were from his second, more successful, ascent of Mount Sinai. The broken tablets are symbols of our failures.

Most of us tend to leave our failures behind, to delete the names from our electronic devices, and to excise whole chapters from our sacred autobiographies. Biblical myth comes to gently remind us: Your broken tablets are holy. Love them. Sparkling manuscripts come only from rough drafts. The rough drafts, too, must be given a place in your sacred ark, in the temple of your life.

NO COSMIC VENDING MACHINE

Just as God, to be a lover, must give up control of us, so must we give up control of God. One reason the Bible is so powerfully opposed to idolatry is because it is a method of controlling God. The basic idea in much of ancient idolatry was that the gods could be manipulated. If you said the right prayer or incantation, or performed the right sacrifice, then the god would do whatever you willed. Divinity becomes a cosmic vending machine, where the key is having the right change. For the Hebrew prophets, sacrifice without the intention for transformation was irrelevant.

Prayer also can be a form of controlling God. Prayer healers abound both within and without organized religion, and they promise that prayer can bring healing. Now, there is little question that prayer does affect wellness. Dr. Larry Dossey has collected many studies and written important books on the subject. But as Dossey himself cites from numerous sources, the prayer that is truly effective is the one in which we ask for healing without specifying a particular outcome. We are not sure what the best outcome is. We cannot force the universe's hand.

What we can do through prayer and spiritual practice, though, is to open up what the Kabbalists call the channels of energetic flow. In Kabbalah, these are somewhat like the heart valves of the universe, which get clogged when we do not clean them through prayer and practice.

We try to control God with theology all the time. When preachers, imams, or rabbis give explanations as to why people suffer in the world, it is an act of hubris motivated by a desperate desire to maintain control. A Jewish example is the Holocaust. There are voices in Judaism that seek to explain why the Holocaust happened; usually, they are based on pointing to the spiritual failings of a particular group of Jews. It is, of course, never the group with which the explainer is affiliated. A Christian example is Jerry Falwell's explanation of why the September 11 terrorist attacks happened. They were punishment for the underlying moral malaise in America.

I can promise you that God did not inform Falwell or the Holocaust explainers of his plans. The explanations come from a desire to control and even own God. But they do not come from a real love of God—quite the contrary. In truth, we do not know why people suffer. And no explanation can suffice to justify the horrors of war, hunger, and disease. The lover seeks not to explain or control, but to become a partner in the healing.

Our bodies remind us that we are neither the masters of our fate nor even the sergeants of our destiny. Actually, although we identify with parts of our bodies, we disassociate from most of our physicality. Language always reveals the secrets of the psyche. We say, "I moved my hand," but we do not say, "I circulated my blood." Your ego can identify with your arm, but not with your circulatory system. We identify with our voluntary systems and detach from our involuntary systems.

The reason is as simple as it is obvious: we fear loss of control. We disassociate from the body, for it is essentially not under our control. Most of the body is a well-organized collection of involuntary processes—that is, processes beyond our control: metabolism, digestion, growth, circulation, respiration. We distance these from our identity. We do not call them "self" because they are uncontrollable. Yet isn't it strange that we call only half of our organism "self"? To whom does the other half belong?

When I (Marc) was eighteen years old, I was close friends with Dafna, an incredible Israeli woman. She taught me far more about life and its mysteries than most of my teachers had.

Early one morning, a terrorist bomb exploded in the cafe in which she was having breakfast. She was paralyzed from the neck down. I went to visit her in the hospital the first day she was allowed visitors. She kept repeating to me the same words, "I am trapped in my body, I am trapped in my body." My heart was breaking and tears streamed down my face as I understood that our bodies, sources of wonder and pleasure, were also terrible prisons over which we have little control.

Our lack of control is brought home again by the body's vulnerability to severe damage and pain. Paradoxically enough, the body is also the seat of pleasure. The major locus of pleasure for most people is sexuality, which models, as we have seen, the spiritual ideal of giving up control. Our unwillingness to lose control in the sacred contexts of pleasure can have devastating results. The loss of control will inevitably come, but may take the forms of pain and pathology.

While initially the decision to have sex is voluntary, once we engage in sex, we have little control. As the sexual experience climaxes, all of our illusions of control are swept away in spasms of pleasure. Hebrew Tantra, unlike its Hindu counterpart, revels in the loss of control. Yet the pleasure is not complete. Sexuality has many shadows: the sexual scandals that rock our world on a regular basis, the false accusations driven by the complex ulterior motives of piety, and the very real abuses such as child pornography. The list is nearly endless.

Besides all that, in the realm of healthy sexuality there is still an undercurrent of disease. It expresses itself mostly in the legions of off-color jokes as well as in our general embarrassment when talking about sex. The source of all this uneasiness is that sexuality reminds us that we are not in control of our bodies and therefore not in control of our lives. In a society where control is so vaunted and worshipped, that reminder is a deep, dark secret we don't want revealed to anyone, least of all ourselves.

A RETURN *to* EROS

THE SAGE AND THE COURTESAN

The wisdom masters tell a wonderful story of the sage Eliezer, son of Dordaya, who had visited every courtesan in the land. He was a great master, yet he was driven by something deep inside, a sense of profound emptiness and futility. Even as he began to teach in the academy, he continued to visit the great prostitutes of the land.

Once he heard that there was a prostitute by the sea who took a pouchful of *dinarim* (a very large amount) for her fee. He took a pouchful of *dinarim* and went in search of her. He crossed seven rivers to find her. In the midst of their sexual engagement, he passed wind (expelled gas). She said, "Just as this gas will never return to its source, so too Eliezer ben Dordaya will never return to his source."

Eliezer, electrified by her words, left immediately. He ran to the forest and said to the trees, "Plead mercy for me." They refused. He turned to the stars, to the earth, to all of nature. Each time he cried, "Pray for me," and each time he was refused. In the end he realized, "It depends only on me." He placed his head between his legs and prayed.

What does this strange myth mean? Eliezer was out of control. Driven by emptiness, he sought out sexual encounter after encounter. He wanted to stop but could not. While deeply ashamed of his lack of control, there was little he could do. What the myth suggests is that his healing could not come through fighting for control. Paradoxically, it was only by embracing his essential lack of control that he could change.

The key to the story is in the passing of gas. Did you ever sit in a meeting and need to "pass wind" and yet work mightily to hold it in? Why? Of course we are mortified at "passing wind" because it punctures our false, inflated projection of control. When we give our essential fragility and lack of control a place of respect, then we are less threatened by apparent emptiness and futility. Slowly and gently we can begin to invest our lives with meaning. Honoring our lack of control is the only way to return a measure of control to our lives.

Sexuality can become a sacrament modeling our true position in the world. We no longer need to chase it compulsively to remind us that we matter. We give up the need for obsessive control. In that surrender, the world comes alive. And so it is in life, since sex models Eros. In surrender, we inherit the kingdom.

CHAPTER
TWENTY-FOUR

THE TENTH FACE

PLAY AND LISHMAH

The next quality of love and Eros modeled by the sexual is play. Play is close in meaning to what the Hebrew mystics called *lishmah*, which is usually translated as "for its own sake." We are engaged in the erotic when we do something simply for its own sake—when we stop networking and let go of goal-oriented thinking, when the activity itself is the end and not the means. This is the Eros of self-evident meaning. *Lishmah* is when loving is the motive, for the only ulterior motive of Eros is love. Indeed, the litmus test of true love is that it has no ulterior motive. It stands and endures for its own sake. *Lishmah*!

THE SEXUAL MODELS THE EROTIC: LISHMAH, PLAY FOR ITS OWN SAKE

The overwhelming majority of our sexing is for its own sake. We even call it sexual play, because play, like sex, is an end unto itself. It is not a means to another end. Classical religion failed in its concerted attempt to reduce sex to a means for having children. Of course, sex accomplishes procreation; that is part of its radical wonder. But the allurement to sexual play is for its own sake. Sexual play is self-justifying just like the play of a child is.

Essayist and poet e. e. Cummings captures in the first stanzas of his famous poem "may I feel said he" the sense of play or fun—for it's own sake—that is the erotic quality of the sexual.

> *may i feel said he*
> *(i'll squeal said she*
> *just once said he)*
> *it's fun said she*
>
> *(may I touch said he*
> *how much said she*
> *a lot said he)*
> *why not said she*

In this precise sense, the sexual models the erotic. That which is erotic is not merely instrumental even if accomplishes a goal. The erotic act is playful. It is the play of Eros that liberates life from its boredom, pressing us into the fullness of our being and becoming.

THE EROS OF PLAY: FOR ITS OWN SAKE

To be erotically engaged means to be on the inside, totally filled and satisfied by the activity itself rather than using it as a way of getting somewhere or doing something else. The model for this kind of radical "in and of itself" engagement is the sexual. The sexual invites us inside to its fullness, promising at its highest not a networking opportunity but the richness of the experience itself. Advancement is not the issue; *lishmah* is not goal-oriented. Once you are in the erotic, you have arrived; you are already there. This is the endpoint. There is nowhere else to go. The process itself is the goal. It is this sense that *lishmah* engenders ecstasy. Past and future melt away as the present swells to infinite proportions.

The sexual models *lishmah* and teaches us how to be lovers, living erotically in all facets of existence. Loving either a person or an activity is an end in itself and not a means. There is no expectation other than what is. There is a deep appreciation of the inherent value, wonder, and truth of each moment. The litmus test of *lishmah* for an interpersonal relationship is when the person you are with becomes more important than the activity you are doing. The process becomes the result.

Beauty is *lishmah*. A breathtaking vista, a rainbow, a sunset—they need no excuse for existing. They just are. They are beautiful and need not serve any other purpose. A perfect expression of this *lishmah* quality is the female breast. The rapture that the female breast has provoked in poets, painters, and biblical writers throughout the ages is fully self-validating. It is not because of infantile memories of nourishment or because of the fascination with taboo, it is just because. God is called Shaddai, a Hebrew wordplay on the word for "breasts," *shaddayim*. The point is not only that God nourishes, but that the essence of the Divine also lies in its being enough; it is self-validating.

Art is *lishmah*. It is the end itself and requires no external justification. So while we valorize the commercial businessman who is driven by profit, we tend to frown upon an artist who shares the same quality. We expect him to carry the torch of *lishmah* for society. The same is true of a spiritual teacher who seems driven by commercial motivation. Yes, the teacher has a right to be compensated for his efforts. But somehow we expect him not to violate the quality of *lishmah*, which is so essential to endeavors of the spirit.

If we expect an activity to model *lishmah*, we are collectively horrified when it does not. This is precisely why society never fully accepted prostitution. On a moral plane, there are certainly more ethically serious issues to engage—slander, corporate corruption, manipulative advertising, to name a few. Yet we hold prostitution to a different standard not because it is a violation of any overriding moral principle. Rather, it contravenes, paradoxically, an erotic principle; sex for commercial profit violates the erotic quality of *lishmah*.

ENDS AND MEANS

It would not be incorrect to say that *lishmah* is an animal-like quality. Human beings are the only animals that are both blessed and cursed by their awareness of life and death. Awareness brings in its wake the potential of consciousness. Its shadow, however, is the non-*lishmah* qualities of past and future anxiety, obsessive planning, and fear. By contrast, an animal lives not for the sake of past or future but for its own sake—*lishmah*. It is this contented *lishmah* quality of the animal that made Walt Whitman write, "Turn and live with animals . . . they do not lie awake in the dark and weep for their sins . . . not one is dissatisfied."

The place where human beings are most instinctive and animal-like is the sexual. In its ideal expression, the sexual exists only for its own sake. The sexual, therefore, models the quality of *lishmah*.*

---

* In human beings, *lishmah* is manifested in both higher and lower expressions of consciousness. We call these lower *lishmah* and higher *lishmah*. A core principle of reality is that consciousness unfolds in triads from simple to complex to a higher simplicity. Even though level one and level three look the same on the outside, they each represent a very different interior experience. Levels one and three are worlds apart in their erotic quality. The classic expression of level one, lower *lishmah*, is sex when it is "merely animal-like." Level one is characterized by a lack or loss of awareness. The second level is normal human awareness—in all of its negative and positive manifestations. This is the great evolutionary breakthrough of the human neocortex. It allows us to hold all of the complexity of human life. Because the human being thinks, virtually all activity becomes a means of accomplishing a goal. Much of our sexual engagement, both satisfying and unsatisfying, takes place on this level. The third level is higher *lishmah*. This is not first but second simplicity. One expression of higher *lishmah* is manifested by human beings when we reclaim our animal nature but at a higher level of consciousness. We engage in sex for its

THE TASTE OF THE TREE

The goal of the erotic life is to engage every area of our lives with the mantra of *lishmah* beating in our breasts. This means being fully present for each thing itself without needing always to justify our activity by recourse to some external gain. In the poetry of Hebrew mysticism, this is referred to as *taam haeitz ketaam haperi*, meaning "the taste of the tree is as the taste of the fruit." This phrase has its source in the delightful biblical creation myth where God commands the trees to be "trees of fruit which bear fruit." The stunning implication of a precise reading of the divine instruction is that the tree itself, the bark, should also have the taste of the fruit. The point is, there should be no distinction between means and ends. A coarse tree that brought the fruit into being should share the very taste of its succulent fruit.

In a similar metaphor, Schneur Zalman of Liadi talks about how "the source of the vessels is higher than the source of the lights." Just as a tree holds and sustains the fruit, the vessel holds and sustains the light. The usual distinction is that the vessel is the means to hold the light, which is the end. Schneur Zalman suggests that this distinction is nonerotic and not reflective of the fullness of reality. The vessels themselves, teaches Schneur Zalman, are no more than "congealed" light.

The essence of *lishmah* collapses the distinction between fruit and bark, vessel and light, means and end. The idea that "the ends justify the means" is therefore not only unethical but also nonerotic.

SACRED PLAY, SACRED WORKPLACE

An open portal to the experience of *lishmah* is play. Play is very much for its own sake. If you play to win, you lose. Very often a game is defined

---

own sake—*lishmah*. But sex at this higher level of *lishmah* is characterized not by a lack or loss of awareness but by the *transcending* of awareness into a higher level of being. At this level, the human being reclaims their animal nature not through a regression to level one simplicity but through evolving to the higher simplicity of level three. Level one is regressive. Level three is transcendent.

by purely arbitrary rules governing purely trivial actions. The goal lies in doing the activity itself.

There are few better spiritual lessons than watching the enraptured play of two toddlers. Children are the archetypes of *lishmah*. Yet the same quality of *lishmah* should hold true for adult play. One of the tragedies of the institutionalization of play is that it has lost its very playful, and therefore erotic, character. Sports play is often bound up with intense competition and betting. It has become a bottom-line, win-lose proposition. Competition always drives us harder. Where competition asks, "Couldn't you try just a little bit harder?" play says, "Couldn't you try just a little bit softer?" *Lishmah* invites us to play more softly and gently.

In Hebrew, there are whole sets of words that feature the repetition of one syllable. The repetition expresses a particular intensity. One of the more powerful examples of this intensity through repetition is the word *sha'a shu'ah,* which is translated as the "delight of erotic play." The word is taken in Hebrew mysticism to refer to erotic delight in both its sexual and its mystical forms. *Sha sha* forms the core of the word. In Hebrew, the word *sha* means "turning toward." *Sha sha* is thus explained by the mystics to mean "turning toward for the sake of turning toward." The same formula follows for the Hebrew word *ga'a gu'ah,* which means "yearning," again with both sexually and mystically erotic implications. *Ga ga* is thus understood as "yearning for the sake of yearning." The subtle wisdom of language reminds us that the erotic is *lishmah*—that is, for its own sake. Its goal is to take us to itself, to remind us that we are already there.

One of the central areas of our lives that has been most painfully de-eroticized is work. The Western world has greatly succeeded in reducing the length of the workday. Yet we have failed terribly to erase the dichotomy between work and pleasure. It is clear that such a division can only make our lives miserable. No matter how wonderful it may be, the weekend is still far shorter than the workweek. If we do not transform our work into *lishmah*—that which we do for its own sake—then we are destined for depression.

In Hebrew, the word for "work" is *avodah*. Wonderfully, though, in Hebrew the first connotation of *avodah* is "service in the Temple in Jerusalem." The subtle linguistic association shows up in English as well. The words *work* and *worship* come from common roots in Old English. The implication is clear: all work—like the work in the temple—should be erotic. That is to say, *lishmah*, for its own sake.

At the site of the ancient Sumerian city of Ur, archaeologists were surprised to find a golden harp buried together with a set of golden working tools. It would appear that the Sumerians, like the Hebrews, understood that there can be no division between Eros and work.

"Six days a week you shall work, and on the seventh day you shall rest on the Sabbath," reads the biblical text. We naturally assume that the sacred imperative is to rest on the Sabbath. The wisdom masters read it differently. "Six days you shall work—this is a positive commandment." The sacred imperative is not just to rest on the seventh day, but also to work for the other six!

No matter how noble a goal we claim as the purpose of our work, it is insufficient. We must search for the meaning intrinsic to the work itself. Only then can we have the erotic workplaces envisioned by biblical myth.

Here's a story of yearning for a sacred workplace:

The great master Levi Isaac of Berditchev was walking his usual route in the marketplace. Along came a man rushing madly to somewhere and bowled the master over.

"Why are you running so fast?" asked Levi Isaac as he got up.

"Well," said the man, "I need to make a living."

Levi Isaac asked, "Why are you working so hard to make a living?"

Well, no one had ever asked our mad dashing friend such a question, and he was at a loss as to how to respond. "Well," he stuttered—and then a light bulb went on in his head. "I am working so hard in order to make a living for my children."

It seemed to be a fine answer, and the master wished him good day.

Twenty-five years went by. Again, the master was walking the same path in the marketplace. Again, he was bowled over by a rushing passerby. Masters are consistent, so the same conversation ensued. And again it concluded with the man saying, confidently, "I am rushing so much in order to make a living for my children."

Levi Isaac looked deeply into the man's face. He realized that this was the son of the man who had bowled him over twenty-five years ago. Turning his eyes heavenward, he asked God, "When will I finally meet that one child for whom all the generations labor so mightily?"

These gentlemen running through the market each justified their labor in terms of their children. Though supporting children is a very good reason, it is still insufficient. Every "reason" is ultimately an excuse. Even kids may be used as excuses, a violation of the erotic quality of *lishmah*. It is only truthful to respond, "I am running for the sake of running, working for the sake of working!"

The most common expansion of *lishmah* beyond the sexual to the erotic is in the arena of study. Remember that for the Hebrew mystic, study is an erotic encounter. It is a flirtation with text, a wooing of wisdom that leads to the final full embrace of life-giving learning. A core requirement of Hebrew law is that the study of Torah (sacred wisdom) be *lishmah*. That means the Torah must be studied not for the sake of honor or prestige, but for the sake of the spirit. According to a second school of thought, studying even for the sake of the spirit is not *lishmah*. Study of the Torah must be totally self-validating—Torah purely for its own sake.

LISHMAH: FOR THE SAKE OF THE NAME

The erotic quality of *lishmah* has a second layer of meaning, which takes us even deeper. *Lishmah* derives from the Hebrew letters spelling *sham*, meaning "there." In the first understanding of *lishmah* (acting for its own sake), when you give up getting there, you realize you are already there.

However, *sham*, pronounced "shem," has a second meaning: "name." In this layer of understanding, *lishmah* means "for the sake of the name." In the ultimate expression of *lishmah*, as we will see in a few pages, this quality of *lishmah* is also modeled in the sexual. But before we get there, let's take a look at what "for the sake of the name" actually means. Your name is the face of God that is you and you alone. *Lishmah* means living for the sake of the unique God expression that is you in the world: your name!

In the deepest sense, this second meaning of *lishmah*, "for the sake of the name," is but a facet of the first meaning, "for its own sake." There are two steps here. First, for the sake of the name is the most profound expression of Unique Self, the fifth face of Eros. Here is the second step. This dimension of Unique Self is not so much focused on your unique gift or mission; rather, it is focused on living your name in the world. You live for the sake of your name, because that is who you are. This sense of "being yourself" or living for your name is the quality of doing things "just because." That is what it means to act for its own sake. I act just because, for the sake of my name.

This is not merely a psychological idea but a life-transforming mystical realization. "For the sake of the name" refers to your own name and to the name of God. In this realization of *lishmah*, you understand clearly that both names, your name and the name of God, are one. It is this sense that one lives for the sake of the name. One's actions are self-justifying and not merely instrumental.

It is this identity between your name and the name of God that we will unfold in the rest of the chapter. As we will see below, in this second quality of *lishmah*, the sexual models the erotic.

The second book of the Torah is called the book of Names—*Shemot*. (In English, it is poorly mistranslated as the book of Exodus.) The book of Names opens with a description of the Hebrew people during their prosperous early days of sojourning in Egypt; at the time, they were still free men and women. One major characteristic stands out in the description. The text here, like the genealogies in the book of Genesis, takes great pains to record for us individual names. A name is a symbol of personal identity. Unique among ancient chronicles, the Bible thinks individuals count. This fact expresses itself later in the biblical narrative, which tells of the great census in which people are individually counted.

The crescendo of this description of freedom is the seemingly super-fluous last verse of the section "Joseph was in Egypt." Remember, Joseph, the son of Jacob, has risen to greatness as the viceroy of Egypt. He has an Egyptian name—Tzafnat Paneach—and yet the text tells us "Joseph was in Egypt." Joseph, not Tzafnat Paneach. This deliberate use of his Hebrew name suggests that Joseph has retained his authentic identity, his name, and his roots.

In the very next verse, however, the shift begins. Individual names blur into anonymous pronouns. The text begins to swell with anonymity. Describing the Hebrews, it reads, "They multiplied, they increased, they became strong . . . the land was full of them." This is followed by the chilling announcement: "A new king arose who did not know Joseph." The name, with all its erotic implications, has been forgotten. From this point until the birth of Moses, the text speaks almost exclusively in pronouns. The children of Israel are repeatedly identified as "they" and "them." "A man from the house of Levi marries the daughter of Levi." Names are effaced. Slavery is on the rise. "And they made their lives bitter with bondage, in mortar and in brick, and in all the work of the field . . . they enslaved them with brutality."

The essence of being a slave is the deconstruction of identity and intimacy. Intimacy is dependent on identity. Intimacy, as we have already seen, is not the giving up of self for another but rather merging in a "shared identity." Undermine the name—the symbol of identity—and there is no possibility for intimacy. Slavery in biblical myth is the symbol of nonerotic living. A slave does not make independent decisions. His evaluation of reality, his testimony, is considered inadmissible in a court of law; most critically, he may not initiate his own marriage.

Slavery at its core is nonerotic and therefore an affront to human dignity and holiness. The shift in the biblical story toward transformation and redemption is signaled by the name. A new child is born. "His name is called Moses." A name breaks through the darkness of slavery with the intimacy of personal identity. The Kabbalists point out that Moses' Hebrew name spelled backward is *hashem*: "the name." Slavery still rules—the name is still backward—but freedom is in the air. The name, a glimpse of godliness, has reappeared.

SPIRITUAL MARRIAGE, SPIRITUAL DIVORCE

The essential requirement in Hebrew law for marriage and divorce is that it be done *lishmah*, for the sake of the name. This is an affirmation that the full uniqueness of the other is being engaged in the marital relationship. If this is not so, if the name is somehow effaced, then no relationship can be established or terminated. Changes in personal status must be *lishmah*; that is, they require the full erotic engagement and presence of all the parties involved.

All of this is expressed by the almost exaggerated emphasis that is placed on the correctness of the name in marriage documents. Great ritual care is taken in researching the precise Hebrew spelling of the name as well as in the listing of any nicknames. The point is that marriage must be an affirmation on both sides of the unique soul root of the other, which makes the beloved an end and not a means. Marriage is a commitment to the name of the beloved.

Not just marriage but also divorce needs to be an erotic process. How many divorces are done with radical violations of name, of intimacy? What is petty "name-calling" other than slinging "names" at a person other than her true, soul-printed name? During the divorce process, how many couples refuse even to use each other's names . . . calling their former spouse "him" or "her" in a tone of disgust? Biblical wisdom attempts to assuage the bitter namelessness of divorce by inviting us to a ritual of spiritual divorce. Its essence is the requirement of *lishmah*, for the sake of the name.

WHAT'S IN A NAME?

A name is an expression of relationship, of intimacy. "What's in a name?" asks Shakespeare. "Everything!" answers the Hebrew mystic. Many of the most common Hebrew mystical sayings reveal the magic, power, and invitation of the name. "For the sake of the great name"; "May his name be blessed"; "May his name be blotted out"; "He is as his name"; "Name is primal cause."

In biblical writings, there are two names for the book incorrectly called "Exodus," which tells the story of physical and spiritual emancipation. One of the names, which we mentioned, is *Sefer Shemot*, "The Book of Names." The other name is *Sefer HaGeulah*, "The Book of Emancipation." Why? To remind us that finding our name is the beginning of becoming free. To be a lover is to know the power of the name. A slave has no name, which is why slavery is such a brutal violation of the spirit of biblical myth. And by this we mean slavery of any kind—not only legal juridical slavery but also typological slavery.

Anyplace where you are regarded only as a function, where your name is not known and honored, you are a slave. Anytime you regard another as a mere instrument in your design, you become a slave master and an oppressor. To be a lover is to know the name. It can be the name of the waiter, of the taxi driver, of your accountant's son, or of the mailman's wife. By remembering the name, you become a lover.

This is why the pet names we have for our beloved are the stuff of beauty in our lives. The more you love someone, the more you accumulate pet names. Pet names come from our child selves reaching out to make authentic contact with the delight of innocence that we have a hard time accessing in our more adult persona. The point is that names matter. The more intimate we are, the more unique our names are for each other. The more alienated we are, the more the name fades away.

Remember the scene in that great old movie *The Graduate*, where Dustin Hoffman's character explains to Mrs. Robinson, who is a generation older than he is, why he can't go on with their affair?

"Why not?" asks Mrs. Robinson. "I love you," she says with little conviction.

"I cannot go on," repeats the young man.

"Why not?"

"Because I don't even know your first name, Mrs. Robinson," he says.

It was ten, eleven years ago, and I (Marc) was giving a lecture in a rented hall on the Upper West Side of Manhattan. The topic was exciting, and so the hall was full, far too full for me to speak without a microphone. And as Lady Fate would have it, in the first two minutes of the talk, the sound system went out. The host of the event went running to find the custodian, who, it was hoped, would be able to fix the microphone. The host came back some seven long minutes later and whispered to me, "I'm really sorry, Rabbi. I found the custodian, but he's a really nasty guy and refuses to help."

I was blessed with one of those moments of grace that allows us sometimes to ask the right question. "What's the custodian's name?" I asked.

Flustered, nervous, and impatient, the host blurted out, "Rabbi, we've got five hundred people in here. How do I know what the blank his name is?"

"Ah," I responded, "perhaps that's the problem." Asking the audience to wait a moment, I went out myself and found the custodian glaring in his office, apparently still smarting from his encounter with the evening's chairman.

I walked in and said, "Hi. I'm Marc. What's your name?"

Taken aback, he said, "George." George knew exactly how to fix the microphone and did so graciously and immediately.

The power of the name.

THE NAME OF GOD

Lishmah, "for the sake of the name," is a core feature of the erotic. A name is a symbol of identity, intimacy, and freedom. But a name is all of these in a way far more powerful than one might initially imagine. When we talk about acting "for the sake of the name," we refer to something far deeper than the technical name that we use to identify a human personality. Name is, as we said earlier, the face of God that is you and you alone. Here is where we touch the deepest erotic core of *lishmah*. Your name is not just a reflection of God's face; it is also actually part and parcel of what the mystics called God's great name. In the deepest level of human identity, the distinction between human being and God collapses. It is here that we realize that each of us is part of God.

As with all good biblical wisdom . . . we begin with a question.

In the Hebrew tradition, the prayer that is recited when someone dies is the *Kaddish*. It opens with the words *Yitgadal v'yitakadash sh'mei raba*—"Magnified and exalted be God's great name." Why, you may ask, is the central prayer of mourning so preoccupied with God's name? Why does God need us to magnify his great name? If his name is so great, why can't it take care of magnifying itself? Even more important, is this the best prayer we can say in the face of the open grave? Someone has died—we are sad. Sometimes we are truly broken. We then say *Kaddish*, "Magnified and exalted be the great name." Is this the most profound response we have, standing before death? Would not words of comfort and an embrace be more appropriate? The answer to this quandary holds one of the most sacred mysteries of love, which is rooted in the heart of the cherub mysteries.

There is a story told about Israel ben Eliezer—also known as Baal Shem Tov, "Master of the Good Name." The appellation was a title given to only the holiest adepts of an eighteenth-century secret mystical tradition. This honored appellation suggests that the master had connected to the root of his name, to his unique divinity.

> When Master Isaac heard of the marvelous effect of Master Israel's holy healing amulets, he was angry. He thought that surely amulets could only have such power if they use the holy name of God, but since this would constitute improper use of God's name, Master Isaac decreed, "Because of improper use of God's name, the power of the amulets must pass away." And so it was.
>
> When Master Israel realized that his amulets were no longer healing, he sought the reason. Eventually, it was revealed to him from on high that Isaac's decree was blocking their efficacy. Israel confronted Isaac. "Why do you stop my amulets, which are used only to heal?" Israel demanded.
>
> "Because you have not the right to use God's name in this way," retorted Isaac.
>
> "But I do not use God's name in my amulets," Israel replied.
>
> "You must, or they could not have such power."
>
> "I insist: I do not use God's name," persisted Israel.
>
> So all the amulets of Master Israel were gathered and brought before a tribunal. When the first one was opened, there was an audible gasp. Then the second, the third, and the fourth.

Master Isaac was in shock. For the name of God indeed was not used in any of the amulets.

Instead, in every amulet, in the place where God's name could have been, it read, "Israel ben Eliezer." It was Israel's own name and not the name of God that gave the amulets their special power. Awed at this great wonder, Master Isaac restored the power of Israel's amulets. Some say that after this incident Israel ben Eliezer became the last and greatest master to hold the title Baal Shem Tov, Master of the Good Name.

In this story we sense a potent enmeshing of the name of God and the name of the person. Are they indeed separate names? Or perhaps in some mysterious way, the name of the individual and the name of God are one.

THE SEXUAL MODELS THE EROTIC: FOR THE SAKE OF THE NAME

The Three Texts of Orgasm

This second meaning is one in which we will see very clearly that the second quality of *lishmah*—for the sake of the name—is modeled most powerfully in the sexual. The importance of the name becomes obvious in sex. What do we call out at the moment of sexual climax? Three common possibilities: the first is that we cry out "Oh, God," or its equivalent in whatever the lingua franca happens to be: Elohim, mon Dieu, etc. The second possibility is that we call out the name of the beloved. The third is that we call out, "Yes." At this moment of ultimate vulnerability—and thus authenticity—there is a blurring of names. The name of the other and the name of God become almost interchangeable. Here again the sexual models the erotic, this time in the most dramatic of ways, bringing us to the heart of the cherubs' secret.

Why do God's name and the name of the beloved seem to interchange at the moment when all the outer layers are stripped bare and we call out our highest truth? Because in the deepest place, it is the same name! The name of God is no less than the name of every being from the beginning to the end of time. The "Yes" is the same "Holy Yes," which reality cries out at the moment of the original big bang that birthed reality. The "Yes" is the radical affirmation of the unrelenting goodness of life and our place in the universe. The name of God and the name of the beloved are one. Yes!

IN THE HOLY OF HOLIES

Now let's go one step deeper. The sexual models the erotic. The lover crying out "Oh, God" at the height of sexual rapture models the rapture of the high priest who calls out "Oh, God" in the erotic climax of merging with the Divine, in the Holy of Holies of the Jerusalem Temple. In the cherub tradition, the priest is the incarnation of the flow of love in the universe. The high priest in the Jerusalem Temple would enter the cherub-crowned Holy of Holies once a year. What would he do there? What was the nature of the mystery rite he performed? This was the only rite that was witnessed by the sexually entwined cherubs. So undoubtedly the mystery rite in the Holy of Holies lies at the very heart of the mystery of love.

As we already know, this day of entering the Holy of Holies is called the Day of Atonement, At-one-ment. It was a time of radical ecstasy, union, and joy. The priest is described in the Zohar as the incarnation of the male organ, while the Holy of Holies is the feminine Divine, the Shechinah. In some Zohar passages, Shechinah is the archetypal expression of the yoni.

So the mystery rite is the priest and the Shechinah merging in erotic union. What did the priest actually do in the Holy of Holies? Tradition answers unequivocally: he called out the name. Not just any name, mind you; but the unpronounceable name of God, the name that was so true and had so much power that it was never said except at this one time of great intimacy. In the ecstasy of the erotic spirit, the priest, the lover par excellence, cried out the name! Mystical orgasm, pure and simple.

In the language of Kabbalah, mystical orgasm brings the priest into the *ayin*—"nothingness," no-thing-ness. *Ayin* is the bliss of leaving self behind in the rapture of orgasm. Yet when love is deep, orgasm gives way not to an empty hangover but to a sweet aftertaste. In that aftertaste the self is reborn. In calling out "Oh, God," the lover also rebirths her own name. In the little death of orgasm, self is reborn. The name of God and the name of the person are one.

In a precisely parallel image, God's face is the totality of all human faces from the beginning to the end of time. The Zohar teaches that when all the root souls who form God's will have been born, it will be the dawn of a new age of consciousness. We will have entered the Holy of Holies—otherwise known as the inside of the inside—or in an alternative reading of the same Hebrew phrase, "the face of faces."

When all human beings who form God's face have been born, we will be *lifnei Hashem*—"before God." The deeper translation, however, is on "the inside of God's face"—or the most fully literal translation: on "the inside of the face of the name."

A DIMINISHMENT OF THE NAME

Now let's go one last step before we bring this all together. When a Jewish person dies, the tradition is to say a eulogy and then recite the *Kaddish* meditation. What is the eulogy's purpose? What is its deep intention? What spiritual service does it render?

When I (Marc) first became a rabbi in my early twenties, I was called to the funeral home all too often. I can still remember today, however, the occasion of my first eulogy. A forty-eight-year-old man named Jerry had passed away while jogging. His wife, Fern, called me to do the eulogy and funeral. I had no idea what to say. So I asked Fern and her kids, Doug and Wendy, to sit with me the day before the funeral.

We sat around Fern's living room for a few hours, talking about Jerry. At first the talk was just polite. But as time wore on, with a few drinks to help, it got far more honest and real. All the while, I jotted notes, trying to capture their precise phrases. I spent most of that night awake, trying to weave their sentences and words into a eulogy that would honor Jerry.

What is a eulogy? It is the last—and sometimes the first—opportunity to recognize the soul print of the one who has passed. In the eulogy, we try to paint in fine brushstrokes the person's radical uniqueness that was his life. It is the time when we "receive their name."

The next morning, I shared the eulogy with Fern and her family and friends at the cemetery. It was magic, plain and simple. All of us felt that Jerry had entered the room. Or put better, somehow his presence seemed to surround and encompass us. We were "on the inside." At that very moment, I asked Fern and her children to rise and recite with me the *Kaddish* meditation: "Magnified and exalted be the great name!" Whose name? Why, God's name . . . and Jerry's, the name of the departed beloved. Of course! For in the deepest place, they are the same name.

Death in the mystical tradition of Ezekiel is called a *hillul Hashem*. Usually translated as "a desecration of God," it more literally means "an emptying of the name." Death is a diminishment of divinity. One aspect of God in the world has suddenly disappeared. Death is tragic because a person dies leaving so much of her story untold. Each person is a unique name-face of God. Each death is a dimming of the divine visage.

This truth is not limited to Kabbalistic masters. Walt Whitman understood at least part of it when he wrote in "Song of Myself":

> *In the faces of men and women, I see God, and in my own*
> *face in the glass,*
> *I find letters from God dropt in the street, and every one is*
> *sign'd by God's name.*

At a eulogy, we try to trace God's signature in the name of the departed. Someone has died—a potential emptying of the divine name, a diminishment of divinity. Someone could pass on without having his name recognized. To be recognized is the deepest craving of the soul. So we say a eulogy in a last—and, sadly, sometimes a first—attempt to recognize the person. When we succeed, we are able to recite the *Kaddish*, for we have certainly magnified and exalted the great name. Not only the name of God, but also the name of the departed, which is an infinitely unique expression of God's very own face and name.

FIXING THE NAME

In Kabbalistic language, *Kaddish* is a *tikkun Hashem*, a "fixing (or heal-ing) of God's name." God's name is healed when we fully recognize and receive the name of the one just passed, because the name of the departed is no less than the name of God.

In this light we can better understand a wonderful passage from poet Alfred, Lord Tennyson's *In Memoriam*:

> A kind of waking trance I have frequently had, quite up from boyhood, when I have been all alone. This has generally come upon me thro' repeating my own name two or three times to myself silently, til all at once, as it were out of the intensity of the consciousness of individuality, the individuality itself seemed to dissolve and fade away into boundless being, and this not a confused state, but the clearest of the clearest, the surest of the surest, the weirdest of the weirdest, utterly beyond words, where death was almost a laughable impossibility, the loss of personality (if so it were) seeing no extinction but the only true life.

Tennyson, like the Master of the Good Name before him, under-stands that it is not the abandonment of individuality but rather its rad-ical embrace that is the portal to the Infinite. This is so because at the deepest level of our individuality, we participate in the name of God. One's own name is the portal to the name of God. They are the same. It is in this sense that the mystical master Nahum of Chernobyl wrote:

> They are called by their names . . . for the name of a person is his soul. For the letters of his name are his soul root and divine flow, and with these he serves, studies, and prays. Therefore a wicked person is one who does not know his name.[50]

Name is intended—in this passage—as the Eros of your story. Your story is your gateway to eternity. The litmus test of your story is *lishmah*. Is it for its own sake? For the sake of your name? For the sake of the Name?

For this reason, reciting the *Kaddish* prayer at a funeral and throughout the mourning period was considered in the Hebrew myth tradition such a vital spiritual task. In *Kaddish* we recognize, sometimes for the first time, that the departed did not live to serve us. We affirm the infinite dignity of his or her story.

So often we don't really see those who are closest to us. We somehow view both our partners and our parents as extensions of our story. We are all too often unable to recognize the full and independent dignity of their lives. Often the pain of misrecognition accompanies our closest loved ones to their grave. Yet there is another chance. *Kaddish*! In saying *Kaddish* we declare for all to hear that the beloved who is departed lived not for our sake but for the sake of the Name—theirs and God's. Often this is what opens us up to a deeper love for them and begins the process of healing open wounds.

A KADDISH STORY

In the following tale, it is not the details of the story line that are so important. Rather, it is the full erotic beauty and power of *Kaddish*, where human and God merge into one in the spelling of the name.

> There is an old story from the villages of Europe of a woman, Rebecca, who owed rent to her landlord. But owing rent then was not like owing rent today. Back then, the landlord had full right to take your possessions, put you in jail, or even sell you into slavery. Rebecca, her husband, and her beloved children owed thousands of rubles and were about to be sold as slaves to different buyers. Rebecca would never see her husband or children again.
>
> Rebecca was broken. She walked desperately through the town, door to door, begging for help. By the end of the day, she had a meager three rubles to her name. Hopelessly, she headed home, weeping and weeping over her impossible fate.

In her despair a tragic thought arose in her mind: "I won't even be there the day my dear husband passes away. Who will say *Kaddish* for him?" The thought struck her soul with a strange and desperate urgency. She ran over to a beggar on the road. Handing him one of her rubles, she pleaded, "Dear sir, please, say the mourner's *Kaddish* for my husband. Please, it means the world to me." The beggar was baffled but agreed.

Rebecca walked away, but another desperate thought struck her: what of all the anonymous people who die, and nobody says *Kaddish* for them? What about them? She ran back to the same beggar and thrust the second ruble into his hand. "Please, please, also say *Kaddish* for all the unnamed, departed souls for whom no one has ever said *Kaddish*." Again, the beggar, moved by her impassioned request, agreed.

As Rebecca turned to leave, her heart more and more shrouded in grief, another thought arose. She took her last ruble and placed it in the beggar's hand. With tears streaming down her cheeks, she entreated, "Please, sir, when you say *Kaddish* for all those lost souls, please, please, say it with all of your heart, all of your soul, and all of your might. Hold nothing back!"

As she left, over her shoulder she heard the beggar beginning to pray. He began softly, but then his voice grew more and more powerful, like a trickle that becomes a stream that becomes a flood. He prayed with all of his might, all of his brokenness, all of his pain. Rebecca listened, transfixed. It was as if a fire enwrapped her and lifted her to the highest heavens. There she had a vision of the beggar's prayers, ascending and crashing through the celestial gates, releasing the myriad souls of those who had long been awaiting their *Kaddish* to be said, their name to be called. She felt a great surge of flowing energy and relief.

And then it was over. The flood turned back to a stream and then back to trickle. Rebecca felt lighter, her heart more at ease.

As she continued down the road, a beautiful, shining carriage approached her. It stopped, and a well-dressed man inside asked for directions. Then, quite unexpectedly, he asked if she would like a ride. Rebecca, having never been in such a fine carriage before, declined. But the man insisted. And so she boarded the carriage and there entered into a deep conversation with the gracious man. Her whole story tumbled out effortlessly. How times were so rough with so many children to feed. How a cruel landlord had increased the rent and debt had built up, and all had been lost, and how the whole family was now to be sold into slavery. The man listened thoughtfully, and as Rebecca left the carriage, he did a most incredible thing. He took out of his pocket a check, filled it out for the exact amount of her debt, handed it to her, and before she could protest, sped away.

The next day, Rebecca dashed to the bank. When she handed the check to the clerk, he gave her a suspicious glance and asked her to wait a moment as he scurried away. Rebecca became nervous . . . perhaps the check was not real and this was all a cruel joke. Again distraught, she waited. Finally the clerk returned and escorted her to the office of the president of the bank. She entered the plush room and sat before him, a large and forbidding man behind a sprawling desk. "Where did you get this check?" he demanded.

She explained to him the entire story, about the stranger in the carriage, about her debts and her family, and even about the beggar who had prayed so mightily. The president then asked her, pointing to the dozens of pictures hanging on the walls of the room, "Do you recognize anyone in these portraits?"

Rebecca looked and immediately pointed to the large portrait behind the president's desk. "That man there," she said. "He is the man in the carriage who gave me this check!"

The president turned pale. The portrait behind the desk was of his father. And the check bore his father's exact signature. The only thing was that his father had died three years before. And his son, now president of the bank, had never said *Kaddish* for him.

RETURNING TO THE CHERUBS

The way of *lishmah* is rooted in the mystery of the cherubs. The sexual models the erotic and teaches us how to be lovers in the world. The Name—of God and the beloved, fully merged into one—is at the heart of the sexual. The sexual is the most exemplary expression of Eros. For sexuality at its best is *lishmah*, for its own sake, and not to network some other advantage. It is, simply, for the sake of the name.

The cherubs themselves were held by many Kabbalists to be the masculine and feminine names of God. When united in sexual embrace, the cherubs were engaged in a unification of the Name. Exile of the Shechinah and the archetypal loss of the Ark represents the fragmentation of the Name. Whenever the Name is made whole, the Shechinah is redeemed from her exile.

When one reclaims one's name, when one lives *lishmah*—for its own sake—stepping off the wheel of networking and superficiality, then the names of both God and the individual are healed. Whenever the calling out of the name is limited only to the sexual, when the sexual is the extent of the erotic and not the model of the erotic, then the Shechinah is in exile. The erotic—the calling out of the Name—is exiled into the merely sexual. The cherubs are separated from each other, and in the language of the Zohar, "blessing does not flow in the world."

TO GREET WITH GOD'S NAME

Calling out the name is evoked the world over in greetings. The Spanish hello—*hola*—originated in Arab Spain from the term *O'Allah*—Allah, of course, being the Arab appellation of God. In Austrian German, they say *grias*—which means "God." In Hebrew, the common response when asked how you are doing is *baruch Hashem*—"Praise God," or "Thank God." The Hebrew greeting *shalom* is actually a name of God. In English, we still follow this custom when we part from someone and say, "Good-bye." That word is a contraction for the centuries-old farewell greeting of "God be with you."

In a wonderful and mysterious passage, the wisdom masters talk of a special decree made nearly three thousand years ago. It taught that one should greet his friend with the name of God. Although the Third Commandment proscribes such "idle use" of God's name, this new law legislated special permission to use the divine name in casual greeting. The source for the decree was said to be the verse: "In a time to do for the Name (God), you may override the Torah."

The idea was that greeting a person using God's sacred name was not taking God's name in vain, but rather, recognizing the person as a sacred expression of God. Greeting someone using God's name meant acknowledging the infinite divine specialness in the other.

There is nothing more painful than anonymity. You come to a party alone. No one recognizes you for several long minutes. You feel forlorn, alienated. Then someone taps you on the shoulder and calls your name in warm welcome. The world is transformed. You have been recognized, perceived. Called by name!

Of course, true recognition is deeper than a mere greeting. It requires a true knowing, receiving, and even merging with the name. This is what happens when the name (God's and the beloved's) is called at the height of sexual passion. If the passion is situated in the context of a shared story and commitment, then this calling is the ultimate transcending of loneliness, for both of the lovers.

The wisdom masters wrote that we must greet each other with the name. A simple reading of the text indicates that they were referring to the name of God. But on a deeper level, the name they refer to is that of the person being greeted. In this powerful rereading, the decree is that no person should remain anonymous. Every person should be called by his or her name. Never allow yourself to be served by someone without knowing his name. In knowing the name of the waiter serving you, there is a fixing and healing of God's name.

It is time to fix divinity, to create God. God is created by revealing the infinite Divine in every person. God's name is emptied when people live without having their names recognized, without being called by name. So the wisdom masters decree: "Greet every man with the name"—the name of God and the name of the blessed and beautiful individual before you, for they are one and the same.

In the tradition it is taught that after the temple fell the name was lost. Because the name is erotic, the fall of the temple means the fall of Eros. The exile of the Shechinah is the exile of the name. Shechinah is the sound of your name being called—recognition of who you are. Every time we call a person by name, we redeem the Shechinah and rebuild the temple.

CHAPTER TWENTY-FIVE

THE ELEVENTH FACE

CREATIVITY

The eleventh face of Eros is creativity—an infinite world of depth and delight entwined with agony and ecstasy. Sex is creative. Sex models Eros. The nature of Eros is ceaselessly creative. Creativity is a primary source of aliveness. The aliveness of the universe expresses itself in what Stuart Kauffman calls the inherent, "ceaseless creativity of cosmos." The cosmos moves toward ever-greater levels of emergence; it is perpetually creating. We call something a new emergent when it emerges from all that came before, even as it is greater than the sum of its parts.

Creativity wells up from another face of Eros: uniqueness. Creativity takes place when new and unique configurations of intimacy emerge on both the atomic and cellular levels. New configurations of unique intimacy between atoms and between cells is what causes every breakthrough to new levels of complexity, consciousness, and love. The new interactions are drawn forth from the cosmos by its own inherent creative intelligence, what evolutionary science refers to as the "self-organizing universe." Creativity awakens on the human level when the human being realizes his or her Unique Self. When people find their unique voice, then they become ceaselessly creative. We are not separate from the cosmos. Our creativity—an expression of our uniqueness—is simply the erotic cosmos awakening as us.

THE SEXUAL MODELS THE EROTIC: CREATIVITY

The radical embrace of human creativity is rooted in the Secret of the Cherubs. It is not insignificant that according to Hebrew myth the world was created from the empty space between the two sexually entwined temple cherubs. This "space between" is the axis mundi, the source of all creativity. The temple, you remember, is called in the original Hebrew the *mikdash*, "the place of holiness." Eros is creativity is holiness.

Even more dramatically, the wisdom masters symbolically identify the Holy of Holies with the marital bed of King Solomon. The masters explain: "Just as Solomon's bed was fruitful and multiplied, so the Holy of Holies was fruitful and multiplied." Said differently, "Just as the bed of Solomon was sexually creative, so too is the Holy of Holies erotically creative." That is precisely the cherub tradition saying in its own internal parlance: the sexual models the erotic. And the erotic and the holy are one. Solomon had a thousand wives. Solomon's bed was very much an epicenter of creativity. The natural creativity of the sexual is of course made self-evident in the conception and birthing of a baby. But Solomon and the cherub mystics point to the raw creativity inherent in the sexual itself. We turn to E. E. Cummings again for a taste of the intrinsic creativity of the sexual, well beyond the classical procreation of a baby.

(lady i will
touch you with my mind.)Touch
you,that is all,

lightly and you utterly will become
with infinite ease

the poem which i do not write.

Cummings evokes not just the raw physicality, but the creative gesture inherent in the erotic touch. That is what he means by "i will touch you with my mind." In the lightness of the creative erotic touch, the beloved literally becomes a new creation. In concluding the poem, Cummings describes how the beloved becomes the poem. Lovemaking is the writing of a creative poem with one's lover being the new verse.

In the last verse Cummings declares in understatement that his lover, through their sexing, has become the poem. The creative act of poetry takes place in the sexing itself as his beloved becomes the verse.

Solomon, fired by divine imagination, was the human architect of the Holy of Holies, the builder of the great edifice of Eros. Solomon understood that there was an essential connection between the sexuality of his own bed and the Eros of God's temple. This connection is precisely the Secret of the Cherubs. Sex models Eros; our bedrooms model the temples of our lives.

In its archetypal mode, sex is the ultimate paradigm of erotic creativity. What could be more erotically powerful than the creation of a new life? Indeed, creativity is so bound up with sex that many religions, classical Christianity chief among them, sanctioned sexuality only if it led to procreation. The breaking of the connection between procreation and sex was seen as a fundamental violation of the sexual ethos.

Hebrew mysticism shared the deep correlation between procreation and sex. Sex that created a child was considered ultimately sacred. However, the cherub mystics insisted that every sexual act is creative, whether it creates a child or not. The essential nature of the sexual is creativity.

Sex always creates a new reality. Sometimes that reality expresses itself in the visible material world in the form of a child. But even when there is no physical manifestation, there is always a spiritual creation. Every sexual engagement, no matter how seemingly meaningless, births a new spiritual reality. In the old spiritual language, these new realities were thought to be either angels or demons. A deep reading of these sources shows that angels or demons are really manifestations of our inner soul processes. In this sense, there is no such thing as casual sex. Sex always has meaning and creative impact in the world of the spirit. Thus, sex models the Eros of creativity.

CREATING GOD

In the Secret of the Cherubs tradition, there is no sharp demarcation between human and divine creativity. God and human live on the same continuum. That by itself is a radical affirmation of human adequacy and dignity. This is the erotic humanism that emerges from the temple tradition. But it is more than that. As we will see, human beings—rooted in their unique voice—are so creatively potent that they can even create new divinity.

The Eros of voice and the Eros of creativity are intimately linked. In the self-understanding of Hebrew wisdom, the Torah—the sacred writ—is the word of God. And yet Moses speaks the fifth book of the Bible, thought to be the word of God. How could this be so? How can mortal man speak the word of God? The cherub tradition responds: "God speaks through the voice of Moses." Organized religion has always understood this passage as meaning that Moses is a channel. In the way of a channel, Moses effaces himself in order to be a pure conduit for God.

But there is a second reading, transmitted by Mordechai Leiner of Izbica. This teacher interprets the text to mean that when the human being fully steps inside his erotic essence, he touches divinity. Moses becomes the Divine. The Eros-inspired human being, in his full creative capacity, becomes Godlike and is therefore able to create new Torah, new sacred writ. This is the ultimate creativity. Given that, the notion of Moses creating "new Torah" through finding his voice radically expresses the Eros of creativity. Moses is creating new divine words through the resonance of his own voice. Moses is creating "new God."

This creative capacity is not limited to Moses. Moses is an archetype that is available to anyone who can access her own Moses energy. In the words of the Zohar, "There is a Moses in every generation." To which Hebrew mystics add, "and in every person."

RETURN TO THE LION OF FIRE

Many of the great philosophers and mystics have gone so far as to view creativity and Eros as being identical. For Plato in *The Symposium*, Eros is the creative arousal that drives the world forward. Plato implicitly understands that Eros is most powerfully symbolized in sex.

But the idea is more ancient than Plato. We return to our story from the first chapter, a Talmudic tale from about a century before Plato. Recall that the sexual drive was personified as no less than a lion of fire abiding in the Holy of Holies. When the masters attempted to slay this fiery feline they found very quickly that to uproot sexuality meant to uproot all creative Eros. Chickens no longer laid eggs, businesses did not open, and painters did not paint. The very life force of the world dried up.

Realizing that the sexual drive ignites more than just sex, the masters modified their request, asking for the sex drive to remain in force but without its terrible shadow. The heavens refused, reminding them that genuine creativity cannot exist without shadow. It is a package deal. Understanding their mistake, the masters prayed for the restoration of the sex drive. Their prayer was granted; sex drive and erotic creativity were restored. The world was revivified.

SEX AND CREATIVITY

How does sex model erotic creativity? That it does so through physical procreation is obvious. But what is it about sex that is so essential for our inner creativity?

The answer lies in the nature of the sexual. Sexuality models Eros because sex takes us to the inside. There is a moment in sex where we let go of our observer status and fully merge with the sexual. In this moment, we access our most primal self, the self that underlies our public postures, social masks, and even rational thought. This inner self is the erotic source code of reality. Sex opens the portal to the inner source of creative Eros. All creation is generated by touching this *prima materia* of Eros.

To access the inner operating system of the cosmos and be creative, the sense of separate self must be temporarily bracketed. We must re-immerse ourselves in what the mystics called "the river of light that comes from Eden." This river is the flow of Eros, the throbbing, pulsating primal energy that sustains the universe. One Zohar passage teaches that this river is the virile semen of being, the source of all erotic creativity—sexual, intellectual, emotional, and spiritual. When human beings let themselves be reabsorbed in this river, they attain the mystical level of *ayin*, no-thing-ness. From this place creative Eros is aroused.

Not surprisingly, in the original Hebrew there is only one root word for both primal energy and creativity. *Yetzer* means "primal drives and energy," and *yetzirah* means "creativity." The message is clear: one depends on the other. You cannot create without touching that primal place that is beyond knowing. Plans, logic, and information are all important for the creative process, but they can take you only so far. True creativity happens when the "I"—in Hebrew, the *ani*—becomes the *ayin* ("no-thing"). Creativity happens when the "I" gets out of the way.

THE MUSIC OF EROS

One of the places where such creativity is most apparent is in the creative arts. When the separate self disappears, we are played by the creativity of the cosmos. There is a wonderful documentary, *From Mao to Mozart*, on Isaac Stern's visit to China after the end of the Cultural Revolution. For many years Western music had been strictly forbidden in China. A resurgent interest in classical music had led to the formation of Suzuki schools, where thousands of children were learning to play the violin. But all they had were the music scores—no one could get access to actual recordings of Western music.

Only the kids who were the very best players performed for Stern. There is an exquisite moment in the film when a young Chinese girl comes up on stage and, before a packed stadium, executes a technically flawless rendition of a Mozart piece. There is a storm of applause. Then Stern himself mounts the stage and ever so gently takes the violin from the girl's hand. He starts to play. In his hands the violin comes alive, the music sweeps and soars and then finally climaxes in the most beautiful of cries. When Stern finishes playing, there is silence in the auditorium. He turns to the girl and says, "You see, it is not you who plays the violin. The violin . . . it, it plays you. No, no, something larger plays you both."

When we surrender so much as to allow something larger to play us, when it is only by the infinite compassion of God that we return to play the next note, then we have touched the erotic God of creativity.*

NEW SOULS

The mystical tradition teaches that the destruction of the temple is the spiritual archetype for the exile of creativity. In the symbolic literature of the Zohar, this is expressed by saying, "There are no new souls in the world since the destruction of the temple." A "new soul" for the Zohar means a wholly original soul, one that never existed before in any incarnation. In the mystical reality map, most souls that come into the world are reincarnating to finish their healing paths. However, in order for the world to spiritually evolve to what is called by the mystics *bechinat*

---

*   The medieval philosopher Maimonides suggests that deep study is a form of music. This is especially true of mystical study. A loving surrender is a prerequisite for any mystical study that engenders radical creativity. Scholars have dubbed the Zohar "the Kabbalah that creates." Indeed, in some mystical sources the word *keshot*, meaning "truth," and the word *chiddush*, meaning "original creativity," are virtually synonyms.

Master Nachman of Bratslav teaches that the Babylonian Talmud, one of the great original interpretations of the divine mind, was created by the tears shed by the Rivers of Babylon. The words of the prophet Jeremiah are echoed in a great African American spiritual: "By the Rivers of Babylon, there we sat and wept." Nachman powerfully reinterprets the verse in order to suggest a new meaning. "The Babylonian Talmud was created through our tears . . . Through the crying which discloses the divine place, we are able to create new Torah, which is the word of God."

mashiach, "messianic consciousness," new souls must also be brought into the world.*

The bringing down of a new soul is the ultimate act of human creativity. The catalyst for the creation of new souls is the mystic. In one provocative and powerful image from the Zohar, the mystic becomes the "aroused feminine waters" and seduces the masculine expression of the Godhead to erotic union with the Shechinah. In a second Zoharic passage, interpreted by Kabbalah scholar Yehuda Liebes, the role of the mystic is no less than to excite the clitoris of the Shechinah.

Of course the description is not physical but mythic. That is not to say it is mere allegory. The Kabbalistic symbol is virtually always much more than allegory. It is an expression of a far more substantive relationship between the symbol and the symbolized. What that means in the case of these explicitly sexual symbols is that sexuality accesses the same primal place that is the source of all creative Eros. New souls are formed through the creative Eros of the mystic expressed in meditation, study, and prayer, all of which are modeled by the sexual. Bringing a new soul into the world, then, is not merely a sexual act but a suprasexual mystical act whereby the human being intentionally causes an erotic union with God. This is true not only for the mystic. Whenever we touch the inside and access our creative Eros, we are also bringing new souls into the world and moving the world a step closer to higher consciousness.

What all this tells us is that creative Eros is divine and thus participates with divinity in the very structuring of reality. Indeed, the Zohar goes so far as to say that the human participates in the creation of God! That is not to say that God is a projection, as in German philosopher Ludwig Feuerbach's old understanding of the idea (which we talked about in chapter twenty on imagination). Rather, the human being is a divine miniature who is not only patterned after but also actually participates in divinity.

A dimension of divinity is created in human acts of self-creation. On the canvas of our internal spiritual, emotional, and psychological

---

*   The popular notion that Judaism has no idea of reincarnation is simply incorrect. Reincarnation is a major tenet of mainstream Jewish texts.

processes, as well as through our physical actions, we create God. Our stories—each and every one of them—are part of God's story. So to say we are creators of God, as the Zohar teaches, is to say that we are the creators of our own stories. To use an image from Hebrew myth, we are artists painting the canvas of our lives.

The ultimate erotic creative act is the storying of self. The creative power of sacred originality needs to be channeled not only into writing new Torah but also into writing our unique letter in the Torah. As Isaac Luria writes, "Every person has his own unique letter in the sacred scroll." Your unique letter is your story, your Unique Self.

Creating our stories is the same as finding our voice. The word *voice* derives from the Latin *vocare*, which has the meaning of "calling" or "destiny." To authentically create the vocations of our lives, we must transcend all the external influences that would have their way with us. We need to go deep inside the bubbling cauldron of Eros and from there access the raw ingredients of our unique voice in order to birth the creativity that can only be emergent from our Unique Selves.

Our true birth is not our physical appearance at the end of nine months of gestation. Rather, it is the person you are on the day you die. There is no greater tragedy than to die without ever having been born. To be a great artist of self, one must access the full erotic energy of the universe. Only this energy allows you to defy inertia and create the infinitely unique being that is you. Through inertia we tend toward imitation, to fashion our souls according to everyone's instructions except our own. The person of evolved consciousness is the one who creates her original self and transcends the overwhelmingly powerful urge to be an imitation.

DARK EROS

The mystics understood that all true creativity requires connecting to our primal and even shadow selves. The original source code of personal, creative Eros is referred to by the masters as *tohu*. The word means "primal chaos" and refers to the force by which the world was created. The nineteenth-century mystic Tzadok observed that this is the same force that creates a human being. In the mystical sources, primal chaos has two different expressions in humans. One of these is our primal drives and urges. The other is the shattering experiences, crises, and tragedies of our lives. Both of these are the matrixes of creativity from which human consciousness evolves.

In reality, they are the same. Both are often expressions of shadow in our lives. Shadow means the primary energy systems that we keep hidden and locked away, often even from ourselves. Included in shadow are repressed sexuality, anger, and, conversely, great unexpressed talent. Any part of our life stories that we deny expression becomes *tohu*, shadow energy. Shadow is our unlived stories.

The Maggid of Mezritch likened creative Eros to a seed falling into the darkness of the ground, a "down and dirty" place. It is there in the darkness that the seed is nourished with the ingredients it needs to sprout and blossom into the light of day. We can only engage in self-creation when we re-access our inner energy sources and channel them toward our self-creation. It is the nature of the world that often only in the darkness do we find the access point to our greatness.

In non-crisis mode the place where we most regularly access this primal energy of light and darkness is in the sexual. It is precisely this accessing of erotic source code that gives sexuality its creative power. Similarly, our life shatterings connect us to that same erotic fountain. Often it is crisis and transition that strip away the veneers of imitation and force us to confront and claim our original selves.

The sexual is the focal point where we touch Eros. For not only does sexuality tie us into unmediated Eros, but it also connects us to the darkness. It is through our sexuality that we meet much of our shadow. For this reason the sexual drive is commonly referred to in Hebrew sources as *yetzer hara*. *Yetzer* means "drive" and *ra* is an all-inclusive term for shadow qualities and events in our lives. It is the *ra* in our sacred autobiographies that opens us up to the vital stream of *yetzer*.

As always, sexuality models the erotic, but it does not exhaust the erotic. The goal is to plug into these matrixes of Eros and engage in the artistic recreation of every dimension of our lives. This is the secret of the sexually entwined cherubs that stood at the epicenter of Eros in the Holy of Holies in the temple.

The masters pass down the story of David's attempt to lay the foundation of the temple, which is a mythic image of the quest for consciousness. Realizing that the temple is the seat of Eros, David knew that its erection could only happen if he could access the primal chaos power of the universe. In digging the foundation, David discovered the *shetiya*, which in myth is the cork stone that holds in place all of the primal erotic powers in the universe, the axis mundi. Overcoming his fear, David removed the cork stone from its place. All of the great and terrible power of the *tehom*, the raging depths, the primal Eros and chaos of creation, was unleashed. It almost destroyed David and the world with it. Yet David knew that it was only through this direct engagement with the depths of Eros that the temple could be built and consciousness could evolve.

According to the tradition, the biblical six days of creation were only completed when the temple was built. The point is that human and divine creativity merge, or at the very least complement and complete each other. "Man is God's partner" is the great erotic truth of biblical mysticism.

CHAPTER TWENTY-SIX

THE TWELFTH FACE

PLEASURE AND DELIGHT

The twelfth face of Eros is delight, or pleasure. Eros is a pleasurable experience. Delight is a primary source of aliveness.

THE SEXUAL MODELS THE EROTIC: PLEASURE AND DELIGHT

Pleasure is another way that sexuality models Eros. Sex is the locus of pleasure. Sex and pleasure and delight are virtual synonyms in the consciousness of humanity. It is in sex that we experience the full meaning of delight. The classic poet Swinburne speaks for all of humanity when he writes:

I wist not what, saving one word—Delight.
And all her face was honey to my mouth,
And all her body pasture to mine eyes;
The long lithe arms and hotter hands than fire,
The quivering flanks, hair smelling of the south,
The bright light feet, the splendid supple thighs
And glittering eyelids of my soul's desire.[51]

Sexual pleasure models erotic pleasure, but it does not exhaust erotic pleasure. We need to experience erotic delight in every dimension of our nonsexual lives. Further, within sex there are authentic and pseudo pleasures. The same is true for pleasure in every facet of life. Finally, the desire for sexual pleasure tells us in the most direct of terms that the cosmos evolves through delight. Reality evolves because it is pleasurable is a fair summation of the leading edges of both mysticism and contemporary science.*

Moreover, pleasure is both the path and the destination. The methodology of evolution is pleasure, even as the inherent telos of evolution is the most refined pleasure for the most people. There are several distinct ideas in this sentence. First, evolution evolves because it feels good. Second, the trajectory of evolution is toward higher and deeper pleasure. The more evolved a person, the greater her capacity for pleasure. Third, the arrow of evolution is not just toward deeper pleasure but also toward more pleasure for more and more people. For example, an average person can get at Whole Foods an array of pleasure-inducing foods that were not available two hundred years ago to the king of France. Fourth, evolution's arrow aims toward more and more pleasure not only for people but also for wider and wider swaths of reality, including mammals, animals, forests, and oceans. Humane treatment of animals and saving the rain forests are but two examples. Reality moves toward more pleasure for all of

---

* See my (Marc) forthcoming academic work on pleasure with Lindsay Briner, *Pleasure as Ethics and Evolution*, as well as the more popular *Pleasure Bible* with Kamala Devi. In mysticism, see also Moshe Chaim Luzzatto; in science, see Stuart Hameroff, "The 'Quantum Pleasure Principle' and 'Orch OR'—How Life and the Brain Evolved to Feel Good."

existence at all levels, all the way up and all the way down the magnificent chain of being.

THE EROS OF PLEASURE AND DELIGHT

How to get to the pleasure modeled by sex differs for everyone, but for everyone the goal is the same. Pleasure is always the goal, even if for some of us, or for some part of us, the path to pleasure is through pain. Sex models the metaphysical truth that all creative Eros is deeply delightful. *Noam elyon*, "the higher sweetness," and *oneg*, "pleasure," are but two of a stream of Zoharic idioms that describe delight as the natural bedfellow of Eros.

The *Sefer Yetzirah*, the earliest known Hebrew mystical work, sets up *oneg* as the highest level of good. In one wisdom passage, the great question posed by God to every soul after death is: "Did you derive pleasure from my world?" This is the measure of a life well lived. To live erotically is to live in delight.

COMFORT VERSUS PLEASURE

Pleasure, of course, is not the same as comfort. Pain is usually thought to be the opposite of pleasure. But probing more deeply, we realize this is not quite true. The opposite of pain is comfort. The goal of comfort is to avoid all pain. Pleasure always incorporates a dimension of pain. Indeed, the more profound the pleasure, the more there is potential for necessary pain. Just ask a parent to name his greatest pleasure and his greatest pain and the point becomes abundantly clear. The answer to both is invariably "my children." The essence of wisdom is the ability to distinguish between necessary and unnecessary pain. In classical sources, the goal of the future world is to "receive pleasure from the Shechinah." This future world, however, is fully available in the present.

Another example: a composer works deep into the night on a symphony only he can hear. He is ecstatic, lifted up, as he creates and refines the music revealed in his heart. His back is aching from sitting for too many hours, his eyes are heavy with exhaustion, and he's thirsty but unwilling to break his concentration to go get a drink of water. On a physical level, he experiences pain, but on the level of his emotions and spirit, he is absorbed in delight. His pleasure knows no bounds. Is he comfortable? No. Is he happy? Beyond what words can describe. The opposite of pain is comfort, not pleasure, because pleasure can coexist with pain.

The very process of evolution could be fairly described as the evolution of pleasure. The more evolved or advanced a being, the greater her capacity to experience delight. Pleasure is a skill that increases with every deepening stage of evolution. There are obviously more and less evolved human beings. Mother Teresa, for example, can be fairly described as more evolved than Hitler. The more awake and enlightened a person is, the more access he has to a wider field of pleasure. Mother Teresa lived an ascetic life, without the physical pleasures most of us enjoy, but her spirit dwelled in a state of utter delight, taking pleasure in things most of us take for granted or miss entirely.

We have exiled pleasure to mere physical pleasure. The world of the physical is a wondrous source of pleasure, but it is only one level of pleasure. Other crucial levels of pleasure include love and affection, relationships, standing for a cause, meaningful work, true knowledge and wisdom, creativity, and more.

ADDICTS AND SAGES

What is the difference between an addict and an enlightened sage? The enlightened sage derives virtually infinite pleasure from ordinary life. The air, colors, sounds, and fragrances of life explode upon him with delight. Similarly, human relationship for the enlightened is filled with poignancy and passion, which birth virtually infinite pleasure.

The addict, on the other hand, is unable to get pleasure from ordinary life. Indeed, the inability to derive pleasure from ordinary life is the very definition of addiction. For the addict, the pain of ordinary life is so intense that it must be covered over at all costs. Often addicts are the most sensitive among us, and for that reason they cannot bear the pain. The addict then turns to pseudo Eros—addiction in all its forms—to paper over the dearth of Eros that makes life intolerable. Thus, the healing of addiction cannot come from the classical models of recovery treatment only. Ultimately, addiction can only be healed by a return to Eros. Because addiction is pleasure unwoven, the healing of addiction can only come from pleasure rewoven. The sustained healing of addiction is directly dependent on the addict's ability to re-access delight and to re-eroticize her life.

SACRED EATING

There are many portals through which we can experience delight or pleasure and thereby return to Eros. One of these is eating. The entire biblical story of the Garden of Eden revolves around eating. Adam and Eve eat what they should not. They know that doing so will wreak havoc on their lives, but they are allured by the intoxicating promises of the divine experience that is said to result from the forbidden fruit's ingestion. The first addictive swallowing of intoxicants was no less than the mythical apple in the Garden of Eden.

The Maggid of Mezritch implies that conscious eating in which one merges erotically with the pleasurable taste of the food is an ecstatic Eros (Shechinah) experience. This is the way of the *tzaddik*, the "enlightened one." In fact, the master teaches that the good taste of the food is the physical manifestation of the Shechinah, the Goddess herself. Pleasure is Eros.

We have lost the power of transformative ecstasy, which is rooted in pleasure and delight. Sacred hedonism is somehow associated with decadence. We have a new disease in modernity that psychiatrists call anhedonia, "the inability to experience pleasure." We forget that the primary ritual of the major biblical holy day is to "eat and drink before God."

For the enlightened person—and that is potentially all of us—the simple pleasure of eating opens us to God. Eating is pleasure. Sex is ultimate pleasure. Eating for many of us, and sex for pretty much everyone, is also a source of shame. But that is because we fail to understand the true divine nature of pleasure. Shame is when pleasure stops short of infinity.

THE MOTIVATING FORCE OF EXISTENCE

All genuine pleasure is unique. But that means more than simply that our pleasure preferences are unique, which they are. It means that only within the context of living your Unique Self do all the pleasures of life actually feel good. Food, drink, sex, music, the wind on your face, the dawn sky—all are experienced differently when you are living your story. These same pleasures become stale and even bitter when you know that you are not in your story.

We return to one of the core cherub texts with which we began: "From the day the temple was destroyed, the taste of sex was given to the boundary breakers." The fall of the temple led to the exile of the erotic quality of pleasure into the sexual. It becomes enormously difficult to access erotic pleasure as an integral part of our engagement in every facet of living. Pleasure becomes most easily accessed in the carnal, and then not even in the sexual but only in illicit sexuality. The redemption of the Shechinah begins with the reclaiming of pleasure as our human birthright both in committed sexuality and in all other facets of our lives.

In the Secret of the Cherubs, pleasure is not only our birthright. It is also the motivating force of all existence. Pleasure drives the entire trajectory of emergence. In evolutionary terms, we might say that reality evolves because it feels good to do so. Not only are higher levels of evolutionary development able to have deeper experiences of pleasure, it is also true that the attractor—the motive force of the entire evolutionary process—is pleasure. This was the secret of the Holy of Holies that science is now catching up to, at least on the external level of perception. Leading-edge scientists are talking about a "quantum hedonism" as the structural nature of the cosmos.

Quantum hedonism expresses at the subatomic level and appears as self-evident in our lives. We are moved by pleasure. Wisdom, however, is to truly know your pleasure, to discern between the different levels of pleasure. In a forthcoming work, I (Marc) identity seven levels of pleasure. Within each level, the goal is to cultivate discernment between authentic pleasure and pseudo pleasure. The first six levels include physical pleasure; love, affection, and relationships; standing for a cause and productive work; transformation; true knowledge; and Unique Self-creativity. At the seventh and final level, there is evolutionary pleasure—the delight of awakening as the evolutionary impulse and literally becoming, through your life and transformation, the leading edge of evolution. At this level you experience the pleasure of directly participating in the evolution of culture and consciousness.

Wisdom comes from being able to discern between genuine pleasure and pseudo pleasure. For example, at level one there is the authentic pleasure of eating delicious, healthy food versus the counterfeit pleasure of eating junk food. In the pleasure of relationships, there can be authentic intimacy or counterfeit intimacy, which may be codependent or even abusive. There's the pleasure of standing up for a good cause and the pseudo pleasure of standing for a false cause. Pseudo pleasure is but another form of pseudo Eros.

Pleasure is not opposed to ethics—precisely the opposite. When you live the erotic life, you realize that pleasure is the source of all ethics. The old Greek split between *hedone* ("pleasure") and *daemon* ("meaning") was wrong. The source of all meaning and ethics is pleasure. We need to refine our delights, however. Junk food is a fast and easy delight. If you have ever eaten truly superlative food that makes you almost faint in orgiastic ecstasy, then you know it is a different experience from grabbing a candy bar at the convenience store. Enjoying the superlative meal is not only a greater pleasure, but it also requires a far more refined capacity to experience pleasure. It is something like the difference between the pleasure a tenth-grade, average math student gets from solving a math problem and the undulating, ecstatic delight a world-class, genius mathematician like Ramanujan receives from his erotic vision of the mathematical cosmos.

CHAPTER
TWENTY-SEVEN

UNION

ON THE EROTICS OF IDENTITY
AND UNION: A DEEPER CUT

We have plumbed the mystery of the Secret of the Cherubs and gazed upon Eros' many faces. Each face is both a destination and a portal, a path. In each one, sex models, hints at, and invites us to enter a deeper truth of Eros. Union is where all the paths lead. It is where Eros leads. In pursuing Eros, we seek not only wisdom but also enlightenment, in the realization of union with all that is. All mature individuality is in the context of union.

In biblical myth, the first mention of an idea is always significant. The first appearance in biblical myth of *echad*, the Hebrew word meaning "unity" or "oneness," is made in reference to the sexual. "He shall cleave to his wife, and they shall be as one flesh," states Genesis. The sexual in its highest expression is a moment of union. Similarly, the word *devekut*—meaning "cleaving," which is often the term for *unio mystica*, total absorption into the one—appears for the first time in the same verse, describing sexual union.

We are so overwhelmingly drawn to the sexual because at our core we are all seekers of unity. During loving sexual connection, we realize that the ego walls we have worked so hard to erect and protect are not real. In moments of bliss we experience union with another person, and through that we catch a fleeting glimpse of the ultimate union that underlies all existence. We die to the world of separation and cry out "Oh, God" as we are ushered for a moment into the reality of union.

Union does not mean that we disappear or dissolve, losing our core integrity as distinct individuals. It does mean, however, that we understand that our separateness is a limited, albeit important, perspective on our story. At a far deeper and more primal level, we are like the cherubs atop the Ark, intertwined with others. And not just with other people but also with all of being. The poet William Blake was right when he wrote: "Everything that lives, lives not alone, nor for itself." This is the deep truth of the erotic interconnectivity of all things.

STAGES OF UNION

We are born into union. We make no distinction in the first few months of consciousness between ourselves and our environment. We feel part of all. Even as we realize our own separate existence, we understand that we are connected to our caretakers on the most primal ontic level. Our natural expectation is that the Shechinah, Mother Earth incarnated in our biological mother, will meet our needs. This is stage one of our human development.

We then grow into stage two. Psychology calls this next stage "individuation." We are treated to the rude surprise of our separateness. Not wanting to be sundered from our caretakers, we often recast the essential contours of our personality to win their love, for we understand that love is the currency of connection. At the same time, we erect ego walls to protect ourselves. The older we get, the more vulnerable we realize we are, and the higher the walls creep.

The walls are important, though; they establish our individuality. They teach us that we are responsible for our actions. If we are lucky, someone lets us know that we have a soul print, a unique story to live that no one else but us can unfold in the world. Yet it is lonely behind those walls. We intuitively reach back to our primal memory of oneness, when belonging to something larger than our individual story was a felt experience.

In reaching for oneness, we are warned against those who would prey on our sense of incompleteness, offering us pseudo-erotic salves that demand we give up our individual integrity as the price for belonging. There are many ways to buy belonging at the price of our integrity. These compromises often come wearing the guises of religion, propriety, economic necessity, or the demands of our professional peers. Sometimes they wear cruder guises: those of cults, racist groups, and false gurus. Hopefully, we are able to avoid their seduction.

In stage two we incorporate the sense of individual integrity into the fabric of our being. That is good, even essential. But it is not enough, because it is only a part of the truth of our being. Because it will not satisfy us. Because, if we do not move to stage three, the shadows of individuality may well destroy us. In a world where twenty million people die of hunger every year, after a century in which a hundred million people were brutally murdered in war games of ego and power, on a planet that cannot sustain us for another century if it continues being so ecologically abused, this idea hardly needs elaboration.

The third stage is the experience of unity consciousness as the guiding principle of our lives. This is the final stage on our human journey. It is aleph consciousness. Aleph is the first letter of the Hebrew alphabet. In Hebrew, each letter is also a number. So aleph is *echad*, "one." Aleph has no sound of its own. Aleph is the ecstasy that is beyond. It is an invitation to experience the highest and deepest part of our soul, which is part of the oneness of God. Experience it even for a moment, and life will never be quite the same again.

We saw how love is actually a perception. When we are in love, we are in love with all creation, because lovers perceive, in the bliss of their erotic experience, the essential oneness of all existence. The *Shema*—"Listen so you know God is one"—is the only prayer mantra that Jews recite daily. This mantra is directly preceded by the word *love* and directly followed by the word *love*. It is a love sandwich. Love in an ultimate sense cannot be commanded. Law can demand that a person act lovingly. Feeding the hungry and clothing the naked can be legislated by a government and executed by governmental bodies. Old-school religion can demand that we behave charitably. Both government and religion are important in this regard and should be heeded and honored. But they are both woefully insufficient. In a world as traumatized as our own, it is painfully apparent that something is seriously lacking in our ethical motivation.

The ultimate motivation for loving must be self-interest. Self-interest does not mean selfishness. It means an expanded notion of self. When you fall in love, what you are really doing is moving your boundary of self to include someone else. Before you meet your beloved, her moods, desires, and dreams have no impact on your life. When she becomes your lover, all that changes. She becomes part of your identity. For that is what intimacy is: shared identity. All love is self-interest, whether it's for someone in our close family circle or for someone in an expanded circle of love. When we willingly do a charitable deed, it is because we identify with the person we are helping. It feels good to help them, as if we are helping ourselves. Expanding our notion of self means we come to recognize the interconnectivity and union of all beings, and that expands our love beyond our immediate circle. We understand that not just our partner or child, but everyone in the world, is "me."

SEAMLESS COAT OF THE UNIVERSE

Biblical wisdom invites us to become lovers. To do so, all that is required is a shift in perception in which we realize that our identity is so much larger than we were taught in our limited stage-two thinking. To love is to realize that the boundaries aren't real. We are all interwoven in what the scientist and philosopher Alfred North Whitehead called "the seamless coat of the universe." Christians called this unity the body of

Christ, Buddhists talked about the Buddhahood of all beings, and the Kabbalists called this underlying unity *adam kadmon*, loosely translated as "original being."

The Hebrew mystics teach that all souls come from different parts of the body of God. Being one body, there is therefore a natural affinity among all souls and a special affinity among souls who come from the same metaphysical neighborhood. The essence of things is that no one is ever really a stranger. We all share a soul. Given this, it is not surprising that the Kabbalists insist that every action has a cosmic effect that ripples well beyond the obvious.

As we have already noted, what was a mystical realization in the cherub tradition has now been shown to be self-evidently true in the physical world by contemporary systems theory and chaos theory. Modern chaos theory calls this "the butterfly effect." For example, the gentle breeze from a butterfly's wing on one side of the world can, two months later, be the "cause" of a windstorm on the other side of the world. For the Kabbalists, this is a core principle of ethics and Eros.

Let's say you stayed a few extra minutes at home to make a phone call. The purpose of your call was that you just had to share a piece of gossip. That caused you to leave for work late. Leaving late could set in motion infinite physical, physiological, and emotional variables that could eventually ripple into a significant disaster for millions of people. To be a lover means to know that every action not born of love hurts the entire world, even as every action motivated by love heals the entire world.

Love is a radical redrawing of boundaries and complete revisioning of the whole notion of self-interest. A revisioning entails a deepening of perception. The fact is, we all know that our narrow definition of self—closed behind the walls of ego—is not our highest truth.

The underlying metaphysics are really quite simple. We are made of divine substance. This is the homo *imago dei* noted by biblical scholars, who teach that every life is sacred. "There is no place devoid of him," writes the Zohar. "I am the light that illumines all things. I am all. Split a piece of wood and I am there; pick up a stone and you will find me there," teaches the Gospel of Thomas. To love is to perceive the infinite divinity in everyone and everything.

GOD'S DISGUISE

All of us are called to live in the erotic awareness that we are interwoven with all of being. No person is a stranger to us. We cannot eat if everyone cannot eat. If there is brutality in the world, it affects us directly. We do not want to wait until the butterfly effect shows our children why our limited consciousness of living as separate monads destroyed our world. The planet will not go on forever with haves and have-nots. In our global villages, the intolerable proximity of massive starvation and obscene luxury will explode in our faces. When food is thrown out at a fancy uptown restaurant while a mother cannot feed her children in a downtown neighborhood, we can expect no real peace.

In the biblical myth of the Garden of Eden, God asks Adam, "Who ate from the tree?" Adam quickly responds, "My wife did it." She and not he. Disconnection. Shifting of blame. You and not me. Them and not us. That is original sin. The biblical project is to return to the Garden. That means nothing less than a return to Eros—an essential redrawing of boundaries to include all those we have placed on the other side of the tracks.

This kind of inclusiveness is what the Jerusalem Temple with its lost Ark was all about. It was a house of prayer for all the nations. Every form of spiritual service that was ethical and caring had a place in the Jerusalem Temple. This was the radical wisdom insight of Solomon, the temple's spiritual architect. Solomon understood that the temple needed to be a place of expanded consciousness where the interconnectivity of all being was both experienced and showcased to the world. A place where the holiness of the feminine pagan Divine would find expression in the Hebrew ethical matrix. In an ancient world where every nation argued for the supremacy of its god, Solomon tried to redraw the boundary lines as lines of connection. Solomon was ahead of the Hebrew consciousness of his day, which rejected much of his radically inclusive vision.

BROTHERS AND BOUNDARIES
AND CHERUBS

In Hebrew myth the reclaiming of Eros always involves shifting boundaries. An ancient tradition asks how it is that God chose this precise plot of land in Jerusalem as the site of the temple. Does the land have some special holiness built into it from the beginning of time? At least one ancient tradition emphatically rejects such an understanding of temple consciousness as the kind of thinking that creates yet another boundary between those who control the land and those who don't. As we see all too clearly in Jerusalem today, every boundary line is also a potential conflict line. It separates "us" from "them" and eventually "they" will want to overrun "our" boundary.

The biblical myth tradition tells a different kind of story—a story of the temple's origins that is a tale of brotherhood, not boundaryhood.

There were two brothers who long ago lived in the field where the temple would be built. These brothers were partners in the ownership of the field and farmed it together.

One brother had a very large family. He said to his wife, "We have so much together. My brother has never married and raised a family. The produce from the field is all he has. Let me go and move the boundary marker between his portion of the field and mine so he will receive more."

"It is good," said the wife, so every night after midnight, long after the day's harvesting was divided, the man would go and move the boundary between his portion and his brother's.

At the same time, the other brother was thinking, "I have no family, no obligations, no one to support. My brother has so much on his shoulders. Surely he needs a larger portion of the field." So every night before midnight he would go and shift the boundary marker between his and his brother's portion, giving his brother a larger share of the field.

Naturally both brothers were puzzled how it was that the other one was not receiving more. So one night the first brother went a little earlier than usual and the second brother a little later. They came to the field at precisely the same moment, each one to move the boundary in favor of the other. They realized what had been happening and fell weeping upon each other's shoulders.

On the surface, it's just a sweet story about compassion and kindness. But on a deeper level, this temple myth suggests that all kindness and compassion must ultimately be rooted in the recognition of our radical interconnection. The boundaries of the field are the mythic expression both of ego boundaries and of all the other lines that artificially divide reality. Tradition has it that on the very spot where those tears fell, the tears that washed away the illusory boundaries, the temple was one day built. It was in that place that the Ark with its embraced cherubs stood. For the essence of the temple is the ability to expand your boundaries to include your wider self. And your wider self is everything and everyone. Your wider self is the very width and breadth of God.

THE WATER AND THE WAVE

The Zen Buddhists tell the story differently, but it is the same story.

Two waves in the ocean were having a conversation as they flowed toward shore. The larger wave was extremely depressed, and the small wave was peacefully flowing along. "If you could see what I see from up here," said the large wave to the small one, "you would not be so happy."

"Well, what is it?" asked the small wave.

"In not too long we will crash into the shore, and that will be the end of us."

"Oh, that," said the small wave. "That's okay."

"What? Are you crazy?" cried the larger wave.

"I know a little secret that tells me it's all okay," said the little wave. "Would you like me to share it with you?"

At this point the large wave was both curious and suspicious. "Will I have to pay a lot of money to learn this secret?"

"No, not at all."

"Will I have to meditate for thirty years in lotus position?"

"No, not at all," said the small wave. "Really, the whole thing is only eight words."

"Eight words! Well, tell me already!"

So the small wave said ever so gently, "You are not a wave. You are water."

"You are water." This is what we referred to earlier as the realization of the True Self. The deeper evolutionary mystical awakening, however, is that you are both a wave *and* water. That is the awakening to Unique Self. Remember, True Self + Unique Perspective + Unique Intimacy = Unique Self. Unique Self transcends and includes True Self.

But we cannot just pay lip service to True Self. The underlying awakening to the core unity of all being is the change that begins to change everything. In the interior world this unity is revealed in meditation, prayer, and other forms of intense spiritual practice. In the exterior world, this underlying unity is disclosed by systems theory, chaos theory, and complexity theory. Realization of some sense of True Self births an expansive joy and ecstasy that cannot be bypassed.

This is why the symbol of love in Hebrew mysticism is water. For to love humanity is to get beyond the limited boundary of the wave that is bound to crash. The wave is real. It is just limited. To love is to fully experience yourself in the flow of what the Kabbalists called "the river of light that flows from Eden."

For this reason, the prayer mantra prescribed by Hebrew myth to be recited the moment before death is the *Shema*, the meditation on the unity of all being. What we need to realize to face death is that we're not waves, we are water. When we hit the shore of the afterworld we don't disappear; we merely transform into the shape we need for the next part of the journey.

The Zen story understands that one of the primary symbols for Eros is water. The Genesis story tells of the creation of all things yet never mentions the creation of water. Mystic Nachman of Bratslav teaches that water is prior to the creation of the world. Creation begins in the Genesis story with the letter *beit*, which is the second letter of the Hebrew alphabet and stands for the number two. All of creation is about two, about separation and boundaries. All of our mistakes and all of our pain come from the illusion that we are separate. So water, the symbol of Eros, cannot be part of the duality. It precedes creation. Waterfalls and oceans enchant us because they summon up our primal memory of Eros, that all being is interconnected and interdependent.

Water has no singular form in Hebrew. There is only the plural form because there is no such thing as water that is separate or disconnected. Whenever a new water molecule enters a body of water, all the other little water molecules make room to receive it, and they become one. This is the experience of the inside.

To purify ourselves from the nonerotic world of sin and separation, biblical myth invites us to immerse ourselves in a pool of water. Not in a swimming pool, not in a manmade still lake. According to the biblical myth law, ritual immersion must be in running water: a river or an ocean. For being dipped in water is our re-immersion in the erotic flow, in the systems of water that connect all life.

DEFINING YOURSELF

The fundamental question of your existence has always been: "Who are you?" What that question really asks is: "What are your boundaries? What is inside you and what is outside?" How you choose to answer will tell you more about yourself than virtually anything else. In the modern world, identity has become a decision. The word *decision* stems from the Latin *decisio*, which means "cutting" or "limiting." We assume that we have a limited identity, and then we attempt to define that limitation.

When we decide on our identity, we are drawing a boundary. Everything inside the boundary, I claim as myself. Everything outside is not me. An identity crisis occurs when we are not sure where to draw the line. Let's say I call myself religious. Then I have to explain—to myself—my impulses that seem less than religious. Or I could call myself a good person. I then have to disassociate from anything that does not support that identity.

The most important reality map of any age is quite naturally the map of personal identity. We moderns have been engaged in a radical narrowing of identity. We like to use the metaphor of a castle. Imagine a gorgeous castle with winding staircases and hundreds of rooms. Each room holds its own magnificent treasure. The castle halls radiate wonder, curiosity, and innocence. Each and every room is special. One day a visitor to your castle tells you that she didn't like one of the rooms. It's ugly, she says, and it's a shame because that room ruins the rest of the castle. Although you have never thought that room ugly, you certainly don't want it to ruin what people think of your castle. So you have that room carefully sealed away.

A few weeks later, another visitor arrives. He tells you another room in the castle is just awful, ruining the image of the palace. So you hastily have that room locked as well. More and more people come, each one telling you about a different room that they don't like. Room after room you swiftly shut down. Over time you forget about those sealed-off rooms. The castle becomes identified in your mind, and in everyone else's, as only that part which you exhibit. Years pass, and you wake up one morning finding yourself in a meager two-room flat—hoping, still hoping, that people will like this place where you live.

And so it is with us. We are born with a magnificent interior castle, each room sparkling with gemstones of personality, aliveness, and creativity. Each time one of the rooms meets with disapproval, our powerful need for love and acceptance moves us to shut it down. Little by little, we wall off more and more of the self from consciousness. We wind up living in one small room, too frightened to find out what treasures may lie behind all of the long-locked doors. This narrowing is what the Kabbalists would call the exile of the Shechinah or, in a different metaphor, Egypt consciousness. Egypt, you remember, means "narrowness." The Shechinah is our essential erotic vitality. Modernity has exiled our Eros to our psyche and then to a very limited part of the psyche.

THE STRANGER AS YOURSELF

Redeeming the Shechinah from exile entails two steps. First, we need to claim our body as part of our core identity. "Through my body I vision God," states a verse from the book of Job. This is one of the most important mantras of the Kabbalists. Nineteenth-century master Elimelech of Lizhensk teaches that only by trusting our body can we decipher the word of God.

The second step is to reclaim all aspects of our psyche. This includes the furthest reaches of consciousness, including the unconscious. We must embrace all of our light as well as all of our darkness. Any part of me that I split off and reject is in exile. By placing it on the outside, I empty myself. The more I place on the outside, the emptier I become. I de-eroticize myself. My life becomes boring, vapid, and empty. The more of my psyche I include on the inside, the more erotic I become, and the "holier" I become. To be holy is to be erotic is to be on the inside.

Biblical myth expresses the same idea in the language of love, using three love mantras: Love God; love yourself; love the stranger. Deeply understood, all three are the same thing. To love yourself is to love all of you—the God in you and the stranger in you. First I must love the stranger in myself. The commandment to embrace the stranger occurs thirty-six times in biblical text—far more mentions than any other topic.

The idea is deep. Every boundary is a potential battle line. War is too often fought over where the boundary should be drawn. The parts of me that I find strange and inappropriate are my strangers. "Strangers are we, errants at the gates of our own psyche," wrote philosopher George Steiner. We very quickly turn the stranger into an enemy. This is true both spiritually and psychologically on the level of realpolitik. For in the end, it is all one discipline.

If history were to be the judge, the human being would more aptly be termed Homo hostilis than Homo sapiens. Since we cannot locate our own true inside, we create a false Eros by placing the other outside our boundary of self. If they are on the outside, we subconsciously inform ourselves, then we must be on the inside. In order to fill up that primal hole of emptiness, we are thus driven to violence and war. Since our erotic needs are so pressing (we cannot live without feeling like we are on the inside), we create a constant stream of enemies to maintain this pseudo-erotic illusion.

"Love the stranger" means to walk through your void and not try to fill it with false Eros. It means to love that part of you that has been split off and disowned. By loving the stranger, you re-include her in your persona. You redraw your boundary. You escape the narrow walls of your ego's fortress, behind which you have hidden for so many lonely years. You realize that all of you is part of God. In loving the stranger in you, you are therefore loving God. It is specifically the strange places, the unique ways of your pathologies, that hold the key to your divinity. To love the stranger is therefore to love the God in you, which is all of you.

Finally, it is loving the stranger inside of you that opens your heart to loving your neighbor. Remember that in Hebrew the word for "neighbor" (*ra*) also means, amazingly, "evil." Love your evil: that is to say, integrate your shadow, and you will be able to avoid projecting it onto your neighbor. Only then will you be able to love your neighbor. By reintegrating the parts of you that have been split off, you can see your neighbor without the terrible blindness of projection. Biblical myth says it beautifully: "Do not oppress the stranger, for you were strangers in the land of Egypt." The wisdom masters explain: "All who invalidate others always invalidate them with the very defect they themselves possess." All too often the moral crusaders who are especially vicious are themselves deeply tainted with the very vice they so venomously accuse others of having.

If we cannot own the fact that there is a part of us that is a stranger in Egypt, if we deny our own narrowness and pathology, then surely we will project it onto others. If we do so, we will never be able to love them. And of course we will never be able to love ourselves. "Love the stranger," "Love your neighbor," and "Love yourself" all really mean the same thing, for love is indivisible.

You can only be a lover when you have taken back the stranger inside of you. What self-love really means is to draw for your consciousness the widest possible map of self, knowing that all of it is God, all of it is lovable, and all of it is you. You are then ready to reclaim your transpersonal self—that is, the parts of you that are beyond your psyche and body. This includes the awareness of your life as embedded in the great web of universal being.

UNITY CONSCIOUSNESS

There are two primary paths to achieving the expanded awareness called "unity consciousness." The first, often favored by varieties of Eastern mysticism, is cosmic and totally impersonal. The goal is to directly embrace the erotic truth that we are all part of the impersonal, living organism of God. In Zen stories, this is often characterized by startling and spontaneous moments of enlightenment.

The second path, often favored by biblical mystics, is to follow the ethical to the erotic. This is a more gradual path. Hebrew mystical stories are rarely about sudden moments of mystical satori or enlightenment. More typically they are about the famous master who disguises himself as a peasant in order to bring wood kindling to a poor woman living in a forest. In the ethical path to unity consciousness, you expand your identity step by step. You understand that in order to be good, to avoid the evils of projection, you need a wider identity. To care for your body and the body of Mother Earth, you need to include them as part of you. Otherwise, the displaced shadows and boundary lines foment great ethical tragedy.

Start with people you know. Expand your circle of caring and identity to include them in your core identity. Let them enter the inside of your boundary. You will see that your whole relationship to them will change. You might start with your partner, children, or perhaps more extended family or close friends. At the next stage, you might want to move beyond your circle of individuals and include a community in your circle of identity and caring. If you are a Baptist, you might consider the Baptist fellowship part of your identity. If you are Jewish, you might view the Jewish community as within your circle of identity.

But ultimately, you must move beyond these limited expansions. For if you arrest your growth at an early stage, you are left with dangerous boundaries. You may consider yourself part of a superior chosen people that excludes all other peoples. We emphasize the word *superior*, for all peoples should consider themselves chosen and special. It simply must not be at the expense of other peoples.

As the next stage, you might want to expand your circle of identity and caring to include your environment: the earth and all the sentient and nonsentient beings on the planet.

Each of these—personal shadow, body, other individuals, community, or environment—may have been as strangers to you. As you redraw your reality map, your world becomes more and more full. Slowly you expand. You learn to love the stranger.

All of these steps gradually bring you to the breakthrough of unity consciousness. This is the awareness that defined the biblical prophets—Kabbalist, Muslim, Christian, Hindu, and Buddhist mystics—throughout the ages. It is the mystic's ultimate erotic awareness, when she experiences that she is inside the all and the all is inside of her. In unity consciousness, we expand the concept of self to include all sentient and non-sentient beings. We expand ourselves to include everything that is.

How do you expand your boundary at each stage of the journey? In two ways. Open your heart wider and take a concrete action. A beautiful practice that you might want to do right now is to review the last paragraphs and then write what might be the action that you could take at each stage to express your expanded boundary.

COMPASSION AND UNION

Union is the ultimate erotic state. Interconnectivity, the fullness of presence, the inside of God's face, the yearning force of being—they all characterize our experience of unity consciousness. This is enlightenment. Yet for the Hebrew mystic, if union does not lead us to compassion and great love, then we have missed the point. The medieval intellectual Maimonides wrote a great book of mystical philosophy called *Guide for the Perplexed*. In the last sentences, after the book reaches its erotic crescendo (*cheshek*, meaning "raw sensual passion," is the Hebrew translation of the

Arabic term employed by Maimonides), he appends an implicit post-script. Paraphrased: If all this doesn't make you a better lover of people, then you are no lover of God and certainly no lover of yourself. Eros must always lead to ethics.

We all begin our evolutionary journey as part of the circle of nature. In the creation story of Genesis, man and woman are created as part of the natural order. Ancient myth reflects this circle of being, in which mortals and immortals, humans and gods, and all of nature participate together. This is the circle of Eros.

Biblical consciousness injects the line of duality and ethics into the circle. Compassion must always override Eros. Mysticism—in every major system of thought—protests that the line view of reality is distorted and calls us back to the unity consciousness of the circle. This return to Eros, however, is not at the expense of ethics; much to the contrary, ethics becomes the most powerful motive and force for loving in the world.

Isaac Luria explains that rules and ethical obligation can never be sufficient motivation for compassion. It is only when I realize that both my neighbor and I are part of the Shechinah that true ethics begins. When a guilty person is punished, the Shechinah cries out, "My head aches, my arms are in pain." To slap another human being is to slap the Shechinah. When you are kind to a fellow human being, you are befriending the Shechinah. In Hebrew mysticism, the Shechinah is embodied in us.

This is the deep understanding of the most famous of all biblical maxims: love your neighbor as yourself. The ultimate source of loving is knowing your neighbor as yourself. It is knowing that your neighbor is part of yourself. Both of you are woven into the seamless coat of the universe.

When Master Israel, the Baal Shem Tov, would engage in the spiritual practice of ascensions of the soul, his wife would sometimes become very frightened. He would become totally inert, and she was sometimes unable to waken him from his trance. On one such day she had become quite desperate, not knowing how to return him to this world. As she paced to and fro, their baby son pulled on his father's beard. Immediately the master came to and gently asked the child, "What do you need, my boy?" To attend to a person in need, taught Master Israel, is deeper than even the deepest mystical communion. It is said that the Baal Shem Tov, while listening to the language of the birds and eavesdropping on the music of the spheres, could also hear the cries of all the tormented souls in the world. All of his work was for their healing.

The body leads to the soul, and the soul leads back to God. "When I look at the 'I' of my body, I find the 'I' of my soul. When I look at the 'I' of my soul, I find the 'I' of God." The Sufis have a wonderful saying: "Say your praise to Allah, and tie your camel to a post." What this means is, touch the fullness of God and let that inspire even the simplest service.

DROPPING AND CARRYING YOUR BURDEN

To become enlightened, we must let go of the wounds of the past and anxiety for the future. This Zen tale expresses this process beautifully:

There was an old Zen monk who had spent many years in meditation. He had attained deep levels of peace but had never achieved that moment of enlightenment when the "I" and the other collapse into one. So he asked his master, "Please grant me permission to leave the monastery and go practice on the great mountain by myself. There is nothing I want more than to realize the true nature of my nondual self."

The master, sensing that his student's time had come, granted permission. The old monk took his begging bowl and few meager possessions in hand and began the journey to the mountain. It took a while, but he finally left the last village behind and began his ascent of the great peak. Just then he saw coming toward him, down the mountain, an old peasant with a large bundle on his back. The peasant of was none other than Manjushri (the great bodhisattva) in disguise, who—according to some Buddhist traditions—appears to aspirants to give them their last nudge toward enlightenment.

Said the peasant to the monk, "Tell me where you are going, friend." There was something about the old fellow's voice that was kind, so the monk told of his woe at being unable to cut through illusion and achieve illumination. "I've practiced for so many years . . ." His voice trailed away, and he lowered his eyes.

After a moment, glancing up, he saw that the other man was continuing his journey down the mountain. The peasant turned and looked back at the monk with a face so radiant and full of compassion that the monk just had to call after him, "Tell me, sir. Might you know something of enlightenment?"

Abruptly, the old peasant let go of his bundle. It crashed to the ground, and the monk instantly achieved enlightenment. Laughing with joy, he looked at Manjushri and said, "Now what?"

The bodhisattva smiled, picked up his bundle, and walked down the mountain.

For enlightenment to occur, one thing we must do is drop the mental burdens we carry—the worries, needs, doubts, fears, and regrets from the past and our anxious hopes for the future. We need to let our bundles fall, only to then pick them up again and walk down the mountain—but with a new consciousness that changes everything.

Manjushri appeared to the old monk because he was an outrageous lover. *Bodhisattva* is the Buddhist word for "outrageous love." The bodhisattva is dedicated to ending suffering for all sentient beings. Manjushri helped the old monk not out of obligation—any more than one hand washes the other out of obligation. Both hands are of the same body, as every person and living thing is part of the same body. That realization is unity. Unity is outrageous love consciousness—compassionate union with all beings, the highest level of enlightenment.

UNITY THROUGH LOVE

For some passages in the Zohar, the mystery of the cherubs is a virtual synonym for unity consciousness. The Zohar understands the union of the cherubs as symbolic of the union of all opposites. The mystic Abraham

Isaac Kook writes: "While all qualities have their opposite—good and evil, life and death, and even holy and profane—there is no opposite of the Holy of Holies." He means that the Holy of Holies is the place that overwhelms all distinctions. That which unites opposites, he explains, is love. It is love—the perception of the infinite Divine in all of reality—that allows us to embrace both pairs in the opposition as glimmerings of the One. The Chinese master Lao-tzu saw this clearly when he said all opposites arise simultaneously and mutually:

What difference between yes and no?
What difference between success and
failure?
Must you value what others value,
Avoid what others avoid?
How ridiculous!

Under Heaven all can see beauty as beauty only because there is
  ugliness.
All can know good as good only because there is evil.

Therefore having and not having arise together.
Difficult and easy complement each other.

To suggest otherwise, writes Chuang Tzu, is not "to apprehend the great principles of the universe or the nature of creation." What does all this mean? That reality is a unity of opposites. That true wisdom is the sweetness of integration and union. The world of two does not exist in the deepest reality. To love is to reach for the radical divine presence in all that is. To love is to know that ultimately there are no boundaries. And yet the road to the circle in which everything is on the inside is through the line. Ethics is the Hebrew mystic's path to Eros. This is what St. Augustine intended in his subversive passage: "Love God and do what you will."

This paradox of formal ethics and erotic ethics is well captured in the hidden teaching of an enigmatic Hasidic story:

The master of Rhizhin entered the study hall of his disciples unexpectedly. They were greatly embarrassed, for they were engrossed in watching a game of checkers between two students when they should have been studying. The master pretended not to notice their discomfort and went straight for the checkerboard. "There are three rules of the spirit," he said. "All of them are learned from checkers. You can only move forward one step at a time. For most of the match you can only move forward and not backward. When you have reached the highest rung, you can move whichever way you want."

Mordechai Leiner of Izbica called this highest place *hitpashtut*, meaning "the spreading out beyond all boundaries." It is in this highest place that we are able to trust love. Love alone is what guides us. Even if we cannot live in this place all the time, the very awareness that this no-boundary territory exists pulls us toward it and transforms our lives.

NO-BOUNDARY SYMPHONY

Claiming the Lost Ark

There is an extraordinary passage in the wisdom texts describing the Ark in the temple. The text describes the dimensions of the Ark and of the Holy of Holies. But strangely, the sum of their measurements would not allow the Ark to fit into the Holy of Holies. It was simply too big for the space. Yet that is where it stood. How could this be so?

The mystics suggest that according to the higher math of the temple, the Ark with its interlocked cherubs takes up no space. It has no measurements. Of course! The Holy of Holies and her cherubs are the epicenter archetypes of erotic love. They are part of the great unity of being. The Ark is mythically beyond all boundaries. It can have no limiting measurements, for the essence of measurement is limitation and boundary. This is the mystical secret hidden in the math and measurements of the biblical text.

POISON BISCUITS AND STOLEN WATERS

Now we begin to truly understand one of the first core principles of the return to Eros. A Talmudic story of stolen waters is our teacher:

A man comes home to his wife. His wife is in the bedroom. The man sits on the bed and reaches for a biscuit. A voice in the closet cries out, "No, don't eat that, it's poison!" The man opens the closet door and behold, the milkman is hidden behind his wife's clothes.

The question at stake is—do we consider the man in the closet an adulterer or not? Jurists discussed this fifth-century text. On a simple level, they suggested that the person is not an adulterer. For if he had been, he would have wanted the woman. He could have had her if her husband had eaten the poison and died. Because he stopped the husband from eating the poison biscuit, he must not be an adulterer.

However, the text raises a completely different scenario. "Stolen waters are sweet," suggests the narrator, quoting the biblical verse. It could well be that he is an adulterer. Why, then, did he save the husband? Because he only wants the woman . . . if and when she is married. Concludes the Talmud, "From the day the temple was destroyed the passion for sex was moved from licit to illicit sex!"

We asked at the very beginning of our study together: what does the temple have to do with the sexual or even the erotic? What we have seen in myriad ways is that sex models Eros. Now we add one last level of depth. What happened on the mythic level when the temple was destroyed? The temple incarnates no-boundary consciousness. As long as it stood, it was the seat of love, Eros, and ecstasy that shattered the bounds of the finite, reaching for the Infinite. When the temple fell and the rule of law and boundaries replaced it, then the erotic need for no-boundary consciousness had no place to go. It was displaced. Whenever essential human needs are displaced, they reappear as shadow. When law becomes the order of the day, then the core human need to authentically break boundaries is suppressed. It needs expression. Its most natural outlet becomes boundary-breaking sexuality.

The rebuilding of the temple—the rebuilding of the human spirit—is a deep internal process. It is all about filling up the hole, the emptiness, with true Eros. When this happens, the sexual becomes not an ominous threat but a loving guide and teacher.

THE BERDITCHEVER PASSPORT

Listen to a final erotic story of No Boundary, Unique Self consciousness told by the Kabbalists:

It happened in Eastern Europe in the mid-nineteenth century. Wolfie had to travel to St. Petersburg, and he was afraid. He knew it was an unsafe place, and he did not have the papers he needed. But he had to make the journey, for his life depended on it. He went to his teacher, the great master Levi Isaac of Berditchev. "Please, please, help me, Master," he cried, and poured out his tale of woe.

The master listened intently and then left the room, bidding Wolfie to wait. Wolfie could hear that in the next room the master was softly weeping. When Levi Isaac returned, he gave the disciple a blank piece of paper wet with his tears. "This will be your passport," he said. "Take it with you, and it will open all the doors."

Wolfie was not sure what to do, but he trusted his teacher. He took the paper and set out on his journey. When he arrived at the first border, he was stopped by the guards. Shaking, knowing they could kill him on the spot, he took out the paper he had received from the Master of Berditchev. They looked down to examine it and then up at him again with the most intent of eyes. Wolfie was about to faint.

One of the guards began to talk. "We had no idea it was you," he said. "We apologize for even stopping you at the border. What an honor it is to have you travel on our road. Please accept our apologies, sir."

Well, you can imagine how absolutely shocked Wolfie was. Mumbling his thanks, about to faint again—this time from disbelief and joy—he traveled on. He arrived at the next border, and remarkably, the same thing happened. Only this time the guards were so overwhelmed that Wolfie was traveling their road that they gave him an escort of four white stallions. And so it went. At each border crossing he would show the blank piece of paper with the tears of his master, his Berditchever passport. He arrived in St. Petersburg traveling like a prince, with a full escort and laden with gifts.

A story of mystery, to be sure. Passports that open all the gates but not with words or letters. A magical sheet of white, empty space. There are many borders we need to cross when we go on a spiritual quest, when we aim for unity consciousness. There are many guards—internal and external—who would block our way. Know that they cannot stop you. Have the courage to close your eyes, and you will see clearly: they are but the illusions of your mind.

We pray that this book, although filled with words, has been a bit of a Berditchever passport for you. It, too, is soaked with tears. Tears of both sorrow and ecstasy.

We all have the power of blessings. We must all bless one another. So we leave you with a blessing: May all the gates be open. May your life be filled with the erotic and the holy, for they are truly one.

APPENDIX A

ON THE PAIN OF EROS

The sexual models the erotic is true for both the pleasure of Eros and its pain. We have talked much about how sex models Eros in all of her faces, including pleasure. Now we turn to the pain of Eros. Here, too, the sexual models the erotic.

Sexuality leaves so many mortally wounded in her wake. There is so much pain from what is supposed to be the source of so much pleasure. We are confused about sexuality. And that confusion is the source of much of our distress, as Persian poet Hafiz attests below in his poem "A Barroom View of Love."

FIRST THOUGHTS ON
THE PAIN OF EROS

Love is grabbing hold of the Great Lion's mane
And wrestling and rolling deep into Existence

While the Beloved gets rough
And begins to maul you alive.

There was a time when we all believed that there was a way out of the pain of Eros. Some people may believe that we didn't try hard enough; others are correct in asserting that we didn't succeed. But we can tell you that we believed, in theory, in a version of love that is fulfilled through commitment, loving gestures, and good listening skills. We thought that the dilemmas that love presents to us were solvable if we were earnest enough, practiced enough, and learned how to honestly communicate the truth of who we are and what we could offer. Unfortunately, there was a quiet untruth in this approach—not only because all of us have lied to others, but also because most of us have lied to ourselves, saying that if we got it right, we would not have to feel pain in loving.

Our approach didn't take into account the ruthless side of Eros—the aspect of Eros that does not let us cut this kind of a deal in any way, which is wildly uncompromising and insists that we live a fully embodied life, one that includes pain, loss, confusion, and bewilderment. Eros is fierce and unrelenting; it won't be captured, cajoled, or lulled into the realm of the comfortable, particularly when it is the ego trying to settle into an untrue version of love. As the Hafiz puts it:

True Love, my dear,
Is putting an ironclad grip upon

The soft, swollen balls
Of a Divine Rogue Elephant
And
Not having the good fortune to Die!

In the Zen school, there is a famous koan about a master whose teaching is to give a student a thorough beating, and no matter what the student's question is, the beating comes just the same. When the student attempts to answer the question, he receives a beating. When the student remains silent, she gets a beating. When the student attempts to escape or withdraw, a beating comes anyway. Eros often gives us a beating; a complete knocked-down, foot-to-groin, nose-smashed-against-asphalt pummeling. It demands that we experience pain, injury, and ego death, and it presents suffering itself as one of its many (hard to believe) loving touches.

The sexual models the erotic—this is true in all kinds of positive and pleasurable ways, but it is also true in terms of suffering and pain. The sexual life is filled with an array of agonies that are not easily borne by the ego, by the body, or by the identity of a small or limited self. There is the pain of not being seen or desired, and the pain of being seen starkly, in clear light of our most obvious flaws and imperfections. There is the pain of not having the attention we seek, or the pain of having it for a time, and then losing it. There is the startling pain of realizing that we are not special in the way we thought we were. Or worse, recognizing that when we thought our love was exclusive, that we are not the only one. There is the pain of others wanting more from us than we are able to give, and the pain of trying to give and not being wanted. There is the pain of love that turns to hate, of affection that turns to contempt, and of physical exchange, once desired, that becomes repellent. Then there is the overlarge, unbearable pain of betrayal. Betrayal is uniquely excruciating because only someone whom you really love—"someone who would never betray you"—can deliver this particular sad and often vicious blow.

We sometimes are called to enter so deeply into the interiority of the pain of sexual and erotic betrayal that we can no longer believe anything about anything. At these moments, sometimes moments that last in aching reality for months and even years, it hurts so much that we cannot find any ideas around it. The only thing we are able to do is to let ourselves into the feeling, to live on the inside of the pain until it clears. Too often we begrudge pain. But pain will not be begrudged. Do not imagine, the pain says to us, that it should be different than this. Do not let yourself have a lot of ideas of how it should be. Surrender to it. Become it, settle in a deeply humbling way to the energy of how it feels to be hurt.

Sex models life in that it hurts like hell. Eros is radical aliveness moving toward contact. Radical aliveness has a side that is excruciatingly painful. So does contact. Is it any wonder that a vigorous world of sex and pain are coupled in the common practice of S&M, and domination and submission are the two poles around which this practice revolves? We are bound—bound to inflict injury, and bound to receive it. We're sure to be hurt in love, and we're sure to hurt. We are subjected to injury against our will, and no matter how hard we fight against it, we injure others all the time. We say this not to release ourselves or others of responsibility; ignorance, hubris, and grasping demand reckoning in love, and all transgressions against others must be recognized for what they are. But genuine sensitivity, radical responsibility taking, even the vow to end suffering, do not take away pain.

The beautiful rock mystic Bono and the transcendent Mary J. Blige sing from the pain of the Irish and the black American experience:

> *Did I ask too much, more than a lot*
> *You gave me nothing, now it's all I got.*
> *We're one, but we're not the same,*
> *Well, we hurt each other, then we do it again . . .*

It is enough to make you want a drink of good Irish whiskey, but medicating the pain is a short-lived response. We have to be willing to look into pain first, deeply, directly. We need to know it firsthand, entering the interior of pain like we enter the interior of sex—with full presence, with a yearning to see, feel, and know it, and with a mind and heart expanded enough to embrace the whole impossibility at once. For as we saw, presence, wholeness, interiority, and yearning are the primary faces of the erotic modeled in the sexual, both in her pleasure and in her hurt.

How does the hurt feel? What are her qualities? How do we engage her interiority without violating our wholeness, failing to be fully present to what actually is happening inside of us and losing the yearning that once animated our hearts? What is the pain telling us? If we could hear her speak, what sacred secret wisdom might she whisper in our ear? We become the strange lover of pain, and through this, Eros manifests in full display.

And like a lover, we need to attend to our reaction to pain with the same care, and the same discrimination with which we seek our pleasure. Neither pain nor rage can ever justify murder. And murder comes in many disguises.

What is our response to the feelings? What strategies arise to protect us against the experience of pain? Do we withdraw, attack, dull out, or immediately seek another love source like an addict who is dope sick?

What exactly is going on here? Only a lover longs to look directly into the eyes of reality and see things exactly as they are. When we talk about spiritual courage—this is the moment. When we talk about being a lover—this is what we mean. We embrace everything exactly as it is—in excruciating, gorgeous detail. We notice how we hide, slink away, or build up a solid story of breach and betrayal. And our spiritual training again instructs us to surrender instead, to let go, to relinquish our ideas, and to breathe into the unwanted sensations. It promises to help us transcend devastating erotic experience, but in love, the only way out is through. We cannot transcend painful experiences without going through them, without becoming them. Hafiz says, "Love is the funeral pyre / where the heart must lay / its body." Easier said than done. Thankfully, some things are just bigger than we are. Sex compels us beyond ordinary boundaries of self. So, too, Eros in the guise of pain overcomes ego. When the hurt is large, all separation bets are off. When there's no keeping pain at bay, when it hurts so much that explanations and stories won't hold, when emotional escape isn't possible, the dharma gate blows open and realization of all and everything at once pervades. There is no time, no past, and no future. There is no other way than this one, no hurt and no hurting. There is no transgression, mine or yours, and all, even murder, is miraculously forgiven in the truth of complete surrender. Let yourself feel that and breathe another step in the surrender. In the surrender of pain is a radical kind of commonality, even of union and at-one-ness, because everyone shares in the pain. We all hurt. We have that in common and in that dawning consciousness of our interconnectedness is the beginning of some form of realization.

In that realization we begin to feel the embrace of the Shechinah of Eros. She is the most expansive, compassionate, and full universal lover, holding every aspect of us at the deepest core of our being, rocking us, listening to our sobs, even as she caresses our head. The Shechinah holds us all in our pain, and in it, we meet her there. In the comfort of her arms, with the soothing sounds of her voice, pain is none other than compassion herself. "In all of their pain, I am in pain . . ." cries out the erotic mystic Isaiah. "Your left hand is under my head and your right hand embraces me," is ecstatically exclaimed by Solomon, who experiences more than most, the pain of the erotic and the sexual.

There is a deep core in our experience that knows how to hold others in their pain. But we do not do it nearly often enough. That deep knowing that is our birthright is what the Zohar of the Hebrew mystics call the "Shechinah that is I." That knowing is God. It is the same as going into the pleasure so extremely, surrendering and opening to it so you become it. And in that merging with the full openness to love and pain—because it is you—you feel the luminous nothingness of all that is.

Let us say it again. There was a time when we believed that there was a way out of the pain of Eros. Some people may believe that we didn't try hard enough; others are correct in ascertaining that we didn't succeed. But we can tell you that we believe in a version of love which is fulfilled through commitment and which includes betrayal, loving gestures which disappoint, and through listening skills yearning to hear everything even as we are sometimes deaf to those who love us most. We, all of us, must be willing now to feel hurt, and the deepest hurt is the recognition of having hurt others. Rumi said it best in "Huddled Beneath the Sky":

The sadness I have caused any face
by letting a stray word
strike it,

any pain
I have caused you,
what can I do to make us even—
Demand a hundred fold of me—I'll pay it.

We sometimes are called to enter so deeply into the interiority of the pain of sexual and erotic betrayal that we can no longer believe anything about anything. At these moments, sometimes moments which last in aching reality for months and even years, it hurts so much that we cannot

find any ideas around it. The only thing we are able to do is to let ourselves into the feeling, to live on the inside of the pain until it clears. Too
often we begrudge pain. But pain will not be begrudged. Do not imagine,
the pain says to us, that it should be different than this. Do not let yourself have a lot of ideas of how it should be. Surrender to it. Become it,
settle in a deeply humbling way to the energy of how it feels to be hurt.
Let yourself feel that and breathe another step in the surrender. In the
surrender of pain is a radical kind of commonality, even of union and
at-one-ness, because everyone shares in the pain. We all hurt. We have
that in common and in that dawning consciousness of our interconnectedness is the beginning of some form of realization.

In that realization we begin to feel the caress of the Shechinah of
Eros. "Your left hand is under my head and your right hand embraces
me," cries out Solomon, who experiences more than most, the pain of the
erotic and the sexual. There is a deep core in our experience which knows
how to hold others in their pain. But we do not do it nearly often enough.
That deep knowing that is our birthright is what the Zohar of the Hebrew
mystics call the "Shechinah that is I." That knowing is God. It is the same
as going into the pleasure so extremely, surrendering and opening to it so
you become it. And in that merging with the full openness to love which
is your pleasure—it is you—you feel the luminous nothingness of what it
all is. This is true as well if you surrender to pain properly.

Most people do not know how to make love because they do not
know how to expand and open. Most also do not know how to make love
in pain because they do not know how expand into their contraction.

Whenever you truly collapse into the pain, when you surrender into
the hurt, whether yours or of others, what always happens is that you feel
the embrace of the feminine. The pain, if you're truly to enter its inside,
always gives way to the Shechinah's embrace. If you are willing to feel so
deeply into the pain that you no longer exist, then you meet God in pain.
No being should ever die without feel like he is being held by the lover,
by the feminine, by the Shechinah.

This is called by the erotic mystics of the Kabbalah, to participate with
pain of the Shechinah in exile. We we meet the Shechinah in our pain. "In
all of their pain I am in pain," cries out the Hebrew mystic Isaiah. This

is the "Shechinah that is called I." When you recognize that she is you and you carry that quality into the world, you bring redemption to yourself, the world, and the Shechinah. You bring the redemption that always was and already is. To enter the pain in this way, you must, at least for a time, give up the protest. Give up your ideas about what and how people should act and what people should do. That is the teaching of forgiveness. That is the teaching of love.

It is Bono who knows to sing of the pain of Eros:

one love, one life, when it's
one need in the night.

Whenever there is need there is pain. Because there is no one person who can ever fill our emptiness, the pain of unmet needs always accompanies the erotic encounter with other.

Did I disappoint you
or leave a bad taste in your mouth?

The illusion that separate selves can meet and find ultimate oneness is shattered in the realization of separation. Knowing that we are "not the same" must always come before the tenderness of true love that has the capacity to stay open through the pain.

We're one, but we're not the same.
We get to carry each other,
carry each other

Bono, in verse after verse, evokes the impossibility of loving, which must always be recognized before love's true possibility is born.

Have you come here for forgiveness,
Have you come to raise the dead,
Have you come here to play Jesus
to the lepers in your head

He returns again and again to the poignant realization of separation which must always precede true bliss.

We're one, but we're not the same.
Well, we hurt each other, then we do it again.

It is more then mere pain, however. We often feel degraded and humiliated in love. Being willing to bear the ego's humiliation is a prerequisite for great love.

You ask me to enter,
but then you make me crawl

To receive another in love is to be willing to bear the ecstasy of their pain.

And I can't keep holding on to what you got,
when all you got is hurt.

Once you realize that there is no escaping the pain of Eros, you can then settle in to the fierce grace of commitment.

One life, but we're not the same.
We get to carry each other,
carry each other.

From a cognitive perspective, how we relate to this pain born of what we experience as erotic and sexual betrayal is a decision. Neither pain nor rage can ever be a license to commit murder. And murder knows many disguises. To avoid the translation of pain into violence, whether physical or verbal, we need to pay close and unflinching attention to our interiority.

What thoughts arise regarding the pain, what beliefs and ideas do we hold about this moment? Are we against this moment? Are we faulting someone for it? Are we certain that our view of how the world should be is right and correct? Can we identify a feeling of separation, of being alone, of being cut off and isolated from the rest of reality in that moment? Most likely we can, and very subtly, yet profoundly, we can watch how the mechanism of ego works. And we should notice correctly that when we feel cut off, separate, diminished, or abandoned, there is usually a subtle attempt to secure our version of how we would like the world to be.

Sometimes simply seeing the ego at work, relaxing the struggle, and opening to the truth of the moment liberates our awareness. Sometimes the holding is deeper in the emotional and physical body. The yogic traditions ask us to free pain through the body by breathing into the fullness of sensation, and to feel the love in the pain itself, to feel aliveness in actual feelings in the body. A feminist yogini friend of ours once said, "Because you say 'ow' instead of 'ah'—because the sensation appears as a menace instead of a friend—doesn't mean that it's not from the same source."

All phenomena arise from this one source, and the body is none other than God. All of our spiritual traditions, in however many different forms, show us that everything is one thing . . . one beautiful, radical, unknowable and ungraspable, vast, empty gorgeousness . . . and that nothing, absolutely nothing, needs to be rejected. This is the enlightenment born of pain. In the universality of pain is the democratization of enlightenment. It is an enlightenment we all must share, for its knowing can end the pain.

The pain of the sexual is, however, an intense and exacting model for how we engage pain in every facet of being. For the sexual models the erotic. It is in the sexual, whether her pain or her pleasure, that all the sacred secrets are held. It is only in opening ourselves to her wisdom that we can resist the temptation to turn secrets sacred into secrets sordid.

Love is a wound that never heals. We can hold on forever to the wound or be willing to enter and feel the pain now and then open up again in love. The Shechinah is always holding us, even and especially when it hurts so much. But love never stops, especially when we are in pain.

Keep your heart open even as you feel sucked into the vortex of love's wound and can imagine no way out. You can get lost in the pain, but deep down you know it is a lie. For love has already found you. To see your death and betrayal and not stop being a lover—that is the terrible, awesome, and wondrous vow of the Bodhisattva. When we swear to do that, we find our place in the source and remind the source itself of its true nature, which is love. When we take the Bodhisattva's vow, we need not persuade ourselves or others that the legitimate privacy of intimacy was a strange and terrible oath of silence that never was. We need not distort silence of presence and claim it as silence of absence. We need not claim voice that was never taken from us. For our oath to speak the word of love amid the pain will always soften the hurt and restore our courage.

If we learn to live wide open, even as we are hurt by love, then the Divine wakes up to its own true nature of love. To be firm in your knowing of love even when you are desperate, to be strong in your knowing of forgiveness even when you betray and are betrayed, this is what it means to be holy. Sufi mystic Rabia said it beautifully in "It Acts Like Love":

> *My body is covered with wounds*
> *this world made,*
>
> *but I still long to kiss Him, even when God said,*
>
> *"Could you also kiss the hand that caused*
> *each scar,*
>
> *for you will not find me until*
> *you do."*

APPENDIX B

THE MURDER OF EROS

I t is the collapse of Eros that leads to what we have called the murder of Eros. Wilhelm Reich called this "the murder of Christ." By "Christ" he meant Eros or life force. This is one of the most common but hidden dimensions of human existence. To live an erotic life, we must guard against the murder of Eros. This is a fundamentally denied yet ever-present human impulse. Human beings may be ready to confess many sins, but all feign innocence when accused of the murder of Eros. And yet this primal impulse is as old as civilization itself. Despite our genuine moral evolution in many regards, this fundamental human compulsion has changed little. What has changed, however, is that because the murder of Eros is no longer socially acceptable, the impulse is carefully disguised.

It is what moves Cain to murder Abel. It is what has always moved ambitious but broken princes to kill their father the king. It is what has always moved ambitious but broken students to murder their teachers. The human feeling that moves a person to murder Eros is called malice. The murder of Eros is motivated by some combination of greed, envy, and rage. These are three ingredients that nourish malice.

Malice is virtually always hidden, however. If you do not understand that malice is always hiding itself, then you will never see malice functioning even when it does so right in front of your eyes. Not to see malice for itself is a mistake that often brings in its wake the most grave of consequences, including the most heinous forms of injustice. Malice must never admit to itself, so it must always plead other motives.[52] The other motives pleaded are usually those of a rescuer or protector. In psychology this is called the victim triangle, where the perpetrator disguises him- or herself as a rescuer or even as a victim. When someone obsessively tries to destroy someone else, claiming to be rescuing victims, red flags warning of malice should go off in culture. When accusations are made, fair process and fact-based decision making are absolutely necessary as essential expressions of democratic love and consciousness. Authentic victims must always be protected. But we need to be no less wary of perpetrators disguising their malice under the fig leaf of the rescuer. Is the rescuer person genuinely heroic and concerned? Or is he a person of malice disguising the truth that he is perpetrator, under the mask of the victim advocate or even the victim?

PROJECTION

Remember as well that malice is always filled with projection onto, and distortion of, the object of malice. This is the rationalization for the vicious attack that is launched by people of malice. One's pathology is projected onto the object of malice. When the person of malice describes what they see in the one they are moving to destroy, in effect they are but confessing to their own dark interiors. That is why malice is so hidden, even to the perpetrators of malice. It is because the people of malice so cleverly disguise their motives even to themselves. They are forced by social convention and the psychology of self-deception to pretend to profess noble intention.

Malice is both the polar opposite of Eros as well as one of the most sophisticated forms of pseudo Eros. Like all pseudo Eros, it is rooted in the failure of authentic Eros. Wilhelm Reich calls the murder of Eros "the emotional plague of Man." He gives a stunning description of how it plays out in public culture. The murder of Eros plays to sold-out crowds in a subset of the public culture, which we might call the takedown culture. Whether the method is the old Salem witch trials or contemporary internet smear campaigns, the murder of Eros is at play. Replace the word *witch* with a psychological designation—*sociopath* is the most common one—and you have moved from the pre-modern witch trial to the modern smear campaign. Facts are not checked. Motives are not examined. False claims to patterns and manipulation of language are not exposed. The goal is the murder of Eros and its methods are anti-erotic and therefore cruel in the extreme.

THE EMOTIONAL PLAGUE OF MAN

Here is Reich's description of the murder of Eros. When you read it, try and track not only the content but also the feeling of murdered Eros.

> When the emotional plague strikes its victim, it strikes hard and fast. It strikes without mercy or regard for truth or facts or anything else except one thing: to kill the victim.
>
> There are public prosecutors who act as true lawyers, establishing the truth by evidence from many sources. There are other prosecutors whose only goal of the prosecution is killing the victim, no matter whether right or wrong, just or unjust.
>
> And this is the murder of Christ today as it was two thousand and four thousand years ago.
>
> When the emotional plague strikes, its victim is exposed to everybody's eyes and judgment; all accusations against it are spread out in full daylight. The victim stands naked before its judges like a deer in the open clearing in a forest ready to be shot by the hunter well hidden in the bushes. The real accuser rarely appears on the scene; his identity is kept secret until very shortly before the final kill. There exists no law to punish the sniper from ambush.
>
> To be standing in the middle of an open clearing in a dense forest, widely visible to everyone, and to be shot at from the

bushes on all sides is the situation of the victim of the emotional plague, no matter what form it has.

When the emotional plague strikes, justice quietly recedes, weeping. There is nothing in the ancient books for justice to call upon to prevail. The sentence of death is perfected before the investigation of the crime. The true motive of the prosecution never meets the cleaning force of God's daylight. The reason for the killing remains in the bushes well hidden from anybody's eyes.

When you meet the accused but not the accuser, the charge but not the defense, the exact point of formal law but not the true reason for the accusation, you are dealing with a killing by the plague.

When the plague kills, it kills for wretched reasons. Therefore, to assure the murder, it will not permit weighing accusation against the true, full being of the victim. It will tear down the victim's honor, besmirch every bit of innocent intention or act; it will pronounce innocuous details in a tone and with a slant of intonation which is meant to kill the last vestige of love or esteem for the victim in the hearts of the most devoted friends.

And this again is how the plague works and thinks and acts.

The perpetrators of malice cannot bear the Eros of the object of malice. Historical archetypes of this abound. In literature we think of Iago and Othello. In music we think of the movie *Amadeus* and its archetypal depiction of Salieri and Mozart. In both cases, the Eros of the object of malice causes a collapse in the Eros of the perpetrator of malice. Salieri is a well-respected court musician to the emperor of Austria. The intensity of his jealousy for Mozart's music makes him virtually mad. He becomes obsessed. While in other dimensions of life he remains civil and virtuous, when it comes to Mozart, the poison of malice has taken him over. He spends years on covert moves to destroy Mozart. He chooses the usual method, false or distorted complaints about sexuality. In the archetypal film version of the story he spreads rumors that Mozart is sexually engaging his young students, girls in their early teens. The claim is not true. But because of Mozart's apparently post-conventional sexual nature, and because of Mozart's outrageous way of living out loud, the claims are accepted as true without investigation. Mozart is unable to find patrons to support his work. The results are devastating to his personal and public life. Mozart dies in poverty writing his requiem.

None of this is surprising. Malice elicits forceful attacks and even what psychologists in the field have called "annihilating behavior." Malice is not connected with legitimate causes at its core—it always hides behind them. It is painfully private, yet when it bursts out of control, it is publicly dangerous in the extreme. It is fed by what leading British psychoanalyst Joseph Berke calls a distorted "inner world of fact and fantasy, brought about by the confused interplay of perception, memory, and imagination."[53]

Envious destructiveness is deliberate. Envious people deny goodwill or love toward the object of their ire. What they want to do is remove the bilious anger and bitter vindictiveness that lurks just beneath their surface self. Their surface self appears more often than not as spiritual, and filled with ostensible good intention and light. It is also possible that the surface good intention and light are real. Envy is often a vicious streak in an otherwise decent and even good personality. This is precisely why the malice of seemingly good people is so persuasive. Envious people want to get rid of the feelings that they vaguely know exist right beneath their surface personality. They violate their own sense of goodness and even righteousness. Since the envious person (unconsciously) blames the one he envies for how he feels, he sets out to make him feel bad or appear bad. It is no accident that "evil" is "live" spelled backward. Evil stands against the life force. And the life force is nowhere more powerful than in the full bloom of the Unique Self.

Malice arises because the interior brokenness of the perpetrator makes her a vessel incapable of holding her own genuine Eros. In the example with Mozart, Salieri's Eros collapses in the face of Mozart's radical aliveness. This is the dynamic that catalyzes the murder of Eros. Salieri's own music feels, to him, so essentially inadequate in the face of Mozart's compositions that in his darkest moments he feels virtually nonexistent. He can only assert his own existence by attacking, distorting, and ultimately destroying the existence of Mozart.

Malice is a primal form of rivalry that hides an obsessively dark and carefully hidden pseudo Eros. Isaac Luria, the great sage of Kabbalah, writes that obsessive malice occurs when two figures derive from what he calls "a common soul root." The perpetrator feels that if the object of malice—often a brother, a colleague, or a teacher—prospers, it will be at his expense. The interior sense of the perpetrator is that they both occupy the same space in the world. The perpetrator's pathology is rooted in the twisted belief that there is not enough nourishment from their common soul root to allow both to flourish.

SEVEN CHARACTERISTICS OF MALICE

As we alluded to above, the perpetrator of malice is recognizable—paradoxically—by the fact that she works so hard to disguise her motives. However, it is possible to discern between the authentic victim or genuine rescuer and the malice of the perpetrator by identifying the seven characteristics.

The first identifying characteristic of malice is its obsessive and virtually undying nature. The second characteristic of malice is the wild exaggeration and distortion of the person against whom the malice is aimed, coupled with an utter denial of any and all goodness that he or she might possess. The third identifying characteristic of malice is that action is taken, often deadly action, without talking to both sides of the conflict and without checking basic facts or underlying motivations. The fourth characteristic of malice is the radical demonization of the object of malice. Fifth, related but distinct, is the ascription of virtually occult-like powers to the object of malice, coupled with the infantilizing of his or her ostensible victims. Sixth is the active process of manufacturing victims, all of whom receive significant social and psychological reward. And the seventh is the fostering of a group-think context in which "the victims" or "the women" or "the community" speak as a collective in order to avoid personal responsibility.

This is not merely a theoretical conversation. The people of malice live among us. They live not only in politics and business, where power is an obvious currency of achievement. They live no less in the academy, in religion, and in spiritual circles. To return to Eros we must first recognize and disempower malice.

MALICE, EROS, AND THE UNIQUE SELF

The Unique Self is one of the primary faces of Eros. The core motive of malice is the destruction of Eros. Malice seeks to destroy or distort the Unique Self. The opposite of a Unique Self encounter is an encounter motivated by malice. Malice manifests as both the denial of and the attempt to physically or socially deconstruct the Unique Self of another. Paradoxically, this is based on a primal recognition of the other's Unique Self, and a feeling that somehow the other's self makes one less than, or not enough. Most of the literature of the human potential movement and its daughter, the New Age movement, ignores or even denies malice. But you cannot skip malice if you want to truly understand and practice outrageous love. Love is a Unique Self perception that creates pleasure and joy in its wake. Malice is a Unique Self distortion that creates envy and hatred in its wake. Malice is a verb in the same way that love is a verb.

The core identifying characteristic of the people of malice is that they attack, undermine, or demonize others instead of facing their own internal virulence. The attack may be subtle or overt. However, it is always covered by the sophisticated veneer of respectability, or even by noble motives.

Joseph Berke informs us that malice is to moderns what sex was to Victorians. It is to be repressed at any price. It is an obsession that is best denied, avoided, or forgotten. The perpetrators of malice often claim to be "protecting" some imagined victim from harm.

There is nothing the people of malice fear more than having the lie of their motivation or the ugliness of their hidden machinations exposed. There is a ferocity to malice. This makes it intuitively frightening for people to confront. Thus, most people withdraw into the shade of their own cowardice, covering their fear-stained tracks with well-reasoned and plausible disclaimers. Often the coward finds it easier to energetically join with the movement of malice than to oppose it. This is the worst and most deplorable form of laziness, albeit one of the most common, even if hidden from the public eye. It might take the form of blaming the victim or exaggerating their responsibility. If in some sense "he had it coming," it is easier to rationalize joining the executors of malice than it is to arouse the discernment and courage necessary to oppose them.

In the great spiritual traditions, much of the judgment after our death about who we were in this world, as well as the greatest creator of karma, is related to how we behaved when confronted with malice that was disguised as a righteous cause. Did we speak truth to power? Or did we cleverly disguise our cowardice with a thousand rationalizations, even as the Unique Self of your friend, colleague, or teacher was thrown under a bus?

Let's look more closely now at the mechanism of malice, so you will be able to identify it clearly. It is absolutely necessary to liberate the world from malice in order to allow Eros and love to flourish.

Malice operates through a simple four-stage process. Malice (1) perceives genuine flaws, (2) exaggerates or distorts them, (3) minimizes the good in the attacked person's character, and (4) absurdly and insidiously identifies the person with his or her distorted caricatures, painted by the purveyors of malice themselves.

"There is bad intent that arises in the world; there is intent to hurt and do evil to other people—we have to confront that." This sadly correct truth was spoken by my beloved friend Ken Wilber several years back in a public dialogue we did on the topic of evil in the world. Ken was responding to a questioner who made the all-too-common argument that all the tragedy that befalls us is ultimately our own creation, and thus we must take 100 percent responsibility for everything that occurs. The New Age narcissists cannot bring themselves to bow before the mystery, so they claim all power to themselves.

Of course, more often than not, the hidden agenda is that the victim has no right to be outraged or demand justice. Since the victim is the creator of his own reality, the ones who have been hurt should be taking responsibility. This cleverly lets the inflictor of pain off the hook. The moral context of justice and injustice, right and wrong, and good and evil is undermined by a subtle relativism in which no ethical discernments are genuinely possible. Or, in a related scenario, the abusers themselves claim to have been abused, thus legitimizing the pain inflicted by them on the true victim. This type of claim is one of the most aggressive and insidious disguises of malice.

This New Age view has found a strange bedfellow in distorted American presentations of Theravada Buddhism. Since everything is the result of cause and effect, you must be the creator of everything in your reality. If you take total, 100 percent responsibility for everything, you will find your way to spiritual depth and maturity, so the popular dharma goes. What is more accurate is that we must take appropriate responsibility and apologize on our knees for any and all hurt that we have inflicted. And who among us has not inflicted hurt? We must take 100 percent responsibility for whatever our contribution is in the system that created the trauma. For example, if we have 10 percent responsibility in the contribution system, then we need to take 100 percent responsibility for our 10 percent. But it is malice that distorts hurt in the normal arc of human relationships into a pathology of a far more sinister nature. This is the methodology of the murder of Eros.

This is the matrix of the endless cycle of demonizing by those disconnected from their demon and incapable of owning their demon. They lack the spiritual courage to name what moves them in their breast, which is that "he," the always-flawed Christ they seek to destroy, has a light that threatens their light. He has an appeal, a draw, that is different from theirs. They cannot explain it. So they seek out his imperfections, magnify them a hundredfold, distort and add some major dose of lies for good measure, and the necessary mix for murder is set. This is the source of the "Foul whisp'rings . . . abroad" that Shakespeare saw as the source of villainy and even murder.

As author Philip Roth describes it:

> The whispering campaign that cannot be stopped, rumors
> it's impossible to quash . . . slanderous stories to belittle your
> professional qualifications, derisive reports of your business

deceptions and your perverse aberrations, outraged polemics denouncing your moral failings, misdeeds, and faulty character traits—your shallowness, your vulgarity, your cowardice . . . your falseness, your selfishness, your treachery. Derogatory information. Defamatory statements. Insulting witticisms. Disparaging anecdotes. Idle mockery. Bitchy chatter. Galling wisecracks.[54]

It is in this regard that Geoffrey Chaucer wrote, "It is certain that envy is the worst sin that is: for all others sin against one virtue, whereas envy is against all virtue and all goodness."

APPENDIX C

TESTIMONIAL BY DR. KRISTINA KINCAID

When I first met Dr. Marc Gafni four years ago, I was deeply committed to working with women, teaching and leading workshops particularly in the area of sexual trauma and abuse. Helping others heal their sexual wounding had become a deep passion and a calling for me as a way to continue my own lifelong journey toward healing from the trauma of sexual abuse when I was a young child.

Years of trying traditional Western psychotherapeutic methods didn't get to the root of the pain. I traveled the world, experiencing all kinds of healing techniques in hopes of finding the silver bullet that would help me feel my wholeness. Many of these experiences had blessed, graced, and helped me on profound levels, providing me with deep insights into the grand healing puzzle. And yet, they didn't take me all the way there.

Then I met Marc while participating in his workshop, "The Journey to Love." During the weekend, I experienced his teachings as a living transmission, resonating profound truths that pierced my being in a uniquely potent way. As he completed the teaching on Saturday afternoon, I began to feel a strange surge of energy rush through my body. I sat up against a wall, closed my eyes, and felt my body suddenly lurch forward. I found myself lying flat on the floor having a full-bodied Shechinah experience (Shechinah is the feminine Hebrew name of God). Intense waves of powerful Shakti coursed through my body. The energy of the transmission had, with great force, entered me, and the only way I can describe it is that it began to break me open, profoundly and ecstatically loving me open from the inside out. The only thing I could do was surrender and let it move through me.

After the energy receded, I felt deep peace and had a profound awareness that I was part of everything and everyone, and in my mind I heard the words, "This is a path of living with an open heart." For the first time I knew, through my body, what it meant to be totally, wildly loved by Love itself. Through Marc's dharmic transmission, I experienced an embodied awakening, an indescribable inner journey, an encounter with Divine Love that I now know to be a transmission of outrageous love. Thanks to Marc's profound gift, I was at last able to feel my wholeness and finally come home.

In my experience, Marc's work with this love intelligence of radical wholeness, which some call the Goddess, connects human consciousness to the consciousness of the Divine and initiates an evolutionary process, one that opens people up to new ways of being that allow them to express their greatest gifts and unique potential. The energy he anchors and transmits opens and aligns people to the presence of the One Heart, the Divine Heart, bringing with it radical healing and transformation.

Marc, however, is careful not to claim ownership of this potent force of wholeness and has taught me how to embody it as part of my person and power. I now gratefully embody this transmission and am able to pass it on to my students and others, and they to their students. The experience of this energy, which is filled with what Plato called Eros, is the same that has been recorded by many great mystics, poets, and sages who learned to tap into it to produce spiritual power and enlightened consciousness. Wilhelm Reich considered life energy and Eros to be one and the same, and many physicists, evolutionary biologists, and psychologists are now pointing to the same conclusion. Marc has termed this "evolutionary Eros," citing his own teachers, who say, "The insides of reality are lined with love."

The opening of this energy can easily be misunderstood. But Marc's whole point is that Eros is not reducible to sex. The point of his profoundly religious and even conservative teaching is to experience the full force of Eros, not merely in the sexual but in all the other dimensions of life. That is what Marc means when he says that "a person can be radically polyamorous and never touch Eros, or be celibate or monogamous and live in full Eros."

In the four years I have known and worked with Marc, I have never known him to be anything other than totally honoring, deeply loving, and profoundly committed to my own and others' absolute empowerment and to the emergence of our unique gifts. With my own history, I am particularly sensitive to abusive energy and I have never witnessed or experienced abusive behavior of any kind. I have experienced him as a man tirelessly devoted to the evolution of people and to the evolution of love itself. He is a man who truly walks the radical path of an outrageous lover. His out-of-the-box ideas may perturb those who cannot accept his way of being because it conflicts with their conditioning. And his larger-than-life, in-your-face, audacious, unashamed, and unabashed presence calls and sometimes challenges people to live to their fullest.

It is my observation, through my experiences with teachers the world over, that when teachers like Marc hold enormous amounts of transformative energy, shadow often gets triggered in other people. It takes an incredible amount of awareness to take on the fallout from other people's negative shadow projections. I know this from my own personal shadow work and my work as a Reichian therapist, where we consider the emergence of a client's deep shadow as the place where the work of healing truly begins.

As a teacher, Marc can be rigorous and uncompromising in his efforts to help you shed your skin-encapsulated ego, to find the ultimate expression of love that is you. Marc creates a portal to step into one's fullness and distinct expression of the Divine. Through my work with Marc, I have walked through that portal and discovered and claimed extraordinary things within myself.

We are entering a new era of reunion with the bliss and ecstasy of our highest being. New frontiers of consciousness are opening, and many of us are beginning to realize and embody direct experiences of becoming extraordinary by reclaiming our divinity. For the first time we are waking up to a conscious space where Eros and ethos meet, what Marc calls "a higher wholeness," a place experienced and described in the past by a select few.

This new consciousness is already here. It is the consciousness of connection, of listening to all sides, of being open to dialogue and radical healing, of truly living with an open heart and holding all of it—including and especially the shadow—with outrageous love. We are being called to create a new reality, a new story, an outrageous love story that is written in the language of the soul, of the heart, of outrageous love—not the old story of duality and separation. It is up to all of us to make it real.

NOTES

1 Shakespeare, *Macbeth*, Act 5, Scene 5.

2 Daphne Rose Kingma, speaking at the Integral Spiritual Experience Conference.

3 In the thirteenth century, the sexual was identified with the heterosexual. Passages like this need to be reread and rewritten in post-modernity to include the full range of sexual desire.

4 See, for example, Charles Sanders Pierce's classic essay "Evolutionary Love." See also my (Marc's) essay by the same title, "Evolutionary Love," emergent from my own work and years of conversations with Ken Wilber, which is published as the afterword to *Your Unique Self: The Radical Path to Personal Enlightenment*, 2012. See also David Loye on Darwin and love; and Stuart Kauffman, *At Home in the Universe: The Search for Laws of Self-Organization and Complexity*.

5 That is how the mystics interpret the following verse: "For this is the covenant that I will make with the house of Israel. After those days, the word of God: I have placed My Torah within them, and I will write it on their hearts. And no longer will a man say to his comrade and to his brother, 'Know God,' for they will all know Me, from the small to the great" (Jeremiah 31:64–65).

6 Spiritual teacher Adi Da Samraj.

7 See Isaac Luria in the beginning of Eitz Hayim and in the eighth gate. See also Sha'ar HaHakdamaot 8a. See Gafni, *Mystery of Love*, 2003, footnote to pp. 187.

8   Wilhelm Reich, *The Function of the Orgasm: Discovery of the Orgone* (New York: Farrar, Straus and Giroux, 1973, 161–162).

9   Attributed to Albert Einstein.

10 See Reich's *The Murder of Christ: The Emotional Plague of Mankind*.

11 Jean Maalouf, *Jesus Laughed: And Other Reflections on Being Human* (London: Sheed & Ward, 1996).

12 Mechtilde von Magdeburg (1241–1299), as quoted in Carter Lindbery, *Love: A Brief History Through Western Christianity*, 86.

13 We, of course, have to rewrite these passages to transcend heteronormative contexts and to include the power of feminine desire (*Sefer Hasidim*, par. 300, p. 240).

14 Basho, "Finis," *The Narrow Road to the Deep North and Other Travel Sketches* (New York: Penguin Classics, 1967).

15 Joe Arnett, "Coevolution and Pollination," *Washington Native Plant Society, Botanical Rambles* (August 1, 2014), www.wnps.org/blog/coevolution-and-pollination (accessed July 29, 2016); University of Maryland, Undergraduate Program in Plant Biology, Lecture 21: Pollination, www.life.umd.edu/classroom/bsci124/lec21.html (accessed July 29, 2016); PBS, Evolution Library, "Mimicry: The Orchid and the Bee," www.pbs.org/wgbh/evolution/library/01/1/l_011_02.html (accessed July 29, 2016).

16 Douglas Main, "The Amazing Mating Dance of the Peacock Spider," *Live Science* (August 21, 2013), www.livescience.com/39052-peacock-spider-mating-dance.html_(accessed July 29, 2016).

17 Paul Willis, "Dancing Brolga," *ABC Science*, www.abc.net.au/science/articles/2001/06/01/2614588.htm (accessed July 29, 2016).

18 Megan Lane, "The Male Beauty Contest Judged by Women," *BBC News*, January 20, 2011, www.bbc.com/news/world-africa-12215138 (accessed July 29, 2016); Wikipedia, "Wodaabe," en.wikipedia.org/wiki/Wodaabe (accessed July 29, 2016).

19 Personal conversation on a walk in Mill Valley, California, 2016.

20 I will talk about this textualization of Eros on page 149.

21 Exodus 25:22.

22 See, for example, the wonderful independent scholar George Feuer-
    stein, *Sacred Sexuality* (New York: Tarcher, 1993), 120–121, on the
    Christian mystics reinterpreting the Song of Songs as lofty mystical
    experience utterly divorced from the sexual. This is the classical read-
    ing offered by virtually all of the mainstream texts—an interpretation
    diametrically opposed to the Secret of the Cherubs.

23 The verse is read to mean, "as one who finds peace . . . for him."

24 See Gafni, *Mystery of Love* (2003), 63–65.

25 This story was originally written for *Mystery of Love* by Chaya, my
    former wife. Chaya contributed about four pages to *Mystery of Love*
    that have all been removed from this book except for this story.

26 See Babylonian Talmud tractate Sanhedrin 75a and tractate Nedarim
    91b. See also Gafni, *Mystery of Love* (2003), p. 52 and p. 331 footnote
    to p. 52.

27 Job 19:26.

28 But it does not cancel all of the previous canon.

29 Rainer Maria Rilke, *Letters to a Young Poet* (Mineola, NY: Dover
    Publications, 2002), 24.

30 Emily Dickinson, "Part Five: The Single Hound."

31 D. H. Lawrence, "Love on the Farm."

32 Pablo Neruda, "Every Day You Play."

33 Vladimir Nabokov, *The Stories of Vladimir Nabokov* (New York: Vin-
    tage, 1996), 77.

34 Another great turn of phrase from Barbara Marx Hubbard.

35 See, for example, Michael Pollan's wonderful work *The Botany of
    Desire*.

36 Orot Ha-Kodesh, Vol. 3:140.

37 Samuel Taylor Coleridge, "Dejection: An Ode."

38 Nicholson Baker, *Vox* (New York: Vintage, 1993), ch. 4.

39 The Serpent, in George Bernard Shaw, *Back to Methuselah* (1921),
    Part I, Act I.

40 Gaston Bachelard, *Air and Dreams: An Essay on the Imagination of
    Movement* (Dallas: Dallas Institute Publications, 2011).

41 Hosea 12:11.

42 John Donne, "The Good-Morrow."

43 William Blake, "Love to faults is always blind."

44 William Wordsworth, "Intimations of Immortality from Recollections of Early Childhood."

45 R. D. Liang, *The Politics of Experience* (New York: Pantheon, 1983), 14.

46 Ehsan Yarshater, ed., *Mystical Poems of Rumi* (Chicago: University of Chicago Press, 2009), 346.

47 Johann Wolfgang von Goethe, *Elective Affinities.*

48 John Beer, *William Blake: A Literary Life* (New York: Palgrave Macmillan, 2007), 47.

49 I (Marc) first heard this story retold by Robbie Gringras in one of his wonderful plays.

50 As cited in his classic work *Me Or Eynayim.*

51 Algernon Charles Swinburne, "Love and Sleep."

52 Paraphrasing Milan Kundera.

53 See Joseph Berke, *Tyranny of Malice* (Pelican, 1988).

54 Philip Roth, *Operation Shylock: A Confession* (New York: Vintage, 1994).

PERMISSION CREDITS

Excerpt from "Huddled Beneath the Sky" from *Love Poems from God: Twelve Sacred Voices from the East and West*, translated by Daniel Ladinsky. Copyright © 2002 and used with his permission.

"It Acts Like Love" from *Love Poems from God: Twelve Sacred Voices from the East and West*, translated by Daniel Ladinsky. Copyright © 2002 and used with his permission.

ACKNOWLEDGMENTS

MARC GAFNI:

It is a delight to thank with so much love and appreciation so many people who have impacted my life and made me better. For the sake of space, I am not going to talk about each person individually but instead will simply mention names. All of you are close and dear friends or colleagues who either serve now or have served in the past on the board of the Center for Integral Wisdom or have been involved in creating and sharing this book or have impacted my thinking and heart in these last ten years.

Ken Wilber, Warren Farrell, Daniel Schmachtenberger, John P. Mackey, John Gray, Zachary Stien, Claire Molinard, Glenn Yeffeth, Frank Wieman, Adam Bellow, Lisa Engles, Kerstin Tuschik Zohar, Chahat Corten, Michael Wright, Vy Tran, Jordan French, Carrie Kish, Clint Fuchs, Diane Hamilton, Michael Zimmerman, Doug Casey, Sally Ranney, Dalit Arnon, Metuka Benjamin, Stephen Marmer, Terry and Betsy Nelson, Christopher Marston, Kate Maloney, Peter Fiekowsksy and Sharon Fiekowsky, Peter Dunlap, Aftab Omer, Kathleen J. Brownback, Liza Braude Glidden, Reed Glidden, Shoshanna French, Gabrielle Anwar, Sharif Malinik, Martin Burke, Riane Eisler, David Loye, Kristen Ulmer, Gerry Judd, Barbara Alexander, Sam Alexander, Elliot Ingersoll, Arthur Kurzweil, Shep Gordon, Colin Bigelow, Jonny Podell, Mariana Caplan, Suzy Rogovin, Catherine Oxenberg, Liri Zohar, Mike Weiss, Roxanne Depalma, Shawn Ramer, Victoria Myer, Tonya Ridgely, Rand Stagen,

Colleen Walker, Jeff Hilliard, Shelly Reichenbach, Tom Goddard, Elizabeth Helen Bullock, Lesley Freeman, Adam Gilad, Alan Davidson, Brett Lavee, Jamie Wheel, Venu and Vinay Julapali, Brad Blanton, Mike Ginn, Bill Little, Fred Jealous, Nance McGee, Peter Britton, Michael Beckwith, Mark Schillinger, Rob Sidon, Ken Kaufman, Elif Kendrili, Kamala Devi, Maureen Metcalf, Suzy Rogovin, Mary Ann Voories, Steve Raymond, Hillel Goldberg, Gil Kopatch, Justine Musk, Rachel Resnick, Juan Carlos Kaiten, Lawrence Bloom, Mark Donohue, Raj Sisodia, Richard Schwartz, Harville Hendrix and Helen Hunt, Richard Barrett, Ryan Ansin, Kelly Sosan Bearer, Timothy Wilken, Jennifer and Bryan, Eben and Annie, Ruth Engel Eldar and Tzvi Eldar, Zivit Davidovich, Joseph Berke and Shri, Cindy Lou Golin, John Kesler, Rob Mcnamara, Sean Esbjorn Hargens, Keith Bellamy, Helma Buis, Olivier Bockenmeyer, Bryan DeSanto, Terry Shireff, Yossi Amram, Russ Volckman, Jeannie Carlisle, Andreas Waschk, David Karchere, Merlin Yockstick, Ben Jealous, David Seidenberg, Mark Schwartz, my mom, my brother Yossi and his family, especially Yitz and Adi, Shmuel.

My children, whom I love very much, each in their own way: Rachel, Eytan, Yair, and Zion.

And to three people who have, each in different ways, held this dharma. To Marina Kaplan, mother of Zion and dear friend; to Lisa, incredible mother of Eytan and Yair; to Shifra, mother of Rachel.

Deep thanks to my beloved and beyond awesome Evolutionary Partner with whom I stand, Barbara Marx Hubbard.

To my beloved and gorgeous Sally Kempton who has been with me in all of it for the last decade, I have no words.

To Lori Galperin, a wildly wondrous, wise and beautiful woman who partnered with me for five great years and is always with me.

My beloved co-author, partner in this dharma of Eros and in life, Kristina Kincaid, who has mused the incarnation of this dharma for the last four years, evolving with me in so many holy ways. GGIF.

KRISTINA KINCAID:

I am deeply indebted to the many family, friends, colleagues, clients, and students who have given their support and opened their hearts to me so that I might grow and learn to love more. I have followed the blazing trail of many extraordinary teachers who have inspired me. Dr. Marc Gafni is at the forefront of those teachers and the one who continues to push me to the highest of standards of my own unique expression while inspiring me to recommit my life over and over to a path of living with an open heart. He is someone who talks and walks the path of outrageous love courageously, with laughter, with pain, and with many tears. I offer my deepest gratitude to you, Marc, for your profound transmission of a living dharma that has radically transformed my life and for your most generous invitation to be a co-author of this most extraordinary work of art.

The wisdom in this book has been at the core of Marc's teachings for over thirty years and comprises the body, blood, and sweat of his life's work. The teachings are rooted in his lifelong scholarly study of over thousands of Aramaic and Hebrew texts, along with his rigorous research and uncanny ability to crack codes deep within the ancient roots of Zoharic and Lurianic texts known in the Kabbalistic tradition as the Wisdom of Solomon. This, coupled with his work in evolutionary world spirituality, systems theory, Integral theory, and the social sciences, weaves together a new worldview. Marc masterfully visions a post-post-modern framework within which the ancient spark of Eros can reignite herself and transmit and articulate a desperately needed new narrative for our time. His work crafts a detailed map of a liberated sexuality, where we can truly live a fully erotic life. Marc, it has been the greatest delight, pleasure, and privilege of my life to help birth this Magnum Opus of Eros with you. I am so proud and honored to have worked with you to reclaim the lost Goddess heritage, which at last appears as written text on the pages of a book, once more. I also thank Spirit for this once in a lifetime opportunity to participate in freeing Her from exile and allowing for us all to come home, to claim our ecstatic birthright and Return to Eros! HE liberates SHE, SHE liberates HE, and WE all come home . . . Amen!

A very special thank you goes to Martin Burke for his unrelenting support of me for the last fifteen years. Without you, Martin, I would not have come to this place. You are my rock. And to Buddy Burke, who reminds me to smell the roses and savor the small things. Thank you to my family, my beloved mother Margaret and father Joe, Uncle Boot, and my beloved sister Karla Kincaid, deep bow to your Prophetess and Indian Chief whose wisdom and sight continue to inspire, protect, and teach me, love you all the way, Ms. Doobie. To my beloved brother Jodi, who always makes me laugh, his wonderful wife Erin, and my beautiful niece Chais.

I am also indebted to the following individuals for their amazing support and love: our incredible editor Jessi Rita Hoffman, Mark Mandel, Wilhelm Reich, Barbara Marx Hubbard, John Pierrakos, Stuart Black, Warren Moe, Bob and Ann Nunley, Delphine Rossi, Terry Fitch, Shep Gordon, Drew Katz, Jonny Podell, Abdy, Michael Dougherty, Joe Robert, Lucho, Sally Burke, Marty Burke Senior, Marc Packer, Mariana Verkerk, Robin Mee, Michelle Hesse, Pam Anders, Ossie Carlson, Belinda Sawyer, Kim Coulter, Lisa Grey, Matt Mohay, Odie Crossman, Tom Seidenspinner, Stacy Sully, Sarah Lidsey, Sherri Gilbert, and deep appreciation and love to Cynthia Kagoshima, my adopted sister who has stood by me stalwart through thick and thin. This book and my contribution to it would not have been possible without all of you.

And to the Beloved Goddess who has shown me a love of the physical as well as the spiritual and has led me to the knowing that there is no difference. You continue to remain a deep mystery and a profound knowing at the same time. I remain in service and with deepest devotion.

In love,
Kristina

ABOUT THE AUTHORS

© Shawn Ramer

Marc Gafni is a visionary thinker, social activist, passionate philosopher, and author of ten books, including the award-winning *Your Unique Self: The Radical Path to Personal Enlightenment*; the two-volume *Radical Kabbalah*; *Self in Integral Evolutionary Mysticism: Two Models and Why They Matter*; and *Tears: Reclaiming Ritual, Integral Religion, and Rosh Hashanah*. New books are now in preparation being written in collaboration with leading thinkers and activists in key areas of human culture including evolutionary theory, world spirituality, psychology, entrepreneurship, Eros, sexuality, and public culture. In the words of Esalen president, Michael Murphy in regard to his Unique Self Theory, Gafni is "changing the game." According to many he is a catalyzing thinker in evolving the source code of consciousness and culture. Ken Wilber calls his work seminal.

He holds his doctorate in philosophy from Oxford University, and holds rabbinic ordination. He teaches on the cutting edge of philosophy in the West, helping to evolve a new "dharma," or meta-theory of integral meaning that is helping to re-shape key pivot points in consciousness and culture.

He is the co-founder with Ken Wilber and Sally Kempton of The Center for Integral Wisdom. The Center where Barbara Marx Hubbard and Kate Maloney serve as co-chairs is a leading activist think tank dedicated to articulating a practical politics of love, and to catalyzing an emergent personal and global vision of ethics, Eros and meaning. He is the evolutionary scholar in residence at the Foundation for Conscious Evolution and a co-founder of the Integral Evolutionary Tantra School and the Outrageous Love Project.

A rabbinic lineage holder in the Bible, Talmud, and Kabbalah, Gafni self-describes as a "dual citizen" of both Integral World Spirituality and classical Hebrew practice. He has been an editor of the *Journal of Integral Theory and Practice* for the special issues of Unique Self and Integral Spirituality and a faculty member of JFK University.

In 2014 Dr. Gafni was an initiating visionary of the Success 3.0 *Summit and Rise Up* movie, whose method and movement is to bring together key thought leaders and change agents to collaboratively evolve a bold new Integral vision of Success, rooted in the entrepreneurial values of Wake Up, Grow Up, Show Up, and Outrageous Love.

Over the past thirty years, Dr. Gafni has developed evolutionary and activist programs rooted in his commitment to what he has termed "participating in the evolution of love." Together with author and social innovator Barbara Marx Hubbard, Zachary Stein, Daniel Shmactenberger, and other leading thinkers, he is working on a series of new works all around the meta-theme The Universe: A Love Story, Evolutionary Spirituality. Gafni is a leading public intellectual impacting the source code of global culture. He is also a forger of new trails in the evolution of intimacy and love.

He has led international spiritual movements and learning communities, as well as created and hosted for several seasons a popular national Israeli television program on culture, meaning, and spirit on Israel's leading network.

© Fadil Berisha

Dr. Kristina Kincaid is the director of The Institute of Integral Evolutionary Tantra in New York City and is the chairperson and a co-creator of the Outrageous Love Project. She holds an M.A. and doctorate in Energy Medicine from Holos University. A graduate of the Institute of Core Energetics and the prestigious Barbara Brennan School of Healing, she also earned a BA in Anthropology from the University of Texas at Austin.

The Institute is an affiliate division of the Center for Integral Wisdom (CIW). CIW is a nonprofit organization co-founded in 2010 by Marc Gafni, Ken Wilber, Sally Kempton, Lori Galperin, Mariana Caplan, and a leadership team that has expanded to dozens of the most respected spiritual teachers, leaders, authors, and activists in the world. CIW is a think tank that is articulating and advancing a spiritual movement which is evolving the source code of human existence. Kristina is a CIW Scholar and a member of the board of directors.

Kristina is known for her transformative work in personal growth and intimate relationships through the body. She offers residential retreats, workshops, and individual sessions for single men and women as well as couples. She lives in New York City.